Beer Cans

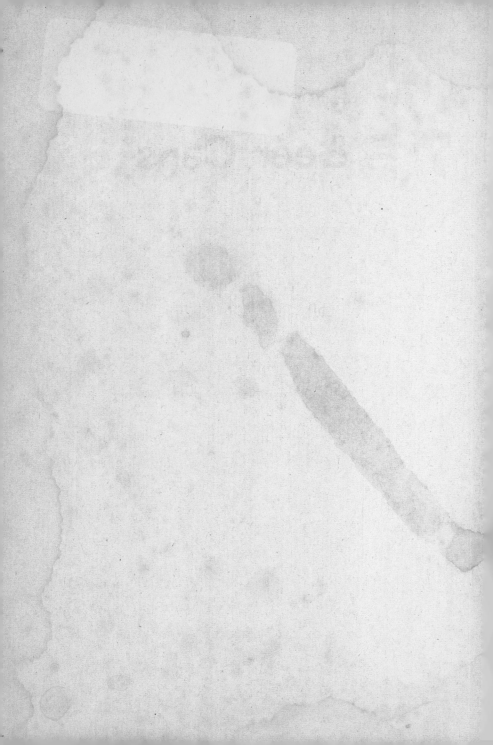

The Official® Price Guide to

Beer Cans

Bill Mugrage

FIFTH EDITION

HOUSE OF COLLECTIBLES • NEW YORK

© 1993 by William E. Mugrage

𝓤𝓒 This is a registered trademark of Random House, Inc.

Published by: House of Collectibles
201 East 50th Street
New York, New York 10022

Distributed by Ballantine Books, a division of Random House, Inc., New York, and simultaneously in Canada by Random House of Canada Limited, Toronto.

Text design by Holly Johnson
Text photos by Ellen Mugrage
Cover design by Kristine V. Mills
Cover photo by George Kerrigan

Manufactured in the United States of America

ISSN: 1069-8426

ISBN: 0-876-37873-4

Fifth Edition: December 1993

10 9 8 7 6 5 4 3 2

Contents

Acknowledgments   vii

INTRODUCTION

A Brief History of the Beer Can   3
Where to Find Cans   8
Cleaning and Restoration   13
Care, Storage, and Display   17
Organizations and Clubs   19
Mandatory Labeling Requirements   21
Brand Names and Breweries   23
How Values Are Determined   51
Definitions   54
Author's Note   56
Beer Can Designs   57

BEER CAN LISTINGS (BY STATE)

Alabama   63
Alaska   64
Arizona   65
Arkansas   69
California   70
Colorado   115
Connecticut   123
Delaware   127

District of Columbia   129
Florida   131
Georgia   139
Hawaii   141
Idaho   142
Illinois   143
Indiana   170
Iowa   184
Kansas   186
Kentucky   187
Louisiana   190
Maine   193
Maryland   194
Massachusetts   204
Michigan   215
Minnesota   225
Mississippi   241
Missouri   242
Montana   249
Nebraska   252
Nevada   255
New Hampshire   257
New Jersey   258
New Mexico   275
New York   276
North Carolina   304
North Dakota   305
Ohio   306
Oklahoma   324
Oregon   326
Pennsylvania   330
Rhode Island   367
South Carolina   371
South Dakota   372
Tennessee   373
Texas   375
Utah   382
Vermont   385
Virginia   386
Washington   391
West Virginia   407
Wisconsin   408
Wyoming   438

Acknowledgments

ELLEN MUGRAGE: For the photography and encouragement and support.

ARLENE MUGRAGE: Thanks Mom!

VAUGHN HUBBARD: For all the help, advise, and encouragement.

R.C. "RIC" BERNDT, PABST BREWING COMPANY: For all the friendship, technical help, and assistance.

CAROL MASNIK, RAINIER BREWING COMPANY: For all the help and friendship and support and trade sessions.

DICK TUCKER: For letting me photograph his collection.

Introduction

A Brief History
of the Beer Can

/

After the end of World War I, American packaging companies began working on putting food and beverages in sealed metal containers. This, of course, was because metal containers were easy to fill, ship, and store with little or no damage to the contents. By the mid-1920s, the technology was sufficiently developed for the mass packaging of food and drink in sealed cans.

As early as 1928, the end of Prohibition was being forecast, and Franklin Roosevelt promised in the 1932 presidential election campaign that if he were elected, he would bring back 3.2 percent beer. By the spring of 1933, 3.2 percent beer was again flowing across the country, and packaging companies were hard at work on using canning technology on beer. The biggest problem faced by the can companies was that beer placed in raw, unlined steel cans picked up a "tinny" taste after only a short while. Attempts to line the inside of the can generally ended with the lining breaking down and badly affecting the taste of the beer.

But in the fall of 1934, the American Can Company approached the Kruger Brewing Company of Newark, New Jersey, with the news that it had solved these problems and was ready to put beer in cans with little or no effect on taste. American Can called the containers produced with their new process "Keglined." Kruger was a small to mid-size brewery with a static market, and they were convinced that packaging beer in cans was the new wave of the post-Prohibition era. American Can went so far as to pay for the installation of the canning equipment and to guarantee Kruger against any losses. With this no-risk situation, Kruger agreed, and Richmond, Virginia, was chosen as the test market. Richmond was far enough way from Kruger's home market that if the test failed, the impact of negative publicity would be kept to a minimum.

The new beer can was introduced with a single ad in a Richmond publication (*see photo A*), and it would be an understatement to say that

FOR YOUR GREATER CONVENIENCE AND ENJOYMENT

KRUEGER'S *now presents the*

KEGLINED* CAN

(Holds 12 ounces — the same as a bottle)

for ALE *and* BEER

Here's the biggest news since repeal—it's the news of a modern way—a more convenient way—to enjoy Krueger's Cream Ale (formerly Boar's Head) in your home. Krueger's, always in the vanguard of brewing science, is the *first* to offer you the advantages of the new keglined can . . . advantages that are truly amazing.

Imagine buying Ale or Beer for your home without paying a bottle deposit, without the trouble and effort of making bottle returns! Imagine being able to get twice as much in the same space in your ice-box! These are the modern conveniences made possible by the astounding keglined can. Of course, you can get your Krueger's in bottles as usual, but we urge you to be one of the first to enjoy the benefits of this remarkable

keglined can development. Get a can of Krueger's Cream Ale or Krueger's Finest Beer today! G. Krueger Brewing Company, Newark, N. J.

Richmond Distributor:
CAVALIER DISTRIBUTING CORP. • RICHMOND, VA. • TEL. 4-8177

Be sure to ask your dealer for a "Quick & Easy" opener and learn the simple little trick of opening your can of ale or beer.

KRUEGER'S CREAM ALE

AND KRUEGER'S *Finest* BEER   *also in bottles and on draught*

Photo A.

the test was a roaring success. By mid-August, 1935, Kruger was producing and shipping almost 200,000 12-ounce cans a day. Watching the success of Kruger, the Premier Pabst Corporation, brewers of Pabst Beer, entered the market and immediately took the beer can nationwide. The American Can Company would continue to add other breweries to its growing list of customers throughout 1935.

Not to be outdone, in mid-1935 the National Can Company entered the market with its own version of the steel flat-top can called "Double Lined," convincing the Northampton Brewing Company of Northampton, Pennsylvania, and the Red Top Brewing Company of Cincinnati, Ohio, that their new can was the packaging of the future.

The Continental Can Company took a different approach to canning beer, developing a "metal bottle" that they called the Cap-Sealed Cone Top. The great advantage of the cone top was easily grasped by the small brewer: Instead of investing huge amounts of money installing a canning line in their factory, they could use their existing bottling machinery to fill the cone top. Crown Cork and Seal also entered the "metal bottle" market with their "Crowntainer." The Gottlieb Heileman Brewing Company of La Crosse, Wisconsin, was the first brewer to use the cap-sealed cone top. By August, 1935, the Joseph Schlitz Brewing Company of Milwaukee, Wisconsin, was using the cone top and was taking it nationwide. By the end of 1935, thirty-seven breweries were putting their products in various cans. By the end of 1937, over ninety percent of United States brewers were canning beer.

The cone top lasted until 1960, when the Rice Lake Brewing Company of Rice Lake, Wisconsin, finally gave them up. Aluminum cans first appeared on April 15, 1958, introduced by the Primo Brewing Company of Honolulu, Hawaii, with their first eleven-ounce cans. Aluminum cans made very little progress with the rest of the nation's breweries until the National Can Company sold the Rainier Brewing Company of Seattle, Washington, on the merits of the light-weight, economical aluminum can. For the first time, a beer container was recyclable. With the obvious advantages aluminum had over steel, the new aluminum can took over the beer container market. The last brewery to give up the steel can was the Pittsburgh Brewing Company of Pittsburgh, Pennsylvania, in 1985.

Since the introduction of aluminum cans, brewers have added many refinements, including combining the aluminum with steel or tin to make bi-metal cans and adding aluminum lids for easier opening. Paper and plastic cans have been tested in various markets around the world, but the beer drinker always seemed to prefer the aluminum can, and for the foreseeable future, the aluminum beer can is here to stay.

Notable Dates in Beer Can History

January 24, 1935: First sale of beer in cans.

June 1, 1935: "Internal Revenue Tax Paid" statement required.

September 1, 1935: First cone top sold.

June 8, 1937: First quart-size cone top introduced.

March 30, 1950: "Internal Revenue Tax Paid" statement no longer required.

June 2, 1954: Schlitz introduces 16-ounce flat-top can.

April 5, 1958: Primo introduces the 11-ounce aluminum can.

October 10, 1960: Coors introduces the 7-ounce aluminum can.

March 3, 1962: Iron City introduces the first pop top.

February 1, 1970: Rainier is the first brewery to go to full aluminum can production.

January 1, 1986: Health warnings required on beer cans by federal government.

Can Producers and Breweries Purchasing Cans 1934–1935

The following is a list of the breweries that bought cans in the early days of canned beer and the companies that produced those first cans.

Date	Brewery	Can Manufactured
1934	Krueger Brewing Company, Newark, NJ	American
5/23/35	Premier-Pabst Corporation, Milwaukee, WI	American
6/11/35	Northampton Brewing Company, Northampton, PA	National
6/27/35	Adam Scheidt Brewing Company, Norristown, PA	American
7/25/35	Ballantine Brewing Company, Newark, NJ	American
8/ 8/35	Red Top Brewing Company, Cincinnati, OH	National
8/12/35	Globe Brewing Company, Baltimore, MD	American
8/13/35	G. Heileman Brewing Company, La Crosse, WI	Continental
8/27/35	J. Schlitz Brewing Company, Milwaukee, WI	Continental
8/28/35	Wehle Brewing Company, New Haven, CT	American
9/ 6/35	Genesee Brewing Company, Rochester, NY	American
9/11/35	Burger Brewing Company, Cincinnati, OH	Continental
9/13/35	Fort Pitt Brewing Company, Pittsburgh, PA	American
9/27/35	Feigenspan Brewing Company, Newark, NJ	American
9/27/35	Fox Brewing Company, Chicago, IL	National
9/27/35	Gunther Brewing Company, Baltimore, MD	American

Date	Brewery	Can Manufactured
9/27/35	Forest City Brewing Company, Cleveland, OH	American
10/17/35	Mankato Brewing Company, Mankato, MN	Continental
10/29/35	Blatz Brewing Company, Milwaukee, WI	Continental
10/29/35	Fitger Brewing Company, Duluth, MN	Continental
10/31/35	Louis F. Neuweiler & Sons, Allentown, PA	American
11/ 2/35	Duquesne Brewing Company, Pittsburgh, PA	Continental
11/ 7/35	Stroudsburg Brewing Company, Stroudsburg, PA	National
11/ 8/35	Fritz Brewing Company, Freeport, IL	Continental
11/12/35	Grace Bros. Brewing Company, Santa Rosa, CA	American
11/13/35	Manhattan Brewing Company, Chicago, IL	American
11/23/35	Kings Brewery Inc., Brooklyn, NY	National
11/26/35	Berghoff Brewing Company, Fort Wayne, IN	Continental
11/29/35	Adolph Coors Company, Golden, CO	American
12/ 7/35	Rainier Brewing Company, San Francisco, CA	Continental
12/ 9/35	Gluek Brewing Company, Minneapolis, MN	Continental
12/10/35	San Francisco Brewing Company, San Francisco, CA	American
12/11/35	Aztec Brewing Company, San Diego, CA	American
12/11/35	General Brewing Company, San Francisco, CA	American
12/12/35	California Brewing Association, San Francisco, CA	American
12/12/35	Theo. Hamms Brewing Company, St. Paul, MN	American
12/18/35	Beverwick Brewing Company, Albany, NY	Continental

Where to Find Cans

/

Indoors
OLD BUILDINGS

A good place to look for cans is in old buildings, especially abandoned farm houses, hunting cabins, and barns. Even outhouses are excellent places to look. Be sure to get permission before entering any abandoned property, and always be careful. Abandoned buildings can be dangerous, so care must be taken to make sure that the structure is still sound enough to enter. That old cone top won't be worth anything if the wall or ceiling falls in on you, or you crash through a rotted floor.

Once you have located a promising site and have inspected it for safety, be sure to check all cupboards, closets, basements, attics, and under the building if it has a crawlspace. I once found a mint-condition quart cone top sitting in a kitchen cupboard. Take the full tour; a surprise might be waiting. If possible, look between old walls, too. Remember to bring gloves and a good flashlight and take care when poking into dark, out-of-the-way spots—those nooks and crannies might be inhabited by a variety of unfriendly creatures, and they usually resent your intrusion.

Hunting cabins usually hosted parties after the day's hunt, and the empty beer cans were put out of sight, generally not very far away. In old barns, check out the hay loft, the walls, and places where machinery was stored or worked on.

In the city, look for houses constructed between 1930 and the late 1950s. When these houses were built, at least one carpenter on the job would have a beer or two with lunch. The empty can would usually go back into the paper sack or lunch pail, but they were also dropped between the walls and boarded up. If you find an old house that is being remodeled or perhaps re-roofed, approach the contractor and ask if you can have any old cans or bottles found during the renovation. I usually offer to trade a full can for any empties that are discovered.

There are still taverns and beer outlets that have outdated beer in the basement or storeroom. Don't be afraid to ask for them. Even offer to pay a fair price for anything of interest. The results could be surprising.

BUYING CANS

Flea markets, antique stores, and antique malls have all come to recognize the fact that beer cans are collectible and offer them for sale. Most cans in these places are overpriced, but an occasional bargain can be found. Always negotiate on the price, especially if you are going to buy more than one can.

OTHER COLLECTORS

When trading with other collectors, you will find that you will probably have better luck if you find someone with a collection and similar interests as yourself. Advanced collectors have very limited needs, and finding a can that this collector needs is not always that easy.

Outdoors

Although a really rare can probably hasn't been thrown away for more than twenty years, there *are* still some out there. The demise of the small brewery in the '50s and '60s, the introduction of aluminum cans in the early '70s, and the increase in returnable cans in many states have all contributed to the decline of outdoor dumping of cans.

There are, however, still cans outdoors that have been virtually untouched by the elements. The biggest enemies of the beer can are, of course, rust and sun. Cans exposed to the sun will fade to the base color—white in the case of steel cans and silver for aluminum cans. Fading is always fatal, as there is no way to restore a faded can. Rust is also damaging, but not necessarily fatal; see the section on cleaning and restoring cans for details on how to deal with rust.

When looking for cans outdoors, it is best to be prepared. Take a raincoat, a change of clothes, and gloves—the weather can change suddenly. A flashlight can be helpful for peering into hollow logs, stumps, and tight spaces under old buildings. A small, three-prong garden cultivator or rake can be very helpful for digging out a buried can, but be careful that you don't add any damage to your find. If you have access to a metal detector, bring it along. Finally, a burlap bag or beer flats will be useful for storing and carrying any treasures you may discover.

If you are going to travel any distance from home, you should start with a full tank of gas, bring along a lunch or something to snack on, and water, especially in remote areas.

Also remember that mice, rats, snakes, bees, and other assorted pests usually don't like to be disturbed and can become quite hostile, so take care when poking around in a dump or by the roadside. Plant life can also be hostile, so learn to recognize nettles, poison ivy, and the like.

THE ROADSIDE

When looking for cans outside, there are a few things to remember, such as the behavior of people who might have been drinking beer outdoors. Before the days of the interstate road system, there were few rest areas on old highways. These old highways, especially in hilly or mountainous areas, are always good places to check for cans. Look for pull-offs where people could get out of their cars. Cans were usually dumped down hillsides and off the shoulders of the road, later to be covered by leaves or needles. These cans can remain virtually intact for years. Look for old roads or highways that have been supplanted by the newer interstates and abandoned.

In really rural areas, check out the dirt roads, especially old hunting or logging roads. In the past, people would often dump their trash on out-of-the-way routes where they couldn't be seen by passers-by on the main road. It is interesting to note that if you find three or four cans of the same brand, the other two or three will be nearby, as this often indicates that a six-pack was drunk on the spot.

Finally, old high-school or college "lovers' lanes" can often produce good results, though, except in rural areas, many of these places are now shopping-mall parking lots.

HUNTING CAMPS AND CABINS

As I've mentioned above, inside old hunting camps or wilderness cabins are good places to look for cans, but don't forget to look around the outside of these buildings. Until recently, people didn't usually take their garbage with them when they left, so look for likely dumping sites. Usually, a small hole was dug near the surface and little or no effort was made to really bury the trash. Cans found in these places are frequently in pretty good condition. Check the trail to the outhouse, if there is one, as the garbage was often taken out while on the way to use it. Be sure to look under the cabin, too.

Don't pass up old beer bottles or tobacco, coffee, or oil tins—or any other old container that may or may not sport advertising. Even if you have no interest in these items, someone else is likely to. Remember that if it's old and in generally fair condition, someone will probably be collecting it. You can use these items to trade for beer cans or sell them and use the proceeds to buy cans.

FARMS

Old farm houses or abandoned buildings in rural farming communities will usually have an old dump nearby that can be a good source for beer cans. But before searching for or disturbing these dumps, be sure to get the permission of the landowner. These dumps were usually not too far from the farm buildings, generally out of sight, but still within walking distance. Cans found in the middle of the dump will usually be in much better shape than those on the outer edges.

THE TOWN DUMP

Up to the early 1950s, most small towns had a town dump. Almost all of these have been long since filled and closed, but if you are lucky enough to get into one of these, the rewards can be great. Remember to take care poking around these old dumps, as they can hide hidden dangers, including sharp metal, broken glass, and various bugs, snakes, rats, and poisonous plants.

OTHER OUTDOOR SITES

Also, be alert to the possibility of cave-ins. If you are not experienced at entering these places, I do not advise you to do so. If you do decide to brave the dangers here, do not go in alone—take along two or three other people. And again, bring along a strong flashlight and gloves, and don't put your hand anywhere where you can't see it.

Cans can also be found on the bottom of lakes, but the quality of such cans is not likely to be good. Even if the can is not already rusted beyond repair, bringing it up into the air accelerates the rusting process and the can quickly crumbles.

Some Final Words

When picking up cans outdoors or from the dump, shake the can lightly with the opening pointed away from you. All kinds of living things make condos out of old beer cans.

One Monday morning, I got into my van to go to work only to find the inside covered with black ants from the cans I'd collected. On another occasion, I stopped for a beer after a hard day's can hunting, and on returning to the van, I was greeted by a lizard eyeballing me from the dashboard. Then there is the collector from Minnesota who found a bunch of cans while wandering through Washington State and returned home with a trunk full of slugs.

The lesson is to be aware of what might be hiding inside the can.

Since beer-can collecting has come of age, don't be afraid to ask the local people you meet on your hunting trips where the local dump or hunting and fishing camps were located. Don't be shy. Go into an old pub or tavern, have a beer, and ask where the cans were dumped before there was a garbage pick-up.

Check the local library or city hall for maps of old roads, farms, dumps, hunting or fishing camps—any place where cans might be waiting for you to find them.

With a little planning and perseverance, you are sure to find some great old beer cans. Good luck!

Cleaning and Restoration

Most cans, other than cans straight from the brewery or store shelf, will need some sort of cleaning, from wiping the dust off to full-scale restoration. Remember, the older and rarer the can, the more the potential buyer will be critical of any damage, including nicks and scratches. If done properly, general cleaning and fixing of minor defects will enhance the value of a can. More extensive restoration might or might not increase the value. It is important to keep track of how much restoration you do on your beer can collection and inform a potential buyer exactly what restoration has been done. Cans that have been heavily restored are not likely to interest an experienced collector, so consider carefully how much restoration you should do before you start. If you intend to trade or sell a can, you might want to talk to the buyer before you begin major restorations; if the can is for your personal enjoyment, feel free to do as much restoration as you feel is warranted.

It is important that you practice on these cleaning and restoring techniques before you use them on a can you care about. First practice on a can that has little value. As you become more proficient, you will move on to restoring more valuable cans with confidence.

Cleaning

First, make sure that the can is empty. As explained above, gently shake the can with the opening pointed away from you. I have encountered all sorts of insects, mice, shrews, snakes, and various other living creatures inside old cans.

A piece of old bed sheet or terry cloth makes an excellent dust cloth. Beyond that, to get the general grime and grit off a can, make sure that the inside has been washed out of all foreign objects, and soak it in warm water with a liquid dish-washing detergent added. Depending on the type and degree of the dirt, this can be done for a few minutes or overnight. When done soaking, rinse the can in clean water and dry. You can let the can air-dry with the opening pointed down to let it drain. Be sure the can is thoroughly dry—water will rust the can.

If the can is beyond simple soap and water, a good cleaning agent is a product called "Simple Green." This is usually available at hardware stores or home centers. A soaking and scrubbing with a *soft-bristle* brush will usually do the trick. Again, either air-dry or wipe dry with a soft cloth. Simple Green is an organic product and can be safely used by the young or inexperienced collector.

Rust

The arch enemies of steel cans are rust and fading. There are few options for restoring a faded can, and I'll talk about that below, but there are a variety of ways to remove rust. The best two ways are by using either citric or oxalic acid. But remember, at this stage you are removing rust, not restoring color.

CITRIC ACID

The best citric acid is simple lemon juice. It is best to use concentrated lemon juice, and there are many brands available at your supermarket. Either soak the can in the concentrated lemon juice or rub it directly on the can with a soft cloth or brush. Again, rinse the can with clear water and dry it. Citric acid is organic and can be used safely by just about anyone. The results can be satisfactory.

OXALIC ACID

If lemon juice doesn't do the trick, a more sophisticated product is oxalic acid. *CAUTION!* **This is a powerful product and should be used *very* carefully. Young collectors should use this only with adult supervision.** If you are not experienced in using this product, find someone to demonstrate it before you use it.

Oxalic acid is an organic product, and while it is generally safe for all collectors to use, care should be taken. It should be used only in a well-ventilated area, and you should wear protective clothing, glasses, and rubber gloves. It is an excellent rust remover, but must be handled with care.

The pharmaceutical grade acid is extremely expensive and for this reason should be avoided. There is an industrial grade that is cheap and usually available by the pound at industrial supply houses. Oxalic acid must be diluted with water, and there are two ways of doing this. One is to mix one ounce of oxalic acid with two gallons of water heated to about 170 degrees. The other method is to mix two pounds in a garbage can full of water at room temperature. The warmer the water, the less oxalic acid is needed—heat increases the strength of the acid.

Be sure the cans are clean before soaking in the acid mixture, as oxalic acid will be badly diluted by dirt.

BUFFING

Rust can be removed from the tops, bottoms, and rims of cans by buffing them on a grinding wheel or, in the case of minor rusting, with a finger-nail file. Be careful not to buff these areas too much—do just enough to remove the rust. Also be careful that you do not scratch these areas.

Fading

Fading is fatal to both aluminum and steel cans, and there is not much that can be done to restore a faded can. Some collectors use Sharpie Pens to restore color. If you become good at this, you can hide some major defects in steel cans that will stand up to all but close examination. Cans that are restored in this manner, however, will generally be of little or no value to other collectors.

Dents

Dents are always a problem. Some dents, especially in aluminum cans, can be worked out with simple finger pressure. A six- or eight-inch metal rod, bent to a right angle (about two inches), can be rotated inside the can with good results. Again, try this first on a can that you don't care about until you become good at it.

Holes

Cans with holes are of little value. But as you become more experienced in cleaning and removing rust and dents, filling holes with liquid steel and replacing missing tops and bottoms will become the next challenge.

But remember, this should be done for personal satisfaction only; cans restored in this manner can be worthless to other collectors.

Preservation

After you have gone as far as you are able to in the restoration of a can, the next step is to preserve your work against further damage from dirt and rust. Let it soak for a couple of minutes in any acrylic floor polish, such as Johnson's Future. What this will do is give the can a shine and brighten the colors. The nice thing about acrylic floor polish is that it not only improves the appearance of the can, but it is barely detectable and won't "yellow" like waxes. If for some reason you want to remove the wax, simply soak the can in hot water and dry it.

Care, Storage, and Display

/

Basically a beer can will take care of itself while on the shelf, needing only an occasional dusting. The exception is that a can may be damaged if it falls off the shelf because of vibrations. Be sure that your shelves are sturdy and securely anchored, and be aware of where they are placed. Vibrations from general foot traffic, from a nearby washing machine or other appliance, or even car traffic if you live close to a road can cause cans to move and fall from the shelf.

Some collectors prefer or come across full cans. Old steel cans have been known to spring leaks and drip down the wall or on the cans on a lower shelf. The substance that leaks from these cans usually has the consistency of molasses and the result will be a sticky mess. If you collect full cans or have a couple in your collection, check them once or twice a year for leakage. If you have full cans that you want to empty, open them from the bottom to leave the top intact.

When traveling to trade meets or to visit other collectors, using cardboard beer flats to transport your cans is not advisable unless newspaper is used to separate the cans. Cans riding in flats will spin, creating spin marks on the cans. This can be avoided by putting newspaper between the cans.

The Beer Can Collectors of America offers its members a cardboard travel and display case called a "Can Tote." It is designed to hold up to forty-eight cans and comes in either twelve- or sixteen-ounce models. The sixteen-ounce model can also hold cone tops. The Can Tote is moderately priced and can be ordered by members from BCCA's office in St.

Louis. When using the Can Tote, newspaper should also be used to avoid metal to metal contact.

If you live in an area of high humidity, you should use a room dehumidifier where your cans are displayed or stored. This will keep unwanted spots from appearing on your cans.

Finally, cans should be stored in a dry place and always out of direct sunlight to avoid fading.

Organizations and Clubs

/

There are several organizations that are oriented toward the beer can collector. If you are a serious collector or simply want to learn more about beer can collecting, these are excellent organizations to join.

The Beer Can Collectors of America
747 Mercus Court
Fenton, MO 83026
   The BCCA is the largest organization of beer can collectors in the United States. Dues are $24 a year, and they issue a quarterly magazine that features timely articles on beer can collecting, including columns on all new can releases both foreign and domestic. Members can also advertise for cans that they want to trade or cans they need for their collection for $3 per ad. The BCCA has approximately 100 chapters worldwide with a membership in excess of 4,000 collectors. There are chapters in virtually every state and major city. In addition to the magazine, this organization issues a roster of these chapters broken down alphabetically and geographically.
   Local chapters usually hold one or more trading meetings a year and issue their own newsletters to local members. Dues to the chapters are generally minimal, just enough to cover expenses. BCCA also holds national "Canventions," usually in the Midwest or East Coast. These Canventions have been known to draw up to a thousand collectors from all over the world.
   BCCA does not attach cash values to cans and encourages trading

among its membership. If your interest is in cans dating after 1965, you can acquire a large collection in a very reasonable time by being somewhat aggressive.

The American Breweriana Association
P.O. Box 11157
Pueblo, CO 81001

The ABA's annual dues are $20 and it has over 3,000 members. It is the fastest growing brewery-oriented club in the world. The ABA's bimonthly magazine covers the full range of breweriana collecting, including beer cans. There is usually an informative feature article in each issue on a particular brewery or piece of breweriana that is submitted by a member. The ABA conventions generally draw up to 500 people and are held in such diverse places as Olympia, Washington; Denver, Colorado; and Fort Mitchell, Kentucky. The ABA also offers breweriana exchanges at no charge, in which members can greatly expand their collections of such breweriana as crowns, openers, coasters, and the like by drawing off the exchange and replacing them with items that the member has duplicates of. The ABA provides a roster for members, which is updated regularly in the magazine, that is arranged both alphabetically and geographically. The ABA encourages members to collect on every level, whether by trading or purchasing the needed items. If you would like a sample of *The American Breweriana Journal*, send $1 (to cover postage) to the address above.

Other Clubs

Two other organizations of merit are:

The East Coast Breweriana Association
Larry Handy
P.O. Box 593
Warrington, PA 18976

The National Association of Breweriana Advertisers
Robert Jaeger
2343 Met To Wee Lane
Wauwatosa, WI 53226

Mandatory Labeling Requirements

/

"Mandatories" are the information that is required on the labels of beer cans by the federal and sometimes the state governments.

Federal Mandatories

When canned beer entered the market, the only mandatory requirements for labeling were the basics: The contents (beer, ale, half and half, porter, or malt liquor), who the brewer was, where it was brewed, the size of the can, and the statement "Internal Revenue Tax Paid."

The tax statement was dropped in March 1950, but since then the government mandatories have been expanded to include: net contents in ounces and milliliters, the size of the word "beer" as well as other words on the can, and a prohibition against words such as "powerful" to describe the strength or alcohol content. There is no requirement to list the alcohol content (though this can be required by the state in which the beer is sold). Also, brewers cannot make claims for protein, fat, or caloric content unless all three are listed.

In 1986, the government required the following warning labels on all beer cans and bottles (as well as wine and other alcoholic beverages):

1. "According to the Surgeon General, women should not drink alcoholic beverages during pregnancy because of risk of birth defects."

2. "Consumption of alcoholic beverages impairs your ability to drive a car or operate machinery and may cause health problems."

State Mandatories

Basically, the states usually pick up where the federal government leaves off. Some states will (or have) required beer over 3.2 percent alcohol content to be labeled "Strong." Other states will limit (or have limited) the size of the container. A few years back, New Mexico passed a law that beer could not be sold in cans 12 ounces or larger. To get around this, Jos. Schlitz produced all their brands in 11¾-ounce cans. New Mexico soon relented, and everything returned to normal. The reason New Mexico outlawed cans twelve ounces or larger is not clear, but the measure was definitely aimed at Schlitz. The larger size cans were usually filled with malt liquors or other stronger beverages. As a side note, some states will leave the size of the container up to the brewer, but limit how many sizes can be marketed.

In the late 1960s, gallons were introduced in the American market following the lead of brewers in Europe. The problem was that the Americans wouldn't drink the gallon as fast as their European counterparts, and the beer went flat before it was consumed. The American gallon soon died out. The largest can currently produced is the Schlitz Malt Liquor can. Stroh and Miller Brewing also puts its Miller brand in a 24-ounce can.

In 1973, Oregon banned all tab tops. For over a year after the ban, if you wanted a beer in Oregon, you needed an opener. But the "sta-on" tab was soon introduced, and this has been the standard tab for beer and soft drinks for the last twenty years. It's strange that the pull tabs on cans were banned, but not the caps on bottles.

For many years, some states, especially those in the South, would require that state tax stamps be put on each individual can. The stamp was usually placed on the lid, but the practice is all but gone today.

Finally, the last of what might be called a mandatory is the UPC bar code. This is not exactly a government requirement, but no mass merchant will buy beer (or any other product, for that matter) that cannot be scanned electronically.

Brand Names and
Breweries

/

The question often comes up, "Why are beers of the same brand name produced by different breweries?" Beers carry the same brand name for a myriad of reasons. In the days before national brands, the brewers really didn't care that a beer with the same or similar name was sold in distant markets.

As late as the early 1940s, for example, Schmidt beer was sold by three different brewers, all independent of each other. Jacob Schmidt Brewing Company in St. Paul, Minnesota, brewed and sold Schmidt Beer from Wisconsin to Washington and south to Kansas and western Illinois. This brewery also produced a beer called Schmidt City Club. The Ekhardt & Becker Brewing Company in Detroit, Michigan, also brewed Schmidt Beer and sold it in the Great Lakes states and the upper Ohio River valley states. In Philadelphia, C. Schmidt & Sons brewed Schmidt's of Philadelphia, which was sold along the Atlantic coast; in 1964, they purchased the old Standard Brewery in Cleveland, Ohio, from the F & M Schaefer Brewing Company, which also produced the Schmidt brand in Cleveland. So, at one point, a beer drinker could go from Seattle to Philadelphia and drink Schmidt (or Schmidt's) beer brewed by three different and independent brewers at four different breweries.

As the brewing industry consolidated, so did the brands. The Schmidt brands in Minneapolis and Detroit were united when the Ekhardt and Becker brewery merged with the Jacob Schmidt brewery in the mid-1960s. A short time later, Piels Brothers in New York and Sterling Brothers in Evansville, Indiana, merged with Ekhardt and Becker to form the

Associated Brewing Company, which in turn merged with G. Heileman
Brewing Company (La Crosse, Wisconsin) in the mid-1970s. Since
C. Schmidt ceased operations in 1985, Heileman calls all the Schmidt
(and Schmidt's) brands "Schmidts," and they are sold nationwide.

Another factor in similar name brands was private labels. Probably
one of the most prominent private labels is Brown Derby Beer. Brown
Derby Beer originated in 1938 at the Humboldt Brewing and Malting
Company (Eureka, California) with a two-million case order placed by
the West Coast Grocery Company (Oakland, California), which was the
chief supplier for Safeway Stores. As Safeway grew, so did the number
of brewers that brewed Brown Derby. It should be noted that there are
some brewers that produced Brown Derby in bottles only, and these
brewers are not included in the following list. At one point, Brown Derby
was virtually sold coast to coast, but when Safeway became victim to
corporate takeovers and retrenched in the late-1980s, Brown Derby faded.

Other private labels of note are 7-11 Beer for Seven-Eleven stores; El
Rancho Beer for Mayfair stores in Los Angeles; Gilt Edge Beer and Ale
for Gilt Edge Markets; Grand Union Beer for the supermarkets of the
same name; Schwegmann Beer for Schwegmann grocery stores; and
9-0-5 Beer for the St. Louis liquor store chain, to name a few.

Still another reason for brand-name confusion was the practice of fran-
chising a label in an attempt to make it a national brand. An example of
this would be KOL Premium Beer. KOL was an effort to give the smaller
grocer or beer retailer a private label. The effort began in the mid-1950s
and was gone by the early 1970s.

A favorite scheme of some brewers, especially the Chicago brewers
of the '40s and '50s, was to let a brewer in a distant market produce
their brand on a royalty basis. This could explain why Best Beer was
produced in Florida—maybe to give Midwesterners a familiar beer to
drink while on vacation there. Also, by paying royalties, the freight and
transportation, as well as other distribution costs, could be reduced when
entering a distant market.

Some brewers used names other than their own to hide the real origin
of their beer. This was done for various reasons, especially when sales
began to fall after a bad beer was put on the market. Brewers have been
known to change the name of the brewery to give the beer a new image.
A good example of this would be when Manhattan Brewing Company in
Chicago changed its name to Canadian Ace Brewing Company. The
armed forces coming home from World War II remembered the bad beer
they drank while stationed overseas and stayed away from those labels
when they returned home. In all fairness, some of the brewers put out
the best product they could; they were hampered by the raw materials
available during the war and the end result was not the same beer as

produced before the war began. A brand would be discontinued by one brewer only to show up from another brewer, sometimes with no change at all in the flavor.

Some brewers operated phantom breweries in other cities. Manhattan Brewing Company also distributed beer under the names of Lubeck Brewing Company (Toledo, Ohio), Whitewater Brewing Company (Philadelphia), Weibel Brewing Company (New Haven, Connecticut), and Schepps Brewing Company (Dallas, Texas). These names, besides masking the origin of the beer, would give the illusion of "local flavor" and give consumers the impression that they were buying a home-town beer.

The more obvious reason for a brand name to change brewers are that either the brewery was sold to another company or it went out of business and sold the brand names to another brewer. A label could also be revived by anyone after its state and/or federal registration expired.

Finally, a brand will often be created for a special event or market and be brewed by different brewers at different times and locations. This is almost a thing of the past today; the cost and other production factors for cans are too high for breweries to do these small production runs efficiently. But the phenomenon will likely live on in the bottled beer market.

Labels (Brand Names) Produced by Different Brewers

The following list shows overlapping or identical labels that were used by more than one brewery. The labels are listed first with the different breweries that produced the label listed immediately below.

7-11 BEER

Altes Brewing Company, Detroit, Michigan
Altes Brewing Company, San Diego, California
Colonial Brewing Company, Hammonton, New Jersey
Garden State Brewing Company, Hammonton, New Jersey
Lexington Brewing Company, Newark, New Jersey

9-0-5 BEER

9-0-5 Brewing Company, Chicago, Illinois
9-0-5 Brewing Company, South Bend, Indiana
Associated Brewing Company, Evansville, Indiana
Atlas Brewing Company, Chicago, Illinois
Drewery's Ltd. U.S.A., Chicago, Illinois

Drewery's Ltd. U.S.A., South Bend, Indiana
Gold Brau Brewing Company, Chicago, Illinois
G. Heileman Brewing Company, La Crosse, Wisconsin

A.B.C. BEER

August Wagner Brewing Company, Columbus, Ohio
Fischer Brewing Company, Auburndale, Florida
Garden State Brewing Company, Hammonton, New Jersey
Maier Brewing Company, Los Angeles, California

ACME BEER

Acme Brewing Company, Los Angeles, California
Acme Brewing Company, San Francisco, California
Blitz-Weinhard Company, Portland, OR
General Brewing Company, San Francisco, CA
Grace Bros. Brewing Company, Santa Rosa, California

ALPINE BEER

General Brewing Company, San Francisco, California
Jos. Huber Brewing Company, Monroe, Wisconsin
Maier Brewing Company, Los Angeles, California
Peter Fox Brewing Company, Chicago, Illinois
Peter Fox Brewing Company, Grand Rapids, Michigan

ALPS BRAU BEER

Alpine Brewing Company, Potosi, Wisconsin
Centlivre Brewing Corporation, Ft. Wayne, Indiana
Grace Bros. Brewing Company, Santa Rosa, California
Maier Brewing Company, Los Angeles, California
Old Crown Brewing Company, Ft. Wayne, Indiana
Peter Hand Brewing Company, Chicago, Illinois

ALTA BEER

Blitz-Weinhard Company, Portland, Oregon
Grace Bros. Brewing Company, Santa Rosa, California

ALTES BEER

Altes Brewing Company, Detroit, Michigan
Altes Brewing Company, San Diego, California
National Brewing Company, Detroit, Michigan
Tivoli Brewing Company, Detroit, Michigan

AMERICAN BEER

American Brewing Company, Baltimore, Maryland
American Brewing Company, Cumberland, Maryland

ARROW BEER

American Brewing Company, Baltimore, Maryland
Globe Brewing Company, Baltimore, Maryland
Globe Brewing Company, Cumberland, Maryland

BALBOA BEER

Balboa Brewing Company, San Diego, California
Grace Bros. Brewing Company, Santa Rosa, California
Monarch Brewing Company, Los Angeles, California
Southern Brewing Company, Los Angeles, California

BAVARIAN

General Brewing Company, Los Angeles, California
Maier Brewing Company, Los Angeles, California

BAVARIANS SELECT BEER

Bavarian Brewing Company, Covington, Kentucky
Bavarians Brewing Company, Evansville, Indiana
Bavarians Brewing Company, South Bend, Indiana
International Brewery Company, Covington, Kentucky
International Brewery Company, Tampa, Florida
International Brewery Company, Buffalo, New York
International Brewery Company, Findlay, Ohio
Iroquois Brewing Company, Columbus, Ohio

BERGHEIM BEER

Old Reading Brewing Company, Reading, Pennsylvania
Reading Brewing Company, Reading, Pennsylvania
C. Schmidt & Sons, Philadelphia, Pennsylvania

BERGHOFF BEER

Berghoff Brewing Company, Fort Wayne, Indiana
Pearl Brewing Company, San Antonio, Texas
Walter Brewing Company, Pueblo, Colorado

BERGHOFF 1887 BEER

Berghoff Brewing Company, Fort Wayne, Indiana
Tennessee Brewing Company, Memphis, Tennessee

BEST BEER

Best Brewing Company, Chicago, Illinois
Cumberland Brewing Company, Cumberland, Maryland
Empire Brewing Company, Chicago, Illinois
Hornell Brewing Company, Hornell, New York
Hornell Brewing Company, Trenton, New Jersey
Spearman Brewing Company, Pensacola, Florida
United States Brewing Company, Chicago, Illinois

BETTER FOODS BEER

Maier Brewing Company, Los Angeles, California
Pacific Brewing, Oakland, California

BIG APPLE BEER

Sunshine Brewing Company, Reading, Pennsylvania
Waukee Brewing Company, Hammonton, New Jersey

BILOW GARDEN STATE BEER

Colonial Brewing Company, Hammonton, New Jersey
Garden State Brewing Company, Hammonton, New Jersey

BISMARCK BEER

Balboa Brewing Company, Los Angeles, California
Bismarck Brewing Company, Chicago, Illinois

BLACK AND WHITE BEER

Maier Brewing Company, Los Angeles, California
St. Claire Brewing Company, San Jose, California

BLACK DALLAS BEER

ABC Brewing Company, St. Louis, Missouri
Manhattan Brewing Company, Chicago, Illinois
Schepps Brewing Company, Dallas, Texas
Time Brewing Company, Dallas, Texas

BLACK DALLAS MALT LIQUOR

Atlantic Brewing Company, Chicago, Illinois
Canadian Ace Brewing Company, Chicago, Illinois
Leisy Brewing Company, Cleveland, Ohio
Walter Brewing Company, Pueblo, Colorado

BLACK HORSE ALE

Black Horse Brewing Company, Dunkirk, New York
Black Horse Brewing Company, Lawrence, Massachusetts
Black Horse Brewing Company, Trenton, New Jersey
Diamond Spring Brewing Company, Lawrence, Massachusetts
Fred Koch Brewery Company, Dunkirk, New York

BLACKHAWK BEER

Atlantic Brewing Company, Chicago, Illinois
Blackhawk Brewing Company, Buffalo, New York
Blackhawk Brewing Company, Davenport, Iowa
Cumberland Brewing Company, Cumberland, Maryland
Leisy Brewing Company, Cleveland, Ohio

BLATZ BEER

Blatz Brewing Company, Milwaukee, Wisconsin
G. Heileman Brewing Company, La Crosse, Wisconsin
Pabst Brewing Company, Milwaukee, Wisconsin

BLUE BOAR BEER

Loewers Brewery Company, New York, New York
Northampton Brewery Company, Northampton, Pennsylvania

BOHEMIAN BEER

Buffalo Brewing Company, Sacramento, California
General Brewing Company, San Francisco, California
Grace Bros. Brewing Company, Santa Rosa, California
Maier Brewing Company, Los Angeles, California
Southern Brewing Company, Los Angeles, California

BOHEMIAN CLUB BEER

Atlantic Brewing Company, Spokane, Washington
Bohemian Breweries, Spokane, Washington
Bohemian Breweries, Boise, Idaho

Bohemian Brewing Company, Chicago, Illinois
Bohemian Brewing Company, Joliet, Illinois
Bohemian Brewing Company, Potosi, Wisconsin
Brewing Company of Oregon, Portland, Oregon
Jos. Huber Brewing Company, Monroe, Wisconsin
Oconto Brewing Company, Oconto, Wisconsin

BONANZA BEER

Garden State Brewing Company, Hammonton, New Jersey
Spearman Brewing Company, Pensacola, Florida

BRAU HAUS BEER

General Brewing Company, Los Angeles, California
General Brewing Company, San Francisco, California
Grace Bros. Brewing Company, Santa Rosa, California
San Francisco Brewing Company, San Francisco, California

BRAUMEISTER BEER

G. Heileman Brewing Company, La Crosse, Wisconsin
Independent Milwaukee Brewery, Milwaukee, Wisconsin
Peter Hand Brewing Company, Chicago, Illinois

BREW 66 BEER

Sicks Brewing Company, Salem, Oregon
Sicks Seattle Brewing & Malting Company, Seattle, Washington
Sicks Rainier Brewing Company, Seattle, Washington

BREWERS BEST BEER

Atlantic Brewing Company, Chicago, Illinois
Grace Bros. Brewing Company, Santa Rosa, California
Maier Brewing Company, Los Angeles, California

BROWN DERBY BEER

Atlantic Brewing Company, Spokane, Washington
Best Brewing Company, Chicago, Illinois
Century Brewing Company, Norfolk, Virginia
Century Brewing Company, San Francisco, California
Grace Bros. Brewing Company, Santa Rosa, California
Humboldt Brewing and Malting Company, Eureka, California
Jos. Huber Brewing Company, Monroe, Wisconsin
Los Angeles Brewing Company, Los Angeles, California

Maier Brewing Company, Los Angeles, California
Pabst Brewing Company, Tumwater, Washington
Pacific Brewing and Malting Company, San Jose, California
Pearl Brewing Company, San Antonio, Texas
Pittsburgh Brewing Company, Pittsburgh, Pennsylvania
Queen City Brewing Company, Cumberland, Maryland
Rainier Brewing Company, San Francisco, California
Silver Springs Brewing Company, Tacoma, Washington
Storz Brewing Company, Omaha, Nebraska
Walter Brewing Company, Pueblo, Colorado

BUCKEYE BEER

Buckeye Brewing Company, Toledo, Ohio
Burgermeister Brewing Company, San Francisco, California
Meister-Brau Inc., Toledo, Ohio
Miller Brewing Company, Milwaukee, Wisconsin

BUCKHORN BEER

Buckhorn Brewing Company, St. Paul, Minnesota
Lone Star Brewing Company, San Antonio, Texas
Olympia Brewing Company, St. Paul, Minnesota
Olympia Brewing Company, Tumwater, Washington
Pabst Brewing Company, Milwaukee, Wisconsin
Pabst Brewing Company, Tumwater, Washington

BUFFALO BEER

Blitz-Weinhard Company, Portland, Oregon
Buffalo Brewing Company, Sacramento, California
General Brewing Company, San Francisco, California

BULL DOG ALE

Acme Brewing Company, Los Angeles, California
Acme Brewing Company, San Francisco, California
California Brewing Association, San Francisco, California
Grace Bros. Brewing Company, Santa Rosa, California
Maier Brewing Company, Los Angeles, California

BULL DOG MALT LIQUOR

Acme Brewing Company, Vernon, California
Acme Brewing Company, San Francisco, California
Atlas Brewing Company, Chicago, Illinois

California Brewing Association, San Francisco, California
Drewry's Ltd. USA, South Bend, Indiana
General Brewing Company, San Francisco, California
Maier Brewing Company, Los Angeles, California

BURGER BEER

Burger Brewing Company, Cincinnati, Ohio
Hudepohl Brewing Company, Cincinnati, Ohio

BURGERMEISTER BEER

Burgermeister Brewing Company, Los Angeles, California
Burgermeister Brewing Company, San Francisco, California
G. Heileman Brewing Company, Portland, Oregon
Jos. Schlitz, Los Angeles, California
Jos. Schlitz Brewing Company, San Francisco, California
Milwaukee Brewery Company, San Francisco, California
Pabst Brewing Company, Portland, Oregon
San Francisco Brewing Company, San Francisco, California
Theo. Hamms Brewing Company, San Francisco, California

CANADIAN ACE BEER

Canadian Ace Brewing Company, Chicago, Illinois
Canadian Ace Brewing Company, Hammonton, New Jersey
Manhattan Brewing Company, Chicago, Illinois
Tivoli Brewing Company, Denver, Colorado
Waukee Brewing Company, Hammonton, New Jersey

CHAMPAGNE VELVET BEER

Associated Brewing Company, Evansville, Indiana
Atlantic Brewing Company, Chicago, Illinois
Blitz-Weinhard Company, Portland, Oregon
Bohemian Breweries, Spokane, Washington
Brewing Company of Oregon, Portland, Oregon
Drewerys Ltd. USA, South Bend, Indiana
G. Heileman Brewing Company, La Crosse, Wisconsin
Jos. Pickett Brewing Company, Dubuque, Iowa
Terre Haute Brewing Company, Terre Haute, Indiana

CHIEF OSHKOSH BEER

Oshkosh Brewing Company, Oshkosh, Wisconsin
Peoples Brewing Company, Oshkosh, Wisconsin

CLUB HOUSE BEER

Grace Bros. Brewing Company, Santa Rosa, California
Maier Brewing Company, Los Angeles, California

COLD BRAU BEER

Associated Brewing Company, Evansville, Indiana
Drewerys Ltd. USA, South Bend, Indiana
Schoenhofen-Edelweiss, Chicago, Illinois

COLUMBIA BEER

Carling Brewing Company, Tacoma, Washington
Carling-National Brewing Company, Tacoma, Washington
Columbia Brewing Company, Tacoma, Washington
Heidelberg Brewing Company, Tacoma, Washington

COOKS BEER

Associated Brewing Company, Evansville, Indiana
F.W. Cook, Evansville, Indiana
G. Heileman Brewing Company, Evansville, Indiana

CREAM TOP BEER

Manhattan Brewing Company, Chicago, Illinois
Whitewater Brewing Company, Whitewater, Wisconsin

DEUTCHE BRAU BEER

General Brewing Company, San Francisco, California
Grace Bros., Santa Rosa, California
Maier Brewing Company, Los Angeles, California

DREWERYS BEER

Associated Brewing Company, South Bend, Indiana
Drewerys Ltd. USA., Chicago, Illinois
Drewerys Ltd. USA., South Bend, Indiana
G. Heileman Brewing Company, La Crosse, Wisconsin

DURST BEER

Atlantic Brewing Company, Chicago, Illinois
Atlantic Brewing Company, Spokane, Washington
Durst Brewing Company, Spokane, Washington
Silver Springs Brewing Company, Tacoma, Washington

E & B BEER

Associated Brewing Company, Evansville, Indiana
Associated Brewing Company, South Bend, Indiana
E & B Brewing Company, Detroit, Michigan
Ekhardt & Becker Brewing Company, Detroit, Michigan

EDELBRAU BEER

General Brewing Company, San Francisco, California
Maier Brewing Company, Los Angeles, California

EDELWEISS BEER

Associated Brewing Company, Evansville, Indiana
Drewerys Ltd. USA, South Bend, Indiana
G. Heileman Brewing Company, La Crosse, Wisconsin
Jos. Pickett, Dubuque, Iowa
Schoenhofen Company, Chicago, Illinois
Schoenhofen-Edelweiss, Chicago, Illinois

EINBOCK BOCK BEER

Arizona Brewing Company, Phoenix, Arizona
Maier Brewing Company, Los Angeles, California
Walter Brewing Company, Pueblo, Colorado

EL RANCHO BEER

Falstaff Brewing Company, San Francisco, California
General Brewing Company, San Francisco, California
Grace Bros. Brewing Company, Santa Rosa, California
Maier Brewing Company, Los Angeles, California

EMBASSY CLUB BEER

Best Brewing Company, Chicago, Illinois
Century Brewing Corporation, Norfolk, Virginia
Embassy Club Brewing Company, Chicago, Illinois
Embassy Club Brewing Company, Chicago, Illinois
Metropolis Brewery Company, Trenton, New Jersey

ENGLISH LAD BEER AND ALE

Prima Brewing Company, Chicago, Illinois
Westminister Brewing Company, Chicago, Illinois

ESSLINGER BEER

Esslinger Inc., Philadelphia, Pennsylvania
Jacob Rupert, New York, New York

EUREKA BEER

Eagle Brewing Company, San Francisco, California
Humboldt Brewing and Malting Company, Eureka, California
Pacific Brewing Company, Oakland, California

EXCELL BEER

Golden West Brewing Company, Oakland, California
Grace Bros., Santa Rosa, California
Maier Brewing Company, Los Angeles, California
Pacific Brewing Company, Oakland, California

FINER FLAVER BEER

Columbia Breweries, Tacoma, Washington
Maier Brewing Company, Los Angeles, California
Monarch Brewing Company, Los Angeles, California
Southern Brewing Company, Los Angeles, California

FISCHERS BEER

Fischer Brewing Company, Auburndale, Florida
Fischer Brewing Company, Cumberland, Maryland
Queen City Brewing Company, Cumberland, Maryland

FISHER BEER

Fisher Brewing Company, Salt Lake City, Utah
General Brewing Company, San Francisco, California
Lucky Brewing Company, San Francisco, California
Lucky Lager Brewery Company, San Francisco, California

FOX DELUXE BEER

Fox Head-Waukesha Corporation, Waukesha, Wisconsin
Fox Head Brewing Company, Waukesha, Wisconsin
G. Heileman Brewing Company, La Crosse, Wisconsin
G. Heileman Brewing Company, Sheboygan, Wisconsin
Peter Fox Brewing Company, Chicago, Illinois

FRANKENMUTH BEER

Associated Brewing Company, South Bend, Indiana
Frankenmuth Brewing Company, Frankenmuth, Michigan
Frankenmuth-Kentucky Brewing Company, Louisville, Kentucky
Geyer Bros. Brewing Company, Frankenmuth, Michigan
International Breweries Incorporated, Buffalo, New York
International Breweries Incorporated, Covington, Kentucky
International Breweries Incorporated, Detroit, Michigan
International Breweries Incorporated, Findlay, Ohio

FREDERICKS 4 CROWN

Fredericks Brewing Company, Thorton, Illinois
South Side Brewing Company, Chicago, Illinois

G.B. BEER

Cleveland-Sandusky Brewing Company, Buffalo, New York
Cleveland-Sandusky Brewing Company, Cleveland, Ohio
Cleveland-Sandusky Brewing Company, Cumberland, Maryland
Cleveland-Sandusky Brewing Company, Findlay, Ohio
Cleveland-Sandusky Brewing Company, Toledo, Ohio
Grace Bros. Brewing Company, Santa Rosa, California
Griesedieck Bros. Brewing Company, St. Louis, Missouri

GAMBRINUS BEER

August Wagner Brewing Company, Chillicothe, Ohio
August Wagner Brewing Company, Columbus, Ohio
Pittsburgh Brewing Company, Pittsburgh, Pennsylvania

GILT EDGE BEER

Bosch Brewing Company, Houghton, Michigan
Buffalo Brewing Company, Sacramento, California
Century Brewing Company, Norfolk, Virginia
Champale Products Incorporated, Norfolk, Virginia
Hornell Brewing Company, Hornell, New York
Rilato Brewing Company, Trenton, New Jersey
Spearman Brewing Company, Pensacola, Florida

GLACIER BEER

Maier Brewing Company, Los Angeles, California
Pacific Brewing Company, Oakland, California

GLUEK BEER

Cold Spring Brewing Company, Cold Spring, Minnesota
Gluek Brewing Company, Minneapolis, Minnesota
G. Heileman Brewing Company, La Crosse, Wisconsin

GOLD COAST BEER

Atlas Brewing Company, Chicago, Illinois
9-0-5 Brewing Company, Chicago, Illinois

GOLD MEDAL BEER

Grace Bros. Brewing Company, Santa Rosa, California
Humboldt Brewing and Malting Company, Eureka, California
Indianapolis Brewing Company, Indianapolis, Indiana
Stegmaier Brewing Company, Wilkes-Barre, Pennsylvania

GOLD SEAL BEER

Mutual Brewing Company, Ellensburg, Washington
Silver Springs Brewing Company, Port Orchard, Washington

GOLDEN BREW

Diamond Spring Brewing Company, Lawrence, Massachusetts
General Brewing Company, Los Angeles, California
Grace Bros. Brewing Company, Santa Rosa, California

GOLDEN CROWN BEER

General Brewing Company, Los Angeles, California
Grace Bros. Brewing Company, Los Angeles, California
Grace Bros. Brewing Company, Santa Rosa, California
Maier Brewing Company, Los Angeles, California

GOLDEN GLOW BEER

Golden West Brewing Company, Oakland, California
Jos. Huber Brewing Company, Monroe, Wisconsin
Pacific Brewing Company, Oakland, California

GOLDEN GRAIN BEER

Harry Mitchell Brewing Company, El Paso, Texas
Maier Brewing Company, Los Angeles, California

GOLDEN HARVEST BEER

General Brewing Company, Los Angeles, California
Maier Brewing Company, Los Angeles, California
Pacific Brewing Company, Oakland, California

GOLDEN LAGER BEER

Burgermeister Brewing Company, San Francisco, California
Maier Brewing Company, Los Angeles, California
Southern Brewing Company, Los Angeles, California
Theo. Hamm Brewing Company, San Francisco, California

GOLDEN VELVET BEER

Blitz-Weinhard Company, Portland, Oregon
Maier Brewing Company, Los Angeles, California
Tivoli Brewing Company, Denver, Colorado

GRAND UNION BEER

Eastern Brewing Company, Hammonton, New Jersey
Gilt Edge Brewing Company, Trenton, New Jersey

GREAT LAKES BEER

Associated Brewing Company, Evansville, Indiana
Drewerys Ltd. USA., South Bend, Indiana
G. Heileman Brewing Company, La Crosse, Wisconsin
Schoenhofen-Edelweiss, Chicago, Illinois

GRETZ BEER

Esslinger Incorporated, Philadelphia, Pennsylvania
Jacob Ruppert, New York, New York
William Gretz Brewing Company, Philadelphia, Pennsylvania

HAMMS BEER

Olympia Brewing Company, Tumwater, Washington
Pabst Brewing Company, Tumwater, Washington
Theo. Hamms Brewing Company, St. Paul, Minnesota

HAPPY HOPS BEER

Grace Bros. Brewing Company, Santa Rosa, California
North Bay Brewing Company, Santa Rosa, California

HAUENSTEIN BEER

G. Heileman Brewing Company, La Crosse, Wisconsin
John Hauenstein Company, Minneapolis, Minnesota

HEIDELBERG BEER

Carling Brewing Company, Tacoma, Washington
Carling-National Brewing Company, Tacoma, Washington
Columbia Breweries Incorporated, Tacoma, Washington
Heidelberg Brewing Company, Tacoma, Washington
G. Heileman Brewing Company, La Crosse, Wisconsin

HERITAGE BEER

Drewrys Ltd. USA, South Bend, Indiana
Jos. Schlitz Brewing Company, Milwaukee, Wisconsin

HERITAGE HOUSE BEER

Pittsburgh Brewing Company, Pittsburgh, Pennsylvania
Queen City Brewing Company, Cumberland, Maryland
Walter Brewing Company, Pueblo, Colorado

HOF-BRAU BEER

General Brewing Company, Los Angeles, California
General Brewing Company, San Francisco, California
Maier Brewing Company, Los Angeles, California
Walter Brewing Company, Pueblo, Colorado

HOLLAND BEER

Eastern Brewing Company, Hammonton, New Jersey
Maier Brewing Company, Los Angeles, California

HOP GOLD BEER

Interstate Brewing Company, Vancouver, Washington
Star Brewing Company, Vancouver, Washington

IMPERIAL BEER

Grace Bros. Brewing Company, Los Angeles, California
Maier Brewing Company, Los Angeles, California
Southern Brewing Company, Los Angeles, California

IROQUOIS BEER

Cleveland-Sandusky Brewing Company, Toledo, Ohio
International Breweries Incorporated, Buffalo, New York
Iroquois Beverage Company, Buffalo, New York
Iroquois Brewing Company, Buffalo, New York
Iroquois Brewing Company, Erie, Pennsylvania
Iroquois Brewing Company, Dunkirk, New York

JAX BEER

Jackson Brewing Company, New Orleans, Louisiana
Jax Brewing Company, Jacksonville, Florida
Pearl Brewing Company, San Antonio, Texas

KC'S BEST BEER

Atlantic Brewing Company, Chicago, Illinois
Empire Brewing Company, Chicago, Illinois
Storz Brewing Company, Omaha, Nebraska

KARLSBRAU BEER

Cold Spring Brewing Company, Cold Spring, Minnesota
Duluth Brewing and Malting Company, Duluth, Minnesota
G. Heileman Brewing Company, La Crosse, Wisconsin

KATZ BEER

Associated Brewing Company, Evansville, Indiana
Drewrys Ltd. USA, South Bend, Indiana
Pearl Brewing, San Antonio, Texas
Schoenhofen-Edelweiss, Chicago, Illinois

KEELEY BEER

Best Brewing Company, Chicago, Illinois
Cumberland Brewing Company, Cumberland, Maryland
Keeley Brewing Company, Chicago, Illinois

KEG BEER

American Brewing Company, Baltimore, Maryland
General Brewing Company, Los Angeles, California
Maier Brewing Company, Los Angeles, California

KINGS TASTE

Rainier Brewing Company, San Francisco, California
St. Claire Brewing Company, San Jose, California

KOL BEER

Atlantic Brewing Company, Chicago, Illinois
Atlantic Brewing Company, Spokane, Washington
Kol Brewing Company, Tampa, Florida
Metz Brewing Company, Omaha, Nebraska
Silver Spring Brewing Company, Tacoma, Washington

LEBANON VALLEY BEER

Eagle Brewing Company, Catasauqua, Pennsylvania
Lebanon Valley Brewing Company, Lebanon, Pennsylvania

MARK V BEER

August Wagner Brewing Company, Columbus, Ohio
Eastern Brewing Company, Hammonton, New Jersey

MEISTER-BRAU BEER

Meister-Brau Inc., Chicago, Illinois
Meister-Brau Inc., Toledo, Ohio
Miller Brewing Company, Milwaukee, Wisconsin
Peter Hand Brewing Company, Milwaukee, Wisconsin

MILE-HI BEER

Mountain Brewing Company, Denver, Colorado
Tivoli Brewing Company, Denver, Colorado

MILWAUKEE'S BEST BEER

A. Gettleman Brewing Company, Milwaukee, Wisconsin
Miller Brewing Company, Milwaukee, Wisconsin

MOUNTAIN BREW BEER

Hatfield-McCoy Brewing Company, Reading, Pennsylvania
Queen City Brewing Company, Cumberland, Maryland

MY BEER

My Brewing Company, Omaha, Nebraska
Walter Brewing Company, Pueblo, Colorado

NECTAR BEER

Ambrosia Brewing Company, Chicago, Illinois
Atlantic Brewing Company, Chicago, Illinois

NEUWEILER BEER

Brewmasters International Brewing Company, Allentown, Pennsylvania
Louis F. Neuweiler & Son, Allentown, Pennsylvania

NORTH STAR BEER

Associated Brewing Company, St. Paul, Minnesota
Cold Spring Brewing Company, Cold Spring, Minnesota
G. Heileman Brewing Company, St. Paul, Minnesota

NORTHERN BEER

Cold Spring Brewing Company, Cold Spring, Minnesota
Northern Brewing Company, Superior, Wisconsin

OLD CROWN BEER

Centlivre Brewing Company, Fort Wayne, Indiana
Old Crown Brewing Company, Fort Wayne, Indiana
Peter Hand Brewing Company, Chicago, Illinois

OLD DUTCH BEER

Associated Brewing Company, Evansville, Indiana
Hornell Brewing Company, Hornell, New York
International Breweries, Findlay, Ohio
Krantz Brewing Company, Findlay, Ohio
Maier Brewing Company, Los Angeles, California
Metropolis Brewing Company, Trenton, New Jersey
Old Dutch Brewers, Brooklyn, New York
Old Dutch Brewing Company, Detroit, Michigan
Pilser Brewing Company, New York, New York
Pittsburgh Brewing Company, Pittsburgh, Pennsylvania
Queen City Brewing Company, Cumberland, Maryland

OLD ENGLISH 600 MALT LIQUOR

Atlantic Brewing Company, Spokane, Washington
Bohemian Breweries Inc., Spokane, Washington
Peoples Brewing and Malting Company, Duluth, Minnesota

OLD ENGLISH 800 MALT LIQUOR

Blitz-Weinhard Company, Evansville, Indiana
Blitz-Weinhard Company, Newark, New Jersey
Blitz-Weinhard Company, Portland, Oregon
Brewing Company of Oregon, Portland, Oregon

OLD EXPORT BEER

Cumberland Brewing Company, Cumberland, Maryland
Pittsburgh Brewing Company, Pittsburgh, Pennsylvania
Queen City Brewing Company, Cumberland, Maryland

OLD GERMAN BEER

Burkhardt Brewing Company, Akron, Ohio
Colonial Brewing Company, Hammonton, New Jersey
Cumberland Brewing Company, Cumberland, Maryland
Eastern Brewing Company, Hammonton, New Jersey
Geo. J. Renner Brewing Company, Akron, Ohio
Grace Bros. Brewing Company, Santa Rosa, California
Maier Brewing Company, Los Angeles, California
Pittsburgh Brewing Company, Pittsburgh, Pennsylvania
Peter Hand Brewing Company, Chicago, Illinois
Queen City Brewing Company, Cumberland, Maryland
Renner Company, Youngstown, Ohio

OLD GOLD BEER

Grace Bros. Brewing Company, Santa Rosa, California
Manhattan Brewing Company, Chicago, Illinois
St. Claire Brewing Company, San Jose, California

OLD MISSION BEER

Los Angeles Brewing Company, Los Angeles, California
Pabst Brewing Company, Los Angeles, California

OLD TIMERS BEER

Cleveland-Sandusky Brewing Company, Buffalo, New York
Cleveland-Sandusky Brewing Company, Cleveland, Ohio
Cleveland-Sandusky Brewing Company, Cumberland, Maryland
Cleveland-Sandusky Brewing Company, Sandusky, Ohio
Cleveland-Sandusky Brewing Company, Toledo, Ohio
West Bend Litha, West Bend, Wisconsin

OLD VIENNA BEER

Grace Bros. Brewing Company, Santa Rosa, California
Maier Brewing Company, Los Angeles, California
Manhattan Brewing Company, Chicago, Illinois
Old Vienna Brewing Company, Chicago, Illinois

OLDBRU BEER

Burgermeister Brewing Company, San Francisco, California
San Francisco Brewing Company, San Francisco, California
Theo. Hamm Brewing Company, San Francisco, California

P.O.C. BEER

Pilsener Brewing Company, Cleveland, Ohio
Pilsener Brewing Company, Pittsburgh, Pennsylvania
Pilsener Brewing Company, Philadelphia, Pennsylvania

PACIFIC BEER

Rainier Brewing Company, San Francisco, California
Southern Brewing Company, Los Angeles, California

PEOPLES BEER

Eastern Brewing Company, Hammonton, New Jersey
Peoples Brewing Company, Oshkosh, Wisconsin
Peoples Brewing Company, Trenton, New Jersey

PFEIFFER BEER

Associated Brewing Company, Evansville, Indiana
Associated Brewing Company, St. Paul, Minnesota
Pfeiffer Brewing Company, Detroit, Michigan
Pfeiffer Brewing Company, Flint, Michigan
Pfeiffer Brewing Company, South Bend, Indiana
Pfeiffer Brewing Company, St. Paul, Minnesota

PHOENIX BEER

International Breweries Incorporated, Buffalo, New York
Iroquois Brewing Company, Buffalo, New York
Iroquois Brewing Company, Columbus, Ohio
Phoenix Brewing Company, Buffalo, New York
Phoenix Brewing Company, Covington, Kentucky

PILSENER CLUB BEER

Gluek Brewing Company, Minneapolis, Minnesota
Pearl Brewing Company, San Antonio, Texas
Storz Brewing Company, Omaha, Nebraska

PRAGER

Atlas Brewing Company, Chicago, Illinois
Drewrys Ltd. USA., South Bend, Indiana
G. Heileman Brewing Company, La Crosse, Wisconsin

PROST BEER

Associated Brewing Company, South Bend, Indiana
Drewerys Ltd. USA, South Bend, Indiana
Schoenhofen-Edelweiss, Chicago, Illinois

RAINIER BEER

Rainier Brewing Company, Seattle, Washington
Rainier Brewing Company, San Francisco, California
Seattle Brewing and Malting Company, Seattle, Washington
Sick's Seattle Brewing and Malting Company, Seattle, Washington
Sick's Spokane Brewing and Malting Company, Spokane, Washington
Spokane Brewery Inc., Spokane, Washington

RAMS HEAD

Adam Scheidt Brewing Company, Norristown, Pennsylvania
C. Schmidt & Sons, Philadelphia, Pennsylvania
Valley Forge Brewing Company, Norristown, Pennsylvania

RED FOX BEER

Century Brewing Company, Norfolk, Virginia
Cumberland Brewing Company, Cumberland, Maryland
Jacob Ruppert-Virginia, Norfolk, Virginia
Largay Brewing Company, Waterbury, Connecticut

REDTOP BEER

Associated Brewing Company, South Bend, Indiana
Atlantic Brewing Company, Chicago, Illinois
C.V. Brewing Company, Chicago, Illinois
Drewerys Ltd. USA., South Bend, Indiana
Terre Haute Brewing Company, Terre Haute, Indiana

REGAL

American Brewing Company, Miami, Florida
American Brewing Company, New Orleans, Louisiana
Anheuser-Busch Inc., Miami, Florida
Associated Brewing Company, Evansville, Indiana
Atlantic Brewing Company, Chicago, Illinois
Drewerys Ltd. USA., South Bend, Indiana
G. Heileman Brewing Company, La Crosse, Wisconsin
Jos. Pickett & Son, Dubuque, Iowa
Regal Brewing Company, Miami, Florida

REGENT

Century Brewing Company, Norfolk, Virginia
Champale Products, Norfolk, Virginia
Metropolis Brewing Company, Trenton, New Jersey
Regent Brewing Company, Pensacola, Florida

REX BEER

August Schell Brewing Company, New Ulm, Minnesota
Fitger Brewing Company, Duluth, Minnesota
Maier Brewing Company, Los Angeles, California

ROYAL BEER

Maier Brewing Company, Los Angeles, California
Reno Brewing Company, Reno, Nevada
Royal Brewing Company, Chicago, Illinois

RUSER BEER

Arizona Brewing Company, Phoenix, Arizona
Grace Bros. Brewing Company, Santa Rosa, California
Maier Brewing Company, Los Angeles, California

SCHMIDT BEER

Associated Brewing Company, St. Paul, Minnesota
G. Heileman Brewing Company, La Crosse, Wisconsin
Jacob Schmidt Brewing Company, St. Paul, Minnesota
Pfeiffer Brewing Company, St. Paul, Minnesota

SCHMIDTS BEER

E & B Brewing Company, Detroit, Michigan
Jacob Schmidt Brewing Company, St. Paul, Minnesota
Schmidt Brewing Company, Detroit, Michigan
C. Schmidt and Sons, Philadelphia, Pennsylvania

SCHWEGMANN BEER

Buckeye Brewing Company, Toledo, Ohio
Gold Brau Brewing Company, Chicago, Illinois
Royal Brewing Company, New Orleans, Louisiana

SHERIDAN BEER

Sheridan Brewing Company, Sheridan, Wyoming
Walter Brewing Company, Pueblo, Colorado

SHOPRITE BEER

Horlacher Brewing Company, Allentown, Pennsylvania
Maier Brewing Company, Los Angeles, California
Old Dutch Brewing Company, Allentown, Pennsylvania

SILVER FOX BEER

Fox Deluxe Brewing Company, Marion, Indiana
Peter Fox Brewing Company, Chicago, Illinois
Peter Fox Brewing Company, Oklahoma City, Oklahoma

SPORTSMAN BEER

Grace Bros. Brewing Company, Santa Rosa, California
Maier Brewing Company, Los Angeles, California
National Brewing Company, Baltimore, Maryland

STAG BEER

Carling Brewing Company, Belleville, Illinois
Carling-National Brewing Company, Belleville, Illinois
Detroit Brewing Company, Detroit, Michigan
Griesedieck-Western Brewing Company, Belleville, Illinois
G. Heileman Brewing Company, La Crosse, Wisconsin
Peoples Brewing Company, Duluth, Minnesota
Stag Brewery, Belleville, Illinois

STERLING BEER

Associated Brewing Company, Evansville, Indiana
G. Heileman Brewing Company, Evansville, Indiana
Sterling Brewing Company, Evansville, Indiana
Sterling Brewers, Evansville, Indiana

TAHOE BEER

Carson Brewing Company, Carson City, Nevada
Grace Bros. Brewing Company, Santa Rosa, California
Maier Brewing Company, Los Angeles, California

TIGER BEER

C. Schmidt & Sons Brewing Company, Philadelphia, Pennsylvania
Jackson Brewing Company, New Orleans, Louisiana
Manhattan Brewing Company, Chicago, Illinois

TIVOLI BEER

Falstaff Brewing Company, San Francisco, California
Tivoli Brewing Company, Denver, Colorado
Tivoli-Union Brewing Company, Denver, Colorado

TROPICAL ALE

Associated Brewing Company, South Bend, Indiana
Cooks Brewing Company, Evansville, Indiana
International Breweries Incorporated, Covington, Kentucky
Tampa Florida Brewing Company, Tampa, Florida

TUDOR BEER or ALE

Best Brewing Company, Chicago, Illinois
Cumberland Brewing Company, Cumberland, Maryland
Five Star Brewing Company, New York, New York
Hornell Brewing Company, Hornell, New York
Metropolis Brewing Company, New York, New York
Metropolis Brewing Company, Trenton, New Jersey
Queen City Brewing Company, Cumberland, Maryland
Tudor Brewing Company, Norfolk, Virginia

TWENTY GRAND ALE

Associated Brewing Company, South Bend, Indiana
Atlantic Brewing Company, Chicago, Illinois
Drewerys Ltd. USA, South Bend, Indiana
Red Top Brewing Company, Cincinnati, Ohio
Terre Haute Brewing Company, Terre Haute, Indiana

VALLEY FORGE BEER

Adam Scheidt Brewing Company, Norristown, Pennsylvania
C. Schmidt and Sons, Norristown, Pennsylvania
Valley Forge Brewing Company, Norristown, Pennsylvania

VALUE LINE BEER

General Brewing Company, Los Angeles, California
General Brewing Company, San Francisco, California
Maier Brewing Company, Los Angeles, California
Theo. Hamm Brewing Company, Los Angeles, California

VAN MERRITT BEER

Old Crown Brewing Company, Fort Wayne, Indiana
Pacific Brewing Company, Oakland, California
Van Merritt Brewing Company, Burlington, Wisconsin
Van Merritt Brewing Company, Chicago, Illinois
Van Merritt Brewing Company, Joliet, Illinois
Van Merritt Brewing Company, Oconto, Wisconsin
Van Merritt Brewing Company, Potosi, Wisconsin

VELVET GLOW BEER

General Brewing Company, Los Angeles, California
Grace Bros. Brewing Company, Santa Rosa, California
Maier Brewing Company, Los Angeles, California

VIKING BEER

Atlantic Brewing Company, Spokane, Washington
Century Brewing Company, Norfolk, Virginia
Sewanee Brewing Company, Pensacola, Florida
Spearman Brewing Company, Pensacola, Florida

WEBER BEER or BOCK

Fox Head Brewing Company, Wausesha, Wisconsin
Weber-Wausesha Brewing Corporation, Wausesha, Wisconsin
Weber-Wausesha Brewing Company, Sheboygan, Wisconsin

WHITE HORSE BEER

Manhattan Brewing Company, Chicago, Illinois
Westminister Brewing Company, Chicago, Illinois

WHITE LABEL BEER

Minneapolis Brewing Company, Minneapolis, Minnesota
Storz Brewing Company, Omaha, Nebraska
White Label Brewing Company, Minneapolis, Minnesota

How Values Are Determined

/

The value of beer cans, like other antiques or collectibles, is determined by demand. And like other price guides, the prices contained in this book are meant only as a guide for the collector. Every effort has been made to give reasonable average values for the cans listed, but, ultimately, a can is worth only what someone is willing to pay for it.

Rarity alone does not determine value—condition plays a large part. One scratch, crease, or other imperfection can and will reduce the value of a beer can by as much as one third. This is not to say, however, that off-grade cans are not without value. I have paid $100 for a can that would cost me $1,000 or more if I had found it in mint condition. In this case, I could likely recover my investment with little effort.

The famous Rosalie can that sold for more than $6,000 in the late 1970s would be greatly reduced in value if a case or even a six-pack of cans in perfect condition were found and put on the market.

Remember, even if a brewery canned only 10,000 barrels of beer in its prime, that would result in approximately 3.3 million cans of beer (a barrel contains thirty-one gallons, or 3,968 ounces, so 10,000 barrels would convert to roughly 3,306,600 12-ounce cans). The question is, of course, how many of those 3.3 million cans survived over the years, and in what condition.

The greatest values lie in the steel cans, produced prior to 1960, and in cone-top cans. Most of the smaller breweries were gone by the end of World War II, and nearly all of them were gone by 1960 or so. Cone top cans were used basically by the smaller breweries because they could be

filled on their existing bottling lines, and the smaller brewer could avoid
an expensive investment in canning equipment. The exception to this was
Pabst, which canned quart-size cone tops into the mid-1950s.

It should also be noted that the reason today's microbreweries do not
put their beer in cans is the same reason the smaller breweries in the past
did not—the high cost of canning equipment. There have been two microbreweries that have bought four- and five-liter cans from Europe and
hand-filled them. These cans carry more novelty value than anything
else. Small labels that appear in can form are usually brewed and filled
on a contract basis by larger breweries.

There are many reasons why aluminum cans will never carry a high
value. Besides the millions and millions of cans that are made, the quality of the graphics and coloring on the cans are not as good as the old
steel cans—some of the old steel cans carried up to eight different colors.
The aluminum cans listed in this book at $10 will increase in value at
the rate of only 5 percent a year, while a steel can will increase in value
at a rate much higher than the 5 percent figure. The value of aluminum
cans will, at some point, reach a ceiling, while steel cans will continue
to rise in value.

For a period of about five years, beginning with the 1976 American
Bicentennial, some of the smaller breweries stayed in business by
changing labels often. The most notable of these was August Schell in
Minnesota. Schell issued commemorative cans for every town festival in
a five-state area. These cans will probably peak in value somewhere
between $5 and $10 in the future.

Another can that should be mentioned is Billy Beer, named for President Jimmy Carter's brother, Billy. Billy Beer was issued by four different breweries, and there were millions of cans produced. There are at
least five different versions of Billy Beer. They are *not* worth hundreds
of dollars, as some people might believe. A price of $2 or $3 is more
than reasonable. Other special issues such as J.R. Beer and M*A*S*H
Beer will carry a similar value.

Finally, if a can is worth putting on the shelf, it is worth at least $1
to the collector. The collector will either have to go to the store to pur-
chase it or trade or buy from another collector. That time and effort—
combined with the can's inherent value—gives us a base price of $1,
which is the base price used in this book.

Prices Listed in This Book

It is important to understand that all the prices quoted in this book are
for cans in absolutely mint condition—no scratches, no dents, no rust or
staining, no damage of any kind.

The rarer the can, the more the slightest flaw will reduce the value. A one-inch scratch on a can worth $1,000 will bring the value down 15 or 20 percent, while the same flaw on a can worth $10 might only reduce the value by a dollar.

All cans in this book have been given individual prices. There are two pricing categories that should be explained.

Exotic is a can worth between $600 and $1,200. This is a rare can and the price should be negotiated between the buyer and seller, but the can will not run over $1,200 in value. *Any* damage to cans in this category greatly affects the value.

Unique is a can worth over $1,200 and there are probably less than a dozen mint-condition cans of this type in circulation. Again, any damage will greatly affect the value of this can.

Another category of can that should be noted is the rusty can or "dumper." These are cans usually found outdoors and carry quite a bit of damage, but due to their rarity or other reasons, they will carry a value between 5 and 25 percent (on rare occasions, 50 percent) of mint-condition value. Don't overlook these cans.

Finally, although there are many aluminum and bi-metal cans in circulation, they are too numerous to list individually in this book. They do, however, carry a collector value of $1 or less. The listings in this book do, therefore, acknowledge which breweries issue aluminum cans.

Buying and Selling

While the prices in this book should guide you in placing a value on your beer cans, it is still true that any collectible is worth only what someone is willing to pay for it. When buying cans for your collection or selling cans to another collector, price should always be negotiated, and you may or may not end up paying or receiving the prices listed here.

Also remember that when selling cans to a dealer there is, as with everything else, a wholesale and a retail value. The dealer must buy low and sell higher to cover expenses and make a profit—after all, it's a business. The wholesale value of a can usually runs from 35 percent to 75 percent of retail value, although commonly closer to 50 percent.

Definitions

/

Mandatory: The requirements of the federal government for labeling cans. This includes the brand name, the brewery name and city, the size of the can (i.e., the amount of beer it contains), and the fill date, which is usually stamped on the bottom of the can. See the "Mandatory Labeling Requirements" chapter.

Internal Revenue Tax Paid: This is also known as IRTP or a similar statement. This is the tax statement required by the federal government from June 1935 through March 1950.

Withdrawn Free: This means that no IRTP statement was required because the beer was brewed for sale outside the United States.

Camouflage: This was beer brewed for the military. Since the beer was intended for troops in combat zones, the can was painted in a camouflage pattern over the original label. This can would not reflect sunlight and would—hopefully—not draw sniper fire.

Opening Instructions (OI): These cans had instructions printed on them on how to open them. This was common on flat tops through World War II. The OI usually show a punch opener along with directions on how to use it.

Versions: This includes *all* differences in the cans produced, including mandatories, brewery name changes, size of the can, can style differences, and can company trademarks—*anything* different from any earlier issued can.

Multi: More than three versions

Minor: Small differences such as can company trademarks or the addition or subtraction of a city name to the mandatory.

Single: Only one version.

Author's Note

/

One of the great things about collecting beer cans is that a collector can collect on any level he or she wishes: a particular brewery or brand; a city, state, or region; a particular type of can—anything goes.

The organizations that are listed in the "Organizations and Clubs" section are well worth joining. These groups can put you in contact with other collectors and give you the latest information on collecting beer cans. I recommend them.

Finally, it is my intent to be as accurate and thorough as possible. The listings in this guide are as complete as countless years of collecting and research can make them. The prices are also as accurate as possible, but remember that these values are intended only as a guide for the collector, not the last word.

If you have any additions, questions, corrections, or comments, please feel free to contact me:

Bill Mugrage
3819 190th Place S.W.
Lynnwood, WA 98036
(206) 774-9849 (7 PM to 12 midnight, Pacific Time, or weekends)

or through the publisher:

House of Collectibles
201 East 50th Street
New York, NY 10022

Beer Can Designs

Lid Designs

FLAT-TOP OR PUNCH LID.

Photo 1.

ALUMINUM OR SOFT-TOP LIDS.

*Photo 2 (left)
and Photo 3.*

ZIP-TOP LID.

Photo 4.

TAB-TOP LID.

Photo 5.

Photo 6.

Photo 7.

Cone-Top Designs

HIGH- AND LOW-PROFILE QUARTS.

Photo 8.

HIGH- AND LOW-PROFILE 12-OUNCE CONE TOP.

Photo 9.

J-SPOUT 12-OUNCE CONE TOP.

Photo 10.

TWELVE-OUNCE CROWNTAINER.

Photo 11.

Examples of Back and Side Panels

Photos 12–18.

Beer Can Listings

Alabama

Alabama had 12 breweries at one time or another with only two operating at the time of national Prohibition. After Prohibition, only the Mobile Brewing Company was issued a federal permit, but it lasted only a year before closing. No beer cans were ever produced.

Alaska

Anchorage

PRINZ BRAU BREWING COMPANY, Huffman Business Park

Prinz Brau Alaska Beer, single-label 12-ounce tab top, metallic gold-yellow vertical stripe, two versions. $5

Prinz Brau Beer, two-label 12-ounce tab top, Lion Crest, single version. ...$5

Two-label 12-ounce tab top, Polar Bears, multiversions including one aluminum. $5

Two-label 12-ounce tab top, "ANNIVERSARY OFFER," single version. $25

Prinz Extra Beer, two-label 12-ounce tab top, "UNCHANGED SINCE 1516," multiversions. $5

Prinz Light Beer, two-label 12-ounce tab top, can never filled, single version. $25

Arizona

Phoenix

ARIZONA BREWING COMPANY, 150 South 12th Street

A-1 Bock Beer, single-label 12-ounce flat top, green can, white label, small white goat, single version. $150

A-1 Pilsner A Premium Beer, single-label 10-ounce flat top, white can, eagle in white, single version. $100

Single-label 12-ounce flat top, white can, eagle in white, multiversions...... $40

Two-label 12- or 16-ounce flat top, white can, red label, minor versions.
12-ounce, ... $40
16-ounce, ... $50

Two-label 16-ounce flat top, silver can, red label, single version. $40

Two-label 16-ounce flat top, white can, red label, single version. $40

A-1 Pilsner Beer, two-label 12-ounce flat top, gold can, white label, "A-1 PIL-SENER" in red, "FLAVOR SEALED," OPENING INSTRUCTIONS, INTERNAL REVENUE TAX PAID, two versions. $150

Single-label 12-ounce flat top, white can, eagle in gold, multiversions. *(See photo 19)* $35

Photo 19. A-1 Pilsner Beer.

65

A-1 Premium Beer, single-label 12-ounce flat top, copper-color desert scene, single version.

12-ounce,.. $40
16-ounce,... $60

Apache Export Beer, 12-ounce low-profile cone top, gold can, Indian profile, single version... Exotic

Argonaut The Light Beer, two-label 12- or 16-ounce flat top, blue can, gold stars, single version.

12-ounce,...$250
16-ounce,.. $300

Dutch Treat Premium Lager Beer, two-label 12-ounce flat top, yellow can with white label, single version. $75

Two-label 12-ounce double flat top, gold can, blue label, single version. $20

Elder Brau Premium Lager Beer, single-label 12- or 16-ounce flat top, white and gold can, green patch on face, single version.

12-ounce,... $60
16-ounce,...: $80

J. F. Lancer's A-1 Beer, two-label 12- or 16-ounce zip top, white can with red, blue, and green triangle, single version.

12-ounce,... $50
16-ounce,... $60

Lancer's A-1 Ale, two-label 12-ounce flat top, green can with white label, single version. *(See photo 20)* $65

Lancer's A-1 Beer, two-label 12- or 16-ounce flat or zip top, white can, blue, green, and white label, multiversions.

12-ounce,... $35
16-ounce,... $30

Lancer's A-1 Pilsener Beer, two-label 12- or 16-ounce flat top, white can, red label with white pennant, minor versions.

12-ounce,... $30
16-ounce,... $25

Rüser The Light Lager Beer, single-label 12- or 16-ounce flat top, blue and gold can, mountain scene, single version of each. *(See photo 21)*

12-ounce,... $400
16-ounce,...$375

Photo 20 (left). Lancers A-1 Ale. Photo 21 (right). Rüser, The Light Lager Beer.

Snowcrest Beer, single-label 12-ounce flat top, multicolored mountain scene, single version.

12-ounce, ...$450
16-ounce, ... $400

CARLING BREWING COMPANY, 112 South 12th Street (successor to Arizona Brewing Company)

Black Label Beer, single-label 12-ounce zip or tab top, red can, black label outlined in white, world or U.S. map, multiversions. $10

Carling A-1 Beer, two-label 12-ounce flat and tab top, white can, blue, red, and green triangle, multiversions 12-ounce, single version 16-ounce.
Flat top, ... $40
Tab top, ... $35

Carling Black Label Beer, two-label 12-ounce zip top, red can, black label outlined in white, "CARLING" on label, single version. $10

J. F. Lancer's A-1 Beer, two-label 12-ounce flat top, white can, red, blue, and green triangle, single version. $20

CARLING NATIONAL BREWING COMPANY, 150 South 12th Street (successor to National Brewing Company)

Tuborg Gold Export Quality Beer, single-label 12-ounce aluminum tab top, special issue cans: "CERTIFICATE OF AUTHENTICITY," "PHOENIX SUNS 77–78," "PHOENIX SUNS 76–77," single version of each. $5

All other brands were produced in aluminum cans with a collector value of $1.

G. HEILEMAN BREWING COMPANY, 150 South 12th Street (successor to Carling National Brewing Company)

All cans produced by G. Heileman at this brewery were produced in aluminum. Collector value is up to $1.

NATIONAL BREWING COMPANY, 150 South 12th Street (successor to Carling Brewing Company)

A-1 Beer, two-label 12-ounce tab top, white can, round triangle, red "A-1," single version. $40

A-1 Premium Beer, two-label 12- or 16-ounce tab top, white can, metallic gold and purple label, single version of each. $15
Brewery also produced this beer in aluminum cans with a collector value of up to $3.

Colt 45 Malt Liquor, two-label 12-ounce flat top, white can, blue label, "MALT LIQUOR" in red, gold horseshoe, single version of each. $5

Colt 45 Stout Malt Liquor, two-label 12-ounce flat top, white can, blue label, "STOUT MALT LIQUOR" in red, gold horseshoe, multiversions. $5
Brand also produced in aluminum cans with a collector value of up to $2.

Photo 22. James Bond's 007 Special Blend.

James Bond's 007 Special Blend, two sets of seven cans each, single-label 12-ounce tab top, label states "A MALT LIQUOR. . . ." or "A subtle blend . . . ," label on both sets pictures beautiful girls and London attractions. Seven labels: GRENADIER GUARDS, TOWER OF LONDON, WESTMINSTER AT DAWN, PARLIAMENT AND ST. PAULS TOWER BRIDGE, PARLIAMENT, LIFE GUARDS. *(See photo 22)* Each can,..$250

Brewery also produced A-1 Light Pilsner Beer, A-1 Premium Beer, Dutch Treat Premium Beer, and Van Lauter Lager Beer in aluminum cans with a collector value of up to $5.

Arkansas

Arkansas, deep in the Bible Belt, has virtually no breweries in its history. Only three breweries have been reported, with the last in 1934. No beer cans were produced.

California

Auburn

In the mid-1970s a beautiful can, Placer Gold (blue and gold in color), appeared in collector circles. The can was never filled, and the only address that was ever found was a vacant lot. The value of the can is around $10. *(See photo 23)*

Azusa

GENERAL BREWING CORPORATION, 819 Vernon Avenue (successor to Lucky Lager Brewing Company)

Fisher Premium Light Beer, single-, two-, or three-label 12- and 16-ounce flat top white can, metallic gold and red label, gold scrolling, "PREMIUM LIGHT" on blue band, multiversions.
12-ounce, ... $20
16-ounce, ... $25
Labatt's Beer, single-label 12- and 16-ounce zip top, white can with red band, single version. *(See photo 24)*
12-ounce, ... $60
16-ounce, ... $85

Photo 23 (left). Placer Gold.
Photo 24 (right). Labatt's Beer.

Lucky Lager Aged For Flavor, two-label 12- and 16-ounce flat or zip top, yellow can, white label outlined in gold, red "X," "AGED FOR FLAVOR" on gold oval, multiversions. All versions, ... $10

LUCKY LAGER BREWING COMPANY, 819 North Vernon Avenue

Fisher Light Beer A Premium Brew, two-label 16-ounce tab top, off-white can, red label, metallic gold bands and scrolling, "A PREMIUM BREW" on white band, single version. $15

Fisher Premium Light Beer, two-label 12- and 16-ounce flat top, white can, red label, metallic gold bands and scrolling, "PREMIUM LIGHT" on blue band, single version each can.
12-ounce, ... $12
15-ounce, ... $15

Lucky Lager Age Dated Beer, two-label 12- or 16-ounce flat top, red and gold can, "LUCKY LAGER" on large red "X," IRTP or non-IRTP, multiversions. *(See photo 25)*
12-ounce IRTP, ... $35
12-ounce non-IRTP, ... $25
16-ounce non-IRTP, ... $30

Two-label 11-, 12-, 15-, or 16-ounce flat top, white can, gold label with red "X," "LUCKY" above label, "LAGER" below label, multiversions.
11-ounce, ... $15
12-ounce, ... $10
15-ounce, ... $15
16-ounce, ... $10

Lucky Lager Age Dated Premium Beer, two-label 12- and 16-ounce flat top, off-white can, gold label, small black circle, "AGE DATED" with no text on gold oval, multiversions.
12-ounce, ... $10
16-ounce, ... $15

Lucky Lager Aged For Flavor, two-label 12- and 16-ounce flat top, yellow can, gold label, small black circle, "AGED FOR FLAVOR" with four cities listed, multiversions.
12-ounce, ... $10
16-ounce, ... $15

Photo 25. Lucky Lager Age Dated Beer.

MILLER BREWING COMPANY, 819 North Vernon Avenue (successor to General Brewing Company)

Miller High Life Beer, single-label 12-ounce tab top, white can, metallic gold bands and trim, "CHAMPAGNE OF BOTTLED BEERS," single version. $10

Two-label 12- and 16-ounce tab top, gold can, white label outlined in green, multiversions. $3

All other cans produced until closing in 1980 carry a collector value of not over $2.

Eureka

HUMBOLDT BREWING AND MALTING COMPANY, 3150 Broadway Street

Associated Beer, single-label 12-ounce flat top, paper label. ....Unique

Brown Derby Pilsner Beer, two-label 12-ounce flat top, silver can, brown label, "BROWN DERBY" in green, OPENING INSTRUCTIONS, INTERNAL REVENUE TAX PAID, two minor versions. *(See photo 26)* $175

Brown Derby Pilsner Type Beer, two-label 12-ounce flat top, silver can, green, brown, and white stripes, OPENING INSTRUCTIONS, INTERNAL REVENUE TAX PAID, single version. $150

Two-sided 12-ounce flat top, silver can, brown label, silver derby, INTERNAL REVENUE TAX PAID, OPENING INSTRUCTIONS, minor versions. $85

"GRACE BROS." stamped on lid, ...Exotic

Eureka Extra Pale Lager Beer, two-label 12-ounce flat top, silver can, brown label, large eagle, OPENING INSTRUCTIONS, INTERNAL REVENUE TAX PAID, single version. $600

Humboldt Extra Pale Beer, two-label 12-ounce flat top, silver can, brown label, large eagle, OPENING INSTRUCTIONS, INTERNAL REVENUE TAX PAID, single version. $200

Fairfield

ANHEUSER-BUSCH, 3101 Busch Drive

All cans produced at this brewery are aluminum. Value to collector is $1 each.

Photo 26. Brown Derby Pilsner Beer.

Irwindale

MILLER BREWING COMPANY, 15801 East 1st Street

All cans produced at this brewery are aluminum. Value to collector is $1 each.

Los Angeles

ACME BREWING COMPANY, 2080 East 49th Street (Vernon)

Acme Beer, two-label 12-ounce flat top, black can, red label, "A" in red, "CME" in black, INTERNAL REVENUE TAX PAID, "NON-FATTENING REFRESHMENT," single version. $60

Two-label 12-ounce flat top, black can, red label, "A" in red, "CME" in black INTERNAL REVENUE TAX PAID, "DELIGHTFUL REFRESHMENT," single version. $60

Two-label 12-ounce flat top, black can, red label, "A" in red, "CME" in black, INTERNAL REVENUE TAX PAID, "DIETETICALLY NON-FATTENING," single version. $60

Two-label 12-ounce flat top, black can, white pinstripes, multicolored label, red "A," black "B" in Acme Beer, IRTP or non-IRTP, multiversions.
IRTP, ... $35
Non-IRTP, ... $30

Acme Bock Beer, two-label 12-ounce flat top, goat head on shield, "BOCK" in red, single version. $300

Acme Bulldog Ale, two-label 12-ounce flat top, green can, "ACME" in red, single version. $40

Acme Englishtown Brand Ale, two-label 12-ounce flat top, INTERNAL REVENUE TAX PAID, gold can, horse and rider, single version. $150

Two-label 12-ounce flat top, woodgrain can, yellow label, IRTP or non-IRTP, multiversions.
IRTP, ... $75
Non-IRTP, ... $60

Acme Genuine Bock Beer, single-label 12-ounce flat top, goat in wreath, "BOCK" in black, single version. $100

Acme Gold Label Light Dry Beer, single-label 12-ounce flat top, yellow can, white band, multiversions. $25

Acme Gold Label Pale Dry Beer, single-label 12-ounce flat top, white can, gold circle, red and black label, single version. $100

Acme Light Dry Beer, single-label 12-ounce flat top, yellow can, white foam label, single version. $25

Acme The Light Dry Beer, single-label 12-ounce flat top, yellow can, white band, single version. $25

Bulldog Extra Stout Malt Liquor, two-label 12-ounce flat top, yellow and black can, "BULLDOG," single version. $40

Bulldog Lager Beer By Acme, two-label 12-ounce flat top, maroon can, red lettering, single version. $50

Bulldog Lager Beer By Acme, two-label 12-ounce flat top, maroon can, red lettering, single version. $50

AMBASSADOR BREWING COMPANY, 1281 East 6th Street

Ambassador Export Beer, two-label, 12-ounce, low-profile cone top, blue can, red ribbon, INTERNAL REVENUE TAX PAID, single version. ....Unique

ANHEUSER-BUSCH, 15800 Rosce Boulevard

Budweiser Lager Beer, two-label 12- and 16-ounce flat top, gold can, red and white label, multiversions.
12-ounce, ... $20
16-ounce, ... $25
Two-label 12- and 16-ounce flat top, white can, red label, multiversions.
12-ounce, ... $10
16-ounce, ... $15
Two-label 12- and 16-ounce flat top, white can, red label, multiversions both sizes. All versions, ...$5
Two-label 12- and 16-ounce flat top, white can, red label, "BREWED AND CANNED BY ANHEUSER-BUSCH INC. OF ST. LOUIS AT LOS ANGELES," multiversions. $3

Busch Bavarian Beer, two-label 12- and 16-ounce flat, zip, and tab top, blue and white can, no circle on face, multiversions in all sizes and tops. $3

Two-label 12- and 16-ounce tab top, blue can, circles on face, blue outer circle, multiversions. $3

Two-label 12- and 16-ounce tab top, blue can, circle on face, red outer circle, multiversions. $3

This plant produced many versions of Budweiser, Natural Light, Busch Bavarian, and Michelob in aluminum cans. These cans are worth up to $1 each to the collector.

GENERAL BREWING COMPANY, 500 East Commercial Street
(successor to Maier Brewing Company)

102 Stout Malt Liquor, two-label 16-ounce tab top, yellow can, red shield, single version. $50

Alpine Beer, two-label 12-ounce tab top, mountain scene, multiversions. .. $20

Amber Brau Lager Beer, two-label 12-ounce tab top, black and white can, gold band top and bottom, multiversions. $35

Bavarian Weiss Pilsner Beer, two-label 12-ounce tab top, white can, mountain scene, red oval, multiversions. $15

Bohemian Pilsner Light Beer, two-label 12-ounce tab top, blue and white can, red lettering, multiversions. $15

Brau Haus Pilsner Beer, two-label 12-ounce flat top, metallic gold and white label, single version. $40

Two-label 12-ounce flat top, dull gold and white label, multiversions. $25

Brew 102 New Pale Dry Beer, two-label 12-ounce tab top, black can, white trim, full beer glass, "6 for $1.09," single version. $20

Two-label 12-ounce tab top, glass of beer on black can, no price, single version. $12

Two-label 12-ounce aluminum tab top, "6 for $1.09," multiversions. $10

Two-label 16-ounce aluminum tab top, "6 for $1.35," multiversions. $10

Two-label 12- and 16-ounce aluminum tab top, glass of beer on black background, no price, single version. $5

Brown Derby Lager Beer, two-label 12- and 16-ounce tab top, white can with orange label outlined in brown, single version. $10

Two-label 12- and 16-ounce aluminum tab top, white can with orange label outlined in brown, multiversions. $5

Bulldog Malt Liquor, two-label 12-ounce tab top, gold can, white label, red and blue lettering, multiversions. $25

Corona Cerveza Extra Beer, two-label 12-ounce tab top, white can, blue and gold trim, single version. $25

Edelbrau Premium Beer, two-label 12-ounce tab top, white can, blue label, single version. $25

Golden Brew Premium Beer, two-label 12-ounce tab top, white can, red label, multiversions. $15

Golden Crown Draft Beer, two-label 12-ounce tab top, blue can, glass of beer, "GOLDEN CROWN DRAFT" in red, single version. $25

Golden Crown Extra Pale Dry Beer, two-label 12-ounce tab top, white can, gold label, red lettering, multiversions. $15

Golden Harvest, two-label 12-ounce tab top, white can, metallic gold trim, multiversions. $25

Hof-Brau Lager Beer, two-label 12-ounce tab top, red can, white label, multiversions. $20

Keg Brand Beer, two-label 12- and 16-ounce tab top, white can, red lettering, multiversions. $15

Maier Select Beer, two-label 12-ounce tab top, red checkerboard can, multiversions. $15

Mule Malt Liquor, two-label 16-ounce tab top, white can, mule in gold circle, single version. $40

Old Heidel Brau Lager Beer, two-label 12-ounce tab top, white can, red stein, multiversions. $20

Padre Pale Lager Beer, two-label 12-ounce tab top, yellow and maroon can, multiversions. $12

Regal Select Light Beer, two-label 12- and 16-ounce tab top, white can, gold, red, and blue ovals, multiversions.
No price on can, ... $10
"6 for 99¢," $15
"6 for $1.29," $15
All aluminum versions, ... $5

Reidenbach Premium Pale Dry Beer, two-label 12-ounce tab top, woodgrain can, gold stripes, multiversions. $15

Spring Lager Beer, two-label 12-ounce tab top, white can, gold oval, blue lettering, multiversions.
No price on can, ... $15
"6 for 89¢," $20

Steinbrau Pale Lager Beer, two-label 12-ounce tab top, white can, silver stein, multiversions. $15

Value Line Lager Beer, two-label 12-ounce tab top, red, white, and gold can, multiversions. $20

Velvet Glow Fine Premium Beer, two-label 12-ounce tab top, white and yellow can, picture of King Gambrius, multiversions. $25

Velvet Glow Pale Dry Beer, two-label 12-ounce tab top, white can, gold triangles, red lettering, multiversions. $20

The General Brewing Company of Los Angeles did produce a variety of aluminum. These cans are worth up to $5 each to the collector.

GRACE BROS. BREWERY, 671 Rio Street (aka: North Bay Brewing, Los Angeles Southern Brewing Company, Los Angeles)

Alta Special Export Beer, Grace Bros. Brewery, single-label 12-ounce flat top, gray and yellow can, blue stripes, OPENING INSTRUCTIONS, INTERNAL REVENUE TAX PAID, two minor versions. Each, ... $300

Balboa Export Premium Pale Beer, Grace Bros. Brewery, single-label 12-ounce flat top, yellow can, red bands, "EXPORT" in red, single version. $150

BB Extra Pale Dry Beer, Southern Brewing Company, single-label 12-ounce flat top, silver can, red shield and band, INTERNAL REVENUE TAX PAID, single version. .... Exotic

BB Special Export Beer, Southern Brewing Company, single-label 12-ounce flat top, blue can, glass of beer, single version. $300

Blue 'N Gold Beer, North Bay and Southern Brewing, single-label 12-ounce flat top, blue and gold can, multiversions. $100

Brown Derby Pilsner Beer, Grace Bros. Brewery, two-label 12-ounce flat top, silver can, brown label, "BROWN DERBY" in green, OPENING INSTRUCTIONS, INTERNAL REVENUE TAX PAID, single version. *(See photo 27)* $125

Photo 27 (left). Brown Derby Pilsner Beer.
Photo 28 (right). Buffalo Brand Extra Pale Beer.

Buffalo Brand Extra Pale Beer, Southern Brewing, single-label 12-ounce flat top, yellow scrolled can, white bands, red and white label, "DON'T SAY BEER, SAY BUFFALO," WITHDRAWN FREE, two versions. *(See photo 28)* $600

Clipper Pale Beer, Grace Bros. Brewery, single-label 12-ounce flat top, multi-colored blue can, airplane label, INTERNAL REVENUE TAX PAID, single version. $600

Dutch Lunch Brand Beer, Grace Bros. Brewery, two-label 12-ounce flat top, silver can, "BEER" in red on black band, OPENING INSTRUCTIONS, INTERNAL REVENUE TAX PAID, minor versions. $100

Finer Flaver Brand Beer, single-label 12-ounce flat top, silver or white can, red circle with mug of beer, with or without red band, IRTP or non-IRTP, single version of each.
Silver can, IRTP, ... Exotic
Silver can, non-IRTP, ... Exotic
White can, non-IRTP, ... $300

Golden Crown Brand Beer, Grace Bros. Brewery, single-label 12-ounce flat top, yellow can, "BEER" in yellow on red patch, OPENING INSTRUCTIONS, INTERNAL REVENUE TAX PAID, single version. .... Exotic

Grace Bros. Age Dated Beer, Grace Bros. Brewery, single-label 12-ounce flat top, yellow can, red bands, "AGE DATED" in red, fourteen-line story, OPENING INSTRUCTIONS, INTERNAL REVENUE TAX PAID, single version. $200

Grace Bros. Ale, Grace Bros. Brewery, single-label 12-ounce flat top, gold can, "ALE" in white on black circle, "GRACE BROTHERS SANTA ROSA" blacked out, "GRACE BROS. LOS ANGELES" overprinted, OPENING INSTRUCTIONS, INTERNAL REVENUE TAX PAID, single version. $300

Imperial Extra Dry Pale Beer, Grace Bros. Brewery or Southern Brewing, single-label 12-ounce flat top, metallic gold can, white label, "EXTRA DRY" in red, IRTP or non-IRTP, minor versions.
IRTP, ... $75
Non-IRTP, ... $65

Kool Beer, Grace Bros. Brewery, single-label 12-ounce flat top, blue and agua-green can, white lettering, OPENING INSTRUCTIONS, INTERNAL REVENUE TAX PAID, single version. $300

Little Imp Extra Dry Pale Beer, Southern Brewing, two-label 12-ounce flat top, gold can, red label and trim, "PALE BEER" in white, single version. .... Exotic

Monogram Beer, Grace Bros. Brewery, single-label 12-ounce flat top, red can, white label, INTERNAL REVENUE TAX PAID, single version. $150

Special Brew Beer, Grace Bros. Brewery or Southern Brewing, single-label 12-ounce flat top, gold can, black lettering, OPENING INSTRUCTIONS, INTERNAL REVENUE TAX PAID, minor versions. $150

THEODORE HAMM BREWING COMPANY, 2080 East 49th Street (successor to Rheingold Brewing Company)

Alpen Glen Beer, two-label 12-ounce aluminum tab top, white can, orange and green scene, single version. $30

Burgermeister Beer, two-label 12-ounce aluminum tab top, white can, blue label outlined in metallic gold, "BURGIE" in red, multiversions. $10

Burgermeister Genuine Draft, two-label 12-ounce aluminum tab top, white can, gold and blue label, single version. $20

Golden Lager Light Export Beer, two-label 12-ounce aluminum tab top, white can, lions holding shield, single version. $25

Hamm's Beer, two-label 11-, 12-, or 15-ounce flat top, gold sunburst can, wide blue band, multiversions.
11-ounce, ... $15
12-ounce, ... $10
15-ounce, ... $15

Two-label 11- or 15-ounce flat, tab, or soft top, blue can, white crown, gold trim, multiversions.
11-ounce flat top, ... $5
11-ounce soft top, ... $8
11-ounce tab top, ... $3
15-ounce flat top, ... $8
15-ounce tab top, ... $5
15-ounce soft top, ... $12

Two-label 11- or 15-ounce tab top, blue can, white crown, with or without silver trim, "FROM THE LAND OF SKY BLUE WATERS," multiversions.
11-ounce, ... $5
15-ounce, ... $8

Matterhorn Beer, two-label 12-ounce flat top, blue and white can, mountain scene, single version. $30

Pantry Pride Oldbru Premium Beer, two-label 11- or 15-ounce aluminum tab top, single version of each.
11-ounce, ... $35
15-ounce, ... $40

All aluminum Hamm's brands carry a collector value of up to $5.

LOS ANGELES BREWING COMPANY, 1910 North Main

Brown Derby Pilsner Type Beer, two-label 12-ounce flat top, silver can, brown label, "BROWN DERBY" in green, OPENING INSTRUCTIONS, INTERNAL REVENUE TAX PAID, two minor versions. $150

Two-label 12-ounce flat top, yellow can, white label, "PILSNER" in red, single version. *(See photo 29)* $75

Eastside Export Beer, single-label 12-ounce flat top, gold can, blue eagle, OPENING INSTRUCTIONS, INTERNAL REVENUE TAX PAID, multiversions. $150

Eastside Genuine Ale, single-label 12-ounce flat top, gold can, red label, OPENING INSTRUCTIONS, INTERNAL REVENUE TAX PAID, single version. $300

Eastside Genuine Bock Beer, two-label 12-ounce flat top, brown can, gold label, goat's head, OPENING INSTRUCTIONS, INTERNAL REVENUE TAX PAID, single version. $300

Eastside Light And Fine Beer, two-label 12-ounce flat top, either solid or checkerboard gold can, multiversions. $60

Old Mission Beer, two-label 12-ounce flat top, orange can, Spanish mission scene, single version. $85

Zobelein's Eastside Beer, single-label, 12-ounce, high-profile cone top, blue can, red label, large eagle, INTERNAL REVENUE TAX PAID, two versions. *(See photo 30)* $90

Single-label 12-ounce flat top, blue can, red oval, gold label, OPENING INSTRUCTIONS, INTERNAL REVENUE TAX PAID, multiversions.

IRTP, ... $60
Non-IRTP, ... $50

Zobelein's Eastside Genuine Bock Beer, single-label 12-ounce flat top, large goat's head on gold label, single version. *(See photo 31)* $350

MAIER BREWING COMPANY, 500 East Commercial (aka: ABC Brewing Company)

102 Continental Dark Beer, single-label 12-ounce tab top, checkerboard can, white shield, red label, single version. *(See photo 32)* $75

102 Genuine Draft Beer, two-label 12- and 16-ounce tab top, white can, metallic blue label, multiversions. Both sizes, ... $30

102 Stout Malt Liquor, two-label 16-ounce tab top, yellow can, red metallic label, single version. $40

ABC Extra Pale Dry Beer, two-label 12-ounce flat and tab top, red, white, and blue, red "ABC" outlined in white, versions: flat top single version, tab top multiversions. *(See photo 33)*
Flat top, ... $60
Tab top, ... $50

ABC Extra Pale Extra Dry Beer, ABC Brewing or Maier Brewing, two-label 12-ounce flat top, red, white, and blue, red "ABC" outlined in blue, single version. $30

ABC Famous Fine Beer, two-label 16-ounce tab top, red, white, and blue, "ABC" outlined in blue, multiversions. $40

(From left to right) Photo 29. Brown Derby Pilsner Type Beer. Photo 30. Zobelein's Eastside Beer. Photo 31. Zobelein's Eastside Genuine Bock Beer. Photo 32. 102 Continental Dark Beer. Photo 33. ABC Extra Pale Dry Beer.

Alpine Beer, two-label 12- and 16-ounce flat and tab top, blue and white can, mountain scene, multiversions.

12-ounce flat top, ... $60
12-ounce tab top, ... $50
16-ounce tab top, ... $50

Two-label 12-ounce tab top, white, blue, and gold can, single version. $25

Alps Brau Beer, two-label 12-ounce flat or tab top, metallic blue and white can, single version each lid. Either version, ... $40

Amber Brau Lager Beer, two-label 12-ounce flat or tab top, black and white can, multiversions. $40

Astro Malt Liquor, two-label 16-ounce tab top, blue and white can, single version..$150

Bavarian Flavor Pilsner Beer, two-label 12-ounce flat top, mountain scene, red circle, single version. $30

Bavarian Flavor Weiss Pilsner Beer, two-label 12- and 16-ounce flat and tab top, mountain scene, label in red circle, minor versions.

Flat top, ... $15
Tab top,... $10

Black And White Lager Beer, two-label 12-ounce flat top, black and white with red trim, two versions... $75

Bohemian Pilsner Light Beer, two-label 12-ounce flat and tab top, white can, blue shield, red lettering, minor versions. All versions,.......................... $15

Brau Haus Pilsner Beer, two-label 12-ounce flat and tab top, white can, blue trim, gold or yellow trim, minor versions.

Flat top, ... $40
Tab top,... $30

Brew 52 Light Lager Beer, two-label 12-ounce flat top, can says "GRACE BROS.," lid stamped "MAIER," dull red can, single version. $100

Brew 102 Pale Dry Beer, two- or single-label 12-ounce flat top, gold or white can, red label, single version of can.

Single-label gold can,... $75
Single-label white can,.. $60
Two-label white can, ... $50

Two-label 12- and 16-ounce flat top, white can, red and purple label, "DRAUGHT BEER FLAVOR," versions: 12-ounce two versions, 16-ounce single version.

12-ounce,... $40
16-ounce,... $50

Two-label 12- and 16-ounce flat top, tab top, or soft top, white can, black label, multiversions all sizes. $15
All "6 for . . . cans,"... $20

Brew 102 Pale Dry Draft Beer, two-sided gallon can, black and white, single version. *(See photo 34)* $400

Brewers' Best Premium Bavarian Type Beer, two-label 12-ounce tab top and 16-ounce flat top, white can, green crest, red label, minor versions.

12-ounce,... $20
16-ounce,... $30

Brewmaster Bavarian Beer, two-label 12- and 16-ounce tab top, mountain scene, red label, single version of each. Each, ... $20

Brewmaster Beer, two-label 12-ounce tab top, Bavarian-type man carrying steins of beer, single version. ....Exotic

Brown Derby Lager Beer, two-label 12- and 16-ounce flat top, tab top, and soft top, white can, brown derby hat, gold trim, multiversions of all varieties of tops and sizes. All versions, ... $25

Two-label 12- and 16-ounce flat and tab top, white can, brown and orange label, multiversions of all varieties of tops and sizes. All versions, ... $20

Bull Dog Ale, two-label 12-ounce flat and tab top, metallic green can, white label, single version of each. *(See photo 35)*
Flat top, ... $35
Tab top, ... $30

Bull Dog Malt Liquor, two-label 12- and 16-ounce flat and tab top, metallic gold can, "ROBUST CHARACTER . . .," multiversions. $25

Cavalier Beer, two-label 12-ounce flat top, gold can, white label, "GRACE BROS. Santa Rosa" on can, "MAIER Los Angeles" on lid, single version. $100

Clear Lake Premium Beer, two-label 12-ounce flat top, multicolored can, red label outlined in metallic gold, "GRACE BROS. Santa Rosa" on can, "MAIER Los Angeles" on lid, single version. $300

Club House Extra Pale Premium Beer, two-label 12-ounce flat top, metallic blue can, blue label, "GRACE BROS. Santa Rosa" on can, "MAIER Los Angeles" on lid, single version. $150

Club Special Premium Beer, two-label 12-ounce flat or tab top, white can, blue lettering, single version of each lid. $90

Custom Club Lager Beer, two-label 12-ounce flat top, red can, white label, "GRACE BROS. Santa Rosa" on can, "MAIER" on lid, single version. $100

Deutche Brau Vienna Type Beer, two-label 12-ounce flat top, "GRACE BROS. Santa Rosa" on can, "MAIER Los Angeles" on lid, single version. $100

Dodger Lager Beer, two-label 12-ounce flat or tab top, white can, gold bars, red letters, multiversions. *(See photo 36)* $80

Draft Brand Beer, two-label 12-ounce flat top, yellow or orange woodgrain can, two versions. $60

Two-label 12-ounce flat top, "MAKES IT A PLEASURE TO BE THIRSTY," single version. $80

Photo 34 (left). Brew 102 Pale Dry Draft Beer. Photo 35 (center). Bull Dog Ale. Photo 36 (right). Dodger Lager Beer.

Edelbrau Premium Beer, two-label 12-ounce flat or tab top, white can, blue ribbon, versions: flat top multiversions, tab top single version.
Flat top, ... $70
Tab top,... $60

Einbock Beer, two-label 12-ounce flat top, yellow can, green trim, two versions.
.... $25

Two-label 12-ounce flat top, white can, green and gold trim, single version, probably a test can. .... Exotic

El Capitan Premium Beer, single-label 12-ounce flat top, gold, blue, and white can, single version. $75

Elder Brau Premium Lager Beer, two-label 12- or 16-ounce flat top, white can, red label, metallic gold trim, single version of each. Either size, ... $60

El Dorado Premium Lager Beer, two-label 12-ounce flat top, gold can, blue label, "GRACE BROS. Santa Rosa" on can, "MAIER Los Angeles" on lid, single version. $100

El Rancho Light Beer, two-label 12-ounce tab top, orange sun and cactus, two versions. $40

El Rancho Premium Lager Beer, two-label 12-ounce tab top, white can, red label, single version. *(See photo 37)* $40

Excell Lager Beer, two-label 12-ounce flat top, white can, red label, single version... $70

GB Dark Bock Beer, two-label 12-ounce tab top, red and black can, large goat's head, single version. $100

Glacier Light Beer, two-label 12-ounce flat top or tab top, metallic or dull gold, white or dull leaves, multiversions. *(See photo 38)*
Metallic,.. $80
Dull gold, ... $70
"6 for 88¢," $100

Golden Brew Premium Beer, two-label 12-ounce flat or tab top, white can, red label, multiversions.
Flat top, ... $25
Tab top,.. $20

Golden Crown Draft Beer, two-label 12-ounce tab top, blue can with glass of beer, two versions. $25

Golden Crown Extra Pale Dry Beer, two-label 12-ounce flat or tab top, metallic or dull gold, multiversions.
Metallic flat top, ... $40
Dull gold, ... $20

Photo 37 (left). El Rancho Premium Lager Beer.
Photo 38 (right). Glacier Light Beer.

Golden Gate Beer, two-label 12- and 16-ounce flat or tab top, blue can picture, Golden Gate Bridge, multiversions.

12-ounce flat top, ...$100
16-ounce flat top, ... $85
12-ounce tab top, ... $60
"6 for 79¢," $125

Golden Grain Beer, two-label 12-ounce flat or tab top, white can, metallic gold trim, maroon label, multiversions. $25

Golden Harvest Pale Dry Beer, two-label 12-ounce tab top, white can, metallic trim, minor versions. $75

Golden Harvest Smooth 'N Mellow, two-label 12-ounce flat or tab top, white can, metallic gold or maroon can, single version of each.

Flat top, ... $80
Tab top, ... $70

Golden Velvet Premium Beer, two-label 12-ounce flat top, white can, maroon label, multiversions. $30

Grace Bros. Bavarian Beer, two-label 16-ounce tab top, white can, red metallic label, single version. $40

Grace Bros. Premium Draft Beer, two-label gallon, white can, red label, "DRAFT" in black, "Brewed and packed by Maier Brewing Company expressly for Grace Bros.," single version. ....Exotic

Hans Leeber Brew Beer, single-label 12-ounce flat top, white can, blue lettering, single version. $300

Hausbrau Premium Lager Beer, two-label 12-ounce flat or tab top, metallic or dull red can, mountain scene, single version.

Metallic red flat top, ...$100
Metallic red tab top, ... $90
Dull red tab top, ... $60

Hof Brau Draft Beer, two-label gallon can, paper label, mock-up gallon can, red can, white label, single version. ....Unique

Hof-Brau Lager Beer, two-label 12-ounce flat or tab top, red can, white label, multiversions. All versions, ... $20

Holland Brand Beer, two-label 12-ounce flat top, white can, country scene, multiversions. $75

Hudson House Lager Beer, two-label 12-ounce tab top, metallic blue, white label, red lettering, multiversions. $60

Imperial Premium Beer, single-label 12-ounce flat top, white can, gold lines top and bottom, single version. $100

Two-label 12-ounce flat top, white and gold can, gold band, top front, single version. $85

Karl's Bavarian Type Beer, two-label 12-ounce flat top, blue can, white oval label, red "K," "GRACE BROS." on can, "MAIER BREWING" on lid, single version. $150

Keg Brand Beer, two-label 12- or 16-ounce flat or tab top, white can, picture of keg on face of can, red lettering, multiversions. $20

King Cole Premium Pale Beer, two-label 12-ounce flat top, white can, metallic red and gold label, single version. $300

King's Taste Extra Pale Dry Beer, two-label 12-ounce flat top, metallic gold can, blue crown and lettering, "GRACE BROS." on can, "MAIER BREWING" on lid, single version. $350

Kol Premium Quality Beer, two-label 12-ounce flat top, blue and white vertical stripes, dark blue label, single version. $20

L & M Aged Lager Beer, two-label 12- and 16-ounce flat top, yellow and black can, versions: 12-ounce two versions, 16-ounce single version. *(See photo 39)* $100

Lassen Bavarian Beer, two-label 12-ounce flat top, mountain scene, blue lettering, "GRACE BROS." on can, "MAIER BREWING" on lid, multiversions. .$125

Maid Rite Premium Beer, two-label 12-ounce flat top, white can, red circle, yellow square "GRACE BROS." on can, "MAIER BREWING" on lid, single version. $300

Maier Export Beer, single-label, low-profile, 12-ounce cone top, silver can, "MAIER" in red, INTERNAL REVENUE TAX PAID, multiversions. *(See photo 40)* $400

Maier Gold Label Ale, single-label, low-profile, 12-ounce cone top, green can, gold oval, "MAIER ALE" in white, INTERNAL REVENUE TAX PAID, single version. $600

Maier Gold Label Beer, single-label, low-profile, 12-ounce cone top or quart cone top, gold can, "MAIER BEER" in red, minor versions.
12-ounce, ... $400
Quart, ...Unique

Maier Pale Dry Beer, single-label 12-ounce flat top, gold can, red label, single version. $200

Maier Select Beer, single-label, 12-ounce, high-profile cone top, solid red can, white lettering, two versions. $100

Single-label 12-ounce flat top, solid red can, white lettering, single version. $85

Single-label 12-ounce flat top, white can with hatched pattern, single version. $75

Single-label 12-ounce flat top, red can with hatched pattern, multiversions. $30

Single-label 12-ounce tab top, red can with hatched pattern, multiversions.. $20

Maier's XXXX Ale, two-label 12-ounce flat top, green can, yellow label, single version. $300

Mann-Chester Extra Pale Beer, single- or two-label 12- and 16-ounce flat or tab top, gold can, red label, multiversions all cans. $40

Single-label, 12-ounce flat or tab top, white can, red label, single version each lid. $20

Photo 39 (left). L & M Aged Lager Beer.
Photo 40 (right). Maier Export Beer.

Medallion Premium Quality Beer, single-label 12-ounce tab top, white can, metallic gold label, two versions. $150

Niborg Beer, two-label 12-ounce flat top, white can, blue oval, single version. ....Exotic

Old Dutch Lager Beer, two-label 12-ounce flat or tab top, white can, windmill scene bottom front, multiversions. $25

Old German Lager Beer, two-label 12-ounce flat or tab top, white can, red metallic label, single version of each. $85

Old Gibraltar Famous Dry Beer, two-label 12-ounce flat top, metallic gold can, maroon label, minor versions. $100

Old Heidel Brau Lager Beer, two-label 12-ounce flat, soft, or tab top, white can, red stein on face, multiversions. $30

Old Vienna Premium Lager Beer, two-label 12-ounce tab top, white can, metallic or dull gold label, two versions. *(See photo 41)*
Metallic,.. $75
"6 for 87¢," $125

Olde Tyme Premium Lager Beer, two-label 12- or 16-ounce flat or tab top, white can, red and blue trim, multiversions. $30

Padre Pale Lager Beer, two-label 12-ounce flat top, creme- or white-color can, maroon drinking scene, multiversions. $30

Pilsner Supreme Beer, two-label 16-ounce flat top, creme-color can, dark red label, two versions... $175

Regal Bock Beer, two-label 12-ounce soft or tab top, white can, "REGAL" in blue oval, "BOCK" in red oval, two versions..................................... $85

Regal Select Beer, two-label 12- or 16-ounce flat, soft, zip, or tab top, white can, six ovals, multiversions. *(See photo 42)*
No script, ... $10
"NOW NO OPENER NEEDED,".. $15
Pre-priced cans,.. $25

Two-label gallon, blue can, white band, glass of beer, single version. $600

Regal Select Genuine Draft Beer, two-label 12- or 16-ounce tab top, blue can with glass of beer, versions: 12-ounce two versions, 16-ounce single version.
.... $35

Regency Premium Pilsner Beer, two-label 12-ounce flat top, woodgrain can, white label, single version. $60

Two-label 12-ounce flat or tab top, yellow can, white oval, red label, single version each top. *(See photo 43)*... $75

Two-label 12-ounce flat or tab top, white can, yellow oval, dark red label, single version each top. $100

Photo 41 (left). Old Vienna Premium Lager Beer.
Photo 42 (center). Regal Select Beer. Photo 43 (right). Regency Premium Pilsner Beer.

Reidenbach Premium Pale Dry Beer, two-label 12-ounce tab top, woodgrain can, multiversions. $50

Rex Pale Lager Beer, two-label 12-ounce flat, soft, or tab top, blue can, white shield, red "REX," multiversions. $40

Royal Award Lager Beer, two-label 12-ounce flat top, white can, blue scroll, two versions. $75

Santa Fe Lager Beer, two-label 12-ounce flat top, gold can, gold open-winged eagle, single version. $250

Snowcrest Beer, two-label 12-ounce flat top, multicolored lake scene, "GRACE BROS." on can, "MAIER" on lid, single version. $500

Soul Mellow Yellow Beer, two-label 12- and 16-ounce tab top, gold can, white band, single version. *(See photo 44)* (A 7-ounce Soul was rumored, but never seen.)
12-ounce,.. $300
16-ounce,..$250

Soul Stout Malt Liquor, two-label 12- and 16-ounce tab top, red can, white band, single version. *(See photo 45)*
12-ounce,..$350
16-ounce,.. $300

Sportsman Premium Beer, two-label 12-ounce flat or tab top, metallic or dull gold can, multiversions. $75

Spring Beer, two-label 12-ounce flat or tab top, white can, gold oval, blue label, multiversions. $25
"6 for 89¢," $35

Steinbeck Lager Beer, two-label 12-ounce flat top, large blue stein, multiversions... $20

Steinbrau Genuine Draft Beer, two-label 12-ounce zip or tab top, brown can, large glass of beer, multiversions. $35

Steinbrau Pale Dry Lager Beer, two-label 12- and 16-ounce flat and tab top, white can, lidded stein, multiversions. $35

Super X Markets Pale Dry Beer, two-label 12-ounce tab top, metallic red bands top and bottom, two versions. $150

Swinger Malt Liquor, two-label 12-ounce tab top, white can, blue band, "SWINGER" on S-shaped label, two versions. $40

Tahoe Lager Beer, two-label 12-ounce flat top, blue can, large glass of beer, single version. $300

Photo 44 (left). Soul Mellow Yellow Beer. Photo 45 (right). Soul Stout Malt Liquor.

Photo 46 (left). Value Line Lager Beer. Photo 47 (center). Zodys Premium Beer. Photo 48 (right). Balboa Export Premium Lager Beer.

Value Line Lager Beer, two-label 12-ounce flat or tab top, white can, gold trim, red lettering, multiversions. *(See photo 46)* $35

Value Line Stout Malt Liquor, single-label 16-ounce tab top, metallic red and white can, maroon label, single version. $250

Velvet Glow Pale Dry Beer, two-label 12- or 16-ounce flat or tab top, white can, gold diamonds, multiversions.
12-ounce, ... $40
16-ounce, ... $75

Western Gold Lager Beer, two-label 12-ounce flat top, gold can, blue-gold label, single version. $85

Zodys Premium Beer, two-label 12-ounce tab top, white can, blue label, red "z," single version. *(See photo 47)* $300

MONARCH BREWING COMPANY, 1850 North Main

Balboa Export Premium Lager Beer, two-label 12-ounce flat top, yellow can, red stripes top and bottom, INTERNAL REVENUE TAX PAID, single version. *(See photo 48)* $300

Brownie Pilsner Beer, single-label 12-ounce flat top, brown and yellow can with elf on side label, INTERNAL REVENUE TAX PAID, single version. $500

Chief Pilsner Beer, single-label 12-ounce flat top, white can, "Chief" in red, INTERNAL REVENUE TAX PAID, single version. .... Exotic

Coronado Pilsner Beer, single-label 12-ounce flat top, red and black can, OPENING INSTRUCTIONS, INTERNAL REVENUE TAX PAID, single version. $400

Finer Flaver Brand Ale, single-label 12-ounce flat top, gray can, blue lettering, red label, OPENING INSTRUCTIONS, INTERNAL REVENUE TAX PAID, single version. .... Exotic

Finer Flaver Brand Beer, single-label 11- or 12-ounce flat top, silver can, stein on red label, OPENING INSTRUCTIONS, INTERNAL REVENUE TAX PAID, three versions:
12-ounce OI, ... $500
11-ounce OI, ... $475
12-ounce non-OI, ... $475

Palomar Pilsner Beer, single-label 12-ounce flat top, blue can, red and white label, OPENING INSTRUCTIONS, INTERNAL REVENUE TAX PAID, single version.
.... $500

Town House Pilsner Beer, single-label 12-ounce flat top, brown can, parchment label, INTERNAL REVENUE TAX PAID, single version. .... Exotic

PABST BREWING COMPANY, 1910 North Main (successor to Los Angeles Brewing Company, 1954–1980)

Big Cat Malt Liquor, two-label 12- or 16-ounce zip or tab top, white can, vertical stripes, running cat, multiversions. $5

Big Cat Stout Malt Liquor, two-label 12-ounce zip top, white can, vertical stripes, running cat, single version. $7.50

Blatz Milwaukee's Finest Beer, two-label 11-, 12-, or 16-ounce flat, tab, or zip top, gold can, maroon or black triangle, multiversions. $30

Blatz Milwaukee's Finest Bock, two-label 11- or 12-ounce flat top, gold can, maroon label, bock along side triangle, single version of each. $10

Burgermeister Beer, two-label 12-ounce steel can, 12- and 16-ounce aluminum, blue and white can, single version steel, multiversion aluminum.
Steel,..$5
Aluminum,...$3

Burgermeister Draft Beer, two-label 12-ounce steel and aluminum can, blue and white can, single version steel, multiversion aluminum.
Steel,..$5
Aluminum,...$3

Burgie Light Golden Beer, two-label 12-ounce aluminum can. Up to.........$3

Eastside Genuine Bock Beer, two-label 12-ounce flat top, gold can, goat on white label, single version. $200

Eastside Lager Beer, two-label 12- and 16-ounce flat, soft, or tab top, white can, red label, multiversions all tops.
Steel,..$5
Aluminum,...$2

Eastside Light And Fine Beer, two-label 12- and 16-ounce flat top, gold can, white label, multiversions.
12-ounce,.. $50
16-ounce,.. $60

Eastside Old Tap Brand Lager Beer, two-label 12- and 16-ounce flat and tab top, white can, red label, gold eagle, multiversions. $5

Eastside Old Tap Brand Bock Beer, two-label 11- and 12-ounce flat top, red label, gold bock, single version of each. $50

Old Mission Beer, two-label 12-ounce flat top, orange can, mission scene, single version. $100

Old Tap Lager Beer, two-label 12-ounce tab top, woodgrain label, multiversions steel and aluminum.
Steel,..$5
Aluminum,...$1

Pabst Blue Ribbon Beer, two-label 12- and 16-ounce flat top and quart cone top, checked gold can, white label, versions: 12-ounce multiversions, 16-ounce single version, 32-ounce single version.
12-ounce flat top, ... $30
16-ounce flat top, ... $35
Quart cone top, ... $85

Two-label 12- and 16-ounce flat top and quart cone top, blue can, white label, versions: 12-ounce multiversions, 16-ounce single version, 32-ounce single version.

12-ounce flat top, ... $15
16-ounce flat top, ... $15
Quart cone top, ... $65

Two-label 12- and 16-ounce flat top and quart cone top, white can with red ribbon, versions: 12-ounce multiversions, 16-ounce multiversions, 32-ounce single version.

12-ounce flat top, ... $10
16-ounce flat top, ... $10
Quart cone top, ... $60

Aluminum Pabst cans are worth up to $1 to the collector.

Pabst Blue Ribbon Bock Beer, two-label 12-ounce flat top, yellow can, large goat, single version. $75

Two-label 12-ounce flat or tab top, two red goats, single version each lid. .. $60

Two-label 12-ounce tab top, Pabst shield, goat on red ribbon, single version. $5

Aluminum, ... $1

Pabst also produced Pabst Extra Light, Pabst Light, Pabst Old Tankard Ale, and Red, White, and Blue Special in aluminum cans. Collector value is up to $1.

RHEINGOLD BREWING COMPANY, 2080 East 49th Street
(successor to Acme Brewing Company)

Rheingold Extra Dry Lager Beer, single-label 12-ounce flat top, white can, red label, single version. $20

Two-label 12- and 16-ounce flat top, white can, red label, single version. Either size, ... $20

JOS. SCHLITZ BREWING COMPANY, 7521 Woodman Avenue

Burgermeister Beer, two-sided 11-, 12-, 15-, or 16-ounce tab, soft, or zip top, white can, blue shield, multiversions. All versions, ... $10

Burgermeister Genuine Draft Beer, two-label 12- or 16-ounce tab top, white can, draft in gold oval, multiversions. All versions, ... $10

Burgermeister Pale Beer, two-label 15-ounce soft top, white can, gold trim, "BURGIE" man, single version. $20

Schlitz Beer, two-label 12- or 16-ounce flat top, white can, brown bands, c. 1954 or 1957, multiversions. All versions, ... $20

Two-label 12- or 16-ounce flat, solf, or tab top, white can, brown label outlined in gold or silver, c. 1960, 1962, or 1969, multiversions, all varieties. All versions, ... $10

Schlitz Malt Liquor, two-label 12- or 16-ounce tab top, white can, silver metals, multiversions. All versions, ... $5

Schlitz Stout Malt Liquor, two-label 12- or 16-ounce tab top, white can, large blue and black bull, multiversions. All versions, ...$3

Schlitz produced Old Milwaukee, Primo, Schlitz, Schlitz Light—A Fine Pilsner Beer, Schlitz Light Natural Pilsner, Schlitz Light Special Lager, Schlitz Malt Liquor, and Schlitz Stout Malt Liquor in aluminum cans. Collector value can range up to $5 for some brands.

SOUTHERN BREWING COMPANY, 671 Rio Street (successor to Grace Bros., et. al.)

Albion Old Stock Ale, single-label 12-ounce flat top, metallic green can, gold oval, single version. *(See photo 49)*.. $300

Balboa Export Premium Pale Beer, single-label 12-ounce flat top, yellow can, red bands, single version..$150

Better Foods Market Lager Beer, single-label 12-ounce flat top, blue and gold can, single version. ....Exotic

Bo-Bohemian Beer, single-label 12-ounce flat top, white can, red "Bo"'s, single version. $200

Bohemian Type Export Beer, single-label 12-ounce flat top, white can, checkered gold label, single version. $75

Single-label 12-ounce flat top, white can, solid gold label, two versions..... $75

Dodger Lager Beer, two-label 12-ounce flat top, white can, gold trim, single version...$100

Golden Crown Lager Beer, two-label 12-ounce flat top, metallic gold can, single version. $85

Golden Lager Premium Beer, two-label 12-ounce flat top, white can, red label outlined in blue, single version. $50

Hofmeister Premium Lager Beer, two-label 12-ounce flat top, single version.
....Exotic

Oakland

GOEBEL BREWING COMPANY, 533 Kirkham Street (successor to Golden West Brewing Company)

Bantam Beer By Goebel, single-label 8-ounce flat top, white can, black label, rooster, two versions. $30

Goebel 22 Beer, two-label 12-ounce flat top, metallic gold can, white label, multiversions. $25

Goebel Bock Beer, single-label 12-ounce flat top, white can, goat on red label, single version. $400

Goebel Extra Dry Beer, single-label 12-ounce flat-top, gold label, "Extra Dry" on black label, multiversions. $60

Goebel Extra Dry Private Stock Beer, two-label 12-ounce flat top, gold can, white label, black "GOEBEL," two versions. $40

Goebel Genuine Bock, single-label 12-ounce flat top, reddish can, goat on white label, single version.. $500

Goebel Light Lager Luxury Beer, single-label 8- or 12-ounce flat top, metallic gold can, red label, 8-ounce single version, 12-ounce two versions.
8-ounce, ... $60
12-ounce, ... $85

Goebel Private Stock Beer, single-label 12-ounce flat top, gold can, white label, multiversions. $50

Keg Brand Beer, two-label 12-ounce flat top, white can, yellow keg, single version. $30

GOLDEN WEST BREWING COMPANY, 533 Kirkham Street

Bull's Eye Beer, single-label 12-ounce flat top, silver can, blue bull's eye, OPENING INSTRUCTIONS, INTERNAL REVENUE TAX PAID, multiversions. $200

Golden Glow Ale, two-label 12-ounce flat top, black stars, "Ale" in script, INTERNAL REVENUE TAX PAID, single version. .... Exotic

Golden Glow Beer, two-label 12-ounce flat top, silver can, blue label, OPENING INSTRUCTIONS, INTERNAL REVENUE TAX PAID, single version. *(See photo 50)*
.... $125

Two-label 12-ounce flat top, gold can, yellow label, INTERNAL REVENUE TAX PAID, single version. $100

Golden Glow Export Beer, two-label 12-ounce flat top, gold can, red label, OPENING INSTRUCTIONS, INTERNAL REVENUE TAX PAID, single version. $150

Golden Glow Grade A Beer, two-label 12-ounce flat top, metallic gold can, blue label, INTERNAL REVENUE TAX PAID, multiversions. $75

Single-label, quart cone top, metallic gold can, blue label, INTERNAL REVENUE TAX PAID, multiversions. $150

Golden Glow Old Stock XXX Ale, single-label 12-ounce flat top, green can, orange label, INTERNAL REVENUE TAX PAID, single version. $75

Two-label 12-ounce flat top, green can, orange label, INTERNAL REVENUE TAX PAID, single version. $75

Single-label, quart cone top, green can, yellow and red label, single version.
.... $200

Golden Glow Pale Dry Beer, two-label 12-ounce flat top, metallic gold can, black label, single version. $60

Single-label, quart cone top, metallic gold can, black label, two versions. $200

Photo 49 (left). Albion Old Stock Ale. Photo 50 (right). Golden Glow Beer.

PACIFIC BREWING COMPANY, 533 Kirkham Street (successor to the Goebel Brewing Company)

Better Foods Market Beer, single-label 12-ounce flat top, blue and gold can, single version. ....Exotic

Buccaneer Stout Malt Liquor, two-label 8- or 12-ounce flat top, metallic gold can, buccaneer on front, single version each size.
8-ounce, ...Unique
12-ounce, ... $300

El Capitan Premium Beer, single-label 12-ounce flat top, gold and white can, blue label, single version. $100

Eureka Pale Dry Beer, two-label 12-ounce flat top, white can, metallic gold label, single version. $200

Excell Pale Dry Beer, two-label, 12-ounce flat top, white can, red and gold label, single version. $100

Falcon Premium Light Lager Beer, two-label 12-ounce flat top, metallic gold can, white oval, single version. $300

Forty Niner Premium Lager Beer, two-label 12-ounce flat top, white can, gold bands and trim, single version. *(See photo 51)* $100

Glacier Premium Light Bright Beer, two-label 12-ounce flat top, mountain scene, single version. ....Exotic

Golden Glow Beer, two-label 8- or 12-ounce flat top, white can, red oval label, single version.
8-ounce, ... $300
12-ounce, ... $75

Golden Harvest Light Bright Beer, two-sided 12-ounce flat top, brown can, white label, single version. $85

Golden West Pale Dry Beer, two-label 12-ounce flat top, white can, gold bottom band, brown trim, single version. $150

Hollywood Ranch Market Lager Beer, two-label 12-ounce flat top, gold can, cowboy, "LAGER BEER" in red, single version. ....Exotic

Hopsburger Premium Lager Beer, two-label 12-ounce flat top, white can, gold label, single version. $400

Keg Brand Beer, two-label 12-ounce flat top, white can, yellow label, single version. $40

Mellow Brew Pale Dry Beer, two-label 12-ounce flat top, white can, blue label, single version. $300

Old Vienna Premium Light Lager Beer, two-label 12-ounce flat top, white can, metallic gold lettering, single version. $100

Ranch Beer, two-label 12-ounce flat top, woodgrain can, white label, single version. ....Exotic

Sierra Beer, two-label 12-ounce flat top, silver can, blue bands and label, single version. $100

Siesta Beer, two-label 12-ounce flat top, gold can, white sunburst, single version. $300

Super X Pale Dry Beer, two-label 12-ounce flat top, red and white can, gold x, single version. *(See photo 52)* $100

Tahoe Pale Dry Beer, two-label 12-ounce flat top, white band, lake scene, single version. $100

Town & Country Beer, two-label 12-ounce flat top, white can, gold bands, red lettering, single version. $250

Van Merritt Beer, two-label 12-ounce flat top, white can, green oval, windmill scene, single version. *(See photo 53)* $100

Velvet Glow Pale Dry Beer, two-label 12-ounce flat top, white can, gold diamonds, single version. $60

Sacramento

BUFFALO BREWERY INC., 1717 21st Street, affiliated with Grace Bros., Santa Rosa, 1942–1948 (successors to Buffalo Brewing Company)

Buffalo Brand Extra Pale Beer, single-label 12-ounce flat top, gold can, INTERNAL REVENUE TAX PAID, single version. ....Exotic

Single-label 12-ounce flat top, silver can, INTERNAL REVENUE TAX PAID, single version. ....Exotic

BUFFALO BREWING COMPANY, 1717 21st Street

Buffalo Brand Beer, single-label 12-ounce flat top, yellow and brown can, brown buffalo, OPENING INSTRUCTIONS, INTERNAL REVENUE TAX PAID, multiversions. $300

Buffalo Brand Extra Pale Beer, single-label, 12-ounce, high- or low-profile cone top, metallic orange can, INTERNAL REVENUE TAX PAID, single version. ......Exotic

Single-label quart cone top, red can, white label, INTERNAL REVENUE TAX PAID, single version. *(See photo 54)* ....Exotic

Single-label 12-ounce flat top, gold can, blue label, INTERNAL REVENUE TAX PAID, single version. $600

Two-label 12-ounce flat top, gold can, blue or white label, INTERNAL REVENUE TAX PAID, single version of each. $600

Gilt Edge Lager Beer, single-label 12-ounce flat top, blue and white can, OPENING INSTRUCTIONS, INTERNAL REVENUE TAX PAID, single version. $300

(From left to right)
Photo 51. Forty Niner Premium Lager Beer.
Photo 52. Super X Pale Dry Beer. Photo 53. Van Merritt Beer. Photo 54. Buffalo Brand Extra Pale Beer.

Ruhstaller's Gilt Edge Lager Beer, single-label 12-ounce flat top, yellow can, red lettering, OPENING INSTRUCTIONS, INTERNAL REVENUE TAX PAID, single version. ....Exotic

Salinas

MONTEREY BREWING COMPANY, 347 North Main

Monterey Beer, single-label, 12-ounce, low-profile cone top, creme-colored can, black label, INTERNAL REVENUE TAX PAID, single version. *(See photo 55)*..$250

San Diego

ALTES BREWING COMPANY, 2301 Main Street (successor to Aztec Brewing Company)

7-11 The Natural Brew Beer, two-label, 12-ounce, high-profile cone top, white can, "7-11" in red, single version. $250

Altes Brisk Lager Beer, two-label, 12-ounce, high-profile cone top, green can, white label, "Brisk" on red, single version. $175

Altes Golden Lager Beer, two-label, 12-ounce, high-profile cone top, white can, gold bands top and bottom, single version. $150

Altes Lager Beer, single-label, 12-ounce, high-profile cone top, green filigree on gold can, IRTP or non-IRTP, minor versions.
Non-IRTP, ... $85
IRTP, ...$100

AZTEC BREWING COMPANY, 2301 Main Street

ABC Famous Quality Plus Beer, single-label, 12-ounce, high- or low-profile cone top, blue can, gold label, INTERNAL REVENUE TAX PAID, single version of each.
Low-profile, ... $90
High-profile, ... $85

ABC Famous World's Gold Metal, single-label, 12-ounce, low-profile cone top, gold can, red label, INTERNAL REVENUE TAX PAID, multi minor versions. ..$150

Single-label 12-ounce flat top, gold can, red label, INTERNAL REVENUE TAX PAID, single version. $125

Associated Brand Lager Beer, two-label, 12-ounce, low-profile cone top, red, white, and blue can, INTERNAL REVENUE TAX PAID, single version.......... $400

Old Dutch Brand Ale, single-label, 12-ounce, low-profile cone top, gold and brown can, INTERNAL REVENUE TAX PAID, single version. $600

Old Dutch Brand Beer, single-label, 12-ounce, low-profile cone top, gold and brown can, "Dutchman," INTERNAL REVENUE TAX PAID, single version... $500

San Francisco

ACME BREWERIES INC., 762 Fulton Street (successor to Cereal Products Refining Corporation)

Acme Beer, two-label or single-label 12-ounce flat top, black can, white bands, red label, slogans on white bands, OPENING INSTRUCTIONS on early cans, INTERNAL REVENUE TAX PAID, multiversions.

OI, ... $75

Non-OI $65

Two-label 12-ounce flat top, WITHDRAWN FREE, camouflage can, single version.
.... $200

Two-label 12-ounce flat top, black can, women in label, multiversions. *(See photo 56)* $40

Acme Bock Beer, single-label 12-ounce flat top, white can, goat on red shield, single version. $400

Acme Bulldog Ale, two-label 12-ounce flat top, green can, white label, multiversions. $80

Acme Englishtown Brand Ale, two- or single-label 12-ounce flat top, gold can, red label, red "A," black "CME," versions IRTP and non-IRTP. *(See photo 57)*

IRTP, ... $300

Non-IRTP $275

Acme Genuine Bock Beer, two-label 12-ounce flat top, white can, large goat's head, single version. *(See photo 58)* $150

Acme Gold Label Light Dry Beer, single-label 12-ounce flat top, yellow can, white band around top, multiversions. $40

Acme Gold Label Pale Dry Beer, single-label 12-ounce flat top, yellow label, white band around top, single version. $50

Acme Light Dry Beer, single-label 12-ounce flat top, yellow can, brand in black, single version. $60

Acme The Light Dry Beer, single-label 12-ounce flat top, yellow can, brand in black, single version. $75

Bull Dog Extra Malt Liquor, two-label 12-ounce flat top, black and white can, bulldog with cap on head, single version. $75

Bull Dog Extra Stout Malt Liquor, two-label 12-ounce flat top, black and white can, bulldog with cap on head, single version. $75

Bull Dog Lager Beer By Acme, two-label 12-ounce flat top, maroon can, white label, single version. $60

(From left to right)
Photo 55. Monterey Beer.
Photo 56. Acme Beer.
Photo 57. Acme
Englishtown Brand Ale.
Photo 58. Acme Genuine
Bock Beer.

ALBION BREWING COMPANY, 5050 Mission Street (successor to El Rey Brewing Company)

Eagle Beer, single-label, 12-ounce, low-profile cone top, white can, large flying eagle, INTERNAL REVENUE TAX PAID, single version. ....Exotic

BURGERMEISTER BREWING CORPORATION, 470 10th Street (successor to San Francisco Brewing Company)

Burgermeister Beer, two-label 11-, 12-, 15-, or 16-ounce flat or soft top, blue and white can, man holding glass of beer, multiversions.
Flat top, ... $15
Soft top, ... $10
Two-label 12- or 16-ounce flat top, "A TRULY FINE PALE BEER" on red ribbon, multiversions. $30
Two-label 11-, 12-, 15-, or 16-ounce flat top, "A TRULY FINE PALE BEER" in script, multiversions. $30

BURGERMEISTER BREWING CORPORATION, DIVISION OF MEISTER BRAU, INC., 470 10th Street (successor to Jos. Schlitz Brewing Company)

Meister Brau, Inc. does *not* appear anywhere on cans.

Alpen Glen Beer, two-label 12- or 16-ounce flat or tab top, white can, orange or green trees, single version. $30

Buckeye Premium Beer, two-label 12- or 16-ounce flat or tab top, metallic or dull red can, multiversions. $20

Burgermeister Beer, two-label 12- or 16-ounce tab top, white can, metallic blue label, multiversions. $10
Two-label 16-ounce tab top, white can, red "BURGIE," multiversions. $10

Burgermeister Genuine Draft Beer, two-label 12- or 16-ounce tab top, white can, metallic gold trim, blue label, multiversions. *(See photo 59)*............. $10

Golden Lager Light Export Beer, two-label 12-ounce tab top, white can, gold stripes, stein of beer center of label, single version. $75

Matterhorn Beer, two-label 12- or 16-ounce flat or tab top, blue can, white mountain, multiversions. $20

Oldbru Beer, two-label 12-ounce flat top and 16-ounce tab top, white can, metallic gold trim, red label, single version. $20

(From left to right)
Photo 59. Burgermeister Genuine Draft Beer.
Photo 60. Acme Beer.
Photo 61. El Rey Beer.
Photo 62. Tornberg's Original Old German Brand Beer.

CALIFORNIA BREWING COMPANY, 762 Fulton Street (successor to Acme Brewing Company)

Bull Dog Ale, two-label 12-ounce flat top, green can, white oval label, two minor versions. $40

Bull Dog 14 Extra Hearty Stout Malt Liquor, two-label 12-ounce flat top, white can, bottom black strip, gold bull dog, single version. $100

Bull Dog Extra Malt Liquor, two-label 12-ounce flat top, white can, black label, single version. $50

Bull Dog Extra Stout Malt Label, two-label 12-ounce flat top, white can, black label, single version. $50

Bull Dog 14 Extra Stout Malt Liquor, two-label 12-ounce flat top, white can, black label, "BULLDOG" in red, single version. $150

California Gold Label Beer, two-label 12-ounce flat top, metallic gold label, white oval, covered wagon, two versions. $40

CEREAL PRODUCTS REFINING CORPORATION, 762 Fulton Street

Acme Beer, single-label 12-ounce flat top, black can, red label, OPENING INSTRUCTIONS, INTERNAL REVENUE TAX PAID, "NON FATTENING," single version. *(See photo 60)* $150

EAGLE BREWING COMPANY, 5050 Mission Street (successor to El Rey Brewing Company)

Eureka Extra Pale Beer, two-label, 12-ounce, low-profile cone top, gold can, flying eagle, INTERNAL REVENUE TAX PAID, single version. $300

EL REY BREWING COMPANY, 5050 Mission Street

Eagle Beer, single-label, 12-ounce, low-profile cone top, gold can, brown trim, flying eagle, INTERNAL REVENUE TAX PAID, single version. $400

El Rey Beer, single-label, 12-ounce, low-profile cone top, yellow can, gold band, crown, INTERNAL REVENUE TAX PAID, WITHDRAWN FREE FOR EXPORT, minor versions of each. *(See photo 61)*
IRTP, ... $300
WFFE, ... $350

Gold Age Beer, single-label, 12-ounce, low-profile cone top, black can, red band, minor, INTERNAL REVENUE TAX PAID, multiversions. $500

Leidig's Dutch Mill Beer, single-label, 12-ounce, low-profile cone top, red and blue can, windmills, INTERNAL REVENUE TAX PAID, single version......... Exotic

Tornberg's Original Old German Brand Beer, single-label, 12-ounce, low-profile cone top, gold can, brown castle, INTERNAL REVENUE TAX PAID, WITHDRAWN FREE. *(See photo 62)*
IRTP, ... $600
WFFE, ... $700

Tornberg's Original Old German Style Beer, single-label low-profile cone top, gold can, yellow label, INTERNAL REVENUE TAX PAID, single version....... $600

FALSTAFF BREWING CORPORATION, 410 10th Street (successor to Burgermeister Brewing Company, Division of Meister Brau, Inc., Chicago, IL)

El Rancho Light Beer, two-label 12-ounce tab top, white can, red label, blue bands, two versions. $10

Heritage House Fine Light Beer, two-label 12-ounce tab top, yellow can, red label, single version. $10

Silver Peak Beer, two-label 12-ounce tab top, white can, blue label, single version. $10

Springfield Beer, two-label 12-ounce flat top, white can, gold band, black and gold label, single-version aluminum can. $5

Tivoli A Light Premium Beer, two-label 12- or 16-ounce tab top, white can, blue label, single version. $10

GENERAL BREWING COMPANY, 2601 Newhall Street (successor to Lucky Breweries, Inc.)

General Brewing took Newhall Street Brewery from Lucky Breweries, Inc. in 1974. It produced nothing but aluminum and bi-metal cans. The brands included Ballantine, Brew 102, Brown Derby, De Light Brew, Falstaff, Fisher, Golden Crown, Heritage House, Hof-Brau, Keg, King Snedley, Lucky, Maier, Padre, Regal Select Padre, Regal Select, Reidenbach, Shortstop, Springfield, Steinbrau, and Tivoli, to name a partial list. Most of the brands carry a collector value of $1 and $2, with exceptions being King Snedley at $20 and Shortstop at $5. The brewery transferred its brands to the Vancouver, WA, plant in 1978.

GENERAL BREWING CORPORATION, 2601 Newhall Street (1933–1948 name changed to Lucky Lager Brewing Company, then back to General Brewing Corporation in October 1963, which was the name used until 1969)

Bankers Ale, single-label 12-ounce flat top, metallic green can, yellow label, INTERNAL REVENUE TAX PAID, single version. $300

Fisher Premium Light Beer, two-label 12- and 16-ounce flat top, white can, gold trim, "FISHER" on red label, multiversions. $20

Frisco Extra Pale Lager Beer, two-label 12-ounce flat top, yellow can, black band, "FRISCO" in white outlined in black, OPENING INSTRUCTIONS, INTERNAL REVENUE TAX PAID, single version... $400

Two-label 12-ounce flat top, metallic gold can, "FRISCO" in black, INTERNAL REVENUE TAX PAID, single version...$350

Glory B Lager Beer, single-label 12-ounce flat top, white can, red label, INTERNAL REVENUE TAX PAID, single version...................................Unique

Gold Metal Extra Pale Lager Beer, single-label 12-ounce flat top, blue and white can, OPENING INSTRUCTIONS, INTERNAL REVENUE TAX PAID, single version. $100

Lisco Lager Beer, single-label 12-ounce flat top, blue and white can, single version. $400

Lucky Ale, two-label 12-ounce flat top, gray can, "LUCKY ALE" on red band, INTERNAL REVENUE TAX PAID, single version. $150

Lucky Dated Ale, single-label 12-ounce flat top, gold can, green "x," OPENING INSTRUCTIONS, INTERNAL REVENUE TAX PAID, single version. $400

Lucky Genuine Draft Beer, two-label 7- or 12-ounce tab top, white and gold can, small "LUCKY X," multiversions of 12-ounce.
7-ounce, ... $20
12-ounce, ... $10

Lucky Lager Age Dated Ale, single-label 12-ounce flat top, red and gold can, diamond label, OPENING INSTRUCTIONS, INTERNAL REVENUE TAX PAID, single version. ....Exotic

Lucky Lager Age Dated Beer, single-label 12-ounce flat top, gold can, large red "x," OPENING INSTRUCTIONS, INTERNAL REVENUE TAX PAID, single version. $75

Single-label 12-ounce flat top, camouflage can, single version. $300

Lucky Lager Aged For Flavor, two-sided 7-, 12-, or 16-ounce soft, zip, or tab top, metallic red "x," multiversions. Up to.................................... $10

Lucky Lager Dated Beer, single-label 12-ounce flat top, gold can, large red "x," OPENING INSTRUCTIONS, INTERNAL REVENUE TAX PAID, single version. *(See photo 63)* $40

Lucky Lager Extra Dry Dated Beer, single-label 12-ounce flat top, gold can, large red "x," INTERNAL REVENUE TAX PAID, single version. $40

Lucky Light Draft Beer, two-label 7-, 12-, or 16-ounce tab top, white can, large gold band, single version. *(See photo 64)*
7-ounce, ... $15
12-ounce, ...$5
16-ounce, ... $10

Old Frisco Extra Pale Lager Beer, single-label 12-ounce flat top, metallic orange can, white label, single version. *(See photo 65)* $150

GLOBE BREWING COMPANY, 1401 Sansone Street

Fort Sutter Beer, two-label 12-ounce flat top, blue can, red label, INTERNAL REVENUE TAX PAID, single version. ....Exotic

Photo 63 (left). Lucky Lager Dated Beer. Photo 64 (center). Lucky Light Draft Beer. Photo 65 (right). Old Frisco Extra Pale Lager Beer.

Log Cabin Beer, two-label 12-ounce flat top, silver can, "LOG CABIN" in large oval label, INTERNAL REVENUE TAX PAID, single version. ....Exotic

Nu-Globe Old Style Lager Beer, two-label 12-ounce flat top, yellow can, black band, "NU-GLOBE" in red, INTERNAL REVENUE TAX PAID, single version. ...Exotic

Primo Beer, two-label 12-ounce flat top, green sunburst, red globe, INTERNAL REVENUE TAX PAID, single version. ....Exotic

THEODORE HAMM BREWING COMPANY, 1550 Bryant (successor to the Rainier Brewing Company, San Francisco, CA)

Buckhorn Premium Lager Beer, two-label 12-ounce tab top, yellow can, buckhorn on black label, multiversions. (Brand also produced in aluminum cans.)..........$3

Buckhorn Special Lager Beer, two-label 11- or 15-ounce flat top, red can, gold label, white bands, multiversions. $15
Aluminum soft top, ...$10

Burgermeister, Burgermeister Genuine Draft, and Burgie Golden Beer were produced in aluminum cans with a collector value of up to $2.

Hamm's Beer, two-label 11-, 12-, 15-, or 16-ounce tab top, gold sunburst can, wide blue band, multiversions.
11- or 15-ounce, ...$15
12- or 16-ounce, ...$10

Two-label 11-, 12-, or 15-ounce flat, soft, zip, or tab top, blue can, white crown, gold trim, multiversions.
11-, 12-, or 15-ounce flat top, ...$5
11-, 12-, or 15-ounce soft top, ...$8
11-, 12-, or 15-ounce zip or tab top, ...$3
All aluminum versions, ...$2

This brewery also produced Hamm's Beer—Genuine Draft Beer and Hamm's Beer—Real Draft in aluminum cans with a collector value of up to $3.

Hamm's Beer—Real Draft, two-label 11-ounce tab top, barrel-shaped can with blue label, multiversions. $3

Hamm's Draft Beer Genuine Draft, two-label 12-ounce tab top, barrel-shaped can with blue label, multiversions. $3

Hamm's Preferred Smooth-Mellow Beer, two-label 12-ounce flat top, gold sunburst, multiversions. $15

Hamm's also produced Alpen Glen, Golden Lager Light Export Beer, Pantry Pride Oldbru Premium, and Value Line Premium Lager Beer at San Francisco. Since these cans are unusual brands, they carry a collector value of up to $25 each.

LUCKY BREWERIES, INC., 2601 Newhall Street (successor to General Brewing Corporation; brewery closed in 1974; brands transferred to Vancouver, WA)

Fisher Light A Premium Beer, two-label 12- and 16-ounce tab top, white can, red label, gold stripes, multiversions. $15

A single-version, aluminum, 12-ounce can was also produced; collector value up to $3.

Fisher Premium Light Beer, two-label 12- and 16-ounce flat or tab top, "Premium Light" on blue band, some varieties pre-priced, multiversions all cans.
Standard variety, ... $15
Pre-priced varieties, ... $20
Brand also produced in 16-ounce aluminum; collector value up to $5.

King Snedley's Beer, two-label 12- or 16-ounce flat top, silver can, black line drawings, single version of each.
12-ounce, ... $40
16-ounce, ... $50

Lucky Bock Beer, two-label 12-ounce tab top, green and white can, goat's head, single version. $25

Lucky Draft Beer, two-label 7-, 12-, and 16-ounce tab top, white can, flowing "LUCKY 'L'," single version 7 ounces, multiversions 12 and 16 ounces.
7-ounce, ... $25
12- and 16-ounce, ... $15

Lucky Lager Aged For Flavor, two-label 12- or 16-ounce tab top, greenish can, small red "x," multiversions. $8

Lucky Lager Beer, two-label 12- or 16-ounce tab top, white can, script, flowing red "LUCKY 'L'," multiversions. *(See photo 66)* $2

Lucky Light Draft Beer, two-label, 7-, 12-, or 16-ounce tab top, white can, metallic gold stripe and lettering, single version of each.
7-ounce, ... $20
12- and 16-ounce, ... $15

Lucky Malt Liquor, two-label 16-ounce tab top, white can, brown shield label, single version. $40

LUCKY LAGER BREWING COMPANY, 2601 Newhall Street
(successor to General Brewing Corporation [1933–1948]; predecessor to General Brewing Corporation [1963–1969])

Fisher Premium Light Beer, two-label 12-, 15-, or 16-ounce flat top, white can, red label, gold stripes, single version each can.
12- and 16-ounce, ... $20
15-ounce, ... $30

Photo 66. Lucky Lager Beer.

Lucky Bankers Ale, two-label 11-, 12-, or 15-ounce flat top, green can, oval white label, Lucky "x," minor versions. *(See photo 67)*

11- or 12-ounce,.. $60
15-ounce,.. $75

Lucky Lager Age Dated Beer, two-label 12- or 16-ounce flat top, quart cone top, large red "x," gold and red can, INTERNAL REVENUE TAX PAID some versions, multiversions all varieties except cone. *(See photo 68)*

IRTP, ... $85
Non-IRTP, ... $75
Quart cone top, ... $125

Two-label 12-, 15-, or 16-ounce flat top and quart cone top, metallic gold bands, Lucky "x" on metallic gold label, multiversions all varieties except cone. $15
Quart cone top, ... $60

Lucky Lager Age Dated Premium Beer, two-label 7- or 12-ounce soft or tab top, metallic gold oval, small red "x" on metallic gold label, multiversions. $15

Lucky Lager Aged For Flavor, two-label 7-, 12-, or 16-ounce flat or zip top, metallic gold oval, small red "x" on metallic gold label, multiversions.

7-ounce, ... $20
12- or 16-ounce, ... $10

RAINIER BREWING COMPANY, 1550 Bryant Street (aka: Tacoma Brewing Company)

All mandatories will read RAINIER BREWING COMPANY except Tacoma Pale Beer.

B B Special Export Beer, single-label, 12-ounce, low-profile cone top, glass of beer on blue label, INTERNAL REVENUE TAX PAID, multiversions. *(See photo 69)*...$350

Brown Derby Pilsner Beer, two-label 12-ounce flat top, silver can, brown label, "BROWN DERBY" in green, OPENING INSTRUCTIONS, INTERNAL REVENUE TAX PAID, single version. $150

Two-label 12-ounce flat top, yellow can, white label, "PILSNER" in red, OPENING INSTRUCTIONS, INTERNAL REVENUE TAX PAID, multiversions. $125

King's Taste Beer, single-label, 12-ounce, low-profile cone top, yellow can, crown over beer, INTERNAL REVENUE TAX PAID, two versions. $500

Krug Pilsener Type Beer, single-label, 12-ounce, low-profile cone top, mug on label, INTERNAL REVENUE TAX PAID, two versions. *(See photo 70)*.........Exotic

(From left to right)
Photo 67. Lucky Bankers
Ale. Photo 68. Lucky Lager
Age Dated Beer. Photo 69.
B B Special Export Beer.
Photo 70. Krug Pilsner
Type Beer.

Leidig's Deluxe Beer, single-label low-profile cone top, "L. H. LEIDIG" on red ribbon, INTERNAL REVENUE TAX PAID, single version. .... Exotic

Lifestaff Pale Lager Beer, single-label, 12-ounce, low-profile cone or flat top, red can, dark blue label, INTERNAL REVENUE TAX PAID, multiversion cone top, single-version flat top.
Cone top, ... $300
Flat top, ... $250

Lisco Lager Beer, single-label, 12-ounce, low-profile cone or flat top, gold can, blue diamond label, INTERNAL REVENUE TAX PAID, two minor versions of cone top, single-version flat top.
Cone top, ... $300
Flat top, ... $250

Pacific Lager Beer, single-label, 12-ounce, low-profile cone or flat top, blue and green can, white lettering, INTERNAL REVENUE TAX PAID, multiversion cone top, single-version flat top.
Cone top, ... $125
Flat top, ... $100

Pilsenbrau Lager Beer, single-label 12-ounce flat top, multicolored can, INTERNAL REVENUE TAX PAID, single version. .... Exotic

Rainier Beer, single-label 12-ounce flat top, gold can, red label, mountain on blue background, INTERNAL REVENUE TAX PAID, single version. $100

Rainier Club Beer, single-label, 12-ounce, high-profile cone or flat top, blue can, red label, INTERNAL REVENUE TAX PAID, versions: WITHDRAWN FREE FOR EXPORT, "Cap sealed panel," flat top. *(See photo 71)*
WITHDRAWN FREE, ... $200
"Cap sealed panel," $150
Flat top, ... $100

Rainier Club Extra Dry Beer, single-label, 12-ounce, high- or low-profile cone or flat top, black can, red label, multiversions.
Low-profile, ... $75
High-profile, ... $75
Flat top, ... $50

Rainier Club Extra Pale Beer, single-label, 12-ounce, low-profile cone or flat top, black can, red label, INTERNAL REVENUE TAX PAID, single version of each. *(See photo 72)*
Low-profile cone top, ... $85
Camouflage cone top, ... $350
Camouflage flat top, ... $300
Flat top, ... $60

Photo 71 (left). Rainier Club Beer.
Photo 72 (right). Rainier Club Extra Pale Beer.

Rainier Old Stock Ale, single-label, 12-ounce, high- or low-profile cone top, or single- or double-label 12-ounce flat top, green can, orange label, IRTP or non-IRTP, multiversions.
Cone top, ... $75
Flat top, ... $40

Rainier Old Time Kräusen Beer, two-label 12-ounce flat top, gold can, metallic red label, multiversions. *(See photo 73)* $100

Rainier Special Export Beer, single-label, 12-ounce, low-profile cone top, white can, red and black lettering, INTERNAL REVENUE TAX PAID, multiversions. *(See photo 74)* $60

Rainier Special Export Genuine Lager, single-label, 12-ounce, low-profile cone top, white can, metallic bands, INTERNAL REVENUE TAX PAID, minor versions.
.... $125

Royal Beer, Rumor?

Royal Finest Lager Beer, single-label, 12-ounce, low-profile cone top, multi-colored can, "FOR GENATO COMMERCIAL CORPORATION," single version.
.... Unique

Salute Brand Lager Beer, single-label, 12-ounce, low-profile cone top, white and gold can, "TERMINAL LIQUORS," INTERNAL REVENUE TAX PAID, multiversions.. $150

Silver Beer, single-label, 12-ounce, low-profile cone top, silver, red, and black can, INTERNAL REVENUE TAX PAID, single version............................. Exotic

Tacoma Pale Beer, single-label, 12-ounce, low-profile cone or flat top, blue can, white label, one version says "TACOMA BREWING," INTERNAL REVENUE TAX PAID, cone tops have minor versions. *(See photo 75)*
Cone top, ... $150
Flat top, ... $100

REGAL AMBER BREWING COMPANY, 675 Treat Street

Blue Boar Ale, single-label 12-ounce flat top, blue can, white lettering, OPENING INSTRUCTIONS, INTERNAL REVENUE TAX PAID, single version.................. $250

Leidig's German Style Beer, single-label 12-ounce flat top, green and white can, OPENING INSTRUCTIONS, INTERNAL REVENUE TAX PAID, single version.
.... $500

Regal Amber Ale, single-label 12-ounce flat top, green can, white letters, OPENING INSTRUCTIONS, INTERNAL REVENUE TAX PAID, single version. $300

Regal Amber Beer, single-label 12-ounce flat top, red can, white lettering, OPENING INSTRUCTIONS, INTERNAL REVENUE TAX PAID, WITHDRAWN FREE FOR EXPORT, single version each can.
WITHDRAWN FREE,... $300
IRTP, ... $250

Regal Pale Beer, two-label 12-ounce flat top, copper-colored can with blue label, single version.. $60

Two-label 12-ounce flat top, white can, gold oval, multiversions. $30

Two-label 12-ounce flat top, white can, gold oval, small red shield, multiversions.. $30

(From left to right) Photo 73. Rainier Old Time Kräusen Beer. Photo 74. Rainier Special Export Beer. Photo 75. Tacoma Pale Beer. Photo 76. Regal Select Beer. Photo 77. Burgermeister Ale.

REGAL PALE BREWING COMPANY, 673 Treat Street (successor to Regal Amber Brewing Company)

Golden Gate Beer, two-label 11-ounce flat top, blue can, bridge scene, single version. $40

Regal Bock Beer, two-label 12-ounce flat top, white can, metallic gold oval, red goat, multiversions. $75

Regal Pale Beer, two-label 12- or 16-ounce flat top, metallic gold oval, blue label, red or blue shield, multiversions. $25

Regal Select Beer, two-label 11-, 12-, or 16-ounce flat top, white can, "REGAL" on blue label, "SELECT" on red label, multiversions. *(See photo 76)* $15

Sierra Beer, two-label 11-ounce flat top, gold can, dark blue lettering, single version. $40

SAN FRANCISCO BREWING CORPORATION, 470 10th Street

Alpen Glen Ale, single-label 12-ounce flat top, gold and green can, OPENING INSTRUCTIONS, INTERNAL REVENUE TAX PAID, single version. .... Exotic

Alpen Glen Beer, single-label 12-ounce flat top, orange and green can, lodge scene, OPENING INSTRUCTIONS, INTERNAL REVENUE TAX PAID, single version. $300

Alpen Glow Ale, single-label 12-ounce flat top, gold and green can, lodge scene, OPENING INSTRUCTIONS, INTERNAL REVENUE TAX PAID, single version. ...Exotic

Alpen Glow Beer, single-label 12-ounce flat top, orange and green can, lodge scene, OPENING INSTRUCTIONS, INTERNAL REVENUE TAX PAID, single version. $350

Brau Haus Beer, single-label 12-ounce flat top, OPENING INSTRUCTIONS, INTERNAL REVENUE TAX PAID, keg-lined panel, single version. ....Exotic

Burgermeister Ale, single-label 12-ounce flat top or quart cone top, orange can, black band, standing man, OPENING INSTRUCTIONS on flat top, INTERNAL REVENUE TAX PAID, multiversions. *(See photo 77)*
Flat top, ... $200
Cone top, ...$250

Burgermeister Beer, single-label 12-ounce flat top or quart cone top, yellow can, black band, standing man, OPENING INSTRUCTIONS on flat top, INTERNAL REVENUE TAX PAID, multiversions.
Flat top, ...$150
Cone top, ... $200

Burgermeister Pale Beer, single- or two-label 12-ounce flat top, light blue can, three-quarter-length man, IRTP or non-IRTP, multiversions.
IRTP, ... $40
Non-IRTP, ... $35

Two-label 12- or 16-ounce flat top, light blue can, bust of man, multiversions except single-version 16-ounce flat top.
12-ounce,.. $30
16-ounce,.. $40

Two-label 12- or 16-ounce flat top or quart cone top, white can, head of man, "A TRULY FINE PALE BEER," multiversions in 12-ounce, all others single. *(See photo 78)*
12-ounce flat top, ... $30
16-ounce flat top, ... $25
Quart cone top, ... $85

Golden State Beer, single-label quart cone top, gold can, yellow label, INTERNAL REVENUE TAX PAID, single version. $350

Krug Pilsner Type Beer, single-label 12-ounce flat top, blue can, red and silver label, INTERNAL REVENUE TAX PAID, single version. ....Exotic

Leidig's Pilsener Style Beer, single-label 12-ounce flat top, green and white can, OPENING INSTRUCTIONS, INTERNAL REVENUE TAX PAID, single version.
....Exotic

Pilsengold Beer, single-label 12-ounce flat top, green and silver can, black band, OPENING INSTRUCTIONS, WITHDRAWN FREE FOR EXPORT, INTERNAL REVENUE TAX PAID, multiversions. $100
WITHDRAWN FREE,...$125

Rishwain Special Beer, single-label 12-ounce flat top, yellow can, blue label, INTERNAL REVENUE TAX PAID, single version....................................Exotic

Willows Lager Beer, single-label 12-ounce flat top, gold can, red lettering, OPENING INSTRUCTIONS, INTERNAL REVENUE TAX PAID, minor versions. ... $400

Wilshire Club Ale, single-label 12-ounce flat top, red can, white mountain, OPENING INSTRUCTIONS, INTERNAL REVENUE TAX PAID, two minor versions.
.... $500

Photo 78. Burgermeister Pale Beer.

Wilshire Club Beer, single-label 12-ounce flat top, blue can, white mountain, OPENING INSTRUCTIONS, INTERNAL REVENUE TAX PAID, two minor versions.
....$350

JOS. SCHLITZ BREWING COMPANY, 470 10th Street (successor to Burgermeister Brewing Company)

Burgermeister Beer, single- or two-label 11-, 12-, or 15-ounce soft, zip, or tab top, white can, metallic gold trim, blue label, multiversions. All versions, . $10
Two-label 12- or 16-ounce tab top, white or blue can, red "BURGIE," multiversions.
12-ounce,..$5
16-ounce,..$8
Burgermeister Genuine Draft, two-label 12- or 16-ounce tab top, white can, blue label, "Genuine Draft" on brown oval, multiversions.
12-ounce,... $10
16-ounce,... $12
Schlitz, two-label 12-ounce soft or tab top, white can, globe, "SCHLITZ" label (c. 1962–1966), multiversions. $10
Schlitz Genuine Draught Beer, two-label 12-ounce tab top, white can, globe, "DRAUGHT" in brown label, single version. $15

San Jose

FALSTAFF BREWING CORPORATION, 1025 Cinnabar (successor to Weiland Brewing Company)

Falstaff Beer, single- or two-label 11-, 12-, 15-, or 16-ounce flat, zip, or tab top, white can, gold bands, Falstaff shield, multiversions. All versions,........... $10
Falstaff Draft Beer, two-label 12- or 16-ounce flat top, white can, gold and maroon shield, "DRAFT" on blue ribbon, single version.
12-ounce,... $10
16-ounce,... $15
Springfield Fine Light Beer was also produced at this brewery and has a collector value of up to $5.

PACIFIC BREWING COMPANY, 1025 Cinnabar

Weiland's Extra Pale Beer, single-label, 12-ounce, high- or low-profile cone top or 12-ounce flat top, gold can, white bands, red label, minor versions.
Cone top, ... $85
Flat top, ... $75

ST. CLAIRE BREWING COMPANY, 1090 West San Salvador

Black And White Fully Aged Lager, single-label 12-ounce flat top, black and white can, red bands, INTERNAL REVENUE TAX PAID, single version. $300
Old Gold Beer, two-label 12-ounce flat top, gold can, green label, INTERNAL REVENUE TAX PAID, single version. $600

Pilsenbrau, single-label 12-ounce flat top, yellow can, man with stein, INTERNAL REVENUE TAX PAID, single version. .... Exotic

St. Claire Bohemian Style Beer, two-label 12-ounce flat top, silver can, blue label, INTERNAL REVENUE TAX PAID, single version. .... Exotic

Two-label 12-ounce flat top, gold can, red label, single version. .... Exotic

St. Claire English Style Ale, single-label 12-ounce flat top, cream colored, green label, INTERNAL REVENUE TAX PAID, single version. .... Exotic

Steinbrau Aged Lager Beer, two-label 12-ounce flat top, gold and white sunburst, stein, INTERNAL REVENUE TAX PAID, single version. .... Exotic

WEILAND BREWING COMPANY, 1090 West San Salvador (successor to Pacific Brewing Company)

Weiland's 100 Year Beer, two-label 12-ounce flat top, gold can, red label, "100 YEAR BEER" in red, single version. $200

Santa Rosa

GRACE BROS. BREWING COMPANY, 218 2nd Street (operated 1933–1950; aka: North Bay Brewing Company, 1950–1953, closed 1953–1958, reopened 1958, closed 1968)

Acme Beer, two-label 12-ounce flat top, white can, blue label, metallic gold trim, single version. $60

Alps Brau Beer, two-label 12-ounce flat top, blue can, mountain scene, silver or gold trim, single version of each.
Gold trim, ... $60
Silver trim, ... $50

Alta Special Export Beer, single-label 12-ounce flat top, yellow and gray can, blue stripes, OPENING INSTRUCTIONS, INTERNAL REVENUE TAX PAID, single version. *(See photo 79)* $250

Balboa Extra Premium Pale Beer, single-label 12-ounce flat top, yellow can, red bands, single version. $150

Bel-Aire Light Beer, two-label 12-ounce flat top, gold can, beer glass outlined in red, single version. $200

Blue 'N Gold Premium Lager Beer, single-label 12-ounce flat top, gold can, blue label, OPENING INSTRUCTIONS, INTERNAL REVENUE TAX PAID, single version. *(See photo 80)* $500

Brau Haus Bavarian Beer, two-label 12- or 16-ounce flat top, white can, blue label, single version.
12-ounce, ... $40
16-ounce, ... $30

Brau Haus Lager, single-label 12-ounce flat top, white can, blue label, single version. $60

Brau Haus Premium Lager Beer, two-label 12-ounce flat top, gold can, maroon can, single version. *(See photo 81)* $150

Brew '52 A Light Lager Beer, two-label 12-ounce flat top, metallic red or enamel red can, single version. *(See photo 82)* $65

(From left to right) Photo 79. Alta Special Export Beer. Photo 80. Blue 'N Gold Premium Lager Beer. Photo 81. Brau Haus Premium Lager Beer. Photo 82. Brew '52, A Light Lager Beer.

Brewer's Best Bavarian Beer, single-label 12- or 16-ounce flat top, white can, "BREWER'S BEST" on red label, two versions of each size.
12-ounce,... $60
16-ounce,... $75
Brewer's Best Bavarian Type Beer, single-label 12- or 16-ounce flat top, off-white can, "BREWER'S BEST" on red label, multiversions 12-ounce, single version 16-ounce.
12-ounce,... $60
16-ounce,... $85
Brown Derby Lager Beer, two-label 12- or 16-ounce flat top, white can, brown derby hat, metallic gold trim, multiversions.
12-ounce,... $40
16-ounce,... $60
Brown Derby Pilsner Beer, two-label 12-ounce flat top, silver can, brown label, "BROWN DERBY" in green, OPENING INSTRUCTIONS, INTERNAL REVENUE TAX PAID, single version. $100
Brown Derby Pilsener Type Beer, two-label 12-ounce flat top, silver can, brown label, "BROWN DERBY" in green, OPENING INSTRUCTIONS, INTERNAL REVENUE TAX PAID, single label. $100
Bull Dog Ale, two-label 12- or 16-ounce flat top, green can, white label, multiversions.
12-ounce,... $40
16-ounce,... $60
Bull Dog 14 Extra Hearty Stout Malt Liquor, two-label 12-ounce flat top, white can, black band, full bulldog, two versions. $40
Bull Dog Extra Malt Liquor, two-label 12-ounce flat top, white can, oval label, "extra" on black label, two versions. $40
Bull Dog Malt Liquor, single-label 8- or 12-ounce flat top, gold can, blue band, white oval label, multiversions.
8-ounce, ... $25
12-ounce,... $20
Bull Dog Stout Malt Liquor, two-label 12-ounce flat top, gold can, blue band, white oval label, two minor versions. $20
Cavalier Beer, two-label 12-ounce flat top, gold can, white oval label, single version. $100

Clear Lake Premium Beer, two-label 12-ounce flat top, green and blue can, red label, minor versions. *(See photo 83)* $200

Clipper Pale Beer, single-label 12-ounce flat top, two-tone blue can, flying airplane, INTERNAL REVENUE TAX PAID, single version. *(See photo 84)* ...Exotic

Club House Extra Pale Premium Beer, two-label 12-ounce flat top, light blue metallic can, dark blue stripe, single version. $60

Cremo Beer, single-label 12-ounce flat top, yellow can, black label, beer in red, minor version. .... Exotic

Custom Club Lager Beer, two-label 12-ounce flat top, red can, white lettering, single version. $60

Deutche Brau Vienna Type Beer, two-label 12-ounce flat top, white can, metallic gold label, blue label, single version. $85

Dutch Lunch Brand Beer, two-label 12-ounce flat top, silver can, red lettering, man holding beer, OPENING INSTRUCTIONS, INTERNAL REVENUE TAX PAID, minor versions. $100

Dutch Lunch Premium Lager Beer, two-label 12- or 16-ounce flat top, white can, red label, beer stein, single version. $150

El Dorado Premium Lager Beer, two-label 12-ounce flat top, gold can, blue label, single version. $100

El Rancho Premium Lager Beer, two-label 12-ounce flat top, off-white can, metallic gold trim, red lettering, minor versions. $60

Two-label 12-ounce flat top, white can, red label, multiversions. $30

El Rey Premium Beer, two-label 12-ounce flat top, metallic gold can, blue label, single version. $100

Elder Brau Premium Lager Beer, two-label 12-ounce or single-label 16-ounce flat top, white can, gold bands and trim, red label, single version 12-ounce, and two versions 16-ounce.

12-ounce, ... $75

16-ounce, ... $70

Excell Pale Beer, single-label 12-ounce flat top, orange can, metallic gold label, OPENING INSTRUCTIONS, INTERNAL REVENUE TAX PAID, single version. $400

Fort Sutter Brand Beer, two-label 12-ounce flat top, blue can, red ribbon, picture of Fort Sutter, OPENING INSTRUCTIONS, INTERNAL REVENUE TAX PAID, single version. $300

(from left to right) Photo 83. Clear Lake Premium Beer.
Photo 84. Clipper Ale Beer. Photo 85. Grace Bros. Extra Pale Beer.
Photo 86. Happy Hops Lager Beer. Photo 87. Hi Lo Lager Beer.

GB Dark Bock Beer, two-label 12-ounce flat top, gold can, black band, red label, white goat's head, multiversions. $75

GB Dark Kulmbacher Type Bock Beer, two-label 12-ounce flat top, gold can, black band, red label, white goat's head, single version. $90

GB Premium Pale Lager Beer, single-label, 12-ounce, high-profile cone or flat top, red can, "GB" in white, INTERNAL REVENUE TAX PAID, single version of each.
Cone top, ... $125
Flat top, ... $75
Single-label 12-ounce flat top, metallic gold can, blue label, multiversions. $85

Gold Medal Extra Pale Beer, single-label 12-ounce flat top, gold can, blue label, OPENING INSTRUCTIONS, INTERNAL REVENUE TAX PAID. $300

Golden Brew Premium Lager, two-label 12- or 16-ounce flat top, metallic gold can, metallic or enamel red label, multiversions. $20

Golden Crown Brand Beer, single-label 12-ounce flat top, black can, creme-colored label, OPENING INSTRUCTIONS, INTERNAL REVENUE TAX PAID, single version. $400

Golden Crown Extra Pale Dry Beer, two-label 12-ounce flat top, white can, metallic gold label, single version. $10

Golden Hops Premium Lager Beer, two-label 12-ounce flat top, yellow or gold can, blue label, multiversions. $75

Grace Bros. Age Dated Beer, single-label 12-ounce flat top, yellow can, red bands top and bottom, OPENING INSTRUCTIONS, INTERNAL REVENUE TAX PAID, two minor versions. $200

Grace Bros. Ale, single-label 12-ounce flat top, gold can, red circle, "ale" on black circle, OPENING INSTRUCTIONS, INTERNAL REVENUE TAX PAID, single version. $600

Grace Bros. Bavarian Beer, two-label 12- or 16-ounce flat top, white can, metallic red label, single version. $60

Grace Bros. Bavarian Type Beer, single-label 8-ounce soft top or 12-ounce flat top, white can, orange label and trim, single version.
8-ounce, ... $60
12-ounce, ... $50
Single-label 12-ounce flat top, off-white can, stripes, orange label, multiversions. $60

Grace Bros. Extra Pale Beer, single-label 12-ounce flat top, orange can, red bands top and bottom, OPENING INSTRUCTIONS, INTERNAL REVENUE TAX PAID, single version. *(See photo 85)* $400

Grace Bros. Premium Extra Pale Beer, single-label 12-ounce flat top, cream can, blue label, single version. .... Exotic

Happy Hops Lager Beer, two-label 12-ounce flat top, metallic gold can, blue circle, single version. *(See photo 86)* $450

Happy Hops Premium Lager Beer, two-label 12-ounce flat top, white can, metallic gold beer, glass, single version. $400

Hi Lo Lager Beer, two-label 12-ounce flat top, gold can, white label, red circle, single version. *(See photo 87)* $100

Hudson House Lager Beer, two-label 12-ounce tab top (one of three tab tops produced by Grace Bros.), blue can, white label, red lettering, single version. $150

Jay Vee Bavarian Beer, two-label 12-ounce flat top, white can, silver stripes, blue label, single version. $85

Karl's Famous Bavarian Type Beer, two-label 12-ounce flat top, brown label, yellow label, single version. *(See photo 88)* $250

Two-label 12-ounce flat top, blue can, off-white label, single version. $225

King's Taste Beer, two-label 12-ounce flat top, gold can, red crown, IRTP or non-IRTP.

IRTP, ...$125

Non-IRTP, ... $115

Two- label 12-ounce flat top, gold can, blue crown, minor versions. $150

Kol Premium Quality Beer, single-label 12-ounce flat top, silver can, white stripes, blue label, minor versions. $40

Kool Beer, single-label 12-ounce flat top, shades of green and blue-green, OPEN-ING INSTRUCTIONS, INTERNAL REVENUE TAX PAID, single version. $400

Lagermeister Beer, two-label 12-ounce flat top, metallic blue can, gold trim, single version. $150

Lassen Bavarian Beer, two-label 12-ounce flat top, silver can, mountain scene, metallic blue or dark blue label, multiversions. $100

Maid Rite Premium Beer, two-label 12-ounce flat top, white can, metallic red label, metallic gold trim, single version. $125

Two-label 12-ounce flat top, white can, two circles, "MAID RITE" on red circle, single version. $100

Monogram, two-label 12-ounce flat top, red can, red oval label, INTERNAL REV-ENUE TAX PAID, single version. $125

Single-label 12-ounce flat top, yellow lettering, OPENING INSTRUCTIONS, INTER-NAL REVENUE TAX PAID, "SFG" or "MM" on shield, two versions. Either ver-sion, ...$175

Nu-Deal Beer, two-label 12-ounce flat top, yellow can, blue shield, OPENING INSTRUCTIONS, INTERNAL REVENUE TAX PAID, single version. $400

Old German Lager Beer, single-label 12-ounce flat top, enamel red label, "TORNBERG'S" above label, single version. $100

Single-label 12-ounce flat top, off-white can, enamel or metallic red label, multi-versions. $60

Photo 88. Karl's Famous Bavarian Type Beer.

Old Gold Beer, single-label 12-ounce flat top, gold can, white stripes, red label, single version. $125

Old Vienna Premium Light Lager Beer, single-label 12-ounce flat top, white can, metallic gold lettering, single version. $75

Rüser The Light Lager Beer, single-label 12-ounce flat top, multicolored label with mountain scene, single version. $600

Snowcrest Beer, single-label 16-ounce flat top, multicolored label, metallic gold bands, minor versions. $500

Special Brew Beer, single-label 12-ounce flat top, gold can, black lettering, OPENING INSTRUCTIONS, INTERNAL REVENUE TAX PAID, two versions......... $150

Sportsman Premium Beer, two-label 12-ounce flat top, white can, metallic gold label, single version. $75

Steinbeck Lager Beer, single-label 12-ounce flat top, white can, stein label, two versions. $60

Super S Beer (Super S Beer is two of three tab tops produced by Grace Bros.), single-label 12-ounce tab top, blue or brown can, glass of beer, single version of each. $150

Tahoe Pale Dry Beer, single-label 12-ounce flat top, white can, lake scene, two versions. $300

Velvet Glow Pale Dry Beer, single-label 12- or 16-ounce flat top, white can, metallic gold bands, multiversions. $20

Western Gold Lager Beer, single-label 12- or 16-ounce flat top, blue-green or off-color purple can, multiversions. $60

Zest Beer, single-label 12-ounce flat top, OPENING INSTRUCTIONS, INTERNAL REVENUE TAX PAID, gold can, black label, single version. $300

NORTH BAY BREWING, 218 2nd Street (predecessor to Grace Bros. Brewing Company, successor to Grace Bros. Brewing Company)

Blue 'N Gold Beer, single-label, 12-ounce, high-profile cone or flat top, INTERNAL REVENUE TAX PAID, blue can, white label, single version.
Cone top, ...$125
Flat top, ... $80

Single-label 12-ounce flat top, metallic gold can, white label, multiversions.
WITHDRAWN FREE, ...$100
Others, ... $85

Single-label 12-ounce flat top, gold can, blue stripes, white label, single version. $85

Blue 'N Grey, Rumor?

Brewer's Best BB Premium Pilsener Beer, single-label 12-ounce flat top, white can, red and green label, single version. $150

Cremo Extra Pale Dry Beer, single-label 12-ounce flat top, gold can, white label, single version. .... Unique

GB Premium Pale Lager Beer, single-label, 12-ounce, high-profile cone or flat top, red can, "GB" on white label, INTERNAL REVENUE TAX PAID, single version of each.

Cone top, ...$125
Flat top, ... $85

Happy Hops Lager Beer, two-label 12-ounce flat top, metallic gold, blue circle label, single version. $300

Salute Brand Lager Beer, single-label 12-ounce flat top, metallic gold can, "Terminal Liquors," INTERNAL REVENUE TAX PAID, single version.........Exotic

Tornberg's Original Old German Pilsener Lager Beer, single-label 12-ounce flat top, metallic gold can, red label, INTERNAL REVENUE TAX PAID or non-IRTP, single version of each.

IRTP, ...$125
Non-IRTP, ... $110

Stockton

EL DORADO BREWING COMPANY, 617 North Stanislaus Street

London Tavern Ale, single-label, 12-ounce, high-profile cone top, INTERNAL REVENUE TAX PAID, white can, red ribbon, tavern scene, single version. *(See photo 89)* ....Exotic

Valley Brew Bock Beer, single-label 12-ounce flat top, silver can, white label, single version. *(See photo 90)* $150

Valley Brew Pale Premium Beer, single-label, 12-ounce, low- or high-profile cone top, gray can, white vertical stripes, white label, INTERNAL REVENUE TAX PAID, single version. *(See photo 91)* $100

Photo 89 (left). London Tavern Ale. Photo 90 (center). Valley Brew Bock Beer. Photo 91 (right). Valley Brew Pale Premium Beer.

Colorado

Denver

TIVOLI BREWING COMPANY, 11342 10th Street (known under this name 1955–1969; aka: Tivoli-Union Brewing Company [1933–1955], and Mountain Brewing Company)

The following mandatories are stamped "BREWED AND PACKAGED BY TIVOLI BREWING COMPANY, DENVER, COLORADO 80204" on lid or bottom of can: CANADIAN ACE BREWING COMPANY, Chicago, WESTMINSTER BREWING COMPANY, Chicago, PILSEN BREWING COMPANY, Chicago, KINGS BREWING COMPANY, Chicago. *(See photo 92)*

Photo 92. Tivoli Brewing Company mandatories.

Aristocrat Premium Beer, Mountain Brewing Company, two-label 12-ounce flat top, red can, metallic gold and black band, single version. $85

Aspen Gold, Tivoli Brewing Company, two-label 12-ounce flat or tab top, white can, blue band, mountain, "ASPEN GOLD" in metallic gold outlined in white, single version of each.
Flat top, ... $20
Tab top, ... $15

Beckers Mellow Premium Beer, Tivoli Brewing Company, two-label 12-ounce flat or tab top, white can, red label, blue trim, single version of each.
Flat top, ... $20
Tab top, ... $15

Big State Beer, Tivoli Brewing Company, two-label 12-ounce flat top, white and orange can, "BIG STATE" in red, single version. $60

Canadian Ace Premium Beer, Canadian Ace or Tivoli Brewing, two-label 12-ounce flat top, brown can, silver bands, white label, single version of each.
Canadian Ace, ... $40
Tivoli, ... $35

Denver Beer, Tivoli Brewing, two-label 12-ounce tab top, blue can, city skyline, single version. $80

Denver Premium Beer, Tivoli Brewing, two-label 12-ounce flat or tab top, blue can, city skyline, single version of each. *(See photo 93)*
Flat top, ... $70
Tab top, ... $65

Denver Tivoli Beer, Tivoli Brewing, two-label 12-ounce flat or tab top, blue can, city skyline, two versions flat top, single version tab top.
Flat top, ... $65
Tab top, ... $60

Golden Velvet Colorado Beer, Tivoli Brewing, two-label 12-ounce flat or tab top, white can, blue label, two versions flat top, single version tab top.
Flat top, ... $20
Tab top, ... $15

Heritage Lager Beer, Tivoli Brewing, single-label 12-ounce flat or tab top, black can, red and white lettering, single version of each. *(See photo 94)*
Flat top, ... $250
Tab top, ... $225

Hi-En Brau Colorado's Spokesman Beer, Tivoli Brewing, single-label 12-ounce tab top, maroon can, white label, story on back, single version. $50

Photo 93 (left). Denver Premium Beer.
Photo 94 (right). Heritage Lager Beer.

Hi-En Brau Premium Beer, Tivoli Brewing, two-label 12-ounce flat, soft, or tab top, white can, light or dark brown label, multiversions.

Flat top, ...$100
Soft top, ...$100
Tab top, ...$100

Jet Malt Liquor, Westminster or Tivoli, white can, metallic blue airplane, single version of each.

Westminster, ...$40
Tivoli, ...$30

Kings Beer, Kings Brewing, two-label 12-ounce tab top, off-white can, gold crown, single version. $75

Land Of Lakes Pale Dry Beer, Pilsen Brewing, two-label 12-ounce tab top, blue can, white arrowhead label, single version.............................$60

Mile Hi Light Premium Beer, Tivoli or Mountain Brewing, two-label 12-ounce flat or tab top, red, white, and blue can, mountain scene, multiversions. *(See photo 95)*

Tivoli, ...$75
Mountain Brewing, ...$90

Old Gibraltar Famous Dry Beer, Tivoli Brewing, two-label 12-ounce flat top, maroon and gold can, single version...$200

Pikes Peak Genuine Light Premium Beer, Tivoli Brewing, two-label 12-ounce flat top, multicolor can, single version. ....Exotic

Silver Peak Beer, Tivoli Brewing, two-label 12-ounce flat or tab top, off-white can, blue label, single version of each.

Flat top, ...$40
Tab top, ...$30

Tivoli Aristocrat Beer, Tivoli-Union, single-label 12-ounce flat top, black can, white label, metallic gold trim, INTERNAL REVENUE TAX PAID, single version of each.

Non-IRTP, ...$175
IRTP, ...$200

Tivoli Beer, Tivoli Brewing, two-label 12-ounce flat top, white can, red label, metallic bands, "Brewed in the Heart of the. . . .," multiversions. $60

Tivoli Brewing, two-label, 12-ounce flat top, metallic gold can, red diamond-shaped label, "From the land. . . .," multiversions.............................$75

Tivoli Brewing, two-label 12-ounce flat top, white can, red diamond label, "OF MEN AND MALT," multiversions. $150

Photo 95. Mile Hi Light Premium Beer.

Tivoli Brewing, two-label 12-ounce flat top, white can, red diamond label, no "OF MEN AND MALT," multiversions... $60

Tivoli Bock Beer, Tivoli Brewing, two-label 12-ounce flat, soft, or tab top, metallic gold can, large goat's head, multiversions. *(See photo 96)*
Flat top, ... $75
Soft or tab top, ... $60

Tivoli Gardens Premium Beer, Tivoli Brewing, two-label 12-ounce flat or tab top, white can, metallic blue label outlined in metallic gold, single version of each.
Flat top, ... $90
Tab top, ... $85

Tivoli Western Premium Beer, Tivoli-Union or Tivoli Brewing, single-label 12-ounce flat top, two versions of each.
Tivoli-Union, ... $125
Tivoli, ... $110

Top Hat Colorado Beer, Tivoli Brewing, two-label 12-ounce flat or tab top, blue can, white "TOP HAT," single version of each. $200

Golden

ADOLPH COORS COMPANY, Golden

Coors Beer, single-label 12-ounce flat top, yellow can, INTERNAL REVENUE TAX PAID, "COORS AMERICA'S FINE LIGHT BEER," minor multiversions: "COORS" in black or "COORS" in red. $40

Coors Banquet Beer, single-label 12-ounce flat top, yellow can, bright gold trim, multiversions. $25

Double-label 7-, 11-, 12-, 15-, or 16-ounce flat, soft, or tab top, yellow can, "BREWED WITH PURE ROCKY MOUNTAIN WATER," multiversions. *(See photo 97)* All versions, up to... $5

Coors also brews the above brand in aluminum cans. Coors was the first brewer to use aluminum cans, introducing them in 1959.

Coors Golden Beer, single-label 12-ounce flat top, gold can, black band, INTERNAL REVENUE TAX PAID, two versions. $50

Single-label 12-ounce flat top, cream-colored can, gold band, INTERNAL REVENUE TAX PAID, two minor versions. $65

Coors Golden Export Lager Beer, single-label 12-ounce flat top, gold can, black band, "EXPORT LAGER" on red label, INTERNAL REVENUE TAX PAID, multiversions. $50

The Adolph Coors Company produces, or has produced, Coors Light Beer, Coors Premium, George Killian's Irish Red Brand, Golden Lager, Herman Joseph's Turbo Malt Liquor, and Keystone in aluminum cans. The collector value will not exceed $2 each.

Pueblo

WALTER BREWING COMPANY, Hickory and La Crosse Streets (aka: General Brewing Company of Colorado, Kol Brewing Company,

Metz Brewing Company, Gold Label Brewing Company, Hoffman Beverage Company, Tivoli Brewing Company)

Berghoff 1887 Beer, Walter Brewing, single-label 12- or 16-ounce flat or tap top, white can, gold bands, multiversions.
Flat top, ... $35
Tab top, ... $30

Berghoff 1887 Draft Beer, Walter Brewing, single-label 12- or 16-ounce flat or tab top, woodgrain can, white and red label, multiversions.
Flat top, ... $30
Tab top, ... $25

Black Dallas Malt Liquor, Walter Brewing, two-label 12-ounce flat or tab top, light or dark blue can, black label, city skyline, single version.
Flat top, ... $85
Light blue tab top, ... $85.88
Dark blue tab top, ... $75

Brown Derby Lager Beer, Walter Brewing, two-label 12- or 16-ounce tab top, white can, dark orange label outlined in brown, single version of each size.
.... $35

Walter Brewing, two-label 12- or 16-ounce tab top, white can, orange label outlined in brown, single version of each size. $25

Canadian Ace Premium Beer, Tivoli Brewing, two-label 12-ounce flat top, brown can, silver and white label, single version. $25

Colorado Gold Label Beer, Walter Brewing, two-label 8-, 12-, or 16-ounce flat or tab top, blue can, mountain scene, red label, single-version 8 and 16 ounce, multiversions 12 ounce. *(See photo 98)*
8-ounce, ... $100
12-ounce, ... $40
16-ounce, ... $65

Crystal Colorado Beer, Walter Brewing, two-label 12-ounce flat or tab top, white can, blue label, red and gold trim, single version.
Flat top, ... $30
Tab top, ... $25

Einbock Bock Beer, Walter Brewing, two-label 12-ounce tab top, yellow can, green trim, two versions. $40

Fisher Light Beer, Walter Brewing or General Brewing of Colorado, two-label 12- or 16-ounce tab top, white can, gold trim, red label, single version of each.
.... $25

Photo 96 (left). Tivoli Bock Beer.
Photo 97 (center). Coors Banquet Beer.
Photo 98 (right). Colorado Gold
Label Beer.

Gold Label Beer, Walter Brewing or Gold Label Brewing, two-label 12-ounce flat or tab top, gold can, diamond-shaped label, single version from Gold Label, multiversions from Walter. *(See photo 99)*
Walter, ... $40
Gold Label, ... $60

Hitts Sangerfest Colorado Beer, Walter Brewing, single-label 12-ounce flat top, blue can, white label, metallic gold trim, single version. .... Exotic

Hoffman House Premium Beer, Walter Brewing or Hoffman Beverage, two-label 12- or 16-ounce flat or tab top, white can, red bands, black lettering, multiversions.
Walter, ... $30
Hoffman, ... $35

Hynne Colorado Beer, Walter Brewing, two-label 12-ounce flat or tab top, yellow can, mountain scene, red lettering, multiversions. $20

Imperial Colorado Beer, Walter Brewing, two-label 12-ounce tab top, single version. $15

Kol Premium Quality Beer, Walter Brewing or Kol Brewing, two-label 12-ounce tab top, blue can, gold label and bands, ''BEER'' in red, single version of each.
Walter, ... $75
Kol, ... $100

Kol Premium Quality Beer, Metz Brewing, white can, blue stripes, blue label, single version. $35

Lucky Lager Beer, Walter Brewing of General Brewing of Colorado, two-label 12- or 16-ounce flat top, white can, script, flowing red Lucky ''L,'' single version of each size and brewery. All versions, ... $15

Metz Premium Beer, Walter Brewing or Metz Brewing, two-label 12- or 16-ounce flat or tab top, red, white, and blue can, metallic gold trim, two 12-ounce versions from Metz, multi 12-ounce versions from Walter, single 16-ounce version from Walter.
12-ounce Metz, ... $30
12-ounce Walter, ... $20
16-ounce Walter, ... $25

My Beer, Walter Brewing or Metz Brewing, two-label 12-ounce flat top, red, white, and blue can, ''MAKE MY BEER YOUR BEER,'' single version each brewery. Either brewery, ... $60

Ox-Bow Beer, Walter Brewing, two-label 12-ounce tab top, metallic gold can, blue oval mountain scene label, single version. *(See photo 100)* $100

Pikes Peak Ale, Walter Brewing, two-label 12-ounce tab top, white can, metallic gold trim, red label, single version. $100

Pikes Peak Malt Lager, Walter Brewing, two-label 12-ounce flat top, white can, metallic gold bands, maroon label, single version. .... Exotic

Pikes Peak Malt Liquor, Walter Brewing, two-label 12-ounce flat top, yellow can, full mountain scene, single version. .... Exotic

Two-label 8- or 12-ounce flat or tab top, white can, metallic gold stripes, maroon label, single version.
8-ounce flat top, ... $75

12-ounce flat top, ... $50

12-ounce tab top, ... $40

Two-label 12- or 16-ounce flat or tab top, white can, metallic gold bands, red label, multiversions 12 ounce, single version 16 ounce.

12-ounce flat top, ... $40

12-ounce tab top, ... $35

16-ounce tab top, ... $35

Pikes Peak Stout Malt Liquor, Walter Brewing, two-label 8-ounce flat top, white can, full mountain scene, single version. .... Exotic

Sheridan Export Beer, Walter Brewing, single-label 12-ounce flat top, yellow can, black bands, single version. $40

Sheridan Premium Beer, Walter Brewing, two-label 12-ounce flat or tab top, white can, metallic gold, red label, single version. *(See photo 101)* $30

Ski Country Premium Beer, Walter Brewing, two-label 12-ounce tab top, white can, winter scene, red label, single version. $30

Walter's Bock Beer, Walter's Brewing, two-label 12-ounce flat, soft, or tab top, white can, white label, goat's head on patch, single version of each. $75

Walter's Draft Beer, Walter's Brewing, two-label gallon can, white can, blue label, single version. $450

Walter's Light Colorado Beer, Walter's Brewing, two-label 12-ounce tab top, white can, black stripes, red label, single version. $60

Walter's Pilsener Beer, Walter Brewing, single-label 12-ounce flat top, yellow can, white label, INTERNAL REVENUE TAX PAID, single version.

IRTP, ... $100

Non-IRTP, ... $85

Walter's Premium Beer, Walter Brewing, two-label 16-ounce tab top, white can, metallic gold bands, red label, minor versions. $20

Walter's Premium Pilsener Beer, Walter Brewing, two-label 12-ounce flat top, metallic gold can, red checkerboard, white label, two versions. $75

Two-label 12-ounce flat top, white can, metallic gold, white label, two versions $60

Walter's Premium Quality Beer, Walter Brewing, two-label 12-ounce flat top, metallic gold can, red label, multiversions. $20

Walter's Ye Olde Ale, Walter Brewing, single-label 12-ounce flat top, yellow can, white label, single version. .... Exotic

Photo 99 (left). Gold Label Beer.
Photo 100 (center). Ox-Bow Beer.
Photo 101 (right). Sheridan Premium Beer.

Wellington Malt Liquor, Walter Brewing, two-label 12- or 16-ounce flat or tab top, white can, red or black lettering, single version.

12-ounce, ... $40

16-ounce, ... $30

Wellington Premium Beer, Walter Brewing, two-label 12-ounce tab top, white can, red "WELLINGTON," single version. $25

Wellington Stout Malt Liquor, Walter Brewing, two-label 12-ounce flat or tab top, white can, red "Stout," single version.

Flat top, ... $60

Tab top, ... $40

Winchester Malt Liquor, Walter Brewing, two-label 12- or 16-ounce tab top, white can, black "WINCHESTER," single version.

12-ounce, ... $40

16-ounce, ... $30

Winchester Stout Malt Liquor, Walter Brewing, two-label 12-ounce flat or tab top, white can, etched label, "Stout" in blue, single version.

Flat top, ... $75

Tab top, ... $60

Trinidad

PHIL SCHNEIDER BREWING COMPANY, 240 North Convent Street

Century Lager Beer, single-label, 12-ounce, low-profile cone top, white can, orange label, INTERNAL REVENUE TAX PAID, single version. .... Exotic

Karl's Famous Pilsener Beer, two-label 12-ounce flat top, maroon can, yellow label, two versions. $150

Old Gibraltar Famous Dry Beer, two-label 12-ounce flat top, gold can, maroon oval label, single version. $150

Silver State Lager Beer, single-label, 12-ounce, low-profile cone top, blue and silver can, INTERNAL REVENUE TAX PAID, single version. .... Unique

Connecticut

Darby

OLD ENGLAND BREWING COMPANY, 324 Derby Avenue

Old England Brand Cream Ale, single-label, 12-ounce, low-profile cone top, gold can, red band outlined in black, INTERNAL REVENUE TAX PAID, single version. $400

Old England Cream Ale, single-label, 12-ounce, low-profile cone top, gold can, red band outlined in black, INTERNAL REVENUE TAX PAID, single version.. $400

Old England Lager Beer, single-label, 12-ounce, low-profile cone top, INTERNAL REVENUE TAX PAID, gold can, red band outlined in black, single version. $300

New Britain

CREMO BREWING COMPANY, Belden Street (aka: Diplomat Brewing Company)

Cremo Ale, Cremo Brewing, single-label, 12-ounce, J-spout cone top, gold can, white label, red band, INTERNAL REVENUE TAX PAID, two versions. $375

Cremo Brewing, single-label, quart cone top, gold can, white label, red band, INTERNAL REVENUE TAX PAID, single version. $500

Cremo Beer, Cremo Brewing, single-label, 12-ounce, J-spout cone top, gold can, white label, blue band, INTERNAL REVENUE TAX PAID, single version. $300

Cremo Lager Beer, Cremo Brewing, single-label, 12-ounce, high-profile cone top, woodgrain can, white label, INTERNAL REVENUE TAX PAID, single version. $250

Cremo Brewing, two-label 12-ounce crowntainer, woodgrain can, white label, INTERNAL REVENUE TAX PAID, single version. $300

Cremo Sparkling Beer, two-label 12-ounce white or silver crowntainer, filigree can, red label, INTERNAL REVENUE TAX PAID, single version of each. $300

Diplomat Select Pilsener Beer, Diplomat Brewing Company, single-label 12-ounce flat top, white can, red lettering and trim, single version. $200

Manhattan Beer, single-label 12-ounce flat top, blue can, yellow city skyline, green ribbon, single version. $300

Old India Pale Ale, single-label 12-ounce flat top, green can, white circle label, single version. $150

Old India Vatted Pale Ale, single-label, 12-ounce, high-profile cone or flat top, green can, red circle inside of white circle, INTERNAL REVENUE TAX PAID, single version of each.
Flat top, ... $200
Cone top, ... $225

New Haven

HULL BREWING COMPANY, 820 Congress Avenue (aka: Diamond Spring Brewing Company)

Dingle Bay Brand Cream Ale, Hull Brewing, single-label 12-ounce flat top, OPENING INSTRUCTIONS, INTERNAL REVENUE TAX PAID, single version. ...Exotic

Holihan's Pilsener Beer, Diamond Spring Brewing, single-label 12-ounce tab top, white can, multi labels, single version. $10

Hull's Ale, Hull Brewing, two-label 12-ounce crowntainer, silver can, blue label, single version. $250

Hull's Beer, Hull Brewing, two-label 12-ounce crowntainer, silver can, blue label, single version. $200

Hull's Bock Beer, Hull Brewing, two-label 12-ounce flat top, gray can, "HULL'S" in red, single version. $300

Hull Brewing, single-label 12-ounce flat top, yellow can, maroon label, single version. $25

Hull's Cream Ale, two-label 12-ounce flat top, silver and blue can, OPENING INSTRUCTIONS, INTERNAL REVENUE TAX PAID, single version. $250

Single-label 12-ounce flat top, green can, yellow label, "CREAM" in red, single version. $125

Single-label 12-ounce flat top, green can, white label, "HULL'S" in green, single version. $100

Hull's Export Ale, single-label 12-ounce flat top, green can, yellow label, single version. $100

Hull's Export Beer, single-label 12-ounce flat top, green can, metallic gold label, "HULL'S" in red, single version. $150

Two-label 12-ounce flat, zip, or tab top, white can, "EXPORT" in red, multiversions. $20

Hull's Lager Beer, two-label 12-ounce flat top, silver and blue can, OPENING INSTRUCTIONS, INTERNAL REVENUE TAX PAID, single version. $300

Hull's Light Beer, single-label 12-ounce flat top, metallic gold can, blue label, WITHDRAWN FREE, single version. $200

Old India Pale Ale, single-label 12-ounce flat top, green can, double circle label, single version. $100

WEIBEL BREWING COMPANY, 270 Legion Avenue

Imperial Extra Pale Ale, single-label 12-ounce flat top, blue and gray can, OPENING INSTRUCTIONS, INTERNAL REVENUE TAX PAID, single version. (Can says "Packaged expressly for WEIBEL BREWING COMPANY." Origin is unknown, although it is thought Manhattan Brewing Company, Chicago, is the origin.) .... Exotic

Waterbury

LARGUY BREWING COMPANY, 1090 Bank Street

Beer, single-label, 12-ounce, high-profile cone top, WITHDRAWN FREE FOR EXPORT, full-color can, single version. .... Exotic

Red Fox Ale, single-label, 12-ounce, high- or low-profile cone top, red can, walking fox on label, single version of each. Either can, ... $200

Single-label quart cone top, red can, walking fox on label, single version.. $350

Red Fox Light Beer, single-label, 12-ounce, high-profile cone top, gold can, red trim, walking fox, two minor versions. $200

Red Fox Premium Beer, single-label, 12-ounce, high-profile cone top, red can, orange and white label, WITHDRAWN FREE FOR EXPORT or INTERNAL REVENUE TAX PAID, multiversions.

WDFE, ...$450

IRTP, ... $400

Single-label quart cone top, red can, orange and white label, single version. $400

West Haven

WEHLE BREWING COMPANY, 1131 Campbell Avenue

Buckingham Ale, single-label 12-ounce flat top, gold can, red label, INTERNAL REVENUE TAX PAID, single version. $300

Cab Cream Ale, single-label 12-ounce flat top, metallic gold can, black trim and line drawings, multiversions. $300

Photo 102. Mule Head Beer.

Mule Head Beer, single-label 12-ounce flat top, metallic gold can, red label and lettering, OPENING INSTRUCTIONS, INTERNAL REVENUE TAX PAID, single version. (*See photo 102*)..$350

Ox Head Beer, single-label 12-ounce flat top, gray can, label outlined in red, OPENING INSTRUCTIONS, INTERNAL REVENUE TAX PAID, minor versions. ... $400

Trumps Ale, single-label 12-ounce flat top, gold can, red bands, one version says "WEHLE BREWING COMPANY," other says "FOR AMERICAN LIQUOR."
Wehle, ...$350
American,...$400

Wehle Beer, single-label 12-ounce flat top, silver can, black label, OPENING INSTRUCTIONS, INTERNAL REVENUE TAX PAID, single version. $300

Wehle Colonial Ale, single-label 12-ounce flat top, orange and gray can, "WEHLE" on orange band, OPENING INSTRUCTIONS, INTERNAL REVENUE TAX PAID, minor versions. $300

Single-label quart cone top, orange and gray can, two versions.............. $400

Wehle Mule Head Stock Ale, single-label 12-ounce flat top or quart cone top, metallic gold can, red or blue lettering, OPENING INSTRUCTIONS, INTERNAL REVENUE TAX PAID, multiversions.
Flat top, ... $400
Cone top, ... $500

Wehle Pale Ale, single-label 12-ounce flat top or quart cone top, silver can, blue label and oval, OPENING INSTRUCTIONS, INTERNAL REVENUE TAX PAID, single version of each.
Flat top, ... $300
Cone top, ... $400

Delaware

/

Wilmington

DIAMOND STATE BREWERY, INC., Fifth and Adams Streets

Diamond State Beer, single-label 12-ounce flat top, metallic gold can, red label, OPENING INSTRUCTIONS or non-OI, INTERNAL REVENUE TAX PAID.
OI, ...$250
Non-OI, ...$225
Diamond State Light Beer, single-label, 12-ounce, high-profile cone top, metallic gold can, white bands, white oval label, single version.................$200
Single-label 12-ounce flat top or quart cone top, metallic gold can, white bands, metallic ribbon, single version of each.
Flat top, ...$125
Cone top, ...Exotic
Stoechle Select Beer, single-label 12-ounce flat top, orange can, King Gambrinus dressed in blue, single version. $300

G. KRUEGER BREWING COMPANY OF DELAWARE, 506 North du Pont Avenue

Krueger Extra Light Dry Beer, single-label, 12-ounce, high-profile cone top, white can, red oval "K," man in red, INTERNAL REVENUE TAX PAID, single version...$125
Krueger Finest Beer, single-label, 12-ounce, high-profile cone top, INTERNAL REVENUE TAX PAID, maroon can, yellow label, multiversions. $85
Single-label 12-ounce crowntainer, maroon label, yellowish label, INTERNAL REVENUE TAX PAID, multiversions. $85

Krueger Finest Light Lager Beer, two-label 12-ounce or quart cone top, yellow can, red bands, INTERNAL REVENUE TAX PAID, single version.

12-ounce,... $90

Quart,..$150

District of Columbia

Washington, DC

CHRISTIAN HEURICH BREWING COMPANY, 26th and K Northwest

Chr. Heurich's Original Lager, two-label 12-ounce flat top, red can, metallic red bands, single version. $150

Old Georgetown Beer, single-label 12-ounce flat top, yellow can, white label with brown outline, multiversions. $150

Old Georgetown Premium Quality Beer, single-label 12-ounce flat top, yellow label, brown bands, white label, multiversions. $75

Senate Ale, single-label 12-ounce flat top, INTERNAL REVENUE TAX PAID, red can, red label, brown trim, minor versions. $250

Senate Beer, single-label 12-ounce flat top, INTERNAL REVENUE TAX PAID, blue or white can, blue label, metallic gold bands, minor versions. *(See photo 103)*
Blue can, ... $2,000
White can, ... $100

Photo 103. Senate Beer.

Senate Bock Beer, single-label 12-ounce flat top, INTERNAL REVENUE TAX PAID, green or red can, blue label, gold bands, minor versions.
Green can, ... $400
Red can, ...Exotic

Senate Extra Fine Beer, single-label 12-ounce flat top, blue can, "EXTRA FINE" on top front, INTERNAL REVENUE TAX PAID, single version. $400

Florida

*

Auburndale

DUNCAN BREWING COMPANY, 202 Gandy Road (successor and predecessor to G. Heileman Brewing Company; aka: Fischer Brewing Company, ABC Brewing Company, Modelo Brewing Company)

Dunk's German Style Beer, Duncan Brewing Company, two-label 12-ounce tab top, blue can, red, white, and blue label, single version. $5

Fischer's Light Beer, Fischer Brewing Company, two-label 12-ounce flat top, white can, red lettering, single version. $2

Fischer's Old English Style Ale, Fischer Brewing Company, two-label 12-ounce tab top, white can, green diamond, multiversions. $2

Fischer's Old German Style Ale, Fischer Brewing Company, two-label 12-ounce tab top, white can, green label, single version. $2

Fischer's Old German Style Beer, Fischer Brewing Company, two-label 12-ounce tab top, white can, red label, vertical pinstripes, multiversions. $3

Two-label 12-ounce tab top, blue can, diamond-shaped label, single version..$2

Master's Choice Bavarian Premium Beer, Duncan Brewing Company, two-label 12-ounce tab top, silver can, blue label, single version. $2

Brand also brewed in aluminum cans; collector value is $1.

Regal Premium Beer, Florida Brewing Company, two-label 12-ounce flat top, white can, blue label, multiversions..$2

TCA Beer, Duncan Brewing Company, two-label 12-ounce flat top, green and white can, multiversions..$3

Duncan Brewing Company also produces or has produced a multitude of brands in aluminum cans. The collector value is up to $2.

G. HEILEMAN BREWING COMPANY, 202 Gandy Road

G. Heileman Brewing Company, La Crosse, WI, operated this brewery from 1980 to 1984 and produced many brands in aluminum cans. Collector value will range up to $2. Look for letter "ɪ" on bottom of can.

Jacksonville

ANHEUSER-BUSCH, INC., 111 Busch Avenue

Anheuser-Busch built this plant in 1969 and has produced all of its brands in aluminum cans. These cans have collector value of up to $1.

JAX BREWING COMPANY, 1701 West 16th Street (aka: Jax Ice and Cold Storage Company)

Jax Hale And Hearty Ale, single-label 12-ounce flat top, metallic gold can, white label, "ALE" in red, single version... $300

Jax Pilsner Style Beer, single-label, 12-ounce, high-profile cone top, orange can, black label, single version. $300

Jax Premium Quality Beer, single-label 12-ounce flat top, gold can, white label, "JAX" in blue, single version. $200

Old Union Lager Beer, two-label 12-ounce flat top, orange can, red label, single version..Exotic

Rhein King Beer, two-label 12-ounce flat top, orange can, maroon label, single version...Exotic

Sans Souci Premium Beer, two-label 12-ounce flat top, black can, red label, single version..Exotic

Skol Premium Beer, single-label 12-ounce flat top, white can, red label, single version. $400

Miami

AMERICAN BREWING COMPANY, 637 Northwest 13th Street

Regal Extra Special Ale, single-label 12-ounce flat top, gold can, green label, single version. *(See photo 104)*.. $85

Regal Genuine Lager Beer, single-label 12-ounce flat top, white can, metallic gold label, single version. $40

Photo 104. Regal Extra Special Ale.

Regal Light Lager Beer, single-label, 12-ounce, high-profile cone top, gold can, pinstripes, white label, single version. $175

Regal Premium Beer, single-label, 12-ounce, high-profile cone top, gold can, pinstripes, white label, single version. $175

Single-label 12-ounce flat top, gold can, pinstripes, white label, "A PREMIUM BREW SINCE 1890," multiversions. $60

Regal Premium Dry Beer, single-label 12-ounce flat top, white can, gold band, "PRINCE REGAL SALUTES YOU," single version. $65

ANHEUSER-BUSCH, INC., 637 Northwest 13th Street (successor to American Brewing Company)

The three years that Anheuser-Busch owned this brewery (February 1958–February 1961) is the only time in the company's history that it produced brands other than brands originating with Anheuser-Busch.

Busch Bavarian Beer, two-label 12-ounce flat top, blue can, white mountain scene, two major versions. $20

Regal Extra Special Ale, two-label 12-ounce flat top, gold can, green and white label, single version. $85

Two-label 12-ounce flat top, gold can, green label, white trim, single version. $80

Two-label 12-ounce flat top, green can, white round label, three white steins, single version. $60

Regal Premium Beer, single-label 12-ounce flat top, white can, metallic gold label, red ribbon, two versions. $40

NATIONAL BREWING COMPANY, 637 Northwest 13th Street (successor to Anheuser-Busch; aka: Florida Brewery, Orbit Brewery, Regal Brewery, S. C. Brewery)

Colt 45 Malt Lager, National Brewing, two-label 12- or 16-ounce tab top, white can, blue label, gold bands, "BY NATIONAL"on blue band, single version of each.
12-ounce, ... $10
16-ounce, ... $15

Colt 45 Malt Liquor, National Brewing, two-label 12-, 14-, or 16-ounce flat, soft, zip, or tab top, white can, blue label, colt inside of horseshoe, multiversions.
14-ounce, ... $10
All others, ... $3

Draft Beer By National, National Brewing, two-label 12-ounce tab top, white can, glass of beer on brown label, single version. $15

Gold Seal Premium Beer, Florida Brewery, two-label 12-ounce aluminum soft top, white can, red label, *aluminum* three-piece can, single version. $50

National Bohemian Light Beer, National Brewing, two-label 12-, 14-, or 16-ounce flat, soft, or tab top, red can, black label, silver trim, multiversions.
14-ounce, ... $20
All others, ... $15

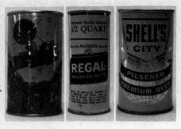

Photo 105 (left). Orbit Premium Beer.
Photo 106 (center). Regal Premium Beer.
Photo 107 (right). Shell's City Pilsener
Premium Beer.

Orbit Premium Beer, Orbit Brewery, single-label 12-ounce flat or tab top, white can, blue mountain scene, metallic gold label, single version. *(See photo 105)*
Flat top, ... $60
Tab top, ... $30

Regal Extra Special Ale, Regal Brewery, single- or two-label 12-ounce flat or soft top, green can, white label, three white steins, single version of each.
Flat top, ... $75
Soft top, ... $65

Regal Premium Beer, Regal Brewery, two-label 12- or 16-ounce flat, soft, or tab top, white can, gold label, red ribbon, multiversions. *(See photo 106)* All versions, ... $25

Two-label 12-ounce tab top, white can, metallic gold trim, blue label, single version. $15

Brand was also produced in aluminum cans with a collector value of up to $5.

Shell's City Pilsener Premium Beer, S. C. Brewery, two-label 12-ounce tab top, white can, blue globe, red lettering, two versions. *(See photo 107)* $40

Whale's White Ale, National Brewing, two-label 12-ounce tab top, white can, black lettering, two major versions. $125

National Brewing, two-label 12- or 16-ounce tab top, dark green, white lettering, single version each size.
12-ounce, ... $30
16-ounce, ... $20

Orlando

MARLIN BREWING COMPANY, 1171 North Orange Street

Marlin Green Hornet Ale, single-label 12-ounce flat top, yellow can, black label, gold trim, single version. ....Exotic
Marlin White Label Beer, single-label 12-ounce flat top, white can, metallic gold and red trim, black letters, single version. ....Exotic

NATIONAL BREWING COMPANY, 1171–1179 North Orange Street (successor to Marlin Brewing Company)

National Bohemian Bock Beer, two-label 12-ounce flat top, black can, red label, goat's head, single version. $150

National Bohemian Light Beer, two-label 12-ounce flat top, red can, black label, silver trim, multiversions. $30

National Bohemian Pale Beer, two-label 12-ounce flat top, red can, black label, "Mr. Boh," single version. $60

Pensacola

SPEARMAN BREWING COMPANY, I Street and Barrancas Street (aka: Embassy Brewing Company, Quality Brewing Company, Sewanee Brewing Company, Best Brewing Company, Chicago)

7–11 Premium Beer, Quality Brewing or Spearman Brewing, two-label 12-ounce flat top, white can, blue label, yellow trim, single version by Spearman, two versions by Quality.

Spearman,.. $75

Quality,.. $85

Best Premium Beer, Spearman Brewing, two-label 12-ounce flat top, white can, red label outlined in gold, single version. $25

Quality Brewing, two-label 12-ounce flat top, white can, red label outlined in gold, two versions. $40

Spearman Brewing, single-label 12-ounce flat top, white can, red and black stripes top and bottom, two versions.. $300

Bon Premium Beer, Spearman Brewing, single-label, 12-ounce, high-profile cone top, white can, yellow label, black label, single version. $150

Embassy Club Beer, Spearman or Embassy Club Brewing, two-label 12-ounce flat top, metallic gold can, red label, single version of each. $60

KC's Best Premium Beer, Spearman Brewing, single-label 12-ounce flat top, white can, red bands, "PREMIUM" in black, single version. $40

Keeley Premium Quality Ale, Best Brewing, two-label 12-ounce flat top, green can, white label, single version. $200

Maverick Premium Quality Beer, Best Brewing Company, Chicago, two-label 12-ounce flat top, maroon can, metallic gold, red, and white label, single version..Exotic

Spearman Ale, Spearman Brewing, single-label, 12-ounce, high-profile cone top or 12-ounce flat top, green can, red label. single-version cone top, multiversion flat top.

Cone top, ... $175

Flat top, ... $75

Spearman Bavarian Style Ale, Spearman Brewing, two-label 12-ounce flat or zip top, white can, yellow label, single version. $100

Spearman English Type Ale, Spearman Brewing, single-label, 12-ounce, high-profile cone top, red can, black label, two versions.

IRTP, ... $300

Non-IRTP, ...$275

Spearman Premium Quality Beer, Spearman or Sewanee Brewing, two-label 12-ounce flat top, white can, metallic gold label, single version from each brewery. Either version, ...$150

Spearman Straight Eight Beer, Spearman Brewing, single-label, 12-ounce, high-profile cone or flat top, white can, yellow label, INTERNAL REVENUE TAX PAID, multiversions.
Cone top, ...$250
Flat top, ...$150

Spearman's Straight Eight Beer, Spearman Brewing, two-label, 12-ounce, high-profile cone or flat top, white can, yellow label, single version.
Cone top, ...$250
Flat top, ...$150

Tudor Premium Quality Beer, Spearman Brewing, two-label 12-ounce flat top, white can, red label, single version. $30
Spearman Brewing, two-label 12-ounce flat top, red can, blue label, single version. $50

Viking Draft Beer, Spearman or Sewanee Brewing, two-label 12-ounce flat top, brown and black can, characters around bottom, single version of each. Either brewery, ...$400

Viking Premium Beer, Spearman or Sewanee Brewing, two-label 12-ounce flat top, white can, red letters, figures, two versions.
Spearman, ...$150
Sewanee, ...$200

Tampa

ANHEUSER-BUSCH, INC., 3000 August Busch, Jr. Boulevard

Budweiser Lager Beer, two-label 12- or 16-ounce flat top, white can, red label, "This is the famous Budweiser Beer especially . . .," multiversions. Up to ..$5
Busch Bavarian Beer, two-label 12- or 16-ounce flat top, blue can, white mountain scene with or without oval on face, multiversions. Up to.....................$5
Brewery is operational. All brands, past and present, were produced in aluminum cans. Collector value is $1.

INTERNATIONAL BREWERIES, INC., Zack and Pierce Streets
(successor to Southern Brewing Company; aka: International Breweries, Frankenmuth Brewing Company, Kol Brewing Company, Orbit Brewing Company, Phoenix Brewing Company, Stolz Brewing Company)

Frankenmuth Melo-O-Dry Ale, International or Frankenmuth, two-label 12-ounce flat top, white can, lime green label, single version. Either version, . $60
Frankenmuth Mel-O-Dry Beer, Frankenmuth Brewing, two-label 12-ounce flat top, white can, red label, single version. $50
International Silver Bar Ale, International Brewing, two-label 12-ounce flat top, white can, green label, two minor versions. $60
International Silver Bar Beer, International Brewing, two-label 12-ounce flat top, white can, red label, single version. $50
Kol Premium Quality Beer, Kol Brewing, two-label 12-ounce flat top, silver can, white vertical stripes, blue label, single version. $50

Orbit Premium Beer, Orbit Brewing, two-label, 12-ounce flat top, white can, blue label, metallic gold label, single version. $60

Silver Bar Ale, International Brewing, single-label 12-ounce flat top, white can, green label, green or brown metal, multiversions. $75

Silver Bar Beer, International Brewing, single-label 12-ounce flat top, white can, red label, red or brown metal, single version of each. Either version, . $75

Stolz Premium Beer, Stolz Brewing, two-label 12-ounce flat top, white can, red lettering, metallic silver trim, single version. $65

PABST BREWING COMPANY, 11111 30th Street (successor to Stroh Brewing Company)

All cans produced by Pabst at this brewery were produced in aluminum cans. The shorter-run, more obscure brands produced by Pabst will command a collector value of up to $5. Pabst's national brands collector value does not exceed $1.

JOS. SCHLITZ BREWING COMPANY, 11111 30th Street

Old Milwaukee, two-label 12-, 14-, or 16-ounce flat, soft, zip, or tab top, red and white can, multiversions.
Flat top, ... $5
All others, ... $1

Old Milwaukee Genuine Draft Beer, two-label 12-, 14-, or 16-ounce flat or tab top, red and white can, multiversions.
Flat top, ... $5
All others, ... $1

Schlitz, two-label 12-, 14-, or 16-ounce flat or tab top, white can, globe, brown label (c. 1962 and 1967), multiversions.
Flat top, ... $15
Tab top, ... $5

All brands were also produced in aluminum cans. Schlitz Malt Liquor was also produced in aluminum. Collector value is $1 or less.

STROH BREWING COMPANY, 11111 30th Street (successor to Jos. Schlitz Brewing Company)

All brands produced in aluminum cans. The collector value is $1 or less.

SOUTHERN BREWING COMPANY, Zack and Pierce Streets

S B Beer, single-label, 12-ounce, high-profile cone top, metallic gold can, red and black label, versions: IRTP and non-IRTP.
IRTP, ... $350
Non-IRTP, ... $325

Silver Bar Premium Beer, single-label 12-ounce flat top, black can, "SILVER BAR" in yellow, single version. $150

Single-label 12-ounce flat top, blue, pink, red, purple, yellow, or orange can, "SILVER BAR" on two lines, single version of each color. $150

Silver Bar Sparkling Ale, single-label, 12-ounce, high-profile cone top, silver can, "SB" on red patch, two versions. $300

TAMPA FLORIDA BREWERY, INC., 13th Street and 5th Avenue

Tropical Ale, single-label, 12-ounce, high-profile cone top, metallic gold can, white label, single version. $300

Tropical Extra Fine Ale, single-label, 12-ounce, high-profile cone or flat top, green can, white band, minor versions.
Cone top, ...$150
Flat top, ...$100

Two-label 12-ounce flat, soft, or zip top, metallic gold can, white label, single version of each top. $40

Tropical Golden All Grain Beer, two-label 12-ounce flat top, white can, metallic gold bands, red label, single version.. $60

Tropical Premium Beer, single-label, 12-ounce, high-profile cone or flat top, brown and white can, single version of each.
Cone top, ...$250
Flat top, ...$150

Tropical Premium Lager Beer, two-label 12-ounce flat top, white can, metallic gold bands, red label, single version... $60

Georgia

Albany

MILLER BREWING COMPANY, Albany

Built in 1979, this plant has produced only Miller brands in aluminum cans. The collector value of these cans is nil.

Atlanta

ATLANTIC BREWING COMPANY, 106 Washington Street

Atlantic Ale, single-label, 12-ounce, high-profile cone top, red can, "ATLANTIC" in metallic gold, versions: IRTP and non-IRTP.
IRTP, ...$250
Non-IRTP, ...$225
Atlantic Beer, single-label, 12-ounce, high-profile cone top, blue can, metallic gold bands, white label, versions: IRTP and non-IRTP.
IRTP, ...$150
Non-IRTP, ...$125

CARLING BREWING COMPANY, 3599 Browns Mill Road Southwest

Black Label Beer, single- or double-label, 12-, 14-, or 16-ounce flat, zip, or tab top, red can, black label outlined in white, map of U.S. or world, multiversions.
All versions, ... $10
Two-label 12- or 16-ounce tab top, red can, black label, gold bands, minor versions.
12-ounce,... $15
16-ounce,... $20

Photo 108. Red Cap Ale.

Single-label 12-, 14-, or 16-ounce tab top, silver tankard can, red label, multiversions. $20

Black Label Draft Beer, single- or double-label 12-, 14-, or 16-ounce flat, zip, or tab top, red can, black label outlined in white, map of U.S. or world.
12-ounce, ... $20
16-ounce, ... $25

Calgary Malt Lager, single-label 12- or 16-ounce tab top, black can, "MALT LAGER" on yellow ribbon, single version of each. $100

Carling Black Label Beer, single-label 12- or 16-ounce flat or zip top, red can, black label outlined in white, "CARLING" on label, multiversions. Up to ... $20

Carling Malt Liquor, single-label 12- or 16-ounce tab top, black can, "MALT LIQUOR" on red ribbon, single version of each. $60

Carling Malt Liquor, single-label 16-ounce zip top, black can, red stripe, single version. $250

Heidelberg Light Pilsner Beer, two-label 12-ounce tab top, white can, brown label, brown bands, single version. $20

Heidelberg Pilsner Beer, two-label 12-ounce tab top, blue can, metallic gold oval and bands, two minor versions. $30

Red Cap Ale, two-label 12-ounce flat top, green can, split orangish label, full head, single version. *(See photo 108)* $20

Pabst

PABST BREWING COMPANY, Georgia Highway 247 Spur

This brewery, built in 1970, has produced only aluminum cans. Pabst national brands carry a collector value of up to $1. The obscure brands will carry a collector value of up to $3.

Perry

G. HEILEMAN BREWING COMPANY, Georgia Highway 247
Spur (successor to Pabst Brewing Company)

Heileman produced a myriad of labels at this brewery, identified by the letter "L" stamped on the bottom of their cans. All cans carry a collector value of up to $1.

Hawaii

HAWAII BREWING COMPANY, 721 Kapiolani Boulevard

Primo Hawaiian Beer, two-label 11-ounce aluminum soft top, red, white, and blue paper label, single version. .... Exotic

JOS. SCHLITZ BREWING COMPANY, 721 Kapiolani Boulevard (successor to Hawaii Brewing Company)

Primo Hawaiian Beer, two-label 12-ounce tab top, metallic gold can, white label, map of islands, single version. $20

Two-label 12-ounce tab top, white can, blue label, map of islands, single version. *(See photo 109)* $15

Two-label 12-ounce tab top, gold can, blue label, two minor versions........ $15

Any brands originating with Schlitz, brewed in Hawaii, are not separated on the label.

Photo 109. Primo Hawaiian Beer.

Idaho

Boise

BOHEMIAN BREWERIES, INC., 601 Idaho Street

Bohemian Club Beer, single-label, 12-ounce, high-profile cone top, metallic orange and flat gray can, single version. *(See photo 110)* $125

Single-label, 12-ounce, high-profile cone top, white can, gold bands, single version. $150

Bohemian Club Light Export Lager Beer, single-label, 12-ounce. high-profile cone top, red, white, black, and gold can, versions: IRTP and non-IRTP.

IRTP, ... $200

Non-IRTP, ... $175

Pocatello

EAST IDAHO BREWING COMPANY, 633 South 1st Avenue

Aero Club Pale Select Beer, single-label, 12-ounce, high-profile cone top, metallic gold can, blue label, white stripe, two versions. *(See photo 111)* $150

Sun Valley Beer, single-label, 12-ounce, high-profile cone top, blue can, white mountain scene, "SUN VALLEY" in gold, two versions. *(See photo 112)* $150

Photo 110 (left). Bohemian Club Beer.
Photo 111 (center). Aero Club Pale
Select Beer. Photo 112 (right). Sun
Valley Beer.

Illinois

Belleville

CARLING BREWING COMPANY, 1201–25 West E Street (successor to Griesedieck Western Brewery Company)

Black Label Beer, single-label 12-ounce flat or tab top, red can, black label outlined in white, map of U.S. or world, multiversions. All versions, ... $10

Single-label 12-ounce tab top, silver tankard can, red label, single version.. $20

Carling Black Label Beer, single-label 12-ounce flat top, red can, black label outlined in white, "CARLING" on label, multiversions. *(See photo 113)*...... $20

Carling Stag Beer, single- or two-label 12- or 16-ounce flat, zip, or tab top, metallic gold can, brown circle, white label, multiversions. $10

Carling Stag Premium Dry Pilsener Beer, single-label 12-ounce flat top, black can, metallic gold-striped and oval white label, multiversions. $20

Red Cap Ale, two-label 12-ounce flat top, gold diamonds, white label, red cap, red vertical band, single version. $20

Two-label 12-ounce flat top, green can, split orangish label, full head, single version. $20

Photo 113. Carling Black Label Beer.

CARLING-NATIONAL BREWING COMPANY, 1201–25 West
E Street (successor to Carling Brewing Company)

This company operated from 1976 to 1979 before merging with G. Heileman Brewing Company. All cans produced were aluminum or bi-metal. Collector value will not exceed $1.

GRIESEDIECK WESTERN BREWERY COMPANY, 1201–25
West E Street

Stag Extra Dry Pilsener Beer, single-label, 12-ounce, high-profile cone top, white can, black label, red letter, INTERNAL REVENUE TAX PAID, multiversions.
.... $60

Stag Premium Dry Pilsener Beer, single-label, 12-ounce, high-profile cone or flat top, black can, yellow label, multiversions.
Cone top, ... $60
Flat top, ... $20

G. HEILEMAN BREWING COMPANY, 1201–25 West E Street
(successor to Carling-National Brewing Company)

All cans produced in Belleville by G. Heileman were in aluminum cans. The collector value of these cans does not exceed $1. To determine these codes, look for the letter "B" stamped on the bottom of the cans.

STAR PEERLESS BREWERY COMPANY, 1125 Lebanon Avenue

Oldtimer Genuine Premium Beer, single-label, 12-ounce, high-profile cone top, red can, gold bands, white label, versions: IRTP and non-IRTP. *(See photo 114)*
IRTP, ... $125
Non-IRTP, ... $115

Chicago

AMBROSIA BREWING COMPANY, 3700 South Halstad Avenue
(successor to South Side Brewing Company)

Ambrosia Lager Beer, single-label 12-ounce flat top, tall or standard gold can, red and yellow label, OPENING INSTRUCTIONS, INTERNAL REVENUE TAX PAID, single version.
Tall can, ... $450
Standard can, ... $400

Photo 114 (left). Oldtimer Genuine Premium Beer.
Photo 115 (right). Katz Premium Beer.

Nector Premium Beer, single-label 12-ounce flat top, gold can, white label, red scrolling, IRTP or non-IRTP, minor versions.
Non-IRTP, ... $175
IRTP, ... $200
Single-label 12-ounce flat top, gold can, white label, "N" on red circle, minor version. $60

ASSOCIATED BREWING COMPANY, 1900–1946 West 18th Street (successor to Drewrys Ltd., U.S.A.; aka: Drewrys Limited U.S.A., 9–0–5 Brewing Company)

9–0–5 Premium Beer, 9–0–5 Brewing, two-label 12-ounce flat or tab top, white can, red circle label, minor versions.
Flat top, ... $15
Tab top, ... $12
Atlas Praeger Bohemian Light Lager Beer, Associated Brewing, two-label 12-ounce flat top, white can, red label, three figures, single version. $10
Champagne Velvet Beer, Associated Brewing, two-label 12-ounce tab top, gold can, white glass, blue band, single version. $10
Drewrys Beer, Drewrys U.S.A., two-label 12- or 16-ounce tab top, red can, white outlined oval label, "THE AMERICAN BEER WITH THE GERMAN ACCENT," single version of each.
12-ounce, ... $10
16-ounce, ... $12
Drewrys Draft Beer, Drewrys U.S.A., two-label 12- or 16-ounce tab top, yellow can, brown label, picture of a keg, single version.
12-ounce, ... $15
16-ounce, ... $20
Great Lakes Premium Beer, Associated Brewing, two-label 12-ounce tab top, blue can, silver stripes and map of Great Lakes, single version. $15
Home Dry Lager Beer, Associated Brewing, two-label 12-ounce tab top, white can, oval red label, single version. $10
Katz Premium Beer, Associated Brewing, two-label 12-ounce tab top, white can, red label, black cat, single version. *(See photo 115)* $12
Old Dutch Brand, Associated Brewing, two-label 12-ounce tab top, white can, red bands, "THE GOOD BEER," single version. $15
Regal Famous Premium Beer, Associated Brewing, two-label 12-ounce flat top, white can, square red label, single version. $10
SGA Premium Beer, Associated Brewing, two-label 12-ounce tab top, white, gold, and blue can, blue diamond label, "YOURS FOR BETTER LIVING," single version. $15
Tavern Pale Dry Beer, Associated Brewing, two-label 12-ounce tab top, "SURE IT'S DIFFERENT," blue, red, and metallic gold can, single version. $20

ATLANTIC BREWING COMPANY, 1549 West Fullerton Avenue (aka: Champagne Velvet Brewing Company, C V Brewing Company,

Excell Brewing Company, Lederer Brewing Company, Savoy Brewing Company, Tuxedo Brewing Company)

Barbarossa Beer, Atlantic Brewing, single-label 12-ounce flat top, red and white can, single version. $25

Black Dallas Malt Liquor, Atlantic Brewing, two-label 12-ounce flat top, light blue can, city skyline, single version. $80

Blackhawk Premium Beer, Atlantic Brewing, two-label 12-ounce flat top, light blue can, Indian head in red, single version. $150

Brewer's Best Premium Pilsener Beer, Atlantic Brewing, single-label 12-ounce flat top, white can, "BREWER'S BEST BEER" on two red bands, single version. .... Exotic

Champagne Velvet Beer, Atlantic or C V Brewing, two-label 12- or 16-ounce flat top, metallic gold can, white champagne glass, single version of each.
12-ounce, ... $20
16-ounce, ... $25

Champagne Velvet Gold Label Beer, Atlantic or C V Brewing, two-label 12- or 16-ounce flat top, metallic gold can, "cv" on red circle, single version of each.
12-ounce, ... $30
16-ounce, ... $50

Durst Premium Quality Beer, Atlantic Brewing, two-label 12-ounce flat top, blue can, yellow label, multiversions. $20

Excell Lager Beer, Atlantic or Excell Brewing, two-label 12-ounce flat top, blue and silver can, "EXCELL" in red, single version of each. *(See photo 116)*
Atlantic, ... $50
Excell, ... $75

Extra Select 82 Premium Beer, Atlantic Brewing, two-label 12-ounce flat top, red can, blue label, single version. $100

Fischer's Light Dry Beer, Atlantic Brewing, single-label 12-ounce flat top, white can, blue band, single version. $60

Goldcrest 51 Premium Beer, Atlantic or Lederer Brewing, two-label 12-ounce flat top, metallic red can, white label, single version each brewery. Either,
.... $300

Goldhoff Pale Extra Dry Beer, Atlantic Brewing, two-label 12-ounce flat top, white can, narrow red bands and diamond, single version. $300

Grand Select Cream Ale, Atlantic Brewing, two-label 12-ounce flat top, green can, yellow label, single version. $20

KC's Best Premium Pilsener Beer, Atlantic Brewing, single-label 12-ounce flat top, white can, metallic red bands and trim, two versions. $100

(From left to right)
Photo 116. Excell Lager Beer.
Photo 117. Tavern Pale Beer.
Photo 118. 49er Premium Beer.

Kol Premium Quality Beer, Atlantic Brewing, single-label 12-ounce flat top, silver can, white vertical stripes, blue label, multiversions. $30

Kold Brau Eastern Premium Beer, Atlantic Brewing, single-label 12-ounce flat top, white can, silver stripes, blue label, multiversions. $50

Lederbrau Genuine Draft Beer, Atlantic Brewing, two-label half-gallon can, metallic brown can, single version. ....Exotic

Two-label gallon can, metallic brown can, single version. $400

Redtop Ale, Atlantic or Champagne Velvet Brewing, single-label 12-ounce flat top, silver can, red label, multiversions. All versions,........................... $40

Redtop Beer, Atlantic, Champagne Velvet, or C V Brewing, single-label 12-ounce flat top, silver can, red label, multiversions. $35

Regal New Orleans Famous Premium Beer, Atlantic Brewing, two-label 12-ounce flat or tab top, white can, red label, single version of each.
Flat top, ... $25
Tab top,.. $20

Rivera Old Fashioned Special Beer, Atlantic Brewing, two-label 12-ounce flat top, metallic blue can, gold label, single version. $400

Savoy Special Beer, Atlantic or Savoy Brewing, two-label 12-ounce flat top, silver can, blue label, single version. $150

Tavern Pale Beer, Atlantic Brewing Company, single-label 12-ounce flat top, IRTP and non-IRTP, white can, red label outlined in metallic gold, multiversions.
IRTP, ... $60
Non-IRTP, ...·· $50

Atlantic Brewing, two-label 12-ounce flat top, "VINTAGE BREW," multiversions.. $40

Atlantic Brewing, two-label 12- or 16-ounce flat, zip, or tab top, "SURE IT'S DIFFERENT, IT'S FOR MEN," multiversions. *(See photo 117)* All versions..... $35

Tuxedo 51 Premium Beer, Atlantic or Tuxedo Brewing, two-label 12-ounce flat top, red can, metallic gold bands, white label, multiversions. $50

Wild Mustang Malt Liquor, Atlantic Brewing Company, two-label gallon can, yellow woodgrain and white can, single version. ....Unique

ATLAS BREWING COMPANY, 1503 West 21st (aka: 9–0–5 Brewing Company, Brewed and Canned for Schoenhofen-Edelweiss)

9–0–5 Premium Beer, 9–0–5 Brewing Company, single-label 12- or 16-ounce flat top, white can, red oval label, "PROPERLY AGED," "FAMOUS FOR QUALITY," multiversions.
12-ounce,.. $20
16-ounce,.. $30

49er Premium Beer, Atlas Brewing, two-label 12-ounce flat top, white can, totem pole, single version. *(See photo 118)* $100

All-American Beer, Atlas Brewing, single-label 12-ounce flat top, red can, white label, hop stake on label, two versions. $75

All-American Extra Dry Beer, Atlas Brewing, single-label 12- or 16-ounce flat top, white can, red lettering, sports figures, single version.
12-ounce,.. $60
16-ounce,.. $75

Atlas Prager Beer, Atlas Brewing, single-label 12-ounce flat top, red, black, and gold can, OPENING INSTRUCTIONS, INTERNAL REVENUE TAX PAID, multiversions. *(See photo 119)* $80

Atlas Brewing, single-label 12-ounce flat top, gold can, black pinstripes, INTERNAL REVENUE TAX PAID, multiversions.. $40

Atlas Prager Bock Beer, Atlas Brewing, two-label 12-ounce flat top, metallic gold can, red label, goat's head, single version. $80

Atlas Prager Bohemian Light Lager Beer, Atlas Brewing, two-label 12- or 16-ounce flat top, white can, red label, man dancing, multiversions. Either size, ... $40

Atlas Prager Extra Dry Beer, Atlas Brewing, single- or double-label 12-ounce flat top, gold can, red label, multiversions. $50

Atlas Brewing, double-label 12-ounce flat top, white can, red label, multiversions.. $40

Atlas Yorkshire Ale, Atlas Brewing, single-label 12-ounce flat top, metallic green can, yellow label outlined in brown, OPENING INSTRUCTIONS, INTERNAL REVENUE TAX PAID, single version. $300

Brown Derby Lager Beer, Atlas Brewing, two-label 12-ounce flat top, white can, gold braid circle label, brown hat, single version. $60

Bull Dog 14 Extra Hearty Stout Malt Liquor, Atlas Brewing, two-label 12-ounce flat top, white can, bulldog on top of gold circle label, single version. $60

Bull Dog Extra Malt Liquor, Atlas Brewing, two-label 12-ounce flat top, white can, black band, "Extra" on black label, multiversions. $40

Bull Dog Malt Lager, Atlas Brewing, two-label 8-ounce flat top, gold can, white oval label, blue stripe, single version. $50

Bull Dog Malt Liquor, Atlas Brewing, two-label 7-, 8-, or 12-ounce flat top, gold can, white oval label, bulldog on blue patch, single version of each size. 7- or 8-ounce, ... $50
12-ounce,.. $40

Eastern Premium Beer, Atlas Brewing, two-label 12-ounce flat top, red and white can, gold or silver trim. *(See photo 120)* $40

Atlas Brewing, two-label 12-ounce flat top, white can, line drawings of skyline, single version.. $150

Atlas Brewing, two-label 12-ounce flat top, metallic gold can, white label, blue trim, single version.. $75

Photo 119. Atlas Prager Beer. Photo 120. Eastern Premium Beer.

Edelweiss Light Beer, Schoenhofen-Edelweiss, two-label 12-ounce flat top, red and white can, "EDELWEISS" in black, INTERNAL REVENUE TAX PAID, single version. $60

F & G Eastern Premium, Atlas Brewing, single-label 12- or 16-ounce flat top, metallic red and gold can, single version of each size.
12-ounce, ... $125
16-ounce, ... $150

GES Premium Beer, Atlas Brewing, two-label 12-ounce flat top, white can, blue eagle, red letters, single version. $175

Gold Coast Premium Beer, Atlas Brewing or Schoenhofen-Edelweiss, two-label 12- or 16-ounce flat top, metallic gold can, white label, "GOLD COAST" in red, multiversions.
12-ounce, ... $100
12-ounce with blue band, ... $60
16-ounce, ... $50

Home Bock Beer, Atlas Brewing, two-label 12-ounce flat top, white can, brown oval label, single version. $60

Home Brew Lager Beer, Atlas Brewing, two-label 12-ounce flat top, black can, red oval label, single version. $75

Home Dry Lager Beer, Atlas Brewing, two-label 12- or 16-ounce flat top, metallic gold or white can, red label, single version each size, each color. All varieties, ... $25

Jordan Slow Brewed Beer, Atlas Brewing, two-label 12-ounce flat top, metallic gold can, white label, single version. $200

Kol Premium Quality Beer, Atlas Brewing, single-label 12-ounce flat top, silver can, white vertical stripes, blue label, multiversions. $25

Kold Brau Eastern Premium Beer, Atlas Brewing Company, single-label 12-ounce flat top, silver can, white stripes, blue label, "MILD-MELLOW DRY," multiversions. $50

McLab Eastern Premium Beer, Atlas Brewing, two-label 12-ounce flat top, white can, steins outlined with red squares, single version. $75

Reidenbach Extra Dry Beer, Atlas Brewing, two-label 12-ounce flat top, metallic gold can, aqua stein, white label, single version. $50

Salzburg Eastern Beer, Atlas Brewing, two-label 12-ounce flat top, white can, steins outlined with red squares, single version. $75

Skol Eastern Premium Beer, Atlas or 9-0-5 Brewing, two-label 12- or 16-ounce flat top, white can, "SKOL" in red, steins, single version each size, each brewery. All versions, ... $35

Volks Brau Pale Eastern Beer, Atlas Brewing, two-label 12- or 16-ounce flat top, white can, large stein, "VOLKS" in red, single version of each. Either size, ... $25

BIRK BROS. BREWING COMPANY, 2117 North Wayne Avenue

Trophy Beer, single-label, 12-ounce, high-profile cone top, off-white can, orange bands, glass of beer, IRTP and non-IRTP, multiversions.
Non-IRTP, ... $110
IRTP, ... $125

CANADIAN ACE BREWING COMPANY, 3901 Emerald Avenue (successor to Manhattan Brewing Company; aka: Ace Brewing Company, Ace Hi Brewing Company, Allied Breweries, Inc., Bismarck Brewing Company, Cold Brau Brewing Company, Crest Brewing Company, Empire Brewing Company, Essex Brewing Company, Gipps Brewing Company/Chicago, Gipps Brewing Company/Peoria, Gold Brau Brewing Company, Hapsburg Brewing Company, Jester Brewing Company, Kings Brewing Company, Koenig Brau Brewing Company, Kol Brewing Company, Leisy Brewing Company, Lubeck Brewing Company, Malt Marrow Brewing Company, Old Vienna Brewing Company, Pilsen Brewing Company, Prima Brewing Company, Prima-Bismarck Brewing Company, Royal Brewing Company, Schultz Brewing Company, Star Union Brewing Company, Superior Brewing Company, Tudor Brewing Company, United States Brewing Company, Westminster Brewing Company, Windsor Brewing Company)

21st Century Beer, Canadian Ace Brewing Company, two-label 12-ounce flat top, white can, red band, metallic gold oval, "21 CENTURY" in metallic dark red, single version. *(See photo 121)* $150

333 Pilsener Brand Beer, Canadian Ace Brewing Company, single-label 12-ounce flat top, maroon filigree on gold can, white label, multiversions. $60

9-0-5 Premium Beer, Canadian Ace Brewing Company, single-label 12-ounce flat top, white can, red label, "PROPERLY AGED IN BREWERY CELLARS" in white square, single version. $40

ABC Premium Ale, Gold Brau Brewing Company, single-label 12-ounce flat top, green can, white label, single version. $40

ABC Premium Beer, Gold Brau Brewing Company, single-label 12-ounce flat or tab top, red can, white label, multiversions. $30

Ace Hi Malt Lager, Ace Brewing Company, single-label 7-ounce flat top, red can, white label, single version. $100

Ace Hi Malt Liquor, Ace High Brewing Company, single-label 7- or 8-ounce flat top, red can, white label. $75

Ace Hi Premium Ale, Ace High Brewing Company, single-label 12-ounce flat top, white can, green diamond label, line drawings, single version. $75

Photo 121. 21st Century Beer.

Ace Hi Premium Beer, Canadian Ace or Ace Hi Brewing, single-label 7-, 8-, 12-, or 16-ounce flat top, white can, red diamond label, line drawings, multiversions.
7-, 8-, and 12-ounce, ... $60
16-ounce, ... $75

Armanetti Premium Beer, Gold Brau Brewing Company, two-label 12-ounce flat top, red can, pinstripes, gold trim, multiversions. $100

Best Premium Quality Ale, United States Brewing Company, two-label 12-ounce flat top, white can, green label outlined in yellow, single version. $30

Best Premium Quality Beer, Empire or United States Brewing, two-label 12-ounce flat top, white can, red label outlined in yellow, single version of each brewery. $20

Bismarck Export Beer, Bismarck Brewing Company, single-label 12-ounce flat top, white can, maroon and green trim, two minor versions. $50

Bismarck Premium Beer, Bismarck Brewing Company, single-label 12-ounce flat top, white can, metallic red and green trim, single version. $50

Black Dallas Malt Liquor, Canadian Ace Brewing Company, single-label 12-ounce flat top, blue can, black lettering, city outline, single version. $75

Brown Derby Lager Beer, Empire or United States Brewing, two-label 12-ounce flat top, white can, "BROWN DERBY" in brown outlined in gold, multiversions. $35

Canadian Ace Brand Ale, Canadian Ace Brewing, two-label 12-ounce flat top, woodgrain can, white and silver label, single version. $30

Canadian Ace Brand Beer, Canadian Ace Brewing, two-label 7-, 8-, or 12-ounce flat top, woodgrain can, white label with red band, multiversions.
7- and 8-ounce, ... $25
12-ounce, ... $15

Canadian Ace Brand Bock Beer, Canadian Ace Brewing, single-label 12-ounce flat top, woodgrain can, white label, goat's head, single version. $40

Canadian Ace Brand Extra Pale Ale, Canadian Ace Brewing, single-label, 12-ounce, high-profile cone or flat top, also quart cone top, or 16-ounce two-label flat top, dark brown woodgrain can, red stripe, multiversions.
12-ounce flat top, ... $20
12-ounce cone top, ... $65
16-ounce flat top, ... $35
Quart cone top, ... $85

Canadian Ace Brand Extra Pale Beer, Canadian Ace Brewing, single-label 7-, 8-, or 12-ounce flat top, 12-ounce, high-profile cone top, or quart cone top, light woodgrain can, white label, silver trim, IRTP 12-ounce cone top, non-IRTP all others, multiversions except 8-ounce and quart.
7- or 8-ounce flat top, ... $25
12-ounce flat top, ... $20
12-ounce IRTP cone top, ... $110
12-ounce non-IRTP cone top, ...$100
Quart cone top, ...$125

Canadian Ace Brand Malt Liquor, Canadian Ace Brewing, two-label 7-ounce flat top, woodgrain can, white label, red stripe, single version. $60

Canadian Ace Brand Premium Ale, Canadian Ace Brewing, two-label 12- or 16-ounce flat or tab top, woodgrain can, white label, green stripe, multiversions. $40

Canadian Ace Brand Premium Beer, Canadian Ace Brewing, single-label, 12-ounce, high-profile cone top, or 12- or 16-ounce flat or tab top, woodgrain can, winged emblem, multiversions.
12-ounce flat or tab top, ... $20
12-ounce cone top, ... $65
16-ounce flat or tab top, ... $35

Canadian Ace Brand Premium Draft Beer, Canadian Ace Brewing, two-label 12-ounce flat or tab top, woodgrain can, "DRAFT" in red on white ribbon, multiversions. $40

Canadian Ace Extra Pale Strong Beer, Canadian Ace Brewing, single-label quart cone top, woodgrain can, white label, silver trim, red stripe, INTERNAL REVENUE TAX PAID, single version. $85

Cold Brau Eastern Premium Beer, Cold Brau Brewing, two-label 12-ounce flat top, white can, blue label, single version. *(See photo 122)* $40

Crest Extra Pale Premium Beer, Crest Brewing Company, two-label 12-ounce flat top, white can, metallic red label, single version. $75

Crown Darby Premium Beer, Westminster Brewing Company, two-label 12-ounce flat top, white can, blue label, metallic gold horseshoe, single version. $60

Dorf Bohemian Lager Beer, Schultz Brewing Company, two-label 12-ounce flat top, blue can, white label, large blue stein, single version. $125

Essex Premium Beer, Essex Brewing Company, two-label 12-ounce flat top, white can, blue ribbon, red trim, single version. $60

Gipps Amberlin Beer, Gipps/Chicago or Gipps/Peoria, two-label 12-ounce flat top, brown can, white label, metallic gold trim, single version. $60
Gipps/Chicago, two-label 12-ounce flat top, blue can, white label, silver trim, multiversions. $50

Gipps Premium Beer, Gipps/Chicago, two-label 12-ounce flat top, dark brown can, white label, single version. $60

Gold Brau Beer, Gold Brau Brewing Company, two-label 12-ounce flat top, dark brown can, vertical stripes, white label. *(See photo 123)* $60

Hapsburg Brand Golden Lager, Hapsburg Brewing Company, two-label 12-ounce flat top, white can, blue label, yellow trim, single version. $75

Photo 122 (left). Cold Brau Eastern Premium Beer. Photo 123 (right). Gold Brau Beer.

Hillman's Superb Beer, Empire or United States Brewing, single-label 12-ounce flat top, blue and gold can, "SUPERB" in black, multiversions. $60

Hillman's Superb Bock Beer, United States Brewing Company, single-label 12-ounce flat top, blue and gold can, "SUPERB BOCK" in black, single version. $100

Hoff-Brau Pale Dry Beer, Allied Breweries, two-label 12-ounce flat top, red can, white label, metallic bands top and bottom, single version. $150

Jester Premium Beer, Jester Brewing Company, two-label 12-ounce flat top, blue and white can, figure on face of can, minor versions. $150

Jet Malt Liquor, Westminster Brewing Company, two-label 12-ounce flat or tab top, or 16-ounce zip top, white can, metallic red airplane, multiversions except 16-ounce.
12-ounce, ... $30
16-ounce, ... $35

Jet Near Beer, Westminster Brewing Company, two-label 12-ounce flat top, metallic blue and white can, metallic gold band, single version. $30

Jet Non-Alcoholic Near Beer, Westminster Brewing Company, two-label 12-ounce flat top, metallic blue and white can, metallic gold band, single version. $30

Jet Stout Malt Liquor, Canadian Ace Brewing Company, two-label 12-ounce flat top, white can, metallic blue airplane, single version. $40

KC's Best Premium Pilsener Beer, Empire and United States Brewing Company, white can, metallic red label and trim, single version of each brewery. $60

King's Premium Beer, Kings Brewing Company, two-label 12-ounce flat top, white can, blue label, single version. $65

Koenig Brau Premium Beer, Canadian Ace, Bismarck, Koenig Brau, or Prima-Bismarck, single-label 12-ounce flat top, metallic gold can, white label, red trim, single version of each brewery. $65

Kol Premium Quality Beer, Kol Brewing Company, single-label 12-ounce flat top, silver can, vertical blue stripes and label, single version. $25

Land Of Lakes Pale Dry Beer, Canadian Ace or Pilsen Brewing, single-label 12-ounce flat or tab top, blue can, white arrowhead label, single versions of each. $30

Leisy Pilsener Beer, Leisy Brewing Company, two-label 12-ounce flat top, metallic gold can, orange band, white label, single version. $300

Leisy's Dortmunder Brand Beer, Leisy Brewing Company, single-label 12-ounce flat top, metallic gold can, red label, white lettering, single version. $150

Leisy's Light Full Flavored Beer, Leisy Brewing Company, two-label 12-ounce flat top, blue can, yellow label, gold trim, single version. ....Exotic

Lubeck Premium Beer, Lubeck Brewing Company, single-label 12-ounce flat top, white can, purple band, black label, single version. $100

Lubeck Brewing Company, single-label 12-ounce flat top, gold and yellow can, green label, single version. $125

Lubeck Royal Beer, Lubeck Brewing Company, single-label 12-ounce flat top, white can, purple band, black label, single version. $100

Mayflower Premium Beer, United States Brewing Company, two-label 12-ounce flat top, blue and white can, black label, single version. $150

McAvoy's Malt Marrow, Malt Marrow Brewing Company, two-label 12-ounce flat top, yellow can, metallic gold label, red letters, single version. $250

Old Vienna Premium Beer, Old Vienna Brewing Company, two-label 12- or 16-ounce flat top, silver can, white pinstripes, metallic dark red label, multiversions.
12-ounce, ... $60
16-ounce, ... $75

Prima America's Finest Beer, Canadian Ace or Prima Brewing Company, single-label 12-ounce flat top, blue can, "PRIMA BEER" in white, minor versions. . $60

Prima Premium Beer, Canadian Ace or Prima Brewing Company, two-label 12-ounce flat top, blue can, white letters, multiversions. $30

Reidenbach Extra Dry Beer, Canadian Ace, Empire, or United States Brewing, two-label 12-ounce flat top, yellow can, white label, large stein, single version of each. $150

Royal Premium Beer, Royal Brewing Company, two-label 12-ounce flat top, blue and silver can, minor versions. $65

Schwegmann Premium Bock Beer, Gold Brau Brewing Company, two-label 12-ounce flat top, blue can, white diamond label, goat's head, single version.
.... $150

Schwegmann Premium Light Beer, Gold Brau Brewing Company, two-label 12-ounce flat top, metallic red can, white label, minor versions. $85

Star Model Premium Quality Beer, Star Union Brewing Company, two-label 12-ounce flat top, white can, metallic red ribbon, single version. $60

Superior Premium Beer, Superior Brewing Company, two-label 12-ounce flat top, white can and label, vertical metallic red stripes, single version. $85

Supreme Premium Beer, Supreme Brewing Company, three-label, 12-ounce flat top, silver can, scrolling, red vertical label, single version. $65

Tudor Cream Ale, Tudor Brewery Ltd., two-label 12-ounce flat or tab top, white can, green label with metallic gold outline, "A & P" in circle, multiversions.
.... $25

Tudor Pilsner Beer, Tudor Brewery Ltd., two-label 12-ounce flat top, white can, large red oval label, "A & P" in circle, multiversions. $20

Tudor Premium Quality Ale, Tudor Brewery Ltd., two-label 12-ounce flat top, green can, green label, white lettering, cornet, single version. $40

Tudor Brewery Ltd., two-label 12-ounce flat top, white can, green label, minor versions. $40

Tudor Premium Quality Beer, Tudor Brewery Ltd., two-label 12-ounce flat top, red can, blue label, cornet, single version. $35

Tudor Brewery Ltd., two-label 12-ounce flat top, white can, red label, minor versions. $30

Windsor Premium Beer, Windsor Brewing Company, two-label 12-ounce flat top, blue, silver, and white can, "WINDSOR" in blue, single label. $85

Yusay Pilsen Premium Beer, Pilsen Brewing Company, two-label 12-ounce flat top, red and white can, "YUSAY" in blue, single version. $50

Photo 124. Drewrys Extra Dry Beer.

DREWRYS LTD., U.S.A., INC., 1900–1956 West 18th Street (successors to Schoenhofen-Edelweiss Company; aka: Drewrys Limited, Schoenhofen-Edelweiss)

Dorf Bohemian Lager Beer, Schoenhofen-Edelweiss, two-label 12-ounce flat or tab top, woodgrain can, white label, yellow stein, single version of each top.
.... $50

Drewrys Beer, Drewrys Ltd., two-label 12-ounce zip top or 16-ounce tab top, white can, white shield label on red band, multiversions. $15

Two-label 12-ounce tab top, red can, white label, "THE AMERICAN BEER WITH A GERMAN ACCENT," multiversions. $10

Single-label 12-ounce flat top, issue called "Sports" series, pictures of people playing various sports, two versions within series: oval label on blue, bronze, green, purple, red, or yellow cans, or shield label on green, orange, purple, bronze, dark blue, or gold cans, single version of each. Each, ... $30

Single-label 12-ounce flat top, issue called "Horoscope" series, two horoscopes per can, colors include purple, gold, red, blue, orange, and green (not all colors were used on every can with horoscopes), single version of each. Each, ... $30

Drewrys Extra Dry Beer, single-label 12-ounce flat top, white can, blue shield label, single version. *(See photo 124)* $15

Drewrys Malt Liquor, single-label 12-ounce flat top, yellow can, black bands, "MALT LIQUOR" on red ribbon, single version. $300

Drewrys Stout Malt Liquor, single-label 12-ounce flat top, yellow can, black bands, "STOUT MALT LIQUOR" on red ribbon, single version. $325

Salburg Eastern Beer, two-label 12-ounce flat top, white can, steins outlined by red square, single version. $100

KEELEY BREWING COMPANY, 528 East 28th Street

Keeley Beer, two-label, 12-ounce, high-profile cone top, orange can, white label outlined in black, single version. $125

Keeley Half & Half, single-label, 12-ounce, high-profile cone or quart cone top, woodgrain can, yellow label, "KEELEY" in black, IRTP or non-IRTP, multiversion 12-ounce, single-version quart cone.
12-ounce non-IRTP, ... $100
12-ounce IRTP, ... $110
Quart, ... $125

Photo 125. Koller's Topaz Beer. Photo 126. Royal Pilsener Beer.

Keeley Lager Beer, single-label, 12-ounce, high-profile cone top, brown can, white label outlined in metallic gold, INTERNAL REVENUE TAX PAID, single version. $125

KOLLER BREWING COMPANY, 39th and South Racine Avenue

Koller's Topaz Beer, single-label, 12-ounce, J-spout cone top, yellow can, brown label, single version. *(See photo 125)* $125

Two-label 12-ounce crowntainer, silver can, "KOLLER'S" in red, single version. $100

Royal Pilsener Beer, single-label, 12-ounce, J-spout cone top, red can, yellow label and trim, single version. *(See photo 126)*....................................$125

Single-label 12-ounce crowntainer, silver can, "ROYAL PILSENER" in blue, single version. $110

MANHATTAN BREWING COMPANY, 3901 Emerald Avenue
(predecessors to Canadian Ace Brewing Company; aka: Whitewater Brewing Company, Whitewater, WI; Schepps Brewing Company, Dallas, TX; Class and Nachod, Philadelphia, PA; Lubeck Brewing Company, Toledo, OH; Westminster Brewing Company; Whitewater-Manhattan Brewing Company)

All Star Premium Beer, Manhattan Brewing Company, single-label 12-ounce flat top, blue and gray can, OPENING INSTRUCTIONS, INTERNAL REVENUE TAX PAID, two versions. $150

Autocrat Pilsner Beer, Manhattan Brewing Company, single-label 12-ounce flat top, cream-colored can, gold trim, red and black lettering, OPENING INSTRUCTIONS, INTERNAL REVENUE TAX PAID, single version. ....Unique

Badger Beer, Whitewater or Whitewater-Manhattan Brewing Company, single-label 12-ounce flat top, red can, gray band, black badger, OPENING INSTRUCTIONS, INTERNAL REVENUE TAX PAID, minor versions both breweries. All versions, ...$150

Black Dallas Beer, Manhattan Brewing Company, single-label 12-ounce flat top, blue can, city skyline in black, OPENING INSTRUCTIONS, INTERNAL REVENUE TAX PAID, minor versions. $100

Black Eagle Beer, Class & Nachod Brewing Company, single-label 12-ounce flat top, gold and black can, OPENING INSTRUCTIONS, INTERNAL REVENUE TAX PAID, single version. ....Unique

Class Pilsner Beer, Class & Nachod Brewing Company, single-label 12-ounce flat top, gold can, yellow and red label, OPENING INSTRUCTIONS, INTERNAL REVENUE TAX PAID, single version. ....Exotic

Cream Top Beer, Whitewater Brewing Company, single-label 12-ounce flat top, green can, man examining glass of beer, OPENING INSTRUCTIONS, INTERNAL REVENUE TAX PAID, single version. $350

English Lad Ale, Manhattan or Westminster Brewing, single-label 12-ounce flat top, green and yellow can, black horseshoe, OPENING INSTRUCTIONS, INTERNAL REVENUE TAX PAID, three versions: PACKED EXPRESSLY FOR WESTMINSTER BREWING COMPANY, CHICAGO, ILLINOIS; PACKED EXPRESSLY FOR WESTMINSTER BREWING COMPANY . . . PRIMA BREWING COMPANY, SUCCESSORS; BREWED AND PACKED BY MANHATTAN BREWING COMPANY . . . EXPRESSLY FOR WESTMINSTER BREWING COMPANY, PRIMA BREWING COMPANY SUCCESSORS. All versions, ...$350

English Lad Beer, Manhattan or Westminster Brewing, single-label 12-ounce flat top, orange and green can, black horseshoe, OPENING INSTRUCTIONS, INTERNAL REVENUE TAX PAID, three versions, same text as English Lad Ale......$350

Ilsner Lager Style Beer, Manhattan Brewing Company, black can, "ILSNER" in red, OPENING INSTRUCTIONS, INTERNAL REVENUE TAX PAID, single version. $300

Lubeck Royal Beer, Manhattan or Lubeck Brewing Company, single-label 12-ounce flat top, black can, red shield, OPENING INSTRUCTIONS, INTERNAL REVENUE TAX PAID, single version. $300

Manhattan Premium Ale, Manhattan Brewing Company, single-label 12-ounce flat top, green can, yellow skyline, OPENING INSTRUCTIONS, INTERNAL REVENUE TAX PAID, single version. $300

Manhattan Premium Beer, Manhattan Brewing Company, single-label 12-ounce flat or quart cone top, metallic gold can, black skyline, OPENING INSTRUCTIONS on flat tops, INTERNAL REVENUE TAX PAID, minor versions each size.
Flat top, ...$100
Cone top, ...$125

Manhattan Premium Bock Beer, Manhattan Brewing Company, single-label 12-ounce flat top, OPENING INSTRUCTIONS, INTERNAL REVENUE TAX PAID, gold can, black skyline, goat's head, single version. ....Exotic

Old Gold Seven Star Lager Beer, Manhattan Brewing Company, single-label 12-ounce flat top, dull red or brown and metallic gold can, OPENING INSTRUCTIONS, INTERNAL REVENUE TAX PAID, minor versions. $200

Old Wisconsin Brand Lager Beer, Manhattan Brewing Company, single-label 12-ounce flat top, red and cream can, OPENING INSTRUCTIONS, INTERNAL REVENUE TAX PAID, single version. ....Exotic

Prima Gold Medal Beer, Manhattan Brewing Company, single-label 12-ounce flat top, dark blue can, "PRIMA BEER" in white, OPENING INSTRUCTIONS, INTERNAL REVENUE TAX PAID, single version. $100

Rosalie Pilsner Beer, Manhattan Brewing Company, single-label 12-ounce flat top, yellow can, red and blue label, OPENING INSTRUCTIONS, INTERNAL REVENUE TAX PAID, single version. ....Unique

Schepps Xtra Beer, Schepps Brewing Company, single-label 12-ounce flat top, cream and gold can, red label, OPENING INSTRUCTIONS, INTERNAL REVENUE TAX PAID, single version..Exotic

Sun Gold Beer, Manhattan Brewing Company, single-label 12-ounce flat top, white can, green and red lettering, gold sunrise, OPENING INSTRUCTIONS, INTERNAL REVENUE TAX PAID, single version. .... Exotic

Tiger Beer, Manhattan Brewing Company, single-label 12-ounce flat top, tiger head, yellow and purple can, OPENING INSTRUCTIONS, INTERNAL REVENUE TAX PAID. .... Unique

White Horse Lager Beer, Lubeck Brewing Company, single-label 12-ounce flat top, blue can, red label, silver lettering, OPENING INSTRUCTIONS, INTERNAL REVENUE TAX PAID, single version. .... Exotic

White Horse Pilsener Beer, Manhattan or Westminster Brewing Company, single-label 12-ounce flat top, red and black can, white horse's head, OPENING INSTRUCTIONS, INTERNAL REVENUE TAX PAID, versions: same text as English Lad and Westminster. $250

Windsor Extra Pale Beer, Whitewater Brewing Company, metallic gold can, black label, OPENING INSTRUCTIONS, INTERNAL REVENUE TAX PAID, single version. $300

MEISTER BRAU, INC., 1000 West North Street (successor to Peter Hand Brewery Company; aka: Warsaw Brewing Company)

Burgermeister Premium Beer, Warsaw Brewing Company, two-label 12- or 16-ounce tab top, white can, red label outlined in yellow (the 16-ounce is a paper label), single version.
12-ounce, ... $10
16-ounce, ... $25

Lite Brand Beer, Meister Brau, two-label 12-ounce tab top, white can, blue lettering, yellow trim, multiversions. Note: The Lite—*LITE*—brand originated with Meister Brau, Inc. in the late '60s. $5

Meister Brau Bock Draft Beer, Meister Brau, two-label 12-ounce flat top, grayish can, brown label, "BOCK & DRAFT" in orange, single version. $20

Meister Brau, three-label 12- or 16-ounce zip or tab top, blue can, vertical white stripes, white label, multiversions. $10

Meister Brau Pilsener Beer, Meister Brau, three-label 12-ounce flat or tab top, white can, white label outlined in red and metallic gold, single version of each top. $20

Meister Brau Premium Beer, Meister Brau, three-label 12- or 16-ounce tab top, metallic gold can, white label outlined in blue, single version of each size. Either size, ... $10

Meister Brau Premium Bock Beer, Meister Brau, three-label 12-ounce tab top, white can, white label outlined in red, yelow trim, multiversions. $10

Meister Brau Premium Draft Beer, Meister Brau, three-label 12- or 16-ounce tab top, woodgrain can, white label, glass of beer, multiversions. $15

Meister Brau Real Draft Beer, Meister Brau, two-label 12-ounce flat or tab top, woodgrain can, white label, "DRAFT" in red, single version of each top. Either top, ... $10

MONARCH BREWING COMPANY, 2419–2449 West 21st Street

Bullfrog Beer, single-label 12-ounce flat top, white can, metallic gold "BULL-DOG," green trim, single version. $85

Monarch Beer, single-label, 12-ounce, high-profile cone or flat top, red can, white label, scroll, IRTP or non-IRTP, multiversions.
IRTP cone top, ... $125
Non-IRTP flat top, ... $80

PETER FOX BREWING COMPANY, 2626 West Munroe Street

Alpine Brand Premium Beer, single-label 12-ounce flat top, white can, red stripes, round label, "ALPINE" on red band, single version. $85

Single-label 12-ounce flat top, white can, green stripes, round label, "ALPINE" on green band, single version. $100

Fox Deluxe Beer, single-label 8- or 12-ounce flat top, gold can, black band, hunter with horn, OPENING INSTRUCTIONS, INTERNAL REVENUE TAX PAID, multiversions.
8-ounce, ... $150
12-ounce, ... $125

Single-label 12-ounce flat top, metallic gold can, white oval label, multiversions. $75

Single-label 12-ounce flat top, metallic gold can, square label, single version. $40

Fox Deluxe Bock Beer, single-label 12-ounce flat top, white can, green oval, fox's head, single version. $125

Single-label 12-ounce flat top, cream-colored can, brown label, hunter with horn, single version. $40

Fox Export Beer, two-label 12-ounce flat top, gold can, hunter with horn, black band, OPENING INSTRUCTIONS, INTERNAL REVENUE TAX PAID, single version. $300

Hillman's Export Beer, single-label 12-ounce flat top, yellow can, red and black label, brown trim, OPENING INSTRUCTIONS, INTERNAL REVENUE TAX PAID, single version. $300

Patrick Henry Velvet Smooth Malt Liquor, single-label 12-ounce flat top, green can, white oval label, single version. $250

Silver Fox Deluxe Beer, single-label 12-ounce flat top, camouflage can, OPENING INSTRUCTIONS, WITHDRAWN FREE, single version. .... Exotic

Silver Fox The Nation's Premium Beer, single-label 12-ounce flat top, gray can, white label outlined in red, versions: WITHDRAWN FREE, INTERNAL REVENUE TAX PAID.
WITHDRAWN FREE, ... Exotic
IRTP, ... $100

PETER HAND BREWERY COMPANY, 1000 West North Avenue

Meister Brau Bock, single-label 12-ounce flat top, brown can, white label, large goat's head, minor versions. $150

Single-label 12-ounce flat top, white can, brown label, "THE CUSTOM BREW," minor versions. $30

Two-label 12-ounce flat top, white can, brown label, "MEISTER BRAU" written in stripes, single label. $25

Meister Brau Bock Draft Beer, three-label 12-ounce flat top, white can, "DRAFT" in red, "BOCK" in orange, minor versions. $15

Meister Brau Extra Pale Pilsener Beer, three-label 12-ounce flat top, brown can, white and metallic gold label, multiversions. $50

Meister Brau Pilsener Beer, three-label 12-ounce flat top, metallic gold can, red and white bands, multiversions. $20

Single-label 12-ounce flat top, set of 36 cans called "Hex Designs," copyrighted 1952, six designs with six colored cans, colors all versions: blue, orange, yellowish, light green, dark green, red, versions: stripes, wavy lines, stars, plain, musical symbols, dots. All cans, ... $60

Single-label 12-ounce flat top, set of 20 cans called "Fiesta Pack," copyrighted 1952, 20 designs each on a different color, versions: astronomical symbols, square dance figures, stars, wavy lines, baseball figures, bowling symbols, dots, playing card symbols, western symbols, pipes, hats, musical instruments, musical symbols, horse racing, golf symbols, bottles and glasses, gardening symbols, plain, sailboats, sports. $60

Single-label 12-ounce flat top, set of 40 cans called "Winter Carnival," copyrighted 1953, 20 designs, all designs issued twice: first on a light metallic-colored can, then on a dark-colored can, versions: skiing, snowflakes on green can, snowflakes on blue can, sleighing, inn, penguins, pine boughs, rabbit hunting, reindeer, duck hunting, Eskimos, ice hockey, ice boating, ice fishing, ice skating, yule log, trees, snowmen, tobogganing, townhouse. Each, ... $65

Single-label 12-ounce flat top, set of 40 cans called "Fiesta Pack," copyrighted 1954, 20 designs issued in dull or metallic colors, all designs issued twice, versions: United States, China, Germany, Greece, Thailand, Switzerland, Spain, gypsies, Hawaii, South Seas, South America, Holland, India, Ireland, Italy, Poland, Mexico, Russia, Scandinavia, Scotland. $75

Two-side 12-ounce flat top, set of 14 cans called "Fiesta Pack" (reissued July 1955), versions: each can was produced with two cartoons and two-color combinations, two basic designs: man with a concertina and lidded stein, *man*: carnival barker/woman, base color brown; antique car/horse and buggy, base color light yellow; antique car/horse and buggy, base color green; carnival barker/woman, base color orange; mermaids/sea captain, base color cream; train/engineer, base color yellowish; woman with pan/man chasing chicken, base color orange; *stein*: lion/lion tamer, base color blue; organ grinder/couple on bench, base color green; organ grinder/couple on bench, base color yellow; riverboat/dancers, base color blue; riverboat/dancers, base color orange; square dancers/turkey, base color yellow; woman with bell/barn, base color orange. $60

Single-label 12-ounce flat top, set of 6 cans called "Pastel-Colored Abstracts," copyrighted 1956, versions: yellow and orange; red, white, and gold; light and dark green; green and pink; yellow and light blue; pink and black. $85

Single-label 12-ounce flat top, set of 10 cans called "Your Toast to Happy Days," copyrighted 1957, versions: barbecue, snowman, beachball, boat model, square dancing, bowling, fishing, golfing, moonlight. $40

Meister Brau Real Draft Beer, single-label 12-ounce flat top, woodgrain can, metallic gold bands and trim, single version. $15

Three-label 12-ounce flat top, woodgrain can, metallic gold, "DRAFT" in red above "MEISTER BRAU." $12

Meister Brau Real Draft Bock, three-label 12-ounce flat top, "REAL DRAFT BEER" on red ribbon, single version. $10

Meister Brau The Beer, single-label 12-ounce flat top, metallic gold can, metallic red label, two versions.
IRTP, ... $65
WITHDRAWN FREE, ... $85

Meister Brau The Custom Brew, renamed reissue of "Your Toast to Happy Days," single-label 12-ounce flat top, set of 10 cans, versions: same as "Your Toast to Happy Days." $40

Peter Hand's Extra Pale Beer, single-label 12-ounce flat top, yellow can, maroon label, OPENING INSTRUCTIONS, INTERNAL REVENUE TAX PAID, minor versions. $200

Peter Hand's Meister Brau, single-label 12-ounce flat top, white can, blue bands and label, INTERNAL REVENUE TAX PAID, single version. $60

Peter Hand's Reserve Beer, single-label 12-ounce flat top, set of six cans, copyrighted 1953, blue can, white oval label, figures on back of cans, versions: artist, fisherman, man at bar with dog, man at bar with newspaper, man at dog show, hunter with sleeping dogs. Each, ... $85

Reserve Beer, single-label 12-ounce flat top, set of 12 cans, copyrighted 1957, blue can, gold bands, white oval label, figures on back of cans, versions: artist, fisherman, man at bar with dog, man at bar with newspaper, man at dog show, hunter with sleeping dogs, yachtsman on dock, waiter, man with binoculars, man with bicycle, "A Most Appealing Flavor, by Peter Hand," in blue and black (two cans). (*See photo 127*) Each, ... $75

Photo 127. Reserve Beer. (A) Front of can. (B) Back of can.

PETER HAND BREWING COMPANY, 1000 West North Street
(successor to Meister Brau, Inc.)

Alps Brau Bavarian Style Premium Beer, two-label 12-ounce tab top, blue, white, and silver can, single version. $5

Braumeister Beer, two-label 12-ounce tab top, white can, red label, single version...$5

Braumeister Bock Beer, two-label 12-ounce tab top, white can, red label, single version. $5

Burgemeister Brewmaster's Premium Beer, two-label 12-ounce tab top, white or yellow can, single version of each. Either can, ...$5

Oertel's '92 Light Lager Beer, two-label 12-ounce tab top, white can, single version. $5

Old Chicago Dark Beer, two label 12- or 16-ounce tab top, yellow can, brown label, metallic gold trim, multiversions. $5

Old Chicago Lager Beer, two-label 12-ounce tab top, yellow can, red label, metallic gold trim, multiversions. $5

Old Crown Light Dry Beer, two-label 12-ounce tab top, white can, red label, multiversions. $5

Old Crown Premium Quality Ale, two-label 12-ounce flat top, gold can, green label, single version. $5

Old German Style Beer, two-label 12-ounce flat top, metallic silver or gold can, metallic red label, single version of each. Either can, ...$5

Peter Hand Export Lager Beer, single-label 12-ounce tab top, white can, orange brewing scenes, single version. $5

Peter Hand Extra Light Beer, two-label 12-ounce tab top, white can, "LIGHT" in blue, single version. $5

Peter Hand Premium Lager Beer, single-label 12-ounce tab top, white can, "PREMIUM LAGER" in blue, single version. $5

Van Merritt Beer, two-label 12-ounce tab top, white can, green oval label, single version. (*See photo 128*)..$5

Zodiac Malt Liquor, two-label 12-ounce tab top, silver can, zodiac emblem in blue, single version. $5

PILSEN BREWING COMPANY, 3043–3065 West 26th Street

Land Of Lakes Pale Dry Beer, single-label 12- or 16-ounce flat top, blue can, white arrowhead label, multiversions.
12-ounce,..$40
16-ounce,..$30

Yusay Pilsen Beer, single-label 12-ounce flat top, red and white can, "YUSAY" in blue, multiversions. $40

Yusay Pilsen Premium Beer, single-label 12-ounce flat top, red and white can, eagle, multiversions. $35

Photo 128 (left). Van Merritt Beer.
Photo 129 (right). Koenig Bräu Premium Beer.

PRIMA-BISMARCK BREWING COMPANY, 2700 Archer Street (aka: Prima Brewing Company)

English Lad Brand Ale, Prima Brewing Company, single-label, 12-ounce, high-profile or quart cone top, yellow and green can, horseshoe, INTERNAL REVENUE TAX PAID, single version of each.
12-ounce, ... $200
Quart, ...$225

English Lad Brand Beer, Prima Brewing Company, single-label, 12-ounce, high-profile or quart cone top, yellow and green can, horseshoe, INTERNAL REVENUE TAX PAID, single version of each.
12-ounce, ... $200
Quart, ...$225

Koenig Bräu Premium Beer, Prima-Bismarck Brewing Company, single-label, 12-ounce, high- or standard-profile cone or quart cone top, metallic gold can, white label, IRTP or non-IRTP, multiversions. *(See photo 129)*
Non-IRTP 12-ounce, ...$125
IRTP 12-ounce, ...$135
Quart, ...$175

Old Missouri Brand Beer, Prima Brewing Company, single-label, quart cone top, orange can, "OLD MISSOURI BRAND" on black band, INTERNAL REVENUE TAX PAID, single version. $300

Prima America's Finest Ale, Prima Brewing Company, single-label 12-ounce or quart cone top, blue can, white lettering, INTERNAL REVENUE TAX PAID, single version.
12-ounce, ...$100
Quart, ...$125

Prima America's Finest Beer, Prima Brewing Company, single-label, 12-ounce, high-profile or quart cone top, blue can, white lettering, INTERNAL REVENUE TAX PAID, multiversions.
12-ounce, ... $75
Quart, ...$100

SCHOENHOFEN-EDELWEISS COMPANY, 1900–1956 West 56th Street (aka: B. B. Brewing Company, Great Lakes Brewing Company, Trophy Brewing Company)

Cold Brau Eastern Premium Beer, Schoenhofen-Edelweiss Company, single-

Dorf Bohemian Lager Beer, Schoenhofen-Edelweiss or Great Lakes Brewing Company, two-label 12-ounce flat top, red or brown can, yellow or white label, multiversions.

Red can, ... $75
Brown can, ... $40

Edelweiss Bock Beer, Schoenhofen-Edelweiss Company, single-label 12-ounce flat top, brown can, goat's head, "BOCK" on red oval, single version. $90

Edelweiss Centennial Brew, Schoenhofen-Edelweiss Company, single-label 12-ounce flat top, white can, red bands, multiversions. $40

Edelweiss Light Beer, Schoenhofen-Edelweiss Company, single-label, 12-ounce, low- or high-profile cone or quart cone top, or 12-ounce flat top, red can, white label, INTERNAL REVENUE TAX PAID, multiversions.

12-ounce flat top, ... $40
12-ounce cone top, ... $85
Quart cone top, ...$125

Two-label 12-ounce flat top, white can, steins on label, multiversions. (*See photo 130*) $15

Edelweiss Malt Liquor, Schoenhofen-Edelweiss Company, single-label 12-ounce flat top, red can, black label outlined in metallic gold, single version. $110

Edelweiss Ritz Extra Dry Beer, Schoenhofen-Edelweiss Company, single-label 12-ounce cone top, metallic blue can, cream-colored label, single version.
.... $300

Edelweiss Stout Malt Liquor, Schoenhofen-Edelweiss Company, single-label 12-ounce flat top, red can, black label outlined in metallic gold, single version. (*See photo 131*) $125

Gold Coast Premium Beer, Schoenhofen-Edelweiss Company, single-label 16-ounce flat top, metallic gold can, white label, "HALF QUART" on white band, single version. $40

Golden Stein Eastern Premium Beer, Schoenhofen-Edelweiss Company, two-label 12-ounce flat top, white can, gold steins, single version. $85

Great Lakes Premium Beer, Schoenhofen-Edelweiss Company, single- or two-label 12-ounce flat top, blue can, silver stripes, map in silver, multiversions.
.... $35

Heritage Lager Beer, Schoenhofen-Edelweiss Company, two-label 12-ounce flat top, black can, red and black trim, multiversions. $60

K & J Private Club Beer, Schoenhofen-Edelweiss Company, single-label 12-ounce flat top, white can, metallic blue label, single version. $100

Photo 130 (left). Edelweiss Light Beer.
Photo 131 (right). Edelweiss Stout
Malt Liquor.

Katz Premium Beer, Schoenhofen-Edelweiss Company, two-label 12-ounce flat top, white can, red label outlined in metallic gold, multiversions. $25

Kol Premium Quality Beer, Schoenhofen-Edelweiss Company, white can, vertical silver stripes, blue label, single version. $25

Kold Brau Eastern Premium Beer, Schoenhofen-Edelweiss Company, white can, horizontal white stripes, blue label, multiversions. $40

Prost Pale Pilsener Eastern Beer, Schoenhofen-Edelweiss Company, two-label 12- or 16-ounce flat top, white can, large stein label, single version. $75

Salzburg Eastern Beer, Schoenhofen-Edelweiss Company, two-label 12-ounce flat top, white can, steins in box, single version. $100

SGA Premium Beer, Schoenhofen-Edelweiss Company, two-label 12-ounce flat top, white, blue, and metallic gold can, single version. $40

Trophy Beer, Trophy Brewing Company, single-label 12-ounce flat top, white can, metallic gold bands and trophy, single version. $75

Trophy Premium Beer, B. B. Brewing and Schoenhofen-Edelweiss Company, two-label 12-ounce flat top, yellow can, red bands, white label, minor versions. $50

SOUTH SIDE BREWING COMPANY, 3700 South Halstad

Ambrosia Lager Beer, single-label 12-ounce tall can, gold can, wide black and red bands, OPENING INSTRUCTIONS, INTERNAL REVENUE TAX PAID, single version..Exotic

Frederick's 4 Crown Lager Beer, single-label 12-ounce tall can, gold can, wide black and red bands, OPENING INSTRUCTIONS, INTERNAL REVENUE TAX PAID, single version...Exotic

Golden Armor Lager Beer, single-label 12-ounce tall can, gold and white can, knight on horseback, OPENING INSTRUCTIONS, INTERNAL REVENUE TAX PAID, single version...Exotic

UNITED STATES BREWING COMPANY, 2519 Elston Avenue

Rheingold Extra Pale Super Dry Beer, single-label 12-ounce flat top, metallic gold can, white label, "EXTRA PALE" in red, two versions. $75

VAN MERRITT BREWING COMPANY, 2419–2449 West 21st Street (aka: Bohemian Brewing Company)

Bohemian 93 Extra Dry Premium Beer, Bohemian Brewing Company, single-label 12-ounce flat top, white can, green, black, and gold label, single version. ....Exotic

Bohemian Club Old Fashioned Beer, Bohemian Brewing Company, two-label 12-ounce flat top, black can, red and gold label, multiversions. $75

Van Merritt Beer, Van Merritt Brewing Company, two-label 12-ounce flat top, white can, green bands, minor versions. $40

WESTMINSTER BREWING COMPANY, 3900 South Union Avenue (aka: Old Missouri Sales Company; Westminster Brewing Company, Prima Brewing Company successor)

English Lad Ale, single-label, 12-ounce high-profile cone or quart cone top, yellow can, black horseshoe, INTERNAL REVENUE TAX PAID, minor versions.
12-ounce, ... $150
Quart IRTP, ... $225

English Lad Beer, Westminster, Westminster, Prima Brewing successor, single-label, 12-ounce, high-profile cone or quart cone top, INTERNAL REVENUE TAX PAID, yellow can, black horseshoe, single-version 12-ounce, multiversions quart.
12-ounce, ... $150
Quart, ... $250

English Lad Beer, Westminster Brewing Company or Prima Brewing, single-label, 12-ounce, high-profile cone or quart cone top, yellow can, black horseshoe, INTERNAL REVENUE TAX PAID, single-version 12-ounce, multiversions quart.
12-ounce, ... $150
Quart, ... $250

Old Missouri Beer, Old Missouri Brewery Sales Company, single-label quart cone top, red can, black label, single version. $250

WHITE EAGLE BREWING COMPANY, 3755 South Racine Street

Chevalier Premium Beer, single-label, 12-ounce, high-profile cone top, metallic red can, white label, metallic gold trim, INTERNAL REVENUE TAX PAID, minor versions. .... Exotic

Freeport

FRITZ BREWING COMPANY, 293–321 East Stephenson Street

Fritz Brew Beer, single-label, 12 ounce, low-profile cone top, orange can, black castle, "FRITZ BREW" in white, single version. $250

Joliet

BOHEMIAN BREWING COMPANY, 100–104 Collins Street (aka: Van Merritt Brewing Company)

Bohemian 93 Extra Dry Beer, Bohemian Brewing Company, single-label 12-ounce flat top, white can, metallic gold bands and label, black trim, single version. $75

Bohemian Club Old Fashioned Beer, Bohemian Brewing Company, single-label 12-ounce flat top, black can, red bands, red and gold label, multiversions. $40

Van Merritt Beer, Van Merritt Brewing Company, single- or two-label 12-ounce flat top, white can, green oval, windmill, single version both labels.
Single-label, ... $40
Two-label, ... $25

Peoria

GIPPS BREWING CORPORATION, 500 South Water Street

Gipps Amberlin Beer, single-label, 12-ounce, high-profile cone top, yellow can, metallic gold stripes, red label, green ribbon, single version. $100
Gipps Amberlin Light Lager Beer, single-label, 12-ounce, high-profile cone top, white can, metallic gold stripes, red label, green ribbon, INTERNAL REVENUE TAX PAID, single version. $115
Gipps Premium Quality Beer, single-label, 12-ounce, high-profile cone top, yellow can, white label outlined in metallic gold, single version. $485

Peoria Heights

PABST BREWING COMPANY, 3421 Prospect Road (aka: Premium-Pabst Corporation)

Big Cat Malt Liquor, Pabst Brewing Company, two-label 12-ounce zip tab, white can, running cat, "BIG CAT" in red, vertical stripes, single version. ...$3
Blatz Milwaukee's Finest Beer, Pabst Brewing Company, two-label 12- or 16-ounce flat top, gold can, black or maroon triangle, multiversions.
12-ounce, ... $10
16-ounce, ... $15
Blatz Milwaukee's Finest Bock, Pabst Brewing Company, two-label 12-ounce flat top, gold can, maroon label, "BOCK" outside triangle, single version. . $30
Eastside Old Tap Brand Lager Beer, Pabst Brewing Company, two-label 12-ounce flat top, white can, red label, gold eagle, single version. $10
Old Tankard Ale, Premium-Pabst Corporation, single-label 12-ounce flat top, silver can, black silhouette of standing man, OPENING INSTRUCTIONS, INTERNAL REVENUE TAX PAID, minor versions. $75
Pabst Blue Ribbon Beer, Pabst Brewing Company, single-label 12-ounce flat top, camouflage can, single version. $200
Single-label 12-ounce flat top, silver can, blue band, "PABST" in red, INTERNAL REVENUE TAX PAID, multiversions. $60
Two-label 12-ounce flat top or quart cone top, silver or gold checkerboard can, white label, blue ribbon, multiversions.
12-ounce flat top, ... $35
Quart cone top, ... $60
Two-label 12-ounce flat top, blue can, white label, multiversions. $30
Two-label 12- or 16-ounce flat or tab top, white can, red ribbon, multiversions. Up to $5
Pabst Blue Ribbon was also produced in aluminum cans at this brewery. Collector value is $1.

Pabst Blue Ribbon Bock Beer, Pabst Brewing Company, two-label 12-ounce flat top, yellow can, blue ribbon combined into goat, single label. $75

Two-label 12-ounce flat top, gold can, white label, "BOCK" on blue ribbon, two versions. $60

Brand also was canned in aluminum cans. Collector value is $1.

Pabst Blue Ribbon Export Beer, Premier-Pabst Brewing Company, single-label 12-ounce flat top, gray can, blue band, "PABST" in red, OPENING INSTRUCTIONS, INTERNAL REVENUE TAX PAID, single version. $75

Pabst Old Tankard Ale, Premier-Pabst Corporation, single-label 12-ounce flat top, gray can, black silhouette of man, OPENING INSTRUCTIONS, INTERNAL REVENUE TAX PAID, single version. $100

Pabst Brewing Company, two-label 12-ounce flat top, gold can, metallic gold bands, "PABST" in red, single version. $35

Red White & Blue Special Lager Beer was produced in aluminum cans. Collector value is $1.

Peru

STAR UNION PRODUCTS COMPANY, Brewster and Pike Streets

Star Model Premium Quality Beer, single-label 12-ounce flat top, white can, large red metallic ribbon, single version. (*See photo 132*) $50

Springfield

REISCH BREWING COMPANY, 733 North Rutledge Street

Reisch Beer, two-label 12-ounce flat or tab top, white can, metallic red oval and stripe, single version. $60

Reisch Gold Top Beer, two-label 12-ounce crowntainer, orange can, "GOLD TOP" in red, INTERNAL REVENUE TAX PAID, single version. $125

Two-label, 12-ounce, high-profile cone top, metallic gold can, red label, two versions. $75

Thorton

FREDERICK'S BREWING COMPANY, Blackstone and Homewood-Lansing Road (successor to Illinois Brewing Company)

Frederick's Extra Pale Beer, single-label, 12-ounce, J-spout cone top, red can, white label, INTERNAL REVENUE TAX PAID, "Canned for FREDERICK BROS. BREWING COMPANY CHICAGO," single version. .... Unique

Pilsener Type Light Lager Beer, single-label, 12-ounce, J-spout cone top, white can, "PILSENER" on red label, INTERNAL REVENUE TAX PAID, single version. .... Exotic

Photo 132 (left). Star Model Premium Quality Beer.
Photo 133 (right). Burgermeister Premium Beer.

ILLINOIS BREWING COMPANY, Blackstone and Homewood-Lansing Road

Pilsener Type Light Lager Beer, single-label, 12-ounce, J-spout cone top, IN-TERNAL REVENUE TAX PAID, white can, "PILSENER" on red label, single version.
....Unique

Warsaw

WARSAW BREWING CORPORATION, 920 North 6th Street

Burgermeister Pilsener Beer, single-label, 12-ounce, high-profile cone top or 12-ounce flat top, white can, red label, gold bands, INTERNAL REVENUE TAX PAID, multiversions.
Cone top, ...$100
Flat top, ...$65

Burgermeister Premium Beer, single-label 12-ounce flat or tab top, white can, red label, gold band, multiversions. (*See photo 133*)............................$50

Kol Beer, single-label 12-ounce tab top, metallic blue and metallic gold can, red trim, single version. $60

Old Tavern Premium Lager Beer, single-label 12-ounce flat, zip, or tab top, white can, hunting scene, multiversions..$40

Indiana

Evansville

ASSOCIATED BREWING COMPANY, 1301 Pennsylvania (successors to Sterling Brewers, Inc.; aka: Sterling Brewers, Inc., Bavarian Brewing Company)

9-0-5 Premium Beer, Associated Brewing Company, single-label 12-ounce tab top, blue can, round red label, horseback rider, multiversions. *(See photo 134)* $5

20 Grand Select Cream Ale, Sterling Brewers or Associated Brewing Company, two-label 12-ounce tab top, metallic green can, yellow label, multiversions. *(See photo 135)*.. $10

Bavarian's Select Beer, Bavarian Brewing Company, single-label 12-ounce tab top, yellow can, yellow label outlined in metallic gold, multiversions. $10

Champagne Velvet Beer, Associated Brewing Company, two-label 12- or 16-ounce tab top, metallic gold can, white champagne glass label, multiversions. *(See photo 136)*.. $10

Photo 134 (left). 9-0-5 Premium Beer.
Photo 135 (center). 20 Grand Select
Cream Ale. Photo 136 (right).
Champagne Velvet Beer.

Photo 137. Redtop Beer.

Champagne Velvet Malt Liquor, Associated Brewing Company, two-label 12-ounce aluminum flat top, metallic gold can, "CHAMPAGNE VELVET" in white, single version. $10

Cook's Goldblume Export Beer, Associated Brewing Company, two-label 12- or 16-ounce tab top, white can, "COOK'S" and label in red, multiversions. $5

Lederbrau Genuine Draft Beer, Associated Brewing Company, two-label gallon can, metallic brown can, large glass of beer label, single version. $300

Mickey's Fine Malt Liquor, Associated Brewing Company, single-label 12- or 16-ounce tab top, white can, metallic gold and green can, single version. $5

Pfeiffer 1889 Draught Beer, Associated Brewing Company, two-label gallon can, woodgrain can, brown label, multiversions. $400

Pfeiffer Famous Beer, Associated Brewing Company, two-label 12-ounce tab top, woodgrain can, metallic gold bands, multiversions. $5

Redtop Beer, Associated Brewing Company, two-label 12-ounce tab top, black can, red label, white stripe, single version. *(See photo 137)*.................... $10

Regal Famous Premium Beer, Associated Brewing Company or Sterling Brewers, two-label 12-ounce tab top, white can, red label, metallic gold trim, multiversions. $5

Schmidt Extra Special Beer, Associated Brewing Company, two-label 12-ounce tab top, white can, red label, "DRAFT" in yellow, single version. $5

SGA Premium Beer, Associated Brewing Company, two-label 12-ounce tab top, white can, metallic blue and gold trim, single version. $5

Sterling Premium Pilsner Beer, Associated Brewing Company, two-label 12-ounce tab top, white can, oval red label, multiversions. $10
Brand was also produced in aluminum cans. Collector value is $2.

Sterling Premium Pilsner Draft Beer, Sterling Brewers, two-label 12-ounce tab top, woodgrain can, "STERLING" in white, single version. $20

Tropical Extra Fine Ale, Associated Brewing Company, two-label 12-ounce tab top, metallic gold can, white label, minor versions. $10

F. W. COOK COMPANY, INC., 11 Northwest 7th Street

Cook's 500 Ale, single-label, 12-ounce, high-profile cone top or two-label 12-ounce flat top, metallic green can, checkered flag, race car, single version of each.
Flat top, ... $100
Cone top, ... $150

Cook's Goldblume Beer, single-label, 12-ounce, high-profile cone top, multi-colored can, riverboat scene, multiversions. $100

Single-label, 12-ounce, high-profile cone top, white can, wide blue vertical stripe, multiversions. $85

Tropical Extra Fine Ale, two-label 12-ounce flat top, metallic gold can, white label, single version. *(See photo 138)* $20

G. HEILEMAN BREWING COMPANY, 1301 Pennsylvania Street (successor to Associated Brewing Company)

Atlas Prager Bohemian Light Lager Beer, two-label 12-ounce tab top, red, white, and blue can, single version. $2

Blatz Milwaukee's Finest Beer, two-label 12-ounce tab top, white can, brown trim, single version. $2

Champagne Velvet Beer, two-label 12-ounce tab top, gold can, white champagne glass label, single version. $2

Drewrys Beer, two-label 12-ounce tab top, silver can, red ribbon, black trim, multiversions. $2

Drewrys Draft Beer, two-label 12-ounce tab top, silver can, white label, blue ribbon, single version. $2

Edelweiss Light Beer, two-label 12- or 16-ounce tab top, white can, large steins, multiversions. $2

Great Lakes Premium Beer, two-label 12-ounce tab top, blue can, silver map of Great Lakes, single version. *(See photo 139)* $3

Home Dry Lager Beer, two-label 12-ounce tab top, white can, red label, single version. $3

Old Dutch Brand The Good Beer, two-label 12-ounce tab top, white can, multicolored label, red bands, multiversions. *(See photo 140)* $3

Sterling Premium Pilsner Beer, two-label 12- or 16-ounce tab top, silver can, red ribbon, multiversions..$3

Sterling Pure Beer, two-label 12- or 16-ounce tab top, silver can, red ribbon, "STERLING" in white, multiversions. $2

Sterling Beer produced two sets of Kentucky Derby winners, one can for each year from 1962–1976. One set listed the horse and jockey, while the other set listed the horse only.

Horse and Jockey: Individual cans, ...$5

Full set, ...$85

Photo 138 (left). Tropical Extra Fine Ale. Photo 139 (center). Great Lakes Premium Beer. Photo 140 (right). Old Dutch Brand, The Good Beer.

Horse Only: Individual cans, ...$5
   Full set, ... $85

A series of four cans, called "Landmark" series, was also produced in aluminum. The value of the set is $25.

G. Heileman produced all their brands in aluminum after 1973. Most Heileman national or multiregional brands were produced at the Evansville plant until it closed in 1987. Value of nonlisted cans will not exceed $2.

STERLING BREWERS, INC., 1301 Pennsylvania Avenue (aka: Sterling Brewers, F. W. Cook)

20 Grand Select Cream Ale, Sterling Brewers, two-label 12-ounce tab top, metallic green can, yellow label, single version. $10

Cook's Goldblume Export Beer, Sterling Brewers, two-label 12-ounce tab top, white can, red label, "COOK'S" in red, multiversions. $10

Mickey's Fine Malt Liquor, Sterling Brewers, single-label 12- or 16-ounce tab top, white can, green and metallic gold label, single version. $10

Mickey's Malt Liquor, Sterling Brewers, two-label 8-ounce flat top, green can, white label, single version. $100

Sterling Ale, Sterling Brewers, single-label 12-ounce flat top, gold can, yellow label, OPENING INSTRUCTIONS, INTERNAL REVENUE TAX PAID, single version.
.... $300

Sterling Brewers, two-label 12-ounce flat top, metallic green can, old man with glass of beer, multiversions. $125

Sterling Draught Ale, Sterling Brewers, two-label gallon can, woodgrain can, red oval, "DRAUGHT ALE" in white, single version. $600

Sterling Draught Beer, Sterling Brewers, two-label gallon can, woodgrain can, red oval, "DRAUGHT BEER" in white, single version. $500

Sterling Pilsner Beer, Sterling Brewers, single-label 12-ounce flat top, IRTP and non-IRTP, white can, red oval, "STERLING" in white, single version of each.
IRTP, ...$100
Non-IRTP, ... $85

Sterling Premium Pilsner Beer, Sterling Brewers, two-label 12- or 16-ounce flat or tab top, white can, red oval label, multiversions. $20

Sterling Premium Pilsner Draft Beer, Sterling Brewers, two-label 12-ounce tab top, woodgrain can, red oval, trimmed in metallic gold, multiversions. *(See photo 141)* $30

Photo 141. Sterling Premium Pilsner Draft Beer.

Sterling Premium Quality Pilsner Beer, Sterling Brewers, two-label 12-ounce tab top, flecked white can, red oval, blue band, multiversions. $35

Sterling Super Blu Pilsner Beer, Sterling Brewers, single-label 12-ounce flat top, flecked white can, red oval, OPENING INSTRUCTIONS, INTERNAL REVENUE TAX PAID, single version. $65

Tropical Extra Fine Ale, F. W. Cook, two-label 12-ounce tab top, white can, metallic gold stripes, green label, single version. $35

Fort Wayne

BERGHOFF BREWING COMPANY, 1025 Grant Street

Berghoff 1887 Beer, single-label, 12-ounce, high- or low-profile cone top, black can, orange and yellow stripes, multiversions. *(See photo 142)*
Non-IRTP, ... $65
IRTP, ... $75
WITHDRAWN FREE, ... $90

Berghoff 1887 Pale Extra Dry Beer, single-label, 12-ounce, high-profile cone or flat top, white can, red and gold label, American eagle, multiversions. .. $60

Berghoff Ale, single-label 12-ounce flat top, green can, white label outlined in metallic gold, single version. $150

Berghoff Light Beer, single-label 12-ounce flat top, white can, red and metallic gold label, single version. $65

Berghoff Malt Liquor, two-label 12-ounce flat top, white can, metallic gold band, "BERGHOFF" in red, single version. $250

Hoff-Brau Light Beer, two-label 12-ounce flat top, red can, white label, white oval, single version. $75

CENTLIVRE BREWING CORPORATION, 2501–2531 Spy Run Avenue

Alps Brau Bavarian Style Beer, two-label 12-ounce flat top, blue can, white mountain, gold or silver bands, single version of each. Either version, ... $20

Centlivre Beer, single-label 12-ounce flat top, metallic gold can, red and black label, "CENTLIVRE" in white, OPENING INSTRUCTIONS, INTERNAL REVENUE TAX PAID, single version. $300

Old Crown Ale, single-label 12-ounce flat top, metallic gold can, yellow label, "O," "C," "A" in red, OPENING INSTRUCTIONS, INTERNAL REVENUE TAX PAID, single version. $200

Old Crown Beer, single-label 12-ounce flat top, yellow can, metallic gold bands, red label, OPENING INSTRUCTIONS, INTERNAL REVENUE TAX PAID, single version. $200

Old Crown Bock Beer, two-label 12-ounce flat top, brown can, white label, goat's head, single version. $10

Old Crown Light Dry Beer, single-label 12-ounce flat top, white can, red label outlined in gold, multiversions. $20

Photo 142 (left). Berghoff 1887 Beer.
Photo 143 (right). Falstaff Beer.

Old Crown Premium Quality Ale, single-label 12-ounce flat top, set of four cans known as "Rainbow" set, crown, green label outlined in white, "LAZY AGED," can colors: copper, yellow, green, and gold. $75

Single-label 12-ounce flat top, set of 10 cans known as "Rainbow" set, crown, green label outlined in white, no "LAZY AGED," can colors: violet, green, yellow, gold, purple, copper, dark blue, blue, light blue, red. Each, ... $75

Single-label 12-ounce flat top, set of seven cans know as "Rainbow" set, crown, white label, enamel lettering, can colors: orange, dark blue, blue, red, violet, green, purple. Each, ... $65

Single-label 12-ounce flat top, set of cans known as "Rainbow" set, crown, white label, metallic green lettering, can color: green. (Set was discontinued when brewery was sold to new owners, Old Crown Brewing Corporation. One can was issued.) $75

FALSTAFF BREWING CORPORATION, 1019–1051 Grant Avenue (successor to Berghoff Brewing Corporation)

Falstaff Beer, single-label 12- or 16-ounce flat top, white can, gold and brown Falstaff shield, "THE CHOICEST PRODUCT OF THE BREWERS ART," multiversions.. $10

Two-label 12- or 16-ounce flat, zip, or tab top, white can, gold and brown Falstaff shield, gold bands, "AMERICA'S PREMIUM QUALITY BEER," multiversions. *(See photo 143)*.. $10

Two-label 12- or 16-ounce tab top, white can, Falstaff shield, "FOR OVER FOUR GENERATIONS . . . ," multiversions. $5

Falstaff Draft Beer, two-label 12- or 16-ounce tab top, white can, Falstaff shield, "DRAFT" on blue ribbon, single version. $10

Falstaff produced aluminum cans from 1974 until closing, and produced 50 or more brands with a collector value of up to $5.

HOFF-BRAU BREWING COMPANY, 2226–32 Dwenger Street

Hoff-Brau Ale, single-label, 12-ounce, high-profile cone top, white can, metallic gold bands, green label, IRTP or non-IRTP.
Non-IRTP, ...$150
IRTP, ...$175

Hoff-Brau Beer, single-label 12-ounce crowntainer, silver can, red label, INTERNAL REVENUE TAX PAID, single version. $150

Hoff-Brau Pilsner Beer, single-label, 12-ounce, high-profile cone top, white can, gold bands, red label, single version. $140

Hoff-Brau Gold Star Beer, single-label, 12-ounce, high-profile cone top, metallic gold can, orange label, silver star, single version. $100

Hoff-Brau Golden Ale, two-label 12-ounce crowntainer, silver can, black shield, single version. $400

OLD CROWN BREWING CORPORATION, 2501–2531 Spy Run Avenue (successor to Centlivre Brewing Corporation)

Alps Brau Bavarian Style Premium Beer, two-label 12-ounce flat or tab top, blue can, white mountain, metallic gold stripes, single version of each. Either top, ... $10

Old Crown Bock Beer, two-label 12-ounce tab top, brown can, white label outlined in yellow, goat's head, multiversions. $15

Old Crown Light Dry Beer, two-label 12-ounce flat or tab top, white can, crown, red label, multiversions. $10

Old Crown Premium Quality Ale, two-label 12-ounce flat or tab top, green can, white pinstripes, white label, crown, single version of each top.
Flat top, ... $60
Tab top, ... $50

Two-label 12-ounce tab top, gold can, green label outlined in white, crown, multiversions. $12

Old German Style Beer, single-label 12-ounce flat or tab top, white can, red label, gold trim, single version of each. $10

Renner Golden Amber Beer, single-label 12-ounce flat or tab top, white can, red label, wide metallic gold band, single version of each. *(See photo 144)*. $20

Van Merritt Beer, two-label 12-ounce flat or tab top, white can, green oval, windmill, multiversions. $20

Indianapolis
INDIANAPOLIS BREWING COMPANY, 316 Agnes Street

Crown Select Beer, single-label 12-ounce flat top, white can, red label, "BEER" in red, blue lettering, INTERNAL REVENUE TAX PAID, single version. $400

Gold Medal Lager Beer, single-label 12-ounce flat top, metallic gold can, red label, "GOLD MEDAL" in white, OPENING INSTRUCTIONS, INTERNAL REVENUE TAX PAID, multiversions. .... Exotic

Progress Brand Beer, single-label 12-ounce flat top, red and white can, world globe, OPENING INSTRUCTIONS, INTERNAL REVENUE TAX PAID, single version. .... Exotic

Lafayette
LAFAYETTE BREWING COMPANY, 736–814 North 4th Street

Kopper Kettle Beer, single-label, 12-ounce, high-profile cone top, metallic gold can, yellow label, INTERNAL REVENUE TAX PAID, multiversions. $300

Photo 144 (left). Renner Golden Amber Beer.
Photo 145 (right). Schmidt's First Premium
Lager Beer.

Tavern Beer, single-label, 12-ounce, high-profile cone top, white can, metallic gold bands, horse and coach, IRTP and non-IRTP.
Non-IRTP, ... $175
IRTP, ... $200

Loganport

K. G. SCHMIDT BREWING COMPANY, 412–426 High Street

Schmidt's First Premium Lager Beer, single-label, 12-ounce, high-profile cone top, green can, "SCHMIDT FIRST PREMIUM" in white on green ribbon, minor versions. *(See photo 145)* $175

Marion

FOX BREWING COMPANY, 1500 Railroad Avenue

Fox Deluxe Beer, single-label, 12-ounce, high-profile cone top or quart cone top, metallic gold can, white label, hunter with horn, multiversion 12-ounce, single-version quart.
12-ounce, ... $125
Quart, ... $250

Silver Fox Beer, single-label, 12-ounce, high-profile cone or quart cone top, silver can, red oval label, "SILVER FOX" in black, single version of each size.
12-ounce, ... $125
Quart, ... $175

Mishawaka

KAMM & SCHELLINGER COMPANY, INC., North Center Street

Kamm's Pilsener Light Beer, single-label J-spout cone top or 12-ounce flat top, metallic gold and red checkerboard can, red label, INTERNAL REVENUE TAX PAID, single version of each.
Cone top, ... $300
Flat top, ... $200

Two-label 12-ounce crowntainer, silver can, red label outlined in orange, INTERNAL REVENUE TAX PAID, multiversions. $125

South Bend

ASSOCIATED BREWING COMPANY, 1408 Elwood Avenue (successor to Drewrys Ltd. USA; aka: Associated Brewing, Atlantic Brewing Company, Frankenmuth Brewing Company, Pfeiffer Brewing Company, Piels Bros. Brewing Company)

Atlas Prager Bohemian Light Lager Beer, Associated Brewing, two-label 12-ounce tab top, white can, red label, dancing man, blue trim, single version. .$5

Barbarossa Beer, Atlantic Brewing Company, single-label 12-ounce flat top, metallic gold can, white label, "BARBAROSSA" in black, single version. $15

Champagne Velvet Beer, Atlantic Brewing Company, two-label 16-ounce tab top, gold can, white champagne glass, single version. $20

Drewrys Beer, Associated Brewing, two-label 12- or 16-ounce tab top, red can, white oval label outlined in metallic gold and black, multiversions. $10

Brand was also produced in aluminum cans with a collector value of up to $2.

Drewrys Draft Beer, Associated Brewing, two-label 12- or 16-ounce tab top, gold can, yellow label, brown ribbon, single version of each size. *(See photo 146)*... $10

Brand was also produced in aluminum cans with a collector value of up to $2.

Edelweiss Light Beer, Drewrys Ltd. or Associated Brewing, two-label 12- or 16-ounce tab top, white can, three steins, "EDELWEISS" in orange, multiversions...$5

Brand was also produced in aluminum cans with a collector value of up to $2.

Frankenmuth Bock Beer, Frankenmuth Brewing, two-label 12-ounce tab top, brown and yellow hatched can, yellow label, single version. $40

Great Lakes Premium Beer, Associated Brewing, two-label 12-ounce tab top, blue can, silver map of Great Lakes, multiversions. $10

Katz Premium Beer, Associated Brewing, two-label 12-ounce flat top, white can, red label outlined in metallic gold, black cat, multiversions. $10

Old Dutch Brand Beer, Old Dutch Brewing Company, two-label 12-ounce tab top, white can, red bands, multicolored label, single version. $10

Pfeiffer Famous Beer, Pfeiffer Brewing Company, two-label 12-ounce flat top, woodgrain can, metallic gold stripes, multiversions. $10

Piels Light Lager Beer, Piels Bros. Brewing, single-label 12-ounce flat top, white can, silver bands, "PIELS" in red, single version. $10

Photo 146. Drewrys Draft Beer.

Redtop Beer, Associated Brewing, two-label 12-ounce tab top, black can, white stripe, red label, multiversions. $12

SGA Premium Beer, Associated Brewing, two-label 12-ounce tab top, metallic gold, blue, and white can, blue triangle, single version. $10

DREWRYS LTD. USA, 1408 Elwood Avenue (aka: Drewrys Ltd.,
Atlantic Brewing Company, Frankenmuth Brewing Company, Great Lakes Brewing Company, Old Dutch Brewing Company, Pfeiffer Brewing Company, 9–0–5 Brewing Company, Red Top Brewing Company, Schoenhofen-Edelweiss)

9–0–5 Premium Beer, Drewrys Ltd. and 9–0–5 Brewing Company, two-label 12- or 16-ounce flat or tab top, white can, "9–0–5" in white on red circle label, multiversions.
12-ounce, ... $20
16-ounce, ... $30

All American Extra Dry Beer, Drewrys Ltd., two-label 12- or 16-ounce flat top, blue and white can, sports scenes, single versions.
12-ounce, ... $40
16-ounce, ... $50

Barbarossa Beer, Atlantic Brewing Company, single-label 12-ounce flat top, metallic gold can, white label, "BARBAROSSA" in black, single version. $20

Bull Dog Malt Liquor, Drewrys Ltd., two-label 8- or 12-ounce flat, tab, or zip top, gold can, white label, white dog's head on blue circle, multiversions.
8-ounce, ... $60
12-ounce, ... $75

Champagne Velvet Beer, Atlantic Brewing Company, two-label 16-ounce tab top, metallic gold can, white champagne glass, metallic gold crown on blue band, minor versions. $40

Cold Brau Eastern Premium Beer, Drewrys Ltd. or Schoenhofen-Edelweiss, two-label 12- or 16-ounce flat or tab top, white can, blue label and stripes, "COLD BRAU" in white, multiversions.
12-ounce, ... $30
16-ounce, ... $40

Dorf Bohemian Lager Beer, Drewrys Ltd., two-label 12- or 16-ounce flat or tab top, brown can, white label, large stein, "DORF" in red, multiversions.
.... $40

Drewrys Ale, Drewrys Ltd., single-label 12-ounce flat top, metallic gold can, mountie and horse, OPENING INSTRUCTIONS, INTERNAL REVENUE TAX PAID, multiversions. $125

Drewrys Beer, Drewrys Ltd., two-label 12- or 16-ounce flat, zip, or tab top, white can, orange label, white shield on red band, mountie on shield, multiversions.
12-ounce, ... $15
16-ounce, ... $15

Two-label 12- or 16-ounce tab top, silver can, red ribbon, white label, "THE AMERICAN BEER WITH THE GERMAN ACCENT," multiversions. $7

Drewrys Draft, Drewrys Ltd., two-label 12-ounce tab top, gold can, yellow label, brown ribbon, single version. $10

Drewrys Extra Dry Beer, Drewrys Ltd., single-label 12-ounce flat top, 12-can set, cans called "Sports" series, two versions: oval and shield labels, six colors: blue, yellow, red, bronze, green, purple. $40

Single-label 12-ounce flat top, 24-can set, cans called "Horoscope" series, 12 cans showing zodiac signs in two colors each, colors: gold, green, bronze, orange, blue, purple, red, pink. $40

Single-label 12- or 16-ounce flat top, a 12-can 12-ounce and a six-can 16-ounce set, called "Your Character" series, versions: square face/round face, forehead/eyes, eyebrow/chin, dimples/lips, heart-shaped face/oval face, ear/nose, eyebrows/chin, colors: blue, purple, bronze, red, green, blue, orange.
12-ounce, ... $40
16-ounce, ... $65

Single-label 12- or 16-ounce flat top, white can, white or blue shield label with small mountie, multiversions. All versions, ... $15

Drewrys Genuine Bock Beer, Drewrys Ltd., single-label 12-ounce flat or zip top, light orange or red shield label with mountie, single version of each. .. $30

Drewrys Lager Beer, Drewrys Ltd., single-label 12-ounce flat top, silver can, mountie with horse, black lettering, OPENING INSTRUCTIONS, INTERNAL REVENUE TAX PAID, two versions. $60

Drewrys Malt Liquor, Drewrys Ltd., single-label 12-ounce flat top, yellow and black can, malt liquor on red band, single version. .... Exotic

Drewrys Old Stock Ale, Drewrys Ltd., single-label 12-ounce flat top, green can, gold label outlined in white, mountie, IRTP and non-IRTP.
IRTP, ... $60
Non-IRTP, ... $50

Single-label 12-ounce flat or tab top, black can with gold or white bands top and bottom, multiversions.
Gold bands, ... $40
White bands, ... $20

Drewrys Stout Malt Liquor, Drewrys Ltd., single-label 12-ounce flat top, gold and black can, "STOUT MALT LIQUOR" on red ribbon, single version. .... Exotic

Eastern Premium Beer, Drewrys Ltd., two-label 12-ounce flat top, white can, dark blue label, skyline, single version. $125

Edelweiss Bock Beer, Schoenhofen-Edelweiss, single-label 12-ounce flat top, brown can, white label and bands, "BOCK" in red oval, single version. $85

Edelweiss Light Beer, Drewrys Ltd., single-label 12- or 16-ounce flat or tab top, white can, stein label, "EDELWEISS" in orange, multiversions.
"Cheery-Beery," $20
All others, ... $5

F & G Supreme Lager Beer, Drewrys Ltd., two-label 12-ounce zip top, white can, red label, metallic gold trim, single version. $200

Frankenmuth Bock Beer, Frankenmuth Brewing, single-label 12-ounce tab top, yellow can and brown-hatched can, single version. $40

Friars Club Special Ale, Drewrys Ltd., single-label 12-ounce flat top, white can, brown and yellow label, single version. $50

Single-label 12-ounce flat top, white can, brown and yellow label, "CLUB SPE-CIAL ALE" in black, single version. $70

Ges Premium Beer, Drewrys Ltd., single-label 12-ounce flat top, white can, blue eagle, "PREMIUM BEER" in red, single version. $100

Gold Coast Premium Beer, Drewrys Ltd., two-label 12- or 16-ounce flat top, gold can, white label, "GOLD COAST" in red, single version each size.
12-ounce, ... $60
16-ounce, ... $85

Great Lakes Premium Beer, Drewrys Ltd. and Great Lakes Brewing, two-label 12-ounce flat or tab top, blue can, silver stripes and map of lakes, multiversions. $25

Heritage Lager Beer, Drewrys Ltd., two-label 12-ounce flat top, black or blue can, white label, "LAGER BEER" in red, single version each color.
Black can, ... $60
Blue can, ... $75

Home Bock Beer, Drewrys Ltd., two-label 12-ounce flat top, white can, brown label outlined in metallic gold, single version. $75

Home Old Style Ale, Drewrys Ltd., two-label 12-ounce flat top, white can, green label outlined in metallic gold, single version. $75

K & J Private Club Beer, Drewrys Ltd., single-label 12-ounce flat top, white can, metallic blue label, single version. $150

Katz Premium Beer, Drewrys Ltd., two-label 12- or 16-ounce flat or tab top, white can, red label, black cat, single version. $15

Leisy's Light Full Flavored Beer, Drewrys Ltd., two-label 12-ounce flat top, blue can, yellow label, silver bands and eagle, single version. $100

McLab Eastern Premium Beer, Drewrys Ltd., two-label 12-ounce flat top, white can, steins outlined in red blocks, single version. $60

Prost Pale Pilsner Eastern Premium Beer, Drewrys Ltd., two-label 12-ounce flat top, white can, large stein label, "PROST" on red ribbon, single version. $65

Redtop Beer, Drewrys Ltd. or Redtop Brewing, single-label 12-ounce flat or tab top, silver can, red and white label, single version of each top. $30

Drewrys Ltd. only, two-label 12-ounce tab top, black can, white or yellow stripe, red label, single version of each. $20

Regal Famous Premium Beer, Drewrys Ltd., two-label 12-ounce flat top, white can, red label outlined in metallic gold, single version. $15

Salzburg Eastern Beer, Drewrys Ltd., two-label 12-ounce flat top, white can, steins in red box, single version. $75

SGA Premium Beer, Drewrys Ltd. or Schoenhofen-Edelweiss, two-label 12-ounce flat top, white can, metallic gold and blue label, multiversions. $20

Skol Eastern Premium Beer, Drewrys Ltd., two-label 12- or 16-ounce flat top, white can, steins, "SKOL" in red, single version.
12-ounce, ... $35
16-ounce, ... $25

Tavern Pale Dry Beer, Atlantic Brewing, two-label 12-ounce flat or tab top, blue can, red label outlined in metallic gold, single version of each. $30

Trophy Beer, Drewrys Ltd., two-label 12-ounce flat top, yellow and black can, white label, red bands, single version. $20

Volks Brau Pale Dry Eastern Beer, Drewrys Ltd., two-label 12- or 16-ounce flat top, white can, large blue stein label, "VOLKS" on red stripe, single version. $50

SOUTH BEND BREWING COMPANY, 739 College Avenue

Hoosier Fine Quality Beer, single-label high-profile cone top, red can, gold bands, single version. $300

Terre Haute

TERRE HAUTE BREWING COMPANY, 440 South 9th Street

20 Grand Select Cream Ale, two-label 12-ounce flat top, white and green hatched can, label outlined in yellow, single version. $85

'76 Ale, single-label high-profile cone top, green can, yellow label, "76" in red, IRTP and non-IRTP. $300

Blackhawk Premium Beer, two-label 12-ounce flat top, silver can, thin blue stripes, red Indian head, single version. $400

Champagne Velvet Brand Beer, single-label, 12-ounce, high-profile cone or flat top, gold can, yellow label, "CV '52 ENJOY IT," "CV '52 TRY IT," multiversions of each.
Cone top, ... $75
Flat top, ... $60

Champagne Velvet Brand Gold Label Beer, single-label, 12-ounce, high-profile cone top or two-label 12-ounce flat top, gold can, white champagne glass. *(See photo 147)*
Cone top, ... $85
Flat top, ... $60

Champagne Velvet Brand Premium Pilsner Beer, single-label, 12-ounce, J-spout or high-profile cone, or single-label quart cone top, IRTP, non-IRTP, or WITHDRAWN FREE, gold can, yellow label, black lettering, "THERE IS NO FINER BEER," multiversions. *(See photo 148)*
IRTP, ... $75

Photo 147. Champagne Velvet Brand Gold Label Beer.

Photo 148. Champagne Velvet Brand Premium Pilsner Beer.

Non-IRTP, ... $60
WITHDRAWN FREE, ... $100
Quart, ... $100

Champagne Velvet Gold Label Beer, two-label 12-ounce flat top, set of seven cans, metallic cans, white champagne glasses, colors: metallic green, light blue, dark blue, silver, gold, red, purple. Each, ... $60

Redtop Beer, two-label 12-ounce flat top, white-and-red-hatched can, red label, "PROVED PREMIUM QUALITY," minor versions. $75

Iowa

Davenport

BLACKHAWK BREWING COMPANY, 1801 West 3rd Street

Blackhawk Old Lager Beer, single-label, 12-ounce, high-profile cone top, gold can, red label, "OLD LAGER" on red patch, single version. ....Exotic

Blackhawk Pilsner Beer, single-label, 12-ounce, high-profile cone or quart cone top, gold can, white label, small Indian head, INTERNAL REVENUE TAX PAID, multiversions.

12-ounce, ...$250
Quart, ... $400

Blackhawk Premium Beer, two-label 12-ounce flat top, white can, gold bands, red Indian head, single version. $100

Blackhawk Topping Beer, single-label, 12-ounce, high-profile cone or quart cone top, red can, yellow bands, black label, multiversions.

12-ounce, ... $200
Quart, ...$350

UCHTORFF BREWING COMPANY, 1801 West 3rd Street (successor to Blackhawk Brewing Company; aka: Savoy Brewing Company)

Blackhawk Premium Beer, two-label 12-ounce flat top, blue can, red Indian head, single version. $250

Brew 82 Extra Select Beer, two-label 12-ounce flat top, red can, blue oval label, single version. $75

Savoy Special Beer, Savoy Brewing Company, two-label 12-ounce flat top, silver can, blue label, single version. ....Exotic

Uchtorff Golden Harvest Pilsner Beer, two-label, 12-ounce, high-profile cone or flat top, gold and white can, brown label, single version of each.
Flat top, ... $150
Cone top, ... $300

Dubuque

Brewery at East 4th Street Extension opened in 1972 and has operated under various names, including Dubuque, Dubuque Star, and Joseph Pickett. Cans produced include steel tab tops and aluminum cans under a wide variety of labels. The collector value of these cans is up to $2.

Sioux City

KINGSBURY BREWING COMPANY, 1230 1st Street (successor to Sioux City Brewing Co.)

Kingsbury Pale Beer, two-label 12-ounce flat top, metallic red and gold can, yellow label, single version. $75

SIOUX CITY BREWING COMPANY, 1230 1st Street (predecessor to Kingsbury Brewing Company)

Ace Pilsner Beer, two-label 12-ounce flat top, white can, yellow label, "ACE" in blue, single version. $85

Ace Premium Beer, two-label 12-ounce flat top, red and gold can, "ACE" on black label, single version. $100

Heidel-Brau Mello Light Pilsner Beer, single-label, 12-ounce, high-profile cone top, gold and orange can, white label, multiversions. $100

Western Brew Premium Quality Beer, two-label 12-ounce flat top, white can, red label outlined in metallic gold, single version. $100

Kansas

/

Kansas never had any major breweries after Prohibition and therefore never canned beer.

Kentucky

Covington

BAVARIAN BREWING COMPANY, 520 West 4th Street

Bavarian's Old Style Beer, single-label, 12-ounce, high-profile cone or flat top, white can, metallic gold bands, red "B," IRTP and non-IRTP, single version of each.

IRTP cone, ... $100
Non-IRTP cone, ... $90
Flat top, ... $75

Bavarian's Select Beer, single-label 12-ounce flat top, white can, metallic gold circle, three triangles, multiversions. $30

INTERNATIONAL BREWERIES, INC., 520 West 4th Street (successor to Bavarian Brewing Company)

Bavarian's Select Beer, single-label 12-ounce flat or tab top, white can, gold round label, three triangles, multiversions. $25

International Frankenmuth Ale, two-label 12-ounce flat top, white can, green label, single version. $60

International Frankenmuth Beer, two-label 12-ounce flat or zip top, white can, metallic red label, single version of each. $50

International Frankenmuth Bock, two-label 12-ounce flat top, gold can, red label outlined in white, single version. $75

International Silver Bar Ale, two-label 12-ounce flat top, white can, dull green label, single version. $60

Stolz Premium Beer, two-label 12-ounce flat top, white can, gold trim, red lettering, single version. $75

Tropical Extra Fine Ale, two-label 12-ounce flat or zip top, white can, metallic gold bands, green label outlined in metallic gold, single version of each top. Either top,.. $15

Louisville

FALLS CITY BREWING COMPANY, 3024-3050 West Broadway

Billy Beer, two-label 12-ounce aluminum can, multiversions. $2

Falls City Beer, single-label 12-ounce flat top, red and metallic gold can, OPENING INSTRUCTIONS, INTERNAL REVENUE TAX PAID, multiversions.
Camouflage can, ... $200
All others, ... $90

Single-label 12- or 16-ounce flat or zip top, red can, white oval, red label, multiversions... $20

Falls City Premium Quality Beer, single-label 12-ounce flat top, red and metallic gold can, red label, single version. $50

Falls City Brewing Company also produced Drummond Bros. Preferred Beer and Falls City Beer in aluminum cans. Collector value is up to $3.

FRANK FEHR BREWING COMPANY, 412 Fehr Avenue

Fehr's Liquid Gold Beer, single-label 12-ounce flat top, metallic gold can, white diamond label, single version. $40

Fehr's X/L Beer, single-label, 12-ounce J-spout, high-profile, or crowntainer, silver can, race horses, INTERNAL REVENUE TAX PAID, single version of each. $200

Single-label, 12-ounce, high-profile cone top, crowntainer, or flat top, silver or white can, red horseshoe, single version of each.
Silver can,...$125
White cone top,...$100
White flat top,... $75

Single-label 12-ounce flat top, white can, red block label, silver or gold bands, multiversions. $35

Kentucky Malt Liquor, two-label 12-ounce flat top, white can, metallic gold trim, multiversions. $70

FRANKENMUTH KENTUCKY BREWERY, 1431-1445 South 15th Street

Frankenmuth Air Free Beer, single-label, 12-ounce, high-profile cone top, yellow can, white label, single version...Exotic

OERTEL BREWING COMPANY, 1400-1408 Story Street

Kentucky Malt Liquor, two-label 12-ounce flat top, white can, label outlined with metallic gold band, single version.. $60

Oertel's 92 Beer, two-label 12-ounce flat top, metallic gold can, "OERTEL'S BEER" in white on red patch, multiversions. $40

Photo 149. Oertel's '92 Beer.

Two-label 12-ounce flat, zip, or tab top, white cans with or without silver bands, red label, multiversions. (*See photo 149*).. $20

Single-label 12- or 16-ounce tab top, gold can, red oval, white label, multiversions... $10

Oertel's 92 Lager Beer, single-label crowntainer, silver can, "92" on blue label, single version. $125

Two-label 12-ounce crowntainer, silver can, white stars, INTERNAL REVENUE TAX PAID, single version. $125

Two-label 12-ounce crowntainer, silver can, "92" on black label, silver scrolls, INTERNAL REVENUE TAX PAID, single version. $75

Three-label 12-ounce crowntainer, silver can, "92" on black label, silver scrolls, single version.. $65

Two-label, 12-ounce, high-profile cone top, metallic gold can, square yellow label, multiversions. $85

Two-label 12-ounce flat top, metallic gold can, label outlined in white, single version... $50

Oertel's '92 Old Style Bock, two-label 12-ounce crowntainer, silver can, red label, red bands top and bottom, single version. $400

Oertel's Real Draft, two-label 12-ounce tab top, red can, label on glass of beer, no "Beer" on label, single version. $35

Ortel's Real Draft Beer, two-label 12-ounce zip or tab top, red can, label on glass of beer, "Beer" on label in black or white, multiversions. $25

Ortel's Thoroughbred Malt Liquor, two-label 12-ounce zip top, white can, metallic gold label, single version. $125

Thoroughbred Malt Liquor, two-label 12-ounce zip top, white can, metallic bronze label, two versions. $150

Louisiana

/

New Orleans

AMERICAN BREWING COMPANY, 525 South Johnson Street

Regal Genuine Lager Beer, two-label 12-ounce flat top, white can, metallic gold label, "GENUINE LAGER" on red ribbon, single version. $25

Regal Light Lager Beer, single-label, 12-ounce, high-profile cone top, yellow can, metallic gold stripes, smiling man, single version. $200

Single-label 12-ounce flat top, white can, metallic gold stripes top and bottom, single version. $150

Regal Premium Beer, two-label 12-ounce flat top, white or yellow can, crowns, red label, single version of each. $20

DIXIE BREWING COMPANY, 2401 Tulane Avenue

Dixie 45 Brand Beer, single-label 10- or 12-ounce flat top, white can, gold bands top and bottom, "DIXIE" in green, single version 10-ounce, multiversion 12-ounce.
10-ounce, ... $15
12-ounce, ... $10

Single-label, 12-ounce, high profile cone top, metallic gold can, large white band, "45" in red, single version. $100

Dixie Beer, two-label 12-ounce flat or tab top, white can, with or without silver bands, "DIXIE" in green, multiversions. $5

Dixie Brewing Company has brewed assorted labels not listed here in both steel and aluminum tab tops. These cans have a collector value of up to $3.

FALSTAFF BREWING CORPORATION, 2600 Gravier Street

Falstaff Beer, single-label, 12-ounce, high-profile cone top, brown can, gold bands, "FALSTAFF" shield, IRTP or non-IRTP, single version of each.
Non-IRTP, ... $40
IRTP, ... $50
Single-label 12-ounce flat top, white can, brown and yellow "Falstaff" emblem, "THE CHOICEST PRODUCT OF THE BREWER'S ART," multiversions. $10
Two-label 10-, 12-, or 16-ounce flat or tab top, white can, blue band bottom, brown and yellow emblem, "AMERICA'S PREMIUM QUALITY BEER," multiversions. All sizes, ... $10

JACKSON BREWING COMPANY, 620 Decatur Street

Fabacher Brau, single-label 10- or 12-ounce tab top, gray can, yellow, orange, and black bands around bottom, single version of each size. Each size, ... $10
Jax Beer, single- or two-label 10-, 12-, or 16-ounce flat, zip, or tab top, hatched metallic or dull gold can, gold band and horse, multiversions.
10-ounce, ... $50
12-ounce, ... $60
16-ounce, ... $50
12-ounce "GO TEXAN" $125
Two-label 12- or 16-ounce tab top, white can, blue ribbon, gold bands, single version each size. (*See photo 150*) $20
Two-label 10-, 12-, or 16-ounce tab top, white can, gold bands, "JAX" in red, multiversions. $5
Jax Best Beer In Town, single-label 12-ounce flat top, red and black can, black horse on label, "EXTRA PALE BEER," IRTP or non-IRTP, multiversions.
Non-IRTP, ... $100
IRTP, ... $125
Single-label 12- or 16-ounce flat top, white can, vertical metallic gold or yellow stripe, multiversions. $60
Jax Genuine Draft Beer, two-label 12-ounce tab top, metallic gold can, brown round label, single version. $100
Jax Premium Beer, two-label 12- or 16-ounce tab top, white can, blue ribbon, gold bands top and bottom, multiversions. $20
K & B Pilsenlager Beer, two-label 12-ounce tab top, silver can, metallic maroon and yellow label, single version. $5

Photo 150. Jax Beer.

Photo 151. Tex Premium Beer.

Kassel Beer, two-label 12-ounce tab top, metallic gold can, black tiger outline, vertical red band, single version. $5

Krewes Premium Light Beer, two-label 12-ounce tab top, light blue can, blue tiger, "KREWES" in red, single version. $5

Schwegmann Premium Light Lager Beer, two-label 12-ounce tab top, light blue can, wide metallic gold band, blue lettering, single version. $5

Tex Premium Beer, two-label 12-ounce tab top, silver can, "TEX" in silver, blue star and trim, single version. *(See photo 151)* $10

Tiger Beer, two-label 12-ounce tab top, white can, walking tiger, yellow bands, single version. $200

Maine

/

Maine has not had a brewery since Prohibition except micros. No beer cans were produced.

Maryland

*

Baltimore

AMERICAN BREWERY, INC. 1700 North Gay (aka: American
Brewery, Fort Pitt Brewing Company, Globe Brewing Company, Heil-
brau Ltd., Imperial Beverage Company)

American Beer, American Brewery, single- or two-label, 12-ounce, high-profile
cone or flat top, white can, vertical gold stripes, "AMERICAN" in blue, IRTP or
non-IRTP in cones, single-version cone, multiversion flat top.
ITRP cone top, ...$135
Non-IRTP cone top, ...$125
Flat top, ...$85
American Brewery, two-label 12- or 16-ounce tab top, gold checkerboard can,
red diamond label outlined in white, single version.
12-ounce, ...$40
16-ounce, ...$70
American Brewery, two-label 12-ounce tab top, white can, stars, metallic red
label, multiversions. $10
American The All Grain Beer, single-label 12-ounce flat top, gold checkerboard can, dull or metallic red label, multiversions. *(See photo 152)* $25

Photo 152. American, The All Grain Beer.

Arrow 77 The Globe's Finest, Globe Brewing, two-label 12-ounce tab top, white and red can, "ARROW" on white ribbon, yellow trim, single version. $15

Arrow Premium Beer, Globe Brewing, two-label 12-ounce tab top, white can, red bands, "77" on metallic gold globe, single version. $25

Corona Cerveza Banda Blanca, Imperial Beverage, single-version 12-ounce flat top, gold can, crowns, "CORONA" on white band, single version. $300

Heibrau Premium Bolder Beer, Heibrau Ltd., black and gold can, single version. $20

Imperial Bavarian Light Beer, Imperial Beverage, two-label 12-ounce flat top, metallic gold and white can, red label outlined in metallic gold, multiversions. $100

Keg Beer, American Brewery, four-label 12-ounce and three-label 16-ounce flat top, keg pouring beer into glass, single version. *(See photo 153)* $20

CARLING BREWING COMPANY, Baltimore Beltway (aka: Tuborg Breweries Ltd.)

Black Label Beer, Carling Brewing, single- or two-label 12-ounce flat, zip, or tab top, red can, black label outlined in white, map of the U.S. or world, multiversions. $10

Carling Brewing, two-label 12-ounce tab top, red can, black label outlined in white, gold bands, multiversions. $15

Carling Brewing, two-label 12-ounce tab top, tankard can, multiversions. .. $15

Carling Black Label Beer, Carling Brewing, single-label 12-ounce flat or zip top, red can, black label outlined in white, "CARLING" on label, multiversions. $8

Carling's Red Cap Ale, Carling Brewing, two-label 12-ounce tab top, metallic green can, yellow oval label, single version. $40

Heidelberg Light Pilsener Beer, Carling Brewing, two-label 12-ounce tab top, gold and white can, black lettering, single version. $20

Red Cap Ale, Carling Brewing, two-label 12-ounce tab top, gold diamonds, white label, red vertical band, multiversions. $10

Tuborg Brewed Light Beer, Tuborg Breweries Ltd., two-label 12-ounce tab top, gold can, red label outlined in blue, multiversions. *(See photo 154)* $5

Can was also produced in aluminum. Collector value is $2.

Photo 153 (left). Keg Beer.
Photo 154 (right). Tuborg Brewed Light Beer.

CARLING NATIONAL BREWERIES, INC., 3602 O'Donnell
Street (successor to Carling and National Brewing Companies; aka:
Carling National, Van Lauter Brewing Company)

All cans produced after merger were produced in aluminum with a collector
value of up to $3.

FREE STATE BREWERY CORPORATION, 1108 Hillen Street

Free State Beer, single-label, 12-ounce, high-profile cone top, blue can, red
label, single version. $250

THE GLOBE BREWING COMPANY, 327 South Hanover Street
(aka: Globe Brewing Company, Hals Brewing Company)

Arrow 77 The Globe's Finest, Globe Brewing, two-label 12-ounce flat top,
metallic gold and white can, "77" in white on gold globe, multiversions. . . $25

Arrow Ale, Globe Brewing, single-label 12-ounce flat top, gold can, single ver-
sion. . . . . Exotic

Arrow Beer, Globe Brewing, single-label 12-ounce flat top, metallic gold can,
"ARROW BEER" in black outlined in red, INTERNAL REVENUE TAX PAID, multi-
versions. $100

Arrow Bock Beer, Globe Brewing, single-label 12-ounce flat top, black can,
red label, single version. $250

Arrow English Style Ale, Globe Brewing, single-label 12-ounce flat top, gold
can, OPENING INSTRUCTIONS, INTERNAL REVENUE TAX PAID, single version.
. . . . Exotic

Arrow Imperial Lagered Beer, Globe Brewing, single-label 12-ounce flat top,
black can, metallic red label, "IMPERIAL LAGERED" on red ribbon, multiver-
sions. $125

Eigenbrot's Ale, Globe Brewing, single-label 12-ounce flat top, gold can, black
label, OPENING INSTRUCTIONS, INTERNAL REVENUE TAX PAID, single version.
. . . . Exotic

Eigenbrot's Beer, Globe Brewing, single-label 12-ounce flat top, black can,
yellow label, OPENING INSTRUCTIONS, INTERNAL REVENUE TAX PAID, single ver-
sion. . . . . Exotic

Hals Premium Beer, Hals Brewing, single-label 12-ounce flat top, metallic blue
can, laughing man, single version. $150

Shamrock Pale Ale, two-label 12-ounce flat top, green can, white label, INTER-
NAL REVENUE TAX PAID, single version. . . . . Exotic

GUNTHER BREWING COMPANY, 1211 Conklin Street

Gunther Extra Dry Beer, single-label 12-ounce flat top, yellow-gold can, brown
oval label, single version. $50

Gunther Old English Ale, single-label 12-ounce flat top, brand in green on
brown can, single version. $125

Two-label 12-ounce flat top, white can, square green label, single version. . $35

Photo 155. Gunther Premium Dry Beer.

Gunther Premium Bock Beer, two-label 12-ounce flat top, yellow can, brown lettering, goat's head, single version. $175

Gunther Premium Dry Beer, single-label 12-ounce flat top, yellow can, brown lettering, "PREMIUM DRY" in red, multiversions. *(See photo 155)*............. $30

Gunther's Beer, single-label 12-ounce flat top, red and white can, "COOL BEFORE SERVING," OPENING INSTRUCTIONS, INTERNAL REVENUE TAX PAID, single version. $250

Gunther's Old English Ale, single-label, 12-ounce, high-profile cone or flat top, green and white can, bands top and bottom, IRTP and non-IRTP, multiversions.
ITRP cone top, ...Exotic
Non-IRTP, ...Exotic
Flat top, ...Exotic

Gunther's Premium Bock Beer, single- or two-label 12-ounce flat top, standing goat, bands top and bottom, INTERNAL REVENUE TAX PAID, multiversions. .$250

Gunther's Premium Dry Lager Beer, single-label 12-ounce flat top, yellow can, brown stripes top and bottom, IRTP or non-IRTP, single version of each.
IRTP, ...$125
Non-IRTP, ...$100

Gunther's Special Dry Lager Beer, single-label, 12-ounce, high-profile cone or flat top, yellow can, brown lettering and bands, INTERNAL REVENUE TAX PAID, multiversions.
Cone top, ...$125
Flat top, ... $85

THEO. HAMM BREWING COMPANY, 1211 South Conkling Street (successor to Gunther Brewing Company)

Gunther Premium Dry Beer, two-label 12- or 16-ounce flat or tab top, gold can, red and white label, white bands, multiversions. $10

Hamm's Beer, two-label 12- or 16-ounce flat top, gold sunburst can, white label, single version. $15

Two-label 12-ounce soft top, blue can, "pine tree" design, single version. . $10

G. HEILEMAN BREWING COMPANY, 3602 O'Donnell Street (successor to Carling-National Brewing Company)

All cans produced by Heileman at Baltimore are produced in aluminum. They can be separated from other Heileman breweries by the letter "G" stamped on the bottom of the cans. Collector value will run up to $2 per can.

THE NATIONAL BREWING COMPANY, 3602 O'Donnell Street

Atles Golden Lager Beer, two-label 16-ounce tab top, white can, square red label outlined in metal gold, multiversions. $10

Colt 45 Malt Lager, two-label 8-, 12-, or 16-ounce tab top, white can, "MALT LAGER" in red, gold horseshoe, multiversions.
8-ounce, ... $12
All other versions, ... $10

Colt 45 Malt Liquor, two-label 8-, 12-, or 16-ounce tab top, white can, "MALT LIQUOR" in red, gold horseshoe, multiversions. All versions, ... $5

Colt 45 Stout Malt Liquor, two-label 8-, 12-, or 16-ounce tab top, white can, "STOUT MALT LIQUOR" in red, gold horseshoe, multiversions. All versions, .$5

Colt Malt Lager, two-label 12- or 16-ounce tab or zip top, yellow can, "COLT MALT LAGER" in white on blue band, multiversions. All versions, ... $10

Draft Beer By National, two-label 12-ounce tab top or two-label gallon can, white can, glass of beer on label, two versions of each.
12-ounce, ... $10
Gallon, ... $175

French 76 Malt Liquor, two-label 7-ounce tab top, white can, gold "Eiffel" tower, gold trim, single version. $300

French 76 Sparkling Malt Liquor, two-label 8-ounce tab top, white can, gold "Eiffel" tower, gold trim, single version. $300

Malt Duck A Premium Malt Liquor, two-label 12-ounce tab top, metallic crimson can, "APPLE MALT DUCK" or "GRAPE MALT DUCK," single version.
"APPLE," .... Exotic
"GRAPE," $100

Malt Duck Premium Beer, two-label 12-ounce tab top, metallic purple can, single version. $175

National Ale, single-label, 12-ounce, high-profile cone top, white can, black round label, German eagle, INTERNAL REVENUE TAX PAID, single version. $300

National Bohemian Bock Beer, two-label 12-ounce flat or tab top, black can, red label, metallic gold trim, multiversions. $50

Single-label 12-ounce flat top, black can, red label outlined in yellow, single version. $100

National Bohemian Brand Bock Beer, single-label, high- or low-profile cone top, black can, red label, goat, single version of each. $300

National Bohemian Brand Pale Beer, single-label, 12-ounce, high- or low-profile cone top, red can, "NATIONAL BOHEMIAN" in white on black ribbon, multiversions. *(See photo 156)* $150

National Bohemian Light Beer, single- or two-label 7-, 12-, or 16-ounce flat or tab top, or quart cone top, red can, black label, "NATIONAL BOHEMIAN" in white, "MR. BOH," multiversions. *(See photo 157)*
7-ounce flat top, ... $30
12-ounce flat top, ... $30
16-ounce flat top, ... $40
Quart cone top, ... $125

Two-label 12-ounce flat or zip top, "transition" can, one side red, one side white, two versions.

Steel, ... $50
Aluminum, ... $40

Two-label 12-ounce soft or tab top, white can, script, bands, red label outlined in gold, multiversions. All sizes, ... $30

Single-label 12-ounce bank top, multicolored can called "Cartoon" can, single version. $65

Two-label 12- or 16-ounce tab top, yellow can, vertical black label, red bands, multiversions. $15

National Bohemian Pale Beer, single- or two-label 12- or 16-ounce flat top or 12-ounce or quart high-profile cone top, red can, "NATIONAL BOHEMIAN" in white on black ribbon, IRTP on cone top, multiversions.

12-ounce flat top, ... $50
16-ounce flat top, ... $50
12-ounce cone top, ...$100
Quart cone top, ...$125

National Genuine Ale, single-label, 12-ounce, low-profile cone top, white can, green map of U.S., INTERNAL REVENUE TAX PAID, multiversions. $250

National Light Beer, single-label, 12-ounce, low-profile cone top, white can, red map of the U.S., INTERNAL REVENUE TAX PAID, multiversions. $300

National Premium Pale Dry Beer, single- or two-label 12-ounce flat or tab top, white can, purple and orange label, multiversions.

Flat top, ... $30
Tab top, ... $25

Single-label, 12-ounce, high-profile cone or crowntainer, purple can, "PALE DRY BEER" in orange circle, INTERNAL REVENUE TAX PAID, multiversions. *(See photo 158)*..$125

Old Bohemian Brand Pale Beer, single-label, 12-ounce, low-profile cone top, "OLD BOHEMIAN" in black arc, INTERNAL REVENUE TAX PAID. ....Exotic

Whales White Ale, two-label 12-ounce flat or tab top, white or off-white can, black lettering, yellow trim, single version of each. Either version, ...$125

Two-label 12-ounce tab top, black can, white lettering, minor versions. $20

National produced most of its brands in aluminum. The collector value of some of these brands can run up to $10.

Photo 156 (left). National Bohemian Brand Pale Beer. Photo 157 (center). National Bohemian Light Beer. Photo 158 (right). National Premium Pale Dry Beer.

F & M SCHAEFER BREWING COMPANY, 1211 South Conklin Street (successor to Theo. Hamms Brewing Company)

Schaefer Beer, single-label 12-ounce flat or tab top, white can, 15 circles on can, multiversions. $10

Gunther was produced at this brewery but there is no way to separate them from the Gunther produced at other Schaefer plants.

WEISSNER BREWING COMPANY, 1108 Hillen Street (successor to Free State Brewing Company)

Weissner's Premium Beer, single-label 12-ounce flat top, gray can, red crown, "WEISSNER'S" in black, single version. $150

Weissner's Regal Beer, single-label 12-ounce flat top, yellow can, red crown, "WEISSNER'S REGAL BEER" in black, single version. $150

Cumberland

CUMBERLAND BREWING COMPANY, 711 Centre Street (aka: Cleveland-Sandusky Brewing Company, Globe Brewing Company)

Arrow 77 The Globe's Finest, Globe Brewing, two-label 12-ounce flat, zip, or tab top, multiversions. $10

Banner Extra Dry Beer, Cumberland Brewing, single-label 12-ounce flat top, white can, blue lettering, red banner label, single version. $25

Best Premium Quality Ale, Cumberland Brewing, two-label 12-ounce flat top, white can, green label outlined in yellow, single version. $75

Best Premium Quality Beer, Cumberland Brewing, two-label 12-ounce flat top, white can, red label outlined in yellow, single version. $35

Blackhawk Premium Beer, Cumberland Brewing, two-label 12-ounce flat top, blue and silver can, red Indian head, single version. $75

Bond Hill Premium Lager Beer, Cumberland Brewing, two-label 12-ounce flat top, metallic blue and silver can, "BOND HILL" in red, single version. ... $200

Fischer's Light Dry Beer, Cumberland Brewing, single-label 12-ounce flat top, white can, red and blue label, single version. $10

GB Lager Beer, Cleveland-Sandusky Brewing, two-label 12-ounce flat top, metallic gold can, red and brown label, single version. $85

Goldcrest Premium Beer, Cumberland Brewing, two-label 12-ounce flat top, white can, metallic gold and black label, single label. $75

Keeley Premium Quality Ale, Cumberland Brewing, two-label 12-ounce flat top, metallic green can, yellow label outlined in gold, single version. $150

Keeley Premium Quality Beer, Cumberland Brewing Company, two-label 12-ounce flat top, red can, yellow label outlined in metallic gold, single version. $75

Kol Beer, Cumberland Brewing, two-label 12-ounce flat or tab top, metallic blue can, metallic gold label, "KOL" in white, single version. $60

Kol Premium Quality Beer, Cumberland Brewing, single-label 12-ounce flat top, white can, silver vertical stripes, blue label and band, multiversions. .. $30

Mann's Export Ale, Cumberland Brewing, two-label 12-ounce flat top, white can, blue bands, large red triangles, single version. $125

Old Bohemian Lager Beer, Cumberland Brewing, white can, red oval label, "LAGER," "ALL GRAIN" in red, single version. $40

Old Export Brand Beer, Cumberland Brewing, single-label, 12-ounce, high-profile cone top, metallic gold can, white lettering, IRTP and non-IRTP, multiversions.

IRTP, ... $125
Non-IRTP, ... $115

Cumberland Brewing, single-label, 12-ounce, high-profile cone top, white can, purple oval label, single version. $75

Old Export Light Beer, Cumberland Brewing, single-label, 12-ounce, high-profile cone top, white can, red oval label, single version. $75

Old Export Pilsener Light Beer, Cumberland Brewing, two-label 12-ounce flat top, white can, red oval label, multiversions. $25

Old Export Premium Pilsener Beer, Cumberland Brewing, two-label 12-ounce flat, zip, or tab top, red can, white label outlined in black, multiversions. .. $10

Old Timers Ale, Cleveland-Sandusky, single-label 12-ounce flat top, white and green can, carriage, single version. $75

Red Fox Beer, Cumberland Brewing, two-label 12-ounce flat top, red and white can, red fox, single version. $75

Schwegmann Premium Light Beer, Cumberland Brewing, two-label 12-ounce tab top, metallic red can, white label, single version. $50

Sweet Life Premium Quality Beer, Cumberland Brewing, two-label 12-ounce flat top, blue can, red bands, white label with blue band, single version. . $200

Tudor Cream Ale, Cumberland Brewing, two-label 12-ounce tab top, white can, green label, with or without A&P logo, multiversions.
A&P logo, ... $20
No A&P logo, ... $35

Tudor Pilsner Beer, Cumberland Brewing, two-label 12-ounce tab top, white can, red label, with or without A&P logo, multiversions.
A&P logo, ... $20
No A&P logo, ... $35

Tudor Premium Quality Ale, Cumberland Brewing, two-label 12-ounce flat top, green can, white label, single version. $25

Cumberland Brewing, two-label 12-ounce flat top, white can, green label outlined in metallic gold, single version. $25

Tudor Premium Quality Beer, Cumberland Brewing, two-label 12-ounce flat top, red label, blue label outlined in metallic gold, single version. $20

Cumberland Brewing, two-label 12-ounce flat top, white can, red label outlined in metallic gold, single version. $20

Tudor Premium Quality Cream Ale, Cumberland Brewing, two-label 12-ounce flat top, green can, white label. $30

QUEEN CITY BREWING COMPANY, 208 Market Street (aka: American Brewing Company, Cumberland Brewing Company [zip 21502], Fischer Brewing Company, Home Brewing Company)

American Beer, American Brewery, two-label 12-ounce tab top, white can, red label, gold trim, diamonds, multiversions. $10

Arrow Premium Beer, American Brewery, two-label 12-ounce tab top, white can, red label, "ARROW" in red, single version. $10

Brown Derby Lager Beer, Queen City Brewing, two-label 12-ounce tab top, white can, orange label, single version. $10

Fischer's Light Dry Ale, Queen City Brewing, single-label 12-ounce flat top, white can, blue and green label, multiversions. $75

Fischer's Brewing, two-label 12-ounce flat or tab top, metallic gold can, green label, "FISCHER'S" in white, multiversions. $75

Queen City Brewing, two-label 12-ounce tab top, white can, vertical green stripes, green label. $10

Fischer's Light Dry Beer, Queen City Brewing, single-label 12-ounce flat top, white can, red and blue label, "LIGHT DRY" on blue band, multiversions. . $75

Fischer's Brewing, two-label 12-ounce flat or tab top, metallic gold can, red label outlined in white, multiversions. $75

Queen City Brewing, two-label 12-ounce flat or tab top, white can, vertical red stripes, red label, multiversions. $10

Fischer's Private Stock Beer, Queen City Brewing, single-label 12-ounce flat top, yellow can, red label outlined in brown, single version. $175

Gamecock Genuine Cream Ale, Cumberland Brewing (21502), two-label 12-ounce tab top, white can, red bird, "GAMECOCK" in green, single version. . $60

Gamecock Genuine Premium Beer, Cumberland Brewing (21502), two-label 12-ounce tab top, white can, red bird, "GAMECOCK" in red, single version. $75

Goldcrest 51 Premium Beer, Queen City Brewing, two-label 12-ounce flat top, metallic red can, white label outlined in metallic gold, single version. $100

Heritage House Premium Beer, Queen City or Cumberland Brewing (21502), two-label 12-ounce tab top, yellow can, red label outlined in white, multiversions. $10

Kings XX Ale, Queen City Brewing, two-label 12-ounce flat top, green can, yellow label, "KINGS" in white on red band, single version. $60

Mountain Brew Beer, Queen City Brewing, two-label 12-ounce tab top, red and white can, "BREW" in metallic gold, single version. $50

"Old Dutch" Brand The Good Beer, Queen City Brewing, two-label 12-ounce flat top, white can, red bands, "THE GOOD BEER" in black, single version. $15

Old Export Premium Beer, Queen City Brewing or Cumberland Brewing (21502), two-label 12- or 16-ounce tab top, red can, white label outlined in metallic gold, multiversions. $20

Old German Brand Beer, Queen City Brewing, single-label, 12-ounce, high-profile cone top, white can, orange and red bands, "BRAND" in red, multiversions. $85

Queen City Brewing, white can, red bands and label, single version. $60

Old German Brand Premium Lager Beer, Queen City Brewing, two-label 12- or 16-ounce flat or tab top, or 12-ounce high-profile cone or quart cone top, white can, red label, "OLD GERMAN" in white, multiversions.
12-ounce flat top, ... $10
16-ounce flat top, ... $12
12-ounce cone top, ... $40
Quart cone top, ... $75

Queens Brau Select Beer, Queen City Brewing, single-label 12-ounce flat top, purple can, metallic gold label, multiversions. $180

Queen City Brewing, single-label 12-ounce flat top, white can, metallic gold label, "QUEENS BRAU" in red, single version. $150

Queen City Brewing, two-label 12-ounce tab top, white can, large black label, single version. $20

Richbrau Premium Beer, Queen City Brewing or Home Brewing, two-label 12- or 16-ounce tab top, white can, black label, "RICHBRAU" on red bar, multiversions. $25

Tudor Ale, Queen City or Cumberland Brewing (21502), green can, square black label, with or without A&P logo, single version of each.
A&P logo, ... $25
No A&P logo, ... $30

Tudor Bock Beer, Cumberland Brewing (21502), two-label 12-ounce tab top, white can, brown label, A&P logo, single version. $75

Tudor Pilsner Beer, Cumberland Brewing (21502), two-label 16-ounce tab top, white can, red label outlined in metallic gold, A&P logo, single version. $25

Tudor Premium Beer, Queen City Brewing or Cumberland Brewing (21502), two-label 12-ounce tab top, yellow and gold can, square black label, with or without A&P logo, single version of each.
A&P logo, ... $15
No A&P logo, ... $20

Massachusetts

Boston

BOSTON BEER COMPANY, 245 West 2nd Street

Boston Light Ale, single-label, 12-ounce, J-spout cone or quart cone top, metallic gold can, cream label, lighthouse, INTERNAL REVENUE TAX PAID, single version of each.
12-ounce,...$250
Quart... $400

Single-label 12-ounce crowntainer, white can, brown hatching, INTERNAL REVENUE TAX PAID, single version. $325

Single-label 12-ounce crowntainer, silver can, brown solid or hatched background, single version of each. Solid background, ...$350
Hatched background, ... $400

Boston Stock Ale, single-label quart cone top, metallic gold can, red, white, and black label, INTERNAL REVENUE TAX PAID, single version. $150

CROFT BREWING COMPANY, 165 Terrace Street

Croft All Malt Cream Ale, single-label 12-ounce flat top or quart cone top, three heads, "keg-lined panel," single version of each.
12-ounce flat top, ... $400
Quart cone top, ...$450
Croft Cream Ale, single-label 12-ounce or quart flat top, green can, yellow lettering, INTERNAL REVENUE TAX PAID, OPENING INSTRUCTIONS, multiversions.
12-ounce,... $85
Quart,.. $200

Single-label 12-ounce flat top, or high-profile cone or quart cone top, green can, yellow lettering, three heads, INTERNAL REVENUE TAX PAID, multiversions.

12-ounce flat top, ... $100
12-ounce cone top, ... $125
Quart cone top, ... $125

Single-label 12-ounce flat top, or 12-ounce high-profile cone top, or quart cone top, green can, oval label, "CROFT ALE" in yellow, multiversions.

12-ounce flat top, ... $75
12-ounce cone top, ... $100
Quart cone top, ... $125

Croft Pilgrim Ale, single-label 12-ounce flat top, "keg-lined" panel or box, INTERNAL REVENUE TAX PAID, with or without OPENING INSTRUCTIONS, single version of each.

OI, ... $400
Non-OI, ... $375

Croft Red Label Ale, single-label 12-ounce flat top, lists six Croft products, "keg-lined" panel, INTERNAL REVENUE TAX PAID, single version. $300

Croft The Champion Ale, single-label 12-ounce flat top, beige can, metallic or dull gold oval label, single version of each. $85

Gamecock Ale, single-label 12-ounce flat top, metallic green can, white label, single version. $250

Pilgrim Ale, single-label 12-ounce flat top, silver can, red pilgrim, OPENING INSTRUCTIONS, INTERNAL REVENUE TAX PAID, single version. $350

Stock Ale By Croft, single-label 12-ounce flat top, or high-profile cone or quart cone top, vertical gold and white stripes, red label, single version of each.

12-ounce flat top, ... $85
12-ounce cone top, ... $175
Quart cone top, ... $250

HAFFENREFFER & COMPANY, 26 Germania Street

ENTERPRISE BREWING COMPANY also used as a mandatory on Boh Bohemian Beer.

Boh Bohemian Beer, Haffenreffer & Co. or Enterprise Brewing, single-label 12-ounce flat top, white can, gold square label, red lettering, single version of each. $15

Boylston Extra Fine Lager Beer, two-label 12-ounce flat top, white can, red label, single version. $125

Two-label 12-ounce flat top, yellow can, red label, single version............ $125

Haffenreffer Lager Beer, two-label 12-ounce flat or tab top, white can, red label, single version of each top.

Flat top, ... $65
Tab top... $60

Haffenreffer Private Stock Malt Liquor, single-label 12-ounce flat top, gold can, yellow label, "PRIVATE STOCK" in red, single version. $85

Haffenreffer Real Draught Beer, two-label 12-ounce tab top, red can, black and white lettering, single version. $65

Pickwick Ale, single-label, 12-ounce, high-profile cone or quart cone top, white can, gold label, INTERNAL REVENUE TAX PAID, single version.

12-ounce, ... $125

Quart, ... $275

Single-label 12-ounce flat top, gold and black can, white label, IRTP or non-IRTP, single version of each.

IRTP, ... $125

Non-IRTP, ... $115

Two-label 12-ounce flat or tab top, red can, white label, multiversions. $60

Pickwick Beer, single-label 12-ounce flat top, metallic gold and black can, white label, single version. .... Exotic

Pickwick Brew, single-label 12-ounce flat top, brown or red can with white label, multiversions. $85

Pickwick Brew Beer, single-label 12-ounce flat top, gold can, white label, single version. $85

Pickwick Lager Beer, single-label 12-ounce flat top, white can, black lettering, "BEER" outlined in red, single version. $85

Pickwick Light Ale, single-label, 12-ounce, high-profile cone top, white can, "LIGHT" in blue, single version. $125

Pickwick Malt Brew, single-label 12-ounce flat top, brown can, white label, metallic gold trim, single version. $300

Pickwick Pale Ale, single-label 12-ounce flat top, red and gold can, white label, multiversions. $85

STAR BREWING COMPANY, 192 Norfolk Street

Murphy's Ale, single-label, 12-ounce, high- or low-profile cone top, green can, red label, single version of each. $250

Star Banner Ale, single-label low-profile cone top, tan can, "STAR" on red ribbon, single version. .... Exotic

Star Stock Ale, single-label high-profile cone top, red can, scroll label, "STOCK" in red, single version. $300

Fall River

ENTERPRISE BREWING COMPANY, 89-91 President Avenue

Bo Bohemian Lager Beer, single- or two-label 12-ounce flat top, yellow, orange label, black hat, multiversions. $50

Two-label 12-ounce flat top, white can, square gold label, "BOH" in red, single version. $20

Bo Light Lager Beer, single-label 12-ounce tab top, metallic gold can, yellow label, multiversions. $100

Cape Cod Beer, two-label 12-ounce flat top, blue can, white label, single version. $350

Clyde Ale, single-label quart cone top, cream-colored can, single version.
....Exotic

Clyde Cream Ale, single-label, 12-ounce, high- or low-profile cone top, silver or cream-colored can, red hatched label, INTERNAL REVENUE TAX PAID, multi-versions. $125

Clyde Lager Beer, two-label 12-ounce flat top, white can, blue label, red trim, single version. $225

Clyde Premium Lager Beer, two-label 12-ounce flat top, white can, blue label outlined in red, single version. $125

Enterprise Bohemian Brand Beer, single-label quart cone top, gold can, black label, INTERNAL REVENUE TAX PAID, single version. $350

Old Tap Ale, two-label 12-ounce flat top, white can, red label outlined in metallic gold, INTERNAL REVENUE TAX PAID, single version. $85

Old Tap Brand Select Stock Ale, single-label, 12-ounce, high-profile cone or quart cone top, green can, man on red label, INTERNAL REVENUE TAX PAID, single version.
12-ounce,.. $300
Quart,...$350

Single-label, 12-ounce, high-profile cone or quart cone top, metallic gold can, white label, INTERNAL REVENUE TAX PAID, single version.
12-ounce,...$150
Quart,...$175

Old Tap Export Lager Beer, single-label, 12-ounce, low-profile cone top, yellow can, man with glass of beer, INTERNAL REVENUE TAX PAID, single version.
....$350

Old Tap Select Stock Ale, single-label, 12-ounce, low-profile cone top, green can, man with a glass of beer, INTERNAL REVENUE TAX PAID, single version.
....$350

Single-label 12-ounce flat top, gold and red can, white label, single version.
....$100

Two-label 12-ounce flat top, white can, red label outlined in gold, single version... $65

Yankee Trader Beer, two-label 12-ounce flat top, white can, red label, sailing ship, single version. $150

Lawrence

DIAMOND SPRING BREWERY, INC., 50 Diamond Street (aka: Golden Brew Spring Brewery)

Finast Lager Beer, Golden Brew Brewery, two-label 12-ounce flat top, metallic gold can, white bands, small red label, single version. $10

Golden Brew A Premium Product, Diamond Spring Brewery, two-label 12-ounce flat top, white can, "GOLDEN BREW" in white on red label, multiversions. $50

Golden Brew Beer, Golden Brew Brewery, two-label 12-ounce flat top, metallic gold hatched can, white oval label outlined in red, single version. $40

Holihan's Genuine Draft Beer, Diamond Spring Brewery, two-label gallon can, yellow or brown woodgrain can, single version of each.

Brown woodgrain, ... $300

Yellow woodgrain, ... Exotic

Holihan's Light Ale, Diamond Spring Brewery, two-label 12-ounce flat or tab top, green can, white label, "HOLIHAN'S" in red, single version of each. .. $60

Holihan's Pilsener Beer, Diamond Spring Brewery, two-label 12-ounce flat, soft, or zip top, white can, gold oval label, "HOLIHAN'S" in red, multiversion. $25

Diamond Spring Brewery, single-label 12-ounce tab top, white can, "HOLI-HAN'S" in black, three labels, single version. $20

HACKER BREWING COMPANY, 24 Payton Street

Hacker's Amberlite XXX Ale, single-label 12-ounce flat top, metallic gold can, white label, single version. .... Unique

Hacker's Extra Dry Beer, single-label 12-ounce flat top, metallic gold can, white label, single version. $150

Lowell

HARVARD BREWING COMPANY, 24 Payton Street (aka: Merrimack Brewing Company)

Connecticut Yankee Ale, Harvard or Merrimack Brewing, single-label 12-ounce flat top, white can, stars, red and blue bands, "ALE" in yellow or red, single version of each. Either can, ... $300

Connecticut Yankee Lager Beer, Harvard or Merrimack Brewing, single-label 12-ounce flat top, white can, stars, "CONNECTICUT" in white on red band, single version of each. Either can, ... $300

Golden Brau Bock Beer, Harvard Brewing, single-label 12-ounce flat top, metallic gold can, large red label, "BOCK" in white, single version. $200

Golden Brau Premium Ale, Harvard Brewing, single-label 12-ounce flat top, metallic gold can, large green label, "ALE" in white, two versions. $200

Golden Brau Premium Beer, Harvard Brewing, single-label 12-ounce flat top, metallic gold can, large red label, multiversions. $175

Harvard Ale, Harvard Brewing, single-label 12-ounce flat top or single-label quart cone top, silver or gray can, "ALE" on red ball, red trim, OPENING INSTRUCTIONS on flat tops, INTERNAL REVENUE TAX PAID, multiversions.

12-ounce flat top, ... $125

Quart cone top, ... $150

Harvard Brewing, single-label 12-ounce flat top, INTERNAL REVENUE TAX PAID, yellow can, "HARVARD" in black, single version. $85

Harvard Brewing, single-label 12-ounce flat top, IRTP or non-IRTP, brown can, "HARVARD" in red, multiversions.

IRTP, ... $60

Non-IRTP, ... $50

Harvard Brewing, single-label 12-ounce flat top, red and yellow can, white "H," multiversions. $75

Harvard Export Beer, Harvard Brewing, single-label 12-ounce flat top or single-label quart cone top, metallic gold can, red trim, "HARVARD" in black, OPENING INSTRUCTIONS, INTERNAL REVENUE TAX PAID, WITHDRAWN FREE, camouflage can, single versions.

12-ounce IRTP,	$85
12-ounce WITHDRAWN FREE,	$100
Quart IRTP,	$125
Quart camouflage,	$250

Harvard Brewing, single-label 12-ounce flat top, beige can, "HARVARD" in red, "EXPORT BEER" in green, multiversions. $60

Harvard Brewing, single-label 12-ounce flat top, white can, yellow and metallic gold trim, "FOAM FRESH," single version. $100

Old Bohemian Bock Beer, Harvard Brewing, single-label 12-ounce flat top, white can, red lettering and bands, "BOHEMIAN" in black, single version.
.... $150

Old Bohemian Light Beer, Harvard Brewing, single-label 12-ounce flat top, yellow can, red lettering and bands, "BOHEMIAN" in black, multiversions.
.... $100

Natick

CARLING BREWING COMPANY, 1143 Worchester Street

Black Label Beer, single- or two-label 12- or 16-ounce flat or tab top, red can, black label outlined in white, map of U.S. or world, multiversions. $10

Two-label 12- or 16-ounce tab top, red can, black label outlined in white, gold bands, multiversions. $15

Two-label 12- or 16-ounce flat or tab top, tankard can, multiversions......... $15

Black Label Export Premium Malt Liquor, two-label 12- or 16-ounce tab top, black can, metallic gold label on black label, single version of each size.

12-ounce,	$50
16-ounce,	$50

Carling Black Label Beer, single-label 12- or 16-ounce flat or zip top, red can, black label outlined in white, "CARLING" on oval label, multiversions. $8

Brand was also produced in aluminum cans. Collector value is $1.

Single-label 12- or 16-ounce tab top, red can, "HOUSE OF CARLING" in black, multiversions. $3

Brand was also produced in aluminum cans. Collector value is $1.

Carling's Red Cap Ale. Brand was produced in aluminum cans only. Collector value is $1.

Heidelberg Fine Quality Beer, single-label 12-ounce flat top, metallic green can, white label, "HEIDELBERG" in red, single version. $25

Heidelberg Light Pilsener Beer, two-label 12-ounce tab top, gold and white can, black lettering, single version. $20

Red Cap Ale, two-label 12-ounce flat, tab, or zip top, green can, orangish label, red cap, multiversions. $20

Two-label 12-ounce flat, zip, or tab top, gold diamonds, white label, vertical red band, multiversions. $15

Carling issued a series of special issue and commemorative cans using the current Carling Black Label Beer, Carling Black Label Lager Beer, or Black Label Beer brands over the 20 years the brewery operated. *Carling Black Label Beer* cans include: 1,000,000 Man Hours, Harvard Class of '39, Harvard Class of '40, Harvard Class of '41, Harvard Class of '42, Harvard Class of '43, Harvard Class of '44, Harvard Class of '49. *Black Label Beer* cans include: Boston Bruins 1969–70, Dartmouth Class of '46, Harvard Class of '45, Harvard Class of '46, Harvard Class of '47, Harvard Class of '48, Harvard Class of '50, "The men of the 200." *Carling Black Label Lager Beer* cans include: Boston Bruins 1971–72, Harvard Class of '49. Collector value of these cans will run from $25 to $40.

New Bedford

DAWSON'S BREWERY OR DAWSON BREWING COMPANY, 29–43 Brook Street

Dawson Diamond Ale, two-label 12- or 16-ounce flat or zip top, silver can, white label outlined in green, single version.
12-ounce, ... $45
16-ounce, ... $35

Dawson Gold Crown Beer, two-label 12- or 16-ounce flat or zip top, gold can, white label outlined in red, single version.
12-ounce, ... $35
16-ounce, ... $30

Dawson Lager Beer, two-label 12- or 16-ounce flat or zip top, silver can, gold lines, white label outlined in red, single version.
12-ounce, ... $10
16-ounce, ... $8

Dawson Sparkling Ale, two-label 12-ounce flat or tab top, silver can, white label, single version.
12-ounce, ... $20
16-ounce, ... $15

Dawson's Ale, two-label, 12-ounce, low-profile cone top, "KING OF DIAMONDS" label, yellow and red can, INTERNAL REVENUE TAX PAID, multiversions. ...$250

Two-label high- or low-profile cone top, "A ROYAL BREW," yellow and red can, INTERNAL REVENUE TAX PAID, multiversions. $200

Two-label, 12-ounce, high-profile cone or quart cone top, "FIT FOR A KING," orange-yellow can, INTERNAL REVENUE TAX PAID, single version. $100

Two-label 12-ounce flat top, INTERNAL REVENUE TAX PAID, gold can, white label, "DEBBIE DAWSON," single version. $60

Dawson's Beer, two-label, 12-ounce, low-profile cone top, "KING OF DIAMONDS" label, red and yellow can, INTERNAL REVENUE TAX PAID, single version. $200

Two-label, 12-ounce, high- or low-profile cone or quart cone top, or 12-ounce camouflage can, "A ROYAL BREW," orange or yellow can, INTERNAL REVENUE TAX PAID, single version.

12-ounce cone top, ... $200
12-ounce camouflage can, ... $400
Quart cone top, ...$350

Two-label, 12-ounce, high-profile cone or quart cone top, silver can, "BEER" in red, INTERNAL REVENUE TAX PAID, single version.

12-ounce, ...$100
Quart, ...$150

Two-label 12-ounce flat top, gold can, white label, "DEBBIE DAWSON," single version. $60

Dawson's Calorie Controlled Ale, two-label 12-ounce flat top, white can, green label, "ALE" in script or block letters, single version of each.

Script letters, ... $50
Block letters, ... $50

Dawson's Calorie Controlled Bock, two-label 12-ounce flat top, white can, red label, "BOCK BEER" in script, single version. $125

Dawson's Calorie Controlled Lager, two-label 12-ounce flat top, white can, red or brown label, "LAGER BEER" in script or block letters, single version of each. Either can, ... $75

Dawson's Extra Dry Ale, two-label 12-ounce flat top or quart cone top, yellow can, green label, multiversions.

Flat top, ... $60
Cone top, ...$125

Dawson's Extra Dry Lager Beer, two-label 12-ounce flat top, yellow can, red label, "DAWSON'S" on white ribbon, multiversions. $65

Dawson's Gold Crown Ale, two-label, 12-ounce, high-profile cone or quart cone top, metallic gold can, "A ROYAL BREW," single version.

12-ounce, ...$125
Quart, ...$250

Dawson's Master Ale, two-label, 12-ounce, low-profile cone top, "KING OF DIAMONDS" label, gold and orange can, INTERNAL REVENUE TAX PAID, multiversions. $200

Two-label, 12-ounce, high- or low-profile cone or quart cone top, "A ROYAL BREW," orange-yellow can, INTERNAL REVENUE TAX PAID, multiversions.

12-ounce, ... $65
Quart, ...$125

Dawson's Pale Ale, two-label, 12-ounce, low-profile cone top, "KING OF DIAMONDS" label, red and orange can, INTERNAL REVENUE TAX PAID, single version. $200

Two-label, 12-ounce, high- or low-profile cone or quart cone top, "A ROYAL BREW," orange-yellow can, INTERNAL REVENUE TAX PAID, multiversions.

12-ounce, ... $65
Quart, ...$125

Dawson's Premium Quality Ale, two-label, 12-ounce, high-profile cone or quart cone top, "FIT FOR A KING," orange-yellow can, single version.
12-ounce,..$65
Quart,..$125
Two-label 12-ounce flat top or quart cone top, gold can, "DAWSON'S" in red, IRTP or non-IRTP, multiversions.
Flat top,..$100
Cone top, ...$250
Dawson's Premium Quality Lager, two-label 12-ounce flat top, gold can, "DAWSON'S" in black, IRTP or non-IRTP, single version.
Non-IRTP, ...$65
IRTP, ...$75

RHEINGOLD BREWING COMPANY, 29–43 Brook Street (successor to Dawson Brewery, Inc. or Dawson Brewing Company; aka: Forrest Brewing Company, Jacob Ruppert)

Gablinger's Beer, Forest Brewing Company, single-label 12- or 16-ounce tab top, black, brown, or metallic brown label, oval label, multiversions. $5
Malta Rheingold, Rheingold Brewing Company, two-label 12-ounce zip top, white can, black lettering, "RHEINGOLD" on red ribbon, single version. $5
Ruppert Knickerbocker New York's Famous Beer, Jacob Ruppert, two-label 12- or 16-ounce tab top, white can, metallic gold trim, three ribbons, multiversions..$5

Springfield

COMMONWEALTH BREWING CORPORATION, 222 Chestnut Street

Bay State Ale, single-label 12-ounce flat top, green can, yellow or silver label, OPENING INSTRUCTIONS, INTERNAL REVENUE TAX PAID, multiversions.....Exotic
Bay State Beer, single-label 12-ounce flat top, brown can, yellow or silver label, OPENING INSTRUCTIONS, INTERNAL REVENUE TAX PAID, multiversions.....Exotic
New England Ale, single-label 12-ounce flat top, red or yellow label, OPENING INSTRUCTIONS, INTERNAL REVENUE TAX PAID, multiversions. ....Exotic
New England Beer, single-label 12-ounce flat top, red trim, OPENING INSTRUCTIONS, INTERNAL REVENUE TAX PAID, single version. ....Exotic

Willamansett

HAMPDEN BREWING COMPANY, HAMPDEN-HARVARD BREWERIES, INC., DREWRYS LTD. USA, INC., PIEL BROS., INC., 45–95 North Chicopee Street (aka: Dawson Brewing Company, Fitzgerald Bros., Hedrick Brewing Company, Regional Brewing Company)

Dawson Lager Beer, Dawson Brewing Company, two-label 12-ounce tab top, gold can, white lines, "DAWSON" in black or red, multiversions. $5

Dawson Sparkling Ale, Dawson Brewing Company, two-label 12-ounce tab top, silver can, white lines, "DAWSON" in black or green, multiversions. $5

Dobler Private Seal Beer, Hampden-Harvard Breweries, two-label 12-ounce flat top, metallic gold can, vertical red lines, "SINCE 1895" in red or green, single version. $20

Dobler XXX Amber Ale, Hampden-Harvard Breweries, two-label 12-ounce flat top, metallic gold or silver can, vertical red or green lines, "SINCE 1895" in red or green, multiversions. $20

Fitz Ale, Fitzgerald Bros., two-label 12-ounce flat top, white can, "ALE" in black or green, single version of each. $60

Fitz Beer, Fitzgerald Bros., two-label 12-ounce flat top, white can, "BEER" in black or red, single version of each. $45

Hampden Ale, Hampden-Harvard Breweries, single-label 12-ounce flat top, green can, white label, "HAMPDEN ALE" in black, multiversions. $35

Hampden Dry Lager Beer, Hampden Brewing Company, yellow can, white label, "HAMPDEN BEER" in black, multiversions. $75

Hampden Mild Ale, Hampden Brewing Company, single-label 12-ounce flat top, green can, yellow label, "MILD" in green, INTERNAL REVENUE TAX PAID, single version. $125

Hampden Brewing Company, single-label 12-ounce flat top or quart cone top, metallic green can, yellow label, "HAMPDEN" in red, multiversions.
Flat top, ... $60
Cone top, ...$100

Hampden Premium Flavor Beer, Hampden-Harvard Breweries, single-label 12-ounce flat top, red can, white label, metallic gold trim, multiversions. $35

Hampden Brewing Company, single-label 12-ounce flat top, yellow can, black label, gold trim, multiversions. $60

Hampden Premium Quality Ale, Hampden-Harvard Breweries, single- or two-label 12-ounce flat top, green can, white label, "HAMPDEN ALE" in green, multiversions. $10

Hampden Premium Quality Beer, Hampden-Harvard Breweries, single- or two-label 12-ounce flat or tab top, white can, metallic blue label and trim, multiversions. $10

Harvard Ale, Hampden-Harvard Breweries, single-label 12-ounce flat top, green can, white label, silver trim, single version. $35

Harvard Export Beer, Hampden-Harvard Breweries, single-label 12-ounce flat top, red can, white label, multiversions. $75

Hedrick Lager Beer, Hedrick Brewing Company, single-label 12-ounce tab top, gold or silver can, red label, single version of each. $10

Norvic Pilsener Lager Beer, Regional Brewing Company, two-label 12-ounce flat top, white can, "NORVIC" in red, metallic gold band, multiversions. ... $60

Piels Draft Ale, Piels Bros., two-label 12-ounce tab top, green can, "PIELS" in red, "DRAFT ALE" in white, single version. $25

Piels Light Lager Beer, Piels Bros., two-label 12-ounce flat, zip, or tab top, white can, "PIELS" in red, gold trim, multiversions. $12

Piels Real Draft Beer, Piels Bros., two-label 12-ounce flat or soft top, white can, "REAL DRAFT" in woodgrain, multiversions. $10

Piels Real Draft Premium Beer, two-label 12-ounce flat or tab top, white can, "NEW" in silver, "REAL DRAFT" in woodgrain, multiversions. $5

Weiss Beer, Hampden Brewery, single-label 12-ounce flat top, yellow can, black label, single version. $3

This brewery produced various brands, with various mandatories in aluminum cans. The collector value does not exceed $3 each.

Worchester

BROCKERT BREWING COMPANY, 81–87 Lafayette Street

Brockert Pale Ale, single-label, 12-ounce, J-spout cone or quart cone top, yellow can, "BROCKERT" in white on green band, single version.
12-ounce,...$225
Quart, ... $400

Brockert Porter, single-label, 12-ounce, J-spout cone top, green can, INTERNAL REVENUE TAX PAID, single version. ....Exotic

Michigan

/

Battle Creek

FOOD CITY BREWING COMPANY, 200 Elm Street

Cans produced with FOOD CITY mandatories were probably produced in Chicago by the Manhattan Brewing Company.

Old Gold Seven Star Lager Beer, single-label 12-ounce flat top, white or gold panels on back of can, OPENING INSTRUCTIONS, INTERNAL REVENUE TAX PAID, two versions. ....Unique

HONER BREWING COMPANY, 66 South McCamly Street

Honer's Special Pilsener Lager Beer, single-label, 12-ounce, J-spout or high-profile cone top, gold can, red label, "PILSNER" in red on white ribbon, single version of each. Either version, ... $300

Bay City

PHOENIX BREWING COMPANY, 408–10 Arbor Street

Phoenix Lager Beer, single-label, 12-ounce, high-profile cone top, black can, large red oval label, single version. $300

Detroit

ALTES BREWING COMPANY, 10205 Mack Avenue (successor to Tivoli Brewing Company)

7/11 The Natural Brew, two-label 12-ounce flat top, white can, gold bands, "7/11" in red, single version. $65

Altes Brisk Lager Beer, two-label, 12-ounce, high-profile cone or flat top, green can, white oval label, red ribbon, single version of each.
Cone top, ...$100
Flat top, ... $85

Altes Golden Lager Beer, two-label 12-ounce flat top, white can, metallic or dull gold trim, "ALTES" in red, multiversions. $40

Altes Lager Beer, two-label 12-ounce crowntainer, silver or white can, green lettering and trim, INTERNAL REVENUE TAX PAID, single version of each.
Silver can, ... $85
White can, ...$100

Single-label, 12-ounce, high-profile cone top, with or without IRTP, green can, gold filigree and label, single version of each.
IRTP, ... $85
Non-IRTP, ... $75

Altes Sportsman Ale, two-label 12-ounce flat top, red can, metallic gold label and lettering statements, set of 17 cans called "Sportsmans" series, "Muskellunge lifespan 10 to 15 years," "30,000 archers hunted. . . .," "80,000 miles of modern highway . . . ," "Michigan's nickname—Wolverine State," "Michigan's land area larger than Greece," "Detroit baseball world champs—1935," "First cement highway in Michigan . . . ," "Michigan highest point 2,023 ft," "Michigan was 26th state in Union," "Michigan state flower—apple blossom," "First Lansing capital destroyed. . . .," "Michigan ruled by English 1763–1796," "Michigan ruled by French 1634–1763," "Sault Ste. Marie settled in 1668," "Ty Cobb's highest average 420 in 1911," "State capital cost $1,510,130.59," "Spanish flag flew in Michigan—1781." Each, ... $85

ASSOCIATED BREWING COMPANY, 3740 Bellevue Avenue (successor to Pfeiffer Brewing Company; aka: Drewrys Ltd., Detroit, MI, E & B Brewing Company, Old Dutch Brewing Company, Pfeiffer Brewing Company)

Drewrys Beer, Drewrys Ltd., two-label 12-ounce tab top, white can, block orange label with white shield, single version. $10

"Old Dutch" Brand "The Good Beer," Old Dutch Brewing Company, two-label 12-ounce tab top, white can, "OLD DUTCH" outlined in red, single version. $10

Pfeiffer Famous Beer, Pfeiffer Brewing Company, woodgrain can, metallic gold bands, multiversions. $7

Pfeiffer Premium Beer, Pfeiffer Brewing Company, white can, red label, metallic oval label, multiversions. $10

Pfeiffer Brewing Company, two-label 12-ounce flat or zip top, cartoon mugs, multicolored can, single version of each.
Flat top, ... $65
Zip top, ... $60

Schmidt's Premium Quality Beer, two-label 12-ounce zip top, metallic gold can, "SCHMIDT'S" in white on black label, single version. $35

EKHARDT & BECKER BREWING COMPANY, 1551 Winder Street (successor to Regal Brewing Company; aka: E & B Brewing Company, Schmidt Brewing Company)

Cardinal Beer, Ekhardt & Becker Brewing, single-label 12-ounce flat top, red can, white label, bird within loop of "c," single version. $60

E & B Brewing, two-label 12-ounce flat top, gold can, white label, bird within loop of "c," single version. .... Exotic

E & B Brew "103" Light Beer, E & B Brewing, white can, metallic gold label, "E & B" in white on red, multiversions. $65

E & B Brew "103" Pale Dry Beer, E & B Brewing, single-label 12-ounce flat top, white can, metallic gold label, "BREW 103" in black, multiversions. .. $85

E & B Golden Bud Ale, single-label, 12-ounce, high-profile cone top, gold can, red label, INTERNAL REVENUE TAX PAID, multiversions...................... Exotic

E & B Light Lager Beer, E & B Brewing, single-label, 12-ounce, high-profile cone top, blue can, yellow label, "LIGHT LAGER" in white on red, INTERNAL REVENUE TAX PAID, multiversions. $85

E & B Premium Beer, E & B Brewing, single-label, 12-ounce, high-profile cone or flat top, blue can, white label, "PREMIUM" in white on red ribbon, IRTP or non-IRTP on cones, flat non-IRTP, single versions.
Flat top, ... $60
Non-IRTP cone top, ... $85
IRTP cone top, ... $100

E & B Special Beer, Ekhardt & Becker Brewing, single-label, 12-ounce, high-profile cone top, blue can, gold label, "SPECIAL" in white on red ribbon, INTERNAL REVENUE TAX PAID, multiversions. *(See photo 159)*
Non-IRTP, ... $100
IRTP, ... $115

Schmidt's Beer, E & B Brewing, two-label 12-ounce flat top, white can, red label, "NATURAL BREW" in white, single version. $75

E & B Brewing or Old Dutch Brewing, single-label 12-ounce flat top, silver can, black shield, white label, multiversions. $40

E & B Brewing, two-label 12-ounce flat top, white can, red shield, white label, single version. $40

Photo 159. E and B Special Beer.

GOEBEL BREWING COMPANY, Maple and Rivard Streets

Bantam Ale By Goebel, single-label 8-ounce flat top, white can, black label, rooster, multiversions. $60

Bantam Beer By Goebel, single-label 8-ounce flat top, white can, black label, "RIGHT FROM CYPRESS CASKS," "NATIONALLY FAMOUS," multiversions. $50

Goebel 22 Beer, two-label 11- or 12-ounce flat top, metallic gold can, white label, "22" in red circle, multiversions. $40

Goebel Bantam Beer, single-label 8-ounce flat top, gold can, white label, blue oval, multiversions. $35

Goebel Beer, single-label 12-ounce flat top, metallic gold can, thunderbird on black label, OPENING INSTRUCTIONS, INTERNAL REVENUE TAX PAID, multiversions. $175

Single-label 12-ounce flat top, metallic gold can, eagle on black label, OPENING INSTRUCTIONS, INTERNAL REVENUE TAX PAID, multiversions.
Camouflage can, ... $400
Others, ... $200

Single-label 12-ounce flat top, gold can, blue and white label, single version. $25

Goebel Bock Beer, single-label 12-ounce flat top, white can, goat on red circle, single version. $300

Goebel Crystilled Beer, single-label 8- or 12-ounce can, white label outlined in blue, multiversions. $20

Goebel Extra Dry Beer, single-label 12-ounce flat top, metallic gold can, "EXTRA DRY" on black circle, multiversions. $85

Goebel Extra Dry Private Stock Beer, single-label 12-ounce flat top, metallic gold can, white label, multiversions. $45

Goebel Genuine Bock Beer, single-label 12-ounce flat top, maroon can, white label, "BOCK BEER" in black, single version. $250

Goebel Light Lager Luxury Beer, single-label 8- or 12-ounce flat top, metallic gold can, red label, "LUXURY BEER" on black ribbon, multiversions.
8-ounce, ... $60
12-ounce, ... $50

Goebel Light Lager Private Stock 22 Beer, single-label 8-, 12-, or 16-ounce flat top, metallic gold can, red label, "PRIVATE STOCK 22" on black ribbon, multiversions.
8-ounce, ... $60
12-ounce, ... $50
16-ounce, ... $60

Goebel Old Original Ale, single-label 8-ounce flat top, gold can, green and white label, rooster, single version. ....Exotic

Goebel Private Stock 22 Beer, single-label 8-, 12-, or 16-ounce flat top, gold can, blue label, multiversions. $15

Guinness's Ale, single-label 12-ounce flat top, green can, gold and white label, multiversions. $150

Guinness's Lager Beer, single-label 12-ounce flat top, red can, gold and white label, multiversions. $150

NATIONAL BREWING COMPANY, 10205 Mack Avenue (successor to Altes Brewing Company; aka: National Brewing Company of Detroit)

Altes Golden Lager Beer, single- or two-label 12- or 16-ounce flat or zip top, red can, white label outlined in metallic gold, multiversions. $60

Two-label 12- or 16-ounce tab top, white can, gold trim, "ALTES BEER" in red, multiversions. $40

Colt 45 Malt Liquor, two-label 12- or 16-ounce zip or tab top, white can, colt in gold horseshoe, "MALT LIQUOR" in red, multiversions. $5

Colt 45 Stout Malt Liquor, two-label 12- or 16-ounce tab or zip top, white can, colt in gold horseshoe, "STOUT MALT LIQUOR" in red, multiversions. $5

Draft Beer By National, two-label gallon can, white can, glass of beer on label, single version. $450

National Bohemian Light Lager Beer, two-label 12-ounce flat or tab top, red can, black label with or without "Mr Boh," multiversions. $20

National Bohemian Pale Beer, single- or two-label 12-ounce flat top, red can, black label, "Mr Boh," multiversions. $30

National Sportsman Ale, single-label 12-ounce flat top, green can, metallic gold trim, "NATIONAL SPORTSMAN ALE" in white, single version. $100

Van Lauter Bavarian Lager Beer, two-label 12-ounce tab top, blue can, white label, "BAVARIAN" in red, single version. $10

PFEIFFER BREWING COMPANY, 3740 Bellevue Avenue

Pfeiffer Premium Beer, single-label 12-ounce flat top, set cans, two sets of nine each, called "Pfeiffer" scenes, dull or bright gold trim, versions: ore ship, one sailboat, two sailboats, white-tailed deer, pheasant, trout fishing, geese, muskie, skiing, single version of each. $100

Two-label 12-ounce flat top, white can, large red label, small "Johnny Pfeiffer," multiversions. $15

Pfeiffer's Famous Beer, single-label 12-ounce flat top, yellow or camouflage can, large "Johnny Pfeiffer," WITHDRAWN FREE, INTERNAL REVENUE TAX PAID, multiversion of non-IRTP, single-version all others.
Non-IRTP, ... $40
IRTP, ... $50
Camouflage can, ... $350

Two-label 12-ounce flat top, gold can, white stripes and label, "PFEIFFER" in red, multiversions. $25

THE SCHMIDT BREWING COMPANY, 1955 Wilkins Street

Schmidt's Beer, single-label 12-ounce, high-profile cone top, red can, metallic gold bands, white label, INTERNAL REVENUE TAX PAID, "NO SUGAR, NO GLUCOSE ADDED," multiversions. $125

Single-label 12-ounce, high-profile cone top, red can, blue vertical bands, white label, INTERNAL REVENUE TAX PAID, "THE NATURAL BREW," multiversions.
.... $125

Single-label, 12-ounce, high-profile cone top, silver can, white label, gold bands, single version. $100

THE STROH BREWERY COMPANY, 909 East Elizabeth

The Stroh Brewery Company acquired the Goebel Brewing Company in 1964, acquiring the rights to the Goebel brand. They issued a wide variety of Goebel cans, both in steel and aluminum. The collector value of these cans does not exceed $2.

When Stroh acquired the Jos. Schlitz Brewing Company in 1981, it acquired the Schlitz brands. All Schlitz labels issued in steel or aluminum have a collector value of up to $1.

When Stroh acquired the Schaefer Brewing Company in 1976, it acquired all the Schaefer brands. All Schaefer brands issued in steel or aluminum have a collector value of $1.

All other brands originating with Stroh, in aluminum, carry a collector value of $1.

Goebel Beer, Goebel Brewing Company, two-label 12-ounce zip top, gold can, blue and white label, single version. $3

Goebel Draft Beer, Goebel Brewing, two-label 12-ounce tab top, metallic or dull gold can, multiversions. $3

Stroh's Bohemian Style Beer, single- or two-label 12- or 16-ounce flat or tab top, metallic gold and white can, black label, multiversions. *(See photo 160)*
Flat top, ... $10
Tab top, ...$2

TIVOLI BREWING COMPANY, 10205 Mack Avenue

Altes Lager Beer, two-label 12-ounce crowntainer, silver can, green lettering and trim, multiversions. $125

Flint

VALLEY BREWING COMPANY, 201 South Saginaw

Heidelburg Brand Pilsner Beer, single-label, 12-ounce, high-profile cone top, red and black can, white label, INTERNAL REVENUE TAX PAID or non-IRTP, single version of each.
Non-IRTP, ... $85
IRTP, ...$100

Photo 160. Stroh's Bohemian Style Beer.

Frankenmuth

CARLING BREWING COMPANY, 907 South Main (successor to International Breweries)

Black Label Beer, single- or two-label 12-ounce tab top, red can, black label, map of the world or U.S., multiversions. $10

Two-label 12-ounce tab top, red can, black label outlined in white, gold bands, multiversions. $15

Two-label 12- or 16-ounce tab top, tankard can, multiversions. $15

Carling Black Label Beer, single-label 12-ounce flat or zip top, red can, black label outlined in white, "CARLING" on label, multiversions. $8

Carling Black Label Bock Beer, single-label 12-ounce tab top, white can, black label, red goat's head, multiversions. $35

Red Cap Ale, two-label 12-ounce tab top, metallic green can, cream-colored split label, man with cap, single version. $20

Two-label 12-ounce tab top, gold diamonds, white label, red vertical band, single version. $15

This brewery also produced the preceding brands in aluminum cans but cannot be distinguished from other Carling Breweries. Tuborg Brewed Light Beer was brewed here, with mandatories reading TUBORG BREWERIES LTD. U.S.A., Frankenmuth. Collector value is $3

CARLING NATIONAL BREWERIES, 907 South Main Street (successor to Carling Brewing Company)

Carling brands (other than Altes Golden Lager Beer), either in aluminum or steel, *cannot* be assigned to a particular brewery, and are therefore not listed. Altes Golden Lager was produced in multiversions in aluminum cans and has a collector value of $2.

THE FRANKENMUTH BREWING COMPANY, 907 South Main

Frankenmuth Air Free Beer, single-label, 12-ounce, high-profile cone top, black and yellow can, with or without story, single version of each. Either version, ... $100

Frankenmuth Dog Gone Good Beer, single-label, 12-ounce, high-profile cone top, black and yellow can, white label, INTERNAL REVENUE TAX PAID, multiversions. $100

Frankenmuth Mellow-Dry Beer, two-label 12-ounce flat top, black can, yellow label, man on red oval, single version. $75

Frankenmuth Melodry Ale, single-label 12-ounce flat top, metallic gold can, brown label outlined in white, single version. $75

Frankenmuth Melodry Beer, single-label 12-ounce flat top, metallic gold can, white label outlined in brown, single version. $75

Frankenmuth Mel-O-Dry Beer, two-label 12-ounce flat top, black can, yellow label, man on red circle, multiversions. $85

Frankenmuth Nut Brown Bock Beer, two-label 12-ounce flat top, black can, red oval label outlined in white, single version. $125

Frankenmuth Old English Brand Ale, single-label, 12-ounce, high-profile cone top, black can, white label, yellow trim, INTERNAL REVENUE TAX PAID, multi-versions. $125

Two-label 12-ounce flat top, black can, white oval label, man on red circle, single version. $60

Two-label 12-ounce flat top, black can, yellow label, man on red circle, single version. $60

Frankenmuth Premium Dry Beer, two-label 12-ounce flat top, black can, yellow label, "PREMIUM DRY" in red, single version. $65

GEYER BROS. BREWING COMPANY, 415 South Main

Frankenmuth Bavarian Dark Beer, two-label 12-ounce tab top, yellow can, black bands, "FRANKENMUTH" in red, single version. $40

Frankenmuth Bavarian Light Beer, two-label 12-ounce tab top, black can, white label, "FRANKENMUTH" in red, single version. *(See photo 161)* $35

Geyer's Lager Beer, two-label 12-ounce tab top, red can, white bands, "G" on stein, single version. $50

G. HEILEMAN BREWING COMPANY, 907 South Main (successor to Carling National Brewing Company)

All cans produced by Heileman Brewing Company at Frankenmuth were produced in aluminum and do not have a collector value that exceeds $1.

INTERNATIONAL BREWERIES, 907 South Main Street (successor to Frankenmuth Brewing Company)

Frankenmuth Genuine Bock Beer, single-label 12-ounce flat top, metallic gold can, red label outlined in white, single version. $60

Frankenmuth Melodry Ale, single-label 12-ounce flat top, metallic gold can, brown label outlined in white, single version. $75

Frankenmuth Melodry Beer, single-label 12-ounce flat top, metallic gold can, white label outlined in brown, single version. $75

Photo 161. Frankenmuth Bavarian Light Beer.

Grand Rapids

FOX DELUXE BREWING COMPANY, India and Ottawa Streets

Alpine Pilsner Beer, single-label 12-ounce flat top, white can, gold stripes, "PILSNER BEER" in red, single version. $85

Fox Deluxe Beer, single-label 12-ounce flat top, metallic or dull gold can, huntsman with horn, OPENING INSTRUCTIONS, INTERNAL REVENUE TAX PAID, camouflage can, single version of each.
Metallic or dull, ... $300
Camouflage, ... $600

Single-label 12-ounce cone or flat top, or quart cone top, gold can, white oval label, IRTP or non-IRTP, multiversions.
12-ounce flat top, ... $25
12-ounce IRTP flat top, ... $35
12-ounce cone top, ... $75
Quart cone top, ...$100

Patrick Henry Beer, single-label 12-ounce flat top, white can, metallic gold label, drinking scene, single version. $300

Patrick Henry Extra Smooth Premium Beer, single-label 12-ounce flat top, gold and maroon can, pinstripes, white oval label, INTERNAL REVENUE TAX PAID, single version. $250

Patrick Henry Velvet Smooth Malt Liquor, single-label 12-ounce flat top, metallic green can, metallic gold stripes, white label, single version. $225

Hancock

COPPER COUNTY BREWING COMPANY, 600 Emma Street
(successor to A. Haas Brewing Company)

Copper Club Pilsner Beer, two-label, 12-ounce, high-profile cone top, gold and green can, multiversions...$100

A. HAAS BREWING COMPANY, 600 Emma Street

Copper Club Pilsner Beer, two-label, 12-ounce, high-profile cone top, metallic gold can, white label, green trim, multiversions. $85

Houghton

BOSCH BREWING COMPANY, Memorial Road

Bosch Beer, single-label 12-ounce flat top, white can, gold bands, red circle, single version. $40

Single-label 12-ounce flat top, metallic gold can, line drawings, multiversions (not a set can). $25

Bosch Premium Beer, single-label 12-ounce flat top, metallic gold can, line drawings, multiversions (not a set can). $25

Gilt Edge Premium Beer, two-label 12-ounce tab top, metallic gold hatched can, white label outlined in red, multiversions. $25

Two-label 12-ounce tab top, white can, white label outlined in metallic gold and red, single version. $10

A. HAAS BREWING COMPANY, 106 Sheldon Street

Copper Club Pilsner Beer, two-label, 12-ounce, high-profile cone top, metallic gold can, green trim, white label, INTERNAL REVENUE TAX PAID, single version. $100

Haas Pilsner Style Beer, single-label high- or low-profile cone top, metallic gold can, red label, "HAAS & BEER" in white, INTERNAL REVENUE TAX PAID, multiversions. $85

Menominee

MENOMINEE MARINETTE BREWING COMPANY, 1200 Sheridan Road

Big Mac Brand Beer, two-label 12-ounce flat top, white can, "BIG MAC" in red, bridge, single version. $85

Menominee Champion Light Beer, single-label, 12-ounce, high-profile cone top, IRTP or non-IRTP, red and white can, multiversions.
IRTP, ... $50
Non IRTP, ... $45

Silver Cream Beer, single-label, 12-ounce, high-profile cone or flat top, silver can, blue or purple label, multiversions.
Cone top, ... $100
Flat top $60

Sebewaing

SEBEWAING BREWING COMPANY, 221 East Main

Sebewaing Beer, single-label 12-ounce flat top, yellow can, red stripe on bottom, line drawing of pheasant, multiversions. *(See photo 162)*................. $60

Single-label 12-ounce flat or zip top, blue can, pheasant, "BEER" in red, single version of each. $75

Photo 162. Sebewaing Beer.

Minnesota

Cold Spring

COLD SPRING BREWING COMPANY, 219 North Red River Street (aka: Northern Brewing Company, Cold Spring, MN, Arrowhead Brewing Company)

Amana Beer, Northern Brewing, two-label 12-ounce tab top, black can, white lettering, single version. $3

Arrowhead Beer, Arrowhead Brewing or Cold Spring Brewing, two-label 12-ounce tab top, blue can, gold or silver arrowhead and trim, multiversion. (*See photo 163*)..$3

Billy Beer, Cold Spring Brewing, two-label 12-ounce tab top, orange and white can, blue, brown, or orange bands, multiversions. $2

Bowman Beer, Cold Spring Brewing, two-label 12-ounce tab top, white can, "BOWMAN" in brown, single version. $3

Buffalo Brew, Cold Spring Brewing, single-label 12-ounce flat top, orange can, picture of a block house, single version. $2

Photo 163. Arrowhead Beer.

Casselton Centennial Beer, Cold Spring Brewing, two-label 12-ounce tab top, white can, black and white label, single version....................................$3

Cold Spring Beer, Cold Spring Brewing, two-label 12-ounce flat or tab top, metallic gold can, blue label outlined in white, multiversions. $10

Cold Spring Brewing, two-label 12- or 16-ounce tab top, white can, blue label outlined in silver, multiversions. (*See photo 164*)...................................$5

Cold Spring Golden Brew Beer, Cold Spring Brewing, two-label 12-ounce flat top, metallic gold can, blue or black label, multiversions.
Blue label, ... $10
Black label, ... $15

Cold Spring Lager Beer, Cold Spring Brewing, single-label, 12-ounce, high-profile cone top, IRTP and non-IRTP, gray can, black lettering, red trim, multiversions.
IRTP, ... $65
Non-IRTP, ... $60

Cold Spring Brewing, single-label, 12-ounce, high-profile cone top, gold can, white label, red trim, multiversions. $85

Cold Spring Brewing, cream-colored can, white label, red trim, multiversions.
.... $75

Cold Spring Pep Lager Beer, Cold Spring Brewing, single-label, 12-ounce, high-profile cone top, IRTP or non-IRTP, gray can, black lettering, red trim, single version of each.
IRTP, ... $100
Non-IRTP, ... $90

Fox Deluxe Beer, Cold Spring Brewing, two-label 12-ounce tab top, white and metallic gold can, multiversions. $10

Gemeinde Brau, Cold Spring Brewing, two-label 12-ounce flat top, green can, black bands, white lettering, multiversions. $10

Gluek Finest Pilsner Beer, Cold Spring Brewing, two-label 12-ounce tab top, yellow and gold can, multiversions. $3

Harlan Gold Beer, Cold Spring Brewing, two-label 12-ounce tab top, black can, gold label, single version. $3

Jennings Deluxe Beer, Cold Spring Brewing, two-label 12-ounce tab top, metallic gold can, blue or black label, single version of each.
Black label, ...$100
Blue label, ...$85

Karlsbrau Old Time Beer, Cold Spring Brewing, two-label 12-ounce tab top, brown and white can, woodgrain, multiversions. $10

Kegle Brau The Classic Beer, Cold Spring Brewing, two-label 12-ounce tab top, black and metallic gold can, multiversions. $10

Kegle Brau Genuine Draft Beer, Cold Spring Brewing, two-label gallon can, blue can, yellow lettering, single version. $350

Knoxville Race Ways Beer, Cold Spring Brewing, two-label 12-ounce tab top, gold can, single version. $3

Kolonie Brau Beer, Cold Spring Brewing, two-label 12-ounce tab top, black can, single version.(*See photo 165*)...$3

(From left to right)
Photo 164. Cold Spring Beer.
Photo 165. Kolonie Brau Beer.
Photo 166. North Star XXX Beer.

North Star XXX Beer, Cold Spring Brewing or Northern Brewing, two-label 12-ounce tab top, white can, metallic gold bands, red or blue label, single version of each. (*See photo 166*)... $15

Traer Czech Fest Beer, Cold Spring Brewing, two-label 12-ounce tab top, gold can, single version. $3

Western Beer, Cold Spring Brewing, two-label 12-ounce tab top, orange, black, and white can, multiversions. $10

White Label Fine Quality Beer, Cold Spring Brewing, two-label 12-ounce tab top, white can, square metallic gold label, single version. $10

Cold Spring has and is producing a wide variety of brands, both in aluminum and in steel. The value of these cans will not exceed $1.

Duluth

DULUTH BREWING AND MALTING COMPANY, 229–231
South 29th Avenue

Karlsbrau Old Time Beer, single-label 12-ounce flat or cone top, red can, white label, "OLD TIME" in black, multiversions.
Flat top, ... $50
Cone top, ... $90

Royal 58 Beer, two-label 12-ounce flat or zip top, metallic gold and white can, "58" in red, single version of each.
Flat top, ... $40
Zip top, ... $35

Royal Bohemian Style Beer, single-label, 12-ounce, high-profile cone top, white or off-white can, "ROYAL BOHEMIAN" on blue ribbon, multiversions. $75

Royal Bohemian Style Extra Pale, single-label, 12-ounce, high-profile cone top, white or off-white can, "EXTRA PALE" in red, multiversions. $75

FITGER BREWING COMPANY, 532–600 East Superior

Fitger's Beer, single-label high-profile cone top, gold can, white label, red bands, multiversions. $65

Two-label 12-ounce flat top, gold can, horizontal pinstripes, black or red band, multiversions. $20

Fitger's Natural Beer, single-label, 12-ounce low-profile cone top, red can, orange label, black lettering, INTERNAL REVENUE TAX PAID, multiversions. $150

Fitger's Nordlager Natural Brewed Beer, single-label high- or low-profile cone top, gray can, bottom black band, INTERNAL REVENUE TAX PAID, multiversions...$110

Fitger's Rex Imperial Dry Beer, single-label, 12-ounce, high-profile cone or tab top, IRTP or non-IRTP, yellow or off-white can, red and gold label, multiversions.
Cone top, ...$65
Flat top, ...$15

Twins Lager Beer, two-label 12-ounce tab top, white can, red label and twin, single version...$175

PEOPLES BREWING COMPANY, 4230 West 2nd

Olde English "600" Malt Liquor, single-label, 12-ounce, high-profile cone top, metallic gold can, white label, "600" in red, single version. $150

Regal Supreme Beer, single-label, 12-ounce, high-profile cone top, cream-colored can, metallic gold bands, multiversions. $85

Fergus Falls

FALLS BREWING COMPANY, 121 North Peck Street

Falls Premium Pilsner Beer, two-label, 12-ounce, high-profile cone top, gold and white sunburst can, white label, multiversions. $100

Falls Velvet Pilsner Beer, single-label, 12-ounce, high-profile cone top, metallic gold can, black label, INTERNAL REVENUE TAX PAID, two versions. $200

Little Falls

KIEWEL BREWING COMPANY, 7th Street and 5th Avenue

Grain Lager Beer, single-label, 12-ounce, high-profile cone top, white can, red band, gold trim, multiversions. $125

Kiewel's White Seal Beer, single-label, 12-ounce, high-profile cone top, red and black can, INTERNAL REVENUE TAX PAID, two versions. $300

White Seal Beer, single-label high-profile cone top, metallic gold can, white diamond label, multiversions. $75

Mankato

COLD SPRING BREWING COMPANY, 628 Roeck Street (successor to Mankato Brewing Company)

Kato Premium Beer, single-label, 12-ounce, high-profile cone top, gold can, white label outlined in black, multiversions. $125

MANKATO BREWING COMPANY, 628 East Roeck Street

Kato Gold Label Beer, single-label, 12-ounce, low-profile cone top, pink can, black band on bottom face, INTERNAL REVENUE TAX PAID, single version.
....Exotic

Single-label, 12-ounce, low-profile cone top, gold can, red band on bottom face, INTERNAL REVENUE TAX PAID, multiversions. $300

Kato Lager Beer, single-label low-profile cone top, silver can, "KATO" on black label, INTERNAL REVENUE TAX PAID, multiversions. $100

Kato Premium Beer, single-label, 12-ounce, high-profile cone top, silver can, large oval yellow label, multiversions. $100

Kato Super Brew Beer, single-label, 12-ounce, low-profile cone top, red can, "KATO" on black label, gold band, INTERNAL REVENUE TAX PAID, single version. $100

Minneapolis

GLUEK BREWING COMPANY, 2021 Marshall Street Northeast

Gluek Brewing Company canned Pioneer Beer using the mandatory PIONEER BREWING COMPANY.

Gluek Fine Pilsner Beer, single- or two-label 12-ounce flat top, white can, "GLUEK" in black, red lion, multiversions. $30

Gluek Stite Malt Lager, two-label 8-ounce flat top, white can, gray and red shield, "GLUEK" in gray, single version. $35

Gluek Stite Malt Liquor, two-label 8- or 12-ounce flat top, white can, "GLUEK" in black, gold, or gray, two-color shield, multiversions.
8-ounce, ... $35
12-ounce, ... $50

Gluek's Beer, single-label 12-ounce crowntainer, IRTP or non-IRTP, silver can, red or blue label, multiversions.
IRTP, ... $60
Non-IRTP, ... $55

Two-label 12-ounce flat top, white can, red and blue stripes, single version.
.... $50

Gluek's Pilsener Beer, two-label, 12-ounce, low-profile cone top, silver and gold can, INTERNAL REVENUE TAX PAID, single version of each. $300

Gluek's Pilsener Pale Beer, single-label, 12-ounce, low-profile cone top, silver can, "GLUEK'S" in black on blue label, INTERNAL REVENUE TAX PAID, multiversions. $150

Single-label, 12-ounce, low-profile cone top, silver can, "GLUEK'S" in white on gold label, INTERNAL REVENUE TAX PAID, single version. $150

Single-label 12-ounce crowntainer, silver can, blue or purple stripes, multiversions. $65

Gluek's Stite Malt Liquor, single-label 12-ounce crowntainer, paper label, white can, green stripes, two versions. .... Exotic

Two-label 8- or 12-ounce flat top, metallic green can, white label, multiversions. (*See photo 167*)

8-ounce, ... $75

12-ounce, ... $85

Pioneer Beer, two-label 12-ounce flat top, white can, blue stripes, "PIONEER" in red, single version. $35

GRAIN BELT BREWERIES, INC., 1215 Marshall Street Northeast
(successor to Minneapolis Brewing Company)

GBX Malt Liquor, two-label 12- or 16-ounce tab top, blue can, embossed "GBX," multiversions. (*See photo 168*) $25

Grain Belt Beer, two-label 12- or 16-ounce tab top, gold stripes, white diamond label, red diamond inner label, multiversions. $3

Grain Belt Bock Beer, two-label 12-ounce tab top, yellow can, maroon stripes and label, red grain belt diamond, multiversions. $5

Grain Belt Premium Beer, two-label 12-ounce tab top, white can, "PREMIUM" in white on red ribbon, single version. $5

Hauenstein New Ulm Beer, two-label 12-ounce tab top, silver and red can, white label outlined in metallic gold, single version. $5

Two-label 12-ounce tab top, red can, white label, multiversions. (There is a version of this can that lists JOHN HAUENSTEIN CO., Minneapolis, Minn., as the mandatory.) $5

Storz Premium Beer, two-label 12-ounce tab top, white, blue, and gold can, "STORZ" on red label, multiversions. $5

White Label Fine Quality Beer, two-label 12-ounce tab top, white can, metallic gold block label, "WHITE LABEL" in black, single version. $15

MINNEAPOLIS BREWING COMPANY, 1215 Marshall Street
Northeast

Grain Belt Beer, single-label, 12-ounce, low-profile cone top, black can, red diamond label, INTERNAL REVENUE TAX PAID, multiversions. $60

(From left to right) Photo 167. Gluek's Stite Malt Liquor.
Photo 168. GBX Malt Liquor. Photo 169. Grain Belt Premium, The Friendly Beer. Photo 170. White Label Draft Beer.
Photo 171. Wunderbar Pilsner Beer Supreme

Single-label, 12-ounce, high-profile cone top, gold can, yellow or white label, large bottle cap, INTERNAL REVENUE TAX PAID, multiversions. $85

Single- or two-label 12- or 16-ounce flat, zip, or tab top, gold can, large bottle cap, "Beer" in black or red, multiversions. $30

Grain Belt Golden Beer, single-label, 12-ounce, high-profile cone or flat top, metallic orange can, metallic gold hatching, white diamond label, single-version cone top, multiversion flat top.
Cone top, ... $50
Flat top, ... $35

Grain Belt Golden Premium Beer, single-label, 12-ounce, high-profile cone top, gold can, white diamond label, red diamond inner label, multiversions.
.... $60

Grain Belt Premium Beer, two-label 12-ounce flat top, metallic gold can, small white diamonds, white diamond labels, multiversions. $10

Grain Belt Premium The Friendly Beer, two-label, 12-ounce, high-profile cone or flat top, metallic orange can, white diamond label, "GRAIN BELT" in white bottle cap on label, INTERNAL REVENUE TAX PAID, multiversions.(*See photo 169*)
IRTP cone top, ... $65
Non-IRTP cone top, ... $60
Flat top, ... $35

White Label Draft Beer, two-label 16-ounce tab top, white can, metallic gold block label, single version. (*See photo 170*) $20

White Label Fine Quality Beer, two-label 12-ounce flat or tab top, white can, metallic gold block label, multiversions. $15

Wunderbar Pilsner Beer Supreme, two-label 12-ounce tab top, black, gold, and yellow can, blue circle, single version. (*See photo 171*).................... $40

New Ulm

JOHN HAUENSTEIN BREWING COMPANY, 1601 South Jefferson

Hauenstein New Ulm Beer, two-label, 12-ounce, high-profile cone top, red can, white lettering, multiversions. $85

Two-label, 12-ounce, high-profile cone top, red can, white label, "NEW ULM" in black, multiversions. $75

AUGUST SCHELL BREWING COMPANY, South Garden Street
(aka: Stein-Haus Brewing Company, Augie's Brewing Company)

Algona Beer, single-label 12-ounce tab top, white can, blue and silver lettering, single version. $2

American Legion '80 World Series Beer, single-label 12-ounce tab top, white can, with outline of Minnesota, single version. $2

An Clar Beer, single-label 12-ounce tab top, white can, green lettering, single version. $2

Andy's Beer, two-label 12-ounce tab top, set can, set of six with map of Minnesota, versions: blue map, "ANDY'S BEER" in red; yellow map, "ANDY'S BEER" in black; tan map, "ANDY'S BEER" in green; red map, "ANDY'S BEER" in yellow; brown map, "ANDY'S BEER" in tan; green map, "ANDY'S BEER in yellow.
Each,..$2
Set,.. $15

Two-label 12-ounce tab top, set can, set of seven with crest, versions: red crest on yellow background, red crest on white background, blue crest on white background, brown crest on white background, green crest on white background, purple crest on white background, orange crest on white background.
Each,..$2
Set, ... $17.50

Andy's Crossroads 56 Beer, two-label 12-ounce tab top, set can, set of six circle on X on white can, versions: light green circle, dark green lettering; blue circle, yellow lettering; dark green circle, light green lettering; black circle, red lettering; red circle, black lettering; yellow circle, blue lettering.
Each,..$2
Set, ... $15

Andy's Grecian Brand Beer, two-label 12-ounce tab top, white can, gladiator on label, single label. $2

Anoka Halloween Festival Beer, single-label 12-ounce tab top, orange and black can, three versions: 1978, 1979, 1980. Each, ...$2

Anoka The Halloween Beer, single-label 12-ounce tab top, yellow can, black cat, "1981," single label. $2

Aquatennial 81 Beer, single-label 12-ounce tab top, yellow can, "81" in blue, single version. $2

Argyle Minnesota Centennial Beer, single-label 12-ounce tab top, white can, blue and yellow label, single version. $2

Avenue Fine Pilsner Beer, single-label 12-ounce tab top, city skyline in black, "AVENUE" in gold, single version. $2

Beer, three- or two-label 12-ounce tab top, white can, "BEER" vertical or horizontal, multiversions. $1

Bix Beer, two-label, 12-ounce tab top, white can, "BIX BEER" in brown, single version. $2

Blackhawk Beer, single-label 12-ounce tab top, black can, gold label, single version. $2

Bob's Special Beer, single-label 12-ounce tab top, set can, set of six, versions: white can, green lettering; silver can, blue lettering; bronze can, black lettering; gold can, black lettering; gold can, green lettering; pink can, black lettering.
Each,..25¢
Set, ...$2

Catfish Jack's Finest Beer, single-label 12-ounce tab top, multicolored can, single version. $2

Crossroads Pilsner Beer, two-label 12-ounce tab top, red or brown can, single version of each color. Each, ...$2

Denver IA Beer, two-label 12-ounce tab top, multicolored can, single version.
....$2

Photo 172. Fitger's Beer.

Durocher's Kan Kave Beer, single-label 12-ounce tab top, multicolored can, single version. $2

Eagle Grove Iowa Centennial Beer, single-label 12-ounce tab top, gold can, black lettering and label, single version. $2

Eagles Beer, single-label 12-ounce tab top, multicolored can, single version. $2

Esterville Iowa Winter Sports Beer, single-label 12-ounce tab top, blue, white, and red can, snowman, single version. $2

Fitger's Beer, two-label 12-ounce tab top, white or yellow can, red star, single version of each. (*See photo 172*) Either version, ...$3

Fitger's Rex Imperial Dry Beer, two-label 12-ounce tab top, yellow can, red and brown shield, single version. $3

Friendship Lounge Beer, single-label 12-ounce tab top, picture of lounge or covered bridge on label, single version of each. $2

Gackle Beer, single-label 12-ounce tab top, yellow can, duck, single label. ...$2

Garrison Beer, single-label 12-ounce tab top, orange can, white label, single label. $2

G. I. Joe Beer, single-label 12-ounce tab top, black can, yellow label, single version. $1

Gorilla Beer, single-label 12-ounce tab top, yellow can, gorilla, single version. $2

Great St. Louisan Beer, two-label 12-ounce tab top, set can, set of two cans, versions: Alfonso J. Cervantes, William L. Clay. Each, ...$2

Heritagefest Beer, two-label 12-ounce tab top, white can, black lettering, single version. $2

Herman's Monument Pilsner Beer, single-label 12-ounce tab top, blue can, monument, single version. $2

High And Mighty Premium Beer, single-label 12-ounce tab top, picture of AV-88 prototype or F-15, single version of each. (Rumored can was never filled.) $5

Holstein Centennial Beer, two-label 12-ounce tab top, black can, white label, single version. $2

Hubbell House Beer, single-label 12-ounce tab top, brown and yellow can, single version. $2

Hunderjahriges Jubilaum Beer, single-label 12-ounce tab top, white can, blue lettering, covered wagon, single version. $2

JB Beer, single-label 12-ounce tab top, red and white can, single version. ...$2

King Turkey Beer, single-label 12-ounce tab top, red or white can, single version of each can. Each,..$2

Light Beer, two-label 12-ounce tab top, white can, multiversions. $1

Lisbon Centennial Beer, single-label 12-ounce tab top, yellow can, single version..$2

Maverick Beer, single-label 12-ounce tab top, set can, series of five cans, versions: Baltimore breweries, Baltimore skyline, Frigate Constellation, Historical Baltimore, Montental City. Each, ...$2

Moose Brand Beer, two-label 12-ounce tab top, white can, maroon label, single version...$2

North Dakota Premium Centennial Beer, two-label 12-ounce tab top, orange can, single version. $2

O'Keenan's Erinbrew Beer, two-label 12-ounce tab top, green can, single version..Worthless

Old Grimes Beer, two-label 12-ounce tab top, white can, single version. $2

Old Okoboji Beer, two-label 12-ounce tab top, multicolored can, single version..$2

Polish Count's Beer, two-label 12-ounce tab top, red or yellow can, single version of each...$2

Polish Countess Beer, two-label 12-ounce tab top, bronze can, single version.
....$2

Railfans Special Beer, single-label 12-ounce tab top, color photo of train, single version. $5

Rough Rider Centennial Beer, single-label 12-ounce tab top, yellow can, single version. $2

Safari Brand Premium Beer, single-label 12-ounce tab top, set can, 24 cans to series, African wildlife, versions: monkey, monkey hanging on a tree, rhinoceros, gerenuk, elephant, cape buffalo, ostrich, lion, eland, women and children, oryx, zebra, Massi, eland herd, gazelle, hippopotamus, lioness, thatched huts, vultures, spotted leopard, hyena, landscape and sun, wildebeast, giraffe. Each,..$5

Schell's Beer, two-label 12- or 16-ounce flat or tab top, gold can, white label, multiversions. All versions,.. $20

Two-label 12- or 16-ounce tab top, black can, maroon or pinkish "IT'S A GRAND OLD BEER," multiversions. $5

Schell's Bock Beer, single-label 12-ounce tab top, brown or white goat, single version..$3

Schell's Deer Brand Beer, single-label 12-ounce crowntainer or high-profile cone top, yellow label, "DEER RUN" on red band, IRTP or non-IRTP, multiversions.
Cone top, ... $85
Crowntainer,...$100
Non-IRTP flat top,.. $10

Schell's Deer Band Export Beer, two-label 12-ounce tab top, multicolored can, deer, series can, six cans to series, versions: "EXPORT BEER," two versions; "EXPORT I BEER," two versions; "EXPORT II BEER," two versions. Each, ...$5

Schell's Export Light Beer, two-label 12-ounce tab top, woodgrain can, single version. $2

Schell's Farmfest 76 Beer, single-label 12-ounce tab top, white can, flag, single version. $3

Schell's Hunters Special Beer, single-label 12-ounce tab top, multicolored can, pheasant, single version. $5

Schell's Xmas Brew Beer, single-label 12-ounce tab top, yellow or white can, multiversions. $3

Spike Drivers Spirit Beer, single-label 12-ounce tab top, orange can, single version. $2

Spirit Lake Centennial Light Beer, single-label 12-ounce tab top, red can, multi-colored label, single version...$2

State Flag Beer, single-label 12-ounce tab top, Ohio state flag, single version. $2

State Line Beer, two-label 12-ounce tab top, white can, single version. $2

Stein-Haus New Ulm Beer, two-label 12-ounce tab top, yellow can, white label, single version...$5

Two-label 12-ounce tab top, yellow or brown can, white label, single version of each. $5

St. Paul Winter Carnival Beer, single-label 12-ounce tab top, white or yellow can, single version of each...$2

St. Urho's Brew, single-label 12-ounce tab top, brown can, green saint, single version. $2

Sugar & Spice Brand Premium Beer, single-label 12-ounce tab top, set can, series of eight, versions: Mary in bathing suit, Mary standing, Terri in bathing suit, Terri standing, Terri head and shoulders, Sherri in bathing suit, Sherri with sun hat, Sherri head and shoulders. (*See photo 173*) Each, ...$5

Turtle Beer, single-label 12-ounce tab top, yellow and black can, single version. $2

V P Fair Beer, two-label 12-ounce tab top, blue and white can, single version. $2

Wildcat Beer, single-label 12-ounce tab top, red can, single version. $2

Williston Basin Beer, two-label 12-ounce tab top, white can, single version. $2

Wilmington Catfish Days Beer, single-label 12-ounce tab top, red can, single version. $2

Photo 173. Sugar & Spice Brand Premium Beer.

In addition to the brands listed, August Schell also produced many brands in aluminum cans. The collector value of these cans is $1.

Red Wing

GOODHUE COUNTY BREWING COMPANY, Bush and 5th Streets

Red Wing Premium Beer, single-label, 12-ounce, high-profile cone top, white can, Indian, "Premium" in red, multiversions. $300

St. Paul

ASSOCIATED BREWING COMPANY, 882 West 7th Street (successor to Pfeiffer Brewing Company)

North Star XXX Beer, single-label 12-ounce tab top, blue can, silver star and trim, "NORTH STAR" in red, multiversions. $35

Single-label 12- or 16-ounce tab top, blue can, white star and trim, "NORTH STAR" in red, multiversions.
12-ounce,.. $10
16-ounce,... $15

Pfeiffer Famous Beer, two-label 12-ounce tab top, metallic gold can, yellow label, factory scene, single version... $25

Two-label 12-ounce tab top, woodgrain can, dull gold bands, factory scene, multiversions. $10

Pfeiffer Premium Beer, two-label 12-ounce tab top, white can, oval metallic gold label, "JOHNNY PFEIFFER," multiversions. $15

Schmidt Beer, two-label 16-ounce tab top, off-white can, red label outlined in metallic gold, multiversions. $5

Single-label 12-ounce flat top, multicolored can, red label, vertical gold bands along seam, set can, set of four, called "Schmidt Scenes," varieties: buffalo and cows, covered wagon and train, canoe and outboard boat, moose and logging; single version of each. Each, ... $15

Single-label 12-ounce tab top, multicolored can, red label outlined in yellow, set can, 13 cans in original set, four cans added to second set, varieties: buffalo and cows, covered wagon and train, canoe and outboard boat, moose and logging, steamboat and deer, plowhorse, pheasants, geese, bear and iron mine, muskie, collie and sheep, antelope, rodeo, mallard ducks, ice fishing, horse and colt, elk; multi and minor varieties will create new sets. Each,........................ $3

Schmidt Draft Beer, two-label 12- or 16-ounce tab top, white can, red label, "DRAFT" in yellow on black patch, multiversions.
12-ounce, ... $3
16-ounce,... $5

Two-label 12- or 16-ounce tab top, multicolored can, red label outlined in yellow, "DRAFT BEER" in black, set can, called "Schmidt Scenes," 12-ounce has 12 cans in set, 16-ounce has eight cans in set, varieties: cans common to 12- and 16-ounce—antelope, collie and sheep, horse and colt, rodeo, mallard ducks, elk, ice fishing, muskie; additional cans in 12-ounce set only—bear and iron mine, geese, pheasants, plowhorses; multi and minor varieties will create new sets.
12-ounce each, ... $10
15-ounce each, ... $15

Schmidt Extra Special Beer, single-label 12-ounce tab top, yellow can, black label, "SCHMIDT" in white on red patch, multiversions. $5

Schmidt Extra Special Draft Beer, single-label 16-ounce tab top, off-white can, black label, "SCHMIDT" in white on red patch, single version. $3

Schmidt Select Near Beer, single-label 12-ounce flat or tab top, blue can, blue label outlined in metallic gold, multiversions. $2

THEODORE HAMM'S BREWING COMPANY, 720 Payne Avenue

Some Buckhorn and some Burgie Light Golden Beer cans brewed by Hamm's carry BUCKHORN BREWING COMPANY and BURGIE BREWING COMPANY mandatories.

Buckhorn Premium Lager Beer, two-label 12-ounce tab top, pale green can, red or silver sunburst behind deer, multiversions. $5

Buckhorn Special Lager Beer, two-label 12-ounce flat or tab top, red can, line drawing on gold, white or silver background, multiversions. $10

Burgermeister Beer, two-label 12- or 16-ounce tab top, white can, blue label outlined in metallic gold, multiversions. $5

Burgermeister Genuine Draft Beer, two-label 12- or 16-ounce tab top, white can, "GENUINE DRAFT BEER" on oval label, single version. $10

Burgie Light Golden Beer, two-label 12-ounce flat or tab top, yellow can, "ORIGINAL CALIFORNIA BEER," multiversions. $5

Hamm's Beer, single-label 12-ounce flat top, silver can, "HAMM'S BEER" on blue band, OPENING INSTRUCTIONS, INTERNAL REVENUE TAX PAID, multiversions including camouflage can. $50
Camouflage can, ...$150

Single-label 12-ounce flat top, silver can, blue logo on red ribbons, OPENING INSTRUCTIONS, INTERNAL REVENUE TAX PAID, multiversions. (*See photo 174*) $50

Two-label 12- or 16-ounce flat top, metallic gold sunburst can, wide blue band, "FROM THE LAND OF SKY BLUE WATERS" or "REFRESHING AS THE LAND OF SKY BLUE WATERS," multiversions. $20

Two-label 12- or 16-ounce tab top, blue can, white crown, "FROM THE LAND OF SKY BLUE WATERS" or "REFRESHING AS THE LAND OF SKY BLUE WATERS," multiversions including all aluminum versions $3
Message from William Figge, ... $35

Two-label 12- or 16-ounce tab top, gold, blue, and white can, blue lion, multiversions. $1

Photo 174. Hamm's Beer.

Photo 175. Hamm's Preferred Smooth Mellow Beer.

Hamm's Beer Genuine Draft, two-label 12- or 16-ounce tab top, white can, metallic blue label, multiversions. $1

Hamm's Beer Real Draft, two-label 12- or 16-ounce tab top, white can, blue crown, "FROM THE LAND OF SKY BLUE WATERS" or "AMERICA'S CLASSIC PRE-MIUM BEER," multiversions. $1

Hamm's Draft Beer Genuine Draft, two-label 12- or 16-ounce tab top, steel barrel cans, multiversions. $3

Hamm's Preferred Smooth Mellow Beer, two-label 12-ounce tab top, metallic gold sunburst can, wide blue band, multiversions. (*See photo 175*) $20

Hamm's Preferred Stock Beer, two-label 12-ounce tab top, gold can, red ribbon, IRTP or non-IRTP, multiversions.
IRTP, ...$60
Non-IRTP, ...$50

Two-label 12-ounce tab top, white can, black label and lettering, multiversions. $20

Heublein Malt Liquor, two-label 12-ounce tab top, black, white, or tan aluminum can, single version of each. $35

Heublein Velvet Glove Malt Liquor, two-label 12- or 16-ounce tab top, white can, black label, multiversions. $40

G. HEILEMAN BREWING COMPANY, 882 West 7th Street
(successor to Associated Brewing Company)

All cans produced by Heileman at this plant have the letter "D" stamped on the bottom of the can. Almost all the cans produced were in aluminum and carry a collector value of $1. The value of any steel or bi-metal cans are also $1.

    G. Heileman Brewing Company added four cans to the "Schmidt Scenes": snow skiing, water skiing, auto racing, snowmobile. The value of Heileman "Schmidt Scenes" will run up to $1.50 each.

OLYMPIA BREWING COMPANY, 720 Payne Avenue (successor
to Theodore Hamm's Brewing Company)

All cans produced by Olympia were produced in aluminum and carry a collector value of $1.

PABST BREWING COMPANY, 720 Payne Avenue (successor to
Olympia Brewing Company)

All cans produced by the Pabst Brewing Company were produced in aluminum and carry a collector value of $1.

PFEIFFER BREWING COMPANY, 882 West 7th Street (successor to Jacob Schmidt Brewing Company)

North Star XXX Beer, single-label 12-ounce flat top, blue can, white label and star, single version. $25

Pfeiffer Beer, two-label 12-ounce flat top, yellow can, large "JOHNNY PFEIFFER," single version. $25

Schmidt Beer, single-label 12-ounce flat top, series set of 12 called "Schmidt Scenes," versions: bear and iron mine, buffalo and cows, canoe and outboard boat, collie and sheep, covered wagon and train, cowboy, steamboat and deer, mallard ducks, moose and logging, muskie, pheasants, plowhorse; multi and minor varieties will create new sets. Each, ... $10

Schmidt Extra Special Beer, single-label 12-ounce flat top, off-white can, black label, "SCHMIDT" in white on red patch, single version. $5

Schmidt Select Near Beer, single-label 12-ounce flat top, blue can, blue label outlined in metallic gold, single version. $5
Note: A complete set will carry a higher value than the individual cans.

JACOB SCHMIDT BREWING COMPANY, 882 West 7th Street

North Star XXX Beer, single-label 12-ounce flat top, blue can, white label, silver star, multiversions. $30

Schmidt Beer, single-label 12-ounce flat top, blue can, metallic gold stripes on both sides of seam, series set of four cans called "Schmidt Scenes," varieties: buffalo and cows, wagon and train, canoe and motor boat, moose and logging; minor versions. Each,.. $15

Schmidt City Club Beer, single-label, 12-ounce, high-profile cone or flat top, metallic gold hatched can, red label, white circle, multiversions of cone, single version of flat.
Flat top, ... $30
Cone top, ... $65

Schmidt Extra Special Beer, single-label 12-ounce flat top, metallic gold hatched can, red label, white circle, single version. $35

Schmidt Select A Cereal Beverage, single-label, 12-ounce, high-profile cone or 12-ounce flat top, white can, brown label and bands, single version of each.
Flat top, ... $25
Cone top, ... $45

Single-label, 12-ounce flat top, desert scene, "AMERICA'S MOST FAMOUS CEREAL BEVERAGE," single version. $50

Schmidt's City Beer, two-label, 12-ounce, high-profile cone or flat top, white can, yellow stripes, red oval label, multiversions. All same design, but camouflage can is dull army green.
Cone top, ... $75
Flat top, ... $60

Two-label, 12-ounce, high-profile cone top, metallic gold can, red oval label, multiversions.
Cone top, ...$100
Flat top, ... $75
Camouflage can, ... $200

Schmidt's Select A Cereal Beverage, single-label, 12-ounce, high-profile cone top, white can, red label, multiversions. $60

THE STROH BREWING COMPANY, 720 Payne Avenue (successor to the Pabst Brewing Company)

All cans produced by the Stroh Brewing Company were produced in aluminum and carry a collector value of $1.

YOERG BREWING COMPANY, 229 Ohio Street

Yoerg's Cave Aged Beer, two-label 12-ounce crowntainer, gray can, red lettering, multiversions. $100

Winona

PETER BUB BREWING COMPANY, Sugar Loaf Avenue

Bub's Beer, single-label, 12-ounce, high-profile cone top, white can, "BUB'S BEER" in red, "TIME HONORED FOR 80 (or 90) YEARS," multiversions. $85

Single-label, 12-ounce, high-profile cone, flat, or tab top, off-white or white can, "B" in "BUB'S" in red, "IT'S THE GRAIN," multiversions.
Cone top, ... $85
Flat or tab top, ... $40

Mississippi

Mississippi never had a brewery.

Missouri

St. Charles

FISCHBACH BREWING COMPANY, 300 Water Street (aka: Cardinal Brewing Company, Kol Brewing Company, Skooner Brewing Company, Grand Lager Brewing Company)

Cardinal Beer, Cardinal Brewing Company, two-label 12-ounce flat top, red can, white label, red cardinal, multiversions. $60

Export Beer, Fischbach Brewing Company, two-label 12-ounce flat top, red can, white label, multiversions. $30

Two-label 12-ounce flat top, white can, red label outlined in metallic gold, multiversions. $15

Grand Lager Premium Beer, Grand Lager Brewing Company, two-label 12-ounce flat top, white can, red label, "GRAND LAGER" in white, single version. $50

Two-label 12-ounce tab top, white can, red label outlined in metallic gold, single version of each top. $20

Kol Beer, Kol Brewing Company, two-label 12-ounce tab or zip top, blue can, gold label, "BEER" in red, multiversions. $35

National Lager Premium Beer, Fischbach Brewing Company, two-label 12-ounce flat top, white can, red shield label, metallic gold trim, single version. $50

Skooner Beer, Skooner Brewing Company, two-label 12-ounce flat top, blue can, white label, covered wagon, single version. $75

VAN DYKE BREWING COMPANY, 300 Water Street (successor to Fischbach Brewing Company)

Van Dyke Export Beer, two-label 12-ounce zip top, white can, blue label, single version. $50

Two-label 12-ounce zip top, white can, red label, single version. $50

St. Joseph

M. K. GOETZ BREWING COMPANY, 600 Ablemarle

Goetz Country Club Beer, single-label 8- or 12-ounce flat top, or 12-ounce high-profile cone top, red can, metallic gold bands, multiversions. *(See photo 176)*
8-ounce flat top, ... $35
12-ounce flat top, ... $30
Cone top, ... $50

Goetz Country Club Lager Beer, single-label 12-ounce cone top, green can, white lettering, INTERNAL REVENUE TAX PAID, multiversions. $60

Goetz Country Club Malt Lager, single-label 8- or 12-ounce flat top, white can, "GOETZ" in gold, yellow, or blue oval, slogan, multiversions. $15

Goetz Country Club Malt Liquor, single-label 7-, 8-, or 12-ounce flat top, white can, "GOETZ" in gold, yellow, or blue oval, slogan, multiversions. *(See photo 177)* $15

Goetz Country Club Pilsener Beer, single-label, 12-ounce, high- or low-profile cone or flat top, IRTP or non-IRTP, red can, white lettering, multiversions.
12-ounce flat top, ... $40
12-ounce IRTP, ... $45
Cone top, ... $65

Goetz Country Club Stout Malt Liquor, single-label 8- or 12-ounce flat top, white can, "GOETZ" in gold, yellow, or blue oval, slogan, multiversions. .. $10

Goetz Pale Cereal Beverage, single-label, 12-ounce, high-profile cone top, yellow can, "PALE" in red, single version. $100

Goetz Pale Near Beer, single-label, 12-ounce, high-profile cone or flat top, yellow can, gold band, "PALE" in red, multiversions. $75

Single-label 12-ounce flat top, white can, red and yellow label, single version. $5

Photo 176 (left). Goetz Country Club Beer. Photo 177 (right). Goetz Country Club Malt Liquor.

Goetz Premium Quality Beer, single-label 12-ounce flat top, off-white can, blue label, multiversions. $10

PEARL BREWING COMPANY, 600 Ablemarle Street (successor to M. K. Goetz Brewing Company)

Country Club Malt Lager, two-label 8-, 12-, or 16-ounce flat or tab top, white can, solid blue or "xxx" on oval, multiversions. All versions, ...$5

Country Club Malt Liquor, two-label 7-, 8-, 12-, or 16-ounce flat or tab top, white can, solid blue or "xxx" on oval, multiversions. All versions, ...$3

Country Club Stout Malt Liquor, two-label 8-, 12-, or 16-ounce tab top, white can, solid blue or "xxx" on oval, multiversions. All versions, ...$3

Goetz Country Club Malt Lager, single-label 8- or 12-ounce flat top, white can, "GOETZ" on blue oval, multiversions. All versions, ...$5

Goetz Country Club Malt Liquor, single-label 8- or 12-ounce flat top, white can, "GOETZ" on blue oval, multiversions. All versions, ...$3

Goetz Country Club Stout Malt Liquor, single-label 8- or 12-ounce flat top, white can, "GOETZ" on blue oval, multiversions. All versions, ...$3

Goetz Pale Near Beer, single-label 12-ounce flat top, white can, orange and yellow label outlined in metallic gold, single version. $25

Goetz Pale The Famous Near Beer, two-label 12-ounce tab top, white can, orange and yellow label, single version. $2

Goetz Premium Quality Beer, single-label 12-ounce flat top, off-white can, blue label, multiversions. $10

Pale Near Beer, single-label 12-ounce flat or tab top, white can, orange and yellow label outlined in metallic gold, multiversions. $5

Pearl Lager Beer, two-label 12-ounce tab top, white can, red label, river scene, single version. $5

Pilsener Club Premium Beer, two-label 12-ounce tab top, white and blue can, single version. $2

St. Louis

ABC BREWING COMPANY, 2825 Broadway

ABC Old English Type Ale, single-label 12-ounce flat top, blue can, "ABC" on blue ribbon, OPENING INSTRUCTIONS, INTERNAL REVENUE TAX PAID, single version. ....Exotic

ABC Select Pilsener Type Beer, single-label 12-ounce flat top, red can, "ABC" in white on black band, OPENING INSTRUCTIONS, INTERNAL REVENUE TAX PAID, two versions. $250

Black Dallas Beer, single-label 12-ounce flat top, red can, "ST. LOUIS" in white front face, OPENING INSTRUCTIONS, INTERNAL REVENUE TAX PAID, single version...$325

Old St. Louis Ale, single-label 12-ounce flat top, silver can, "OLD ST. LOUIS ALE" in red, riverboat, OPENING INSTRUCTIONS, INTERNAL REVENUE TAX PAID, single version. $300

Old St. Louis Beer, single-label 12-ounce flat top, silver can, "OLD ST. LOUIS BEER" in red, riverboat, OPENING INSTRUCTIONS, INTERNAL REVENUE TAX PAID, single version. $275

ANHEUSER-BUSCH, INC., 721 Pestalozzi Street

Budweiser Bock Beer, single-label 12-ounce flat top, red can, white lettering, goat on letter "B" in "BOCK," single version. $600

Budweiser Lager Beer, two-label 12-ounce crowntainer, silver can, single version (rumored test can). ....Unique

Single-label 12-ounce flat top, gold can, black eagle, red trim, OPENING INSTRUCTIONS, INTERNAL REVENUE TAX PAID, multiversions.
WITHDRAWN FREE, ...$125
OI, IRTP, ... $75
Non-OI, ... $60
Non-OI, non-IRTP, ... $50

Single- or two-label, 10-, 12-, or 16-ounce flat top, gold can, split label, long-neck bottle, multiversions.
10-ounce, ... $50
12-ounce, ... $20
16-ounce, ... $20

Two-label 10-, 12-, or 16-ounce flat top, white can, split label, red lettering, multiversions. $5

Two-label 10-, 12-, or 16-ounce flat, zip, or tab top, white can, red lettering, multiversions. $1

Budweiser Malt Liquor, two-label 12- or 16-ounce tab top, test cans, black, cream, or red cans, four rows of eagles, single version of each color can.
12-ounce black, ... $40
16-ounce black, ... $60
12- or 16-ounce red, ...$100

Two-label 12-ounce tab top, black can, three rows of eagles, multiversions. $10

Busch Bavarian Beer, two-label 12- or 16-ounce flat, zip, or tab top, blue and white can, mountain scene, multiversions. $5

Busch Beer, single-label 12-ounce zip top, test cans, white can, triangle label, multiversions. $75

Busch Lager Beer, two-label 12-ounce flat top, metallic gold and red can, single version. $125

Faust Beer, single-label 12-ounce flat top, black can, white label, "FAUST" in red, two versions. $600

Michelob Beer, two-label 12-ounce tab top, gold can, vertical ribbons, embossed can, multiversions. $5

Anheuser-Busch issued brands in aluminum cans and bi-metal cans not listed here and they carry a collector value of up to $1. In addition, Anheuser-Busch issued a variety of special cans covering a wide variety of subjects. The value of these cans rarely exceeds $10.

CARLING BREWING COMPANY, 3617 North Florrisant (successor to Griesedieck Western Brewery Company)

Red Cap Ale, two-label 12-ounce flat top, green can, orangish label, red cap, multiversions. $15

Stag Premium Dry Pilsener Beer, single-label 12-ounce flat top, black can, yellow label, gold trim, single version. $15

FALSTAFF BREWING COMPANY, 3684 Forest Park Boulevard (1933–1978), 3181 Michigan Avenue (1933–1951), 20th and Madison Streets (1948–1968), 1920 Shenandoah (1957–1978)

Falstaff Beer, single-label 12-ounce crowntainer, brown can, white "FALSTAFF" shield, gold bands, single version. $150

Single-label, 12-ounce, high-profile cone top, brown can, gold bands, "FALSTAFF" shield, multiversions. $40

Two-label 12-, 14-, or 16-ounce flat top, white can, gold and brown "FALSTAFF" shield, "The Choicest Product of The Brewer's Art," multiversions. $10

Two-label 12- or 16-ounce flat, zip, or tab top, white can, gold and brown "FALSTAFF" shield, gold bands, "AMERICA'S PREMIUM QUALITY BEER," multiversions... $15

Two-label gallon can, white can, gold and brown "FALSTAFF" shield, "AMERICA'S PREMIUM QUALITY BEER," single version. ....Unique

Two-label 12-, 14-, or 16-ounce tab top, white can, gold and maroon "FALSTAFF" shield, "FOR OVER FOUR GENERATIONS . . . ," multiversions. *(See photo 178)* $5

Two-label 12-, 14-, or 16-ounce tab top, white can, wide metallic gold band, gold and maroon shield, multiversions. $5

Falstaff Draft Beer, two-label 12- or 16-ounce tab top, white can, gold and maroon shield, "DRAFT" on blue ribbon, single version of each. $10

GB Finest Quality Light Beer, two-label 12-ounce tab top, white can, two-color shield, two versions. $5

Griesedieck Malt Liquor, two-label 12-ounce tab top, blue or maroon can, large glass of beer, single version of each. $100

Hanley Lager Beer, single-label 12-ounce tab top, greenish can, "H" in red circle, multiversions. $3

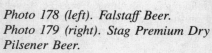

Photo 178 (left). Falstaff Beer.
Photo 179 (right). Stag Premium Dry Pilsener Beer.

Katz Premium Beer, two-label 12-ounce tab top, white can, red label, yellow trim, multiversions. $3

Krueger Pilsner Beer, two-label 12-ounce tab top, gold can, white shield, red bands, multiversions. $3

Falstaff Brewing Company produced some brands in aluminum cans. Collector value is up to $2.

GRIESEDIECK BROS. BREWERY, 1920 Shenandoah (aka: Lami Brewing Company)

GB Light Lager Beer, single-label 12-ounce flat top, set cans, set of four cans, "GRIESEDIECK BROS." in block letters, "GB" on bi-color shield, can colors: white, dark blue, brown, green. $125

Single-label 12-ounce flat top, set cans, set of 12 cans, "THE ORIGINAL GRIESE-DIECK BROS." in script, "GB" on bi-color shield, can colors: white, brown, bronze, light purple, dark purple, blue green, lime green, emerald green, light blue, red, dark blue, gold. $125

Griesedieck Bros. Double Mellow Beer, two-label 12-ounce crowntainer, silver can, "GRIESEDIECK BROS." on blue band, INTERNAL REVENUE TAX PAID, single version. $125

Single-label 12-ounce flat top, gold can, white band, "DOUBLE MELLOW" on red band, single version. $50

Griesedieck Bros. Premium Beer, single- or two-label 12-ounce flat top, gold can, "GRIESEDIECK BROS." in white on red band, multiversions. $50

Single-label 12-ounce flat top, series can, set of eight, called "Rainbow" set, large pilsner glass, western scenes, can colors: orange, blue-green, red, emerald green, blue, lime green, brown, purple. $100

Old St. Louis Beer, mandatory states LAMI BREWING COMPANY, two-label 12-ounce flat top, blue can, white or blue label outlined in metallic gold, single version of each. $85

GRIESEDIECK WESTERN BREWERY COMPANY, 3607 North Florrisant (successor to Hyde Park Breweries Association; aka: Hyde Park Breweries Association)

Hyde Park 75 Premium Pale Beer, Hyde Park Breweries Association, single-label 12-ounce flat top, white can, red ribbon, silver or gold trim, two versions. $85

Hyde Park Beer, Hyde Park Breweries Association, single-label 12-ounce flat top, woodgrain can, red label outlined in white, single version. $75

Stag Premium Dry Pilsener Beer, Griesedieck Western Breweries, single-label 12-ounce flat top or high-profile cone top, white can, black label outlined in metallic gold, single-version cone top, multiversion flat top. *(See photo 179)*
Cone top, ...$50
Flat top, ...$25

Photo 180. Hyde Park Beer.

HYDE PARK BREWERIES ASSOCIATION, 3607 North Florrisant

Hyde Park Beer, single-label 12-ounce flat top, brown can, red label outlined in white, single version. *(See photo 180)* $75

Hyde Park True Lager Beer, single-label 12-ounce flat top, woodgrain can, red label outlined in white, INTERNAL REVENUE TAX PAID, single version. $85

Montana

Anaconda

ANACONDA BREWING COMPANY, 1200 East Park Avenue

Rocky Mountain Beer, single-label, 12-ounce, high-profile cone top, silver can, mountain, "ROCKY MOUNTAIN" on red band, single version. $85

Billings

BILLINGS BREWING COMPANY, 24th Street and Montana Avenue

Billings Pale Beer, single-label, 12-ounce, high-profile cone top, red can, metallic gold bands, single version. $200

Billings Tap Beer, single-label, 12-ounce, high-profile cone top, white can, yellow trim, "BEER" in red, single version. $225

Old Fashion Select Beer, single-label, 12-ounce, high-profile cone top, olive green can, metallic gold can, single version. *(See photo 181)* .... Unique

Photo 181. Old Fashion Select Beer.

Photo 182 (left). Butte Lager Beer.
Photo 183 (center). Butte Special Beer.
Photo 184 (right). Big Sky Pale
Light Beer.

Butte

BUTTE BREWING COMPANY, 220 North Wyoming Street

Butte Lager Beer, two-label 12-ounce flat top, white can, metallic gold bands top and bottom, single version. *(See photo 182)* $60

Butte Special Beer, single- or two-label, 12-ounce, low- or high-profile cone or flat top, white can, "BUTTE" in red outlined in black, single version of each can.
Low-profile, ... $100
High-profile, ... $85
Flat top, ... $60

Single-label, 12-ounce, high-profile cone top, red and gold can, "BUTTE SPECIAL" in red outlined in white, black band around bottom, INTERNAL REVENUE TAX PAID, single version. *(See photo 183)* .... Exotic

Butte Special Quality Controlled Beer, two-label 12-ounce flat top, white can, red oval label, "QUALITY CONTROLLED" in red, single version. $60

Great Falls

GREAT FALLS BREWERIES, INC., American Brewery Addition & 410 14th Street (aka: Sick's Great Falls Breweries, Inc., Brewing Company of Montana)

Big Sky Pale Light Beer, Great Falls Breweries, Inc., two-label 12-ounce flat or tab top, light blue can, white label outlined in metallic gold, multiversions. *(See photo 184)* $75

Bohemian Club Beer, Brewing Company of Montana, two-label 12-ounce tab top, off-white and metallic orange can, single version. $100

Great Falls Select Beer, Great Falls Breweries, Inc., two-label 12-ounce flat or tab top, white can, red label, metallic gold trim, multiversions. $40

Two-label 12- or 16-ounce tab top, white can, red label, "CAREFULLY BREWED BEER," single version of each size.
12-ounce, ... $20
16-ounce, ... $30

Two-label 12-ounce tab top, white can, red label, "BREWED WITH EXTRA CARE," two versions. $20

Great Falls Select Fine Beer, Sick's Great Falls Breweries, Inc., single-label 12-ounce flat top, bands, white label, brewery, red "6," INTERNAL REVENUE TAX PAID, single version. $75

Great Falls Breweries, Inc., single-label 12-ounce flat top, bands, white label, brewery, multiversions. $50

Great Falls Breweries, Inc., two-label 12-ounce flat top, metallic gold can, white label, cowboy, multiversions. $40

Great Falls Breweries, Inc., two-label 12-ounce flat top, metallic gold can, white label, multiversions. $25

Helena

KESSLER BREWING COMPANY, 1 Mile West

Kessler Beer, single-label, 12-ounce, high-profile cone top, blue can, "KESSLER" in silver, single version. *(See photo 185)* $75

Kalispell

KALISPELL BREWING AND MALTING COMPANY, 22 5th Avenue

Gus' Premium Topper Beer, single-label, 12-ounce, high-profile cone top, white can, red bands, "BEER" in black, single version. *(See photo 186)* $125

Missoula

MISSOULA BREWING COMPANY, Head of Madison Street
(aka: Sick's Missoula Brewing Company)

Highlander Beer, Missoula Brewing Company, single-label, 12-ounce, low-profile cone top, gold can, eagle, black band, INTERNAL REVENUE TAX PAID, two versions. *(See photo 187)* $100

Sick's Missoula Brewing Company, single-label 12-ounce flat top, white can, orange bands, "A SICK'S QUALITY PRODUCT," INTERNAL REVENUE TAX PAID, single version. $65

Missoula Brewing Company, single-label 12-ounce flat top, white can, orange bands, IRTP or non-IRTP, multiversions. *(See photo 188)*

Non-IRTP, ... $50

IRTP, ... $50

Highlander Premium Beer, two-label 12-ounce flat top, red and black checkerboard, white label, multiversions. $25

Photo 185. Kessler Beer.
Photo 186. Gus' Premium
Topper Beer.
Photo 187. Highlander Beer.
Photo 188. Highlander Beer.

Nebraska

Columbus

COLUMBUS BREWING COMPANY, 672 15th Avenue

Ronz Beer, single-label, 12-ounce, high-profile cone top, white can, bronze label, "RONZ" in white, single version. ....Exotic

Omaha

FALSTAFF BREWING COMPANY, 25th Street and Deer Park Boulevard

Big E The Western Premium Beer, mandatory reads JAMES HANLEY COMPANY, two-sided 12-ounce steel or aluminum tab top, gold and black can, single version of each. $3

Falstaff Beer, single-label high-profile cone top, brown can, gold band, "FALSTAFF" shield, IRTP or non-IRTP, multiversions.

IRTP, ...$50

Non-IRTP, ...$40

Single- or two-label 12- or 16-ounce flat top, white can, gold and brown "FALSTAFF" shield, "The Choicest Product of the Brewer's Art," multiversions. $10

Two-label 11- or 12-ounce flat, zip, or tab top, white can, gold band, gold and brown "FALSTAFF" shield, "America's Premium Quality Beer," multiversions. $15

Falstaff, Omaha, produced many brands in aluminum and excruded steel, some obscure and with limited distribution. The collector value can range up to $5 for these cans.

METZ BREWING COMPANY, 210 Hickory Street (aka: My Brewing Company)

Kol Premium Quality Beer, single-label 12-ounce flat top, silver can, white vertical stripes, blue label, single version. $50

Metz Extra Dry Beer, single-label 12-ounce flat top, white can, red label, "METZ" in white, single version. $60

Metz Jubilee Beer, single-label, 12-ounce, high-profile cone top, red can, "METZ" in red, IRTP or non-IRTP, multiversions.
IRTP, ... $85
Non-IRTP, ... $75

Metz Malt Liquor, two-label 12-ounce flat top, white can, red lines, single version. $300

Metz Premium Beer, single-label 12-ounce flat top, white can, "METZ" in red, red or metallic gold trim, multiversions. $35

Metz Supreme Beer, single-label 12-ounce flat top, metallic gold can, green label, multiversions. $100

My Beer, Metz Brewing or My Brewing, red and blue quarter panels, white label, single version of each brewery.
My Brewing, ... $60
Metz Brewing, ... $50

STORZ BREWING COMPANY, 1807 North 16th Street

All Grain Beer, two-label 12-ounce flat or tab top, white can, red oval label, single version of each top. $40

Brown Derby Lager Beer, two-label 12-ounce tab top, white can, brown or orange label, multiversions. $20

KC's Best Premium Pilsner Beer, single-label 12-ounce flat or tab top, white can, red bands, multiversions. $50

Pilsener Club Premium Beer, two-label 12-ounce tab top, blue and white can, lion on shield, single version. $20

Pilsener Club Select Beer, two-label 12-ounce tab top, blue and white can, small shield with lion, single version. $25

Storz All Grain Slow Aged Beer, single-label 12-ounce flat top, blue can, red bands, farm scene, INTERNAL REVENUE TAX PAID, single version. .... Exotic

Storz Draft Beer, two-label 12-ounce tab top, white can, red label, "DRAFT" in blue, single version. $25

Storz Fine Lager Beer, single-label 12-ounce flat top, red and blue can, "STORZ" in white, INTERNAL REVENUE TAX PAID, multiversions. $125

Storz Gold Crest Beer, single-label 12-ounce flat top, yellow can, brown label, INTERNAL REVENUE TAX PAID, single version. $200
Single-label 12-ounce flat top, white can, red and white label, INTERNAL REVENUE TAX PAID, single version. $40

Storz Pilsener Premium Beer, two-label 12-ounce flat, zip, or tab top, blue and gold can, red label, single version of each top. $20

Photo 189. Storz Premium America's Light Beer.

Storz Premium America's Light Beer, two-label 12-ounce flat top, white can, red label outlined in metallic gold, single version. *(See photo 189)* $25

Two-label 12-ounce flat or tab top, blue and gold can, red label, gold trim, multiversions. $20

Storz Premium Dry Beer, single-label 12-ounce flat top, white can, metallic red label, multiversions. $60

Storz Premium Dry Select Beer, single-label 12-ounce flat top, white can, red label, single version. $60

Storz Premium The Orchid Beer, two-label 12-ounce flat top, white can, red label, metallic gold trim, multiversions. $40

Storz Tap Genuine Draft Beer, two-label 12-ounce tab top, woodgrain can, "TAP" in white, multiversions. $20

Storz test marketed a gallon can with this label. The value of the Storz Tap gallon is Unique.

Storz Triumph Beer, two-label 12-ounce flat or tab top, white can, "TRIUMPH" in white on blue band, multiversions. $10

Storz Winterbrau Beer, single-label 12-ounce flat top, red can, tavern scene, INTERNAL REVENUE TAX PAID, two versions. .... Exotic

Single-label 12-ounce flat top, white can, tavern scene, INTERNAL REVENUE TAX PAID, single version. .... Exotic

Storzette Beer, single-label 8-ounce flat top, white can, orchid on label, single version. $100

White Label Fine Quality Beer, two-label 12-ounce tab top, white can, metallic gold label, single version. $20

Nevada

Carson City

CARSON BREWING COMPANY, King and Division Streets

Tahoe Beer, single-label, 12-ounce, low-profile cone top, black can, "TAHOE BEER" in red outlined in yellow, INTERNAL REVENUE TAX PAID, multiversions.
.... $200

Reno

RENO BREWING COMPANY, 900 East 4th Street

Royal Beer, single-label, 12-ounce, low-profile, cone top, white can, "ROYAL" on red band, INTERNAL REVENUE TAX PAID, multiversions. *(See photo 190)*
.... $250

Sierra Beer, single-label, 12-ounce, high- or low-profile cone top, off-white can, dark blue label, mountain scene, single version of each. *(See photo 191)* $85

Photo 190 (left). Royal Beer.
Photo 191 (right). Sierra Beer.

Photo 192. Sierra Beer.

Single-label 12-ounce cone top or two-label 12-ounce flat top, silver can, yellow stripes, blue label, mountain scene, single version of each. *(See photo 192)*
Cone top, ...$125
Flat top, ... $85

New Hampshire

Merrimack

ANHEUSER-BUSCH, INC., 1000 Daniel Webster Way

Built in 1970, this plant produced a few steel cans, but most were aluminum. All Anheuser-Busch labels have been produced here. Collector value is $1.

New Jersey

/

Camden

CAMDEN COUNTY BEVERAGE COMPANY, Filmore and Bulsen Streets

Bohio Beer, single-label 12-ounce flat top, white can, "BOHIO" in yellow outlined in brown, single version. $250
Camden Lager Beer, single-label 12-ounce flat top, white can, orange and yellow bands, multiversions. $200

Elizabeth

PETER BREIDT BREWING COMPANY, 600 Pearl Street

Breidt's Half & Half, single-label high-profile cone or quart cone top, maroon and yellow can, black label, outlined in white, single version of each.
12-ounce, ... $500
Quart, ...Unique
Breidt's Pilsner Beer, single-label, 12-ounce, high-profile cone or quart cone top, yellow can, maroon or brown label with matching stripes, INTERNAL REVENUE TAX PAID, WITHDRAWN FREE, single version of all cans.
12-ounce, ... $300
12-ounce WITHDRAWN FREE, ... $400
Quart, ... $350

Hammonton

EASTERN BREWING COMPANY, 329 North Washington (aka: Eastern Beverage Corporation, Canadian Ace Brewing Company, Cerveceria San Juan, Circle Brewing Company, Colonial Brewing Company, Fischer Brewing Company, Fox Head Brewing Company, Garden State Brewing Company, Hampden Brewing Company, Polar Brewing Company)

7-Eleven Premium Beer, Garden State Brewing Company, two-label 12-ounce tab top, metallic gold can, black lettering, single version. $35

7-Eleven Stores Premium Beer, Eastern Brewing Company, two-label 12-ounce flat top, white can, "7-ELEVEN STORES" on label, single version. $85

279 Special Brew Light Beer, Colonial Brewing Company, two-label 12-ounce flat top, white can, "279 SPECIAL BREW" on red patch, single version. $100

ABC Premium Ale, Garden State Brewing Company, single-label 12-ounce tab top, green can, white trim, "ABC PREMIUM ALE" in white, multiversions. $5

ABC Premium Beer, Garden State Brewing Company, single-label 12- or 16-ounce tab top, red can, white trim, "ABC PREMIUM BEER" in white, multiversions...$5

American Dry Extra Premium Beer, Eastern Brewing Company, two-label 12-ounce flat, zip, or tab top, metallic gold can, red, white, and blue label, multiversions. $20

Betts Light Beer, Colonial Brewing Company, two-label 12-ounce flat top, white can, "BETTS" in white on oval red label, single version. $75

Big Apple Premium Beer, Waukee Brewing Company, two-label 12-ounce flat top, white can, "BIG APPLE" in white on blue label, single version. *(See photo 193)* $150

Big E Brand Light Beer, Colonial Brewing Company, two-label 12-ounce flat top, white can, "E" in white on red square, single version. $100

Bilow Garden State Light Beer, Colonial and Garden State Brewing, two-label 12-ounce flat or tab top, white can, red, orange, or green label, multiversions. All versions, ... $10

Blanchard's Quality Product Beer, Waukee Brewing Company, two-label 12-ounce zip or tab top, white can, "BLANCHARD" in white on red bar, stein, multiversions. $10

Bonanza Premium Beer, Garden State Brewing Company, two-label 12-ounce tab top, white can, red label, steins, single version. *(See photo 194)* $10

Photo 193 (left). Big Apple Premium Beer.
Photo 194 (right). Bonanza Premium Beer.

Brown Derby Beer, Eastern Brewing Company, two-label 12-ounce tab top, white can, orange label outlined in brown, single version. $10

Canadian Ace Brand Premium Beer, two-label 12- or 16-ounce tab top or gallon can, brown woodgrain can, silver bands, white label, multiversions.
12-ounce, ... $3
16-ounce, ... $3
Gallon, ... $100

Cee Cee Brand Pilsner Beer, Colonial Brewing Company, two-label 12-ounce flat or tab top, white can, "C" and "BEER" in white on red blocks, single version of each top.
Flat top, ... $15
Tab top, ... $12

Cerveza Premiada Dukesa, Eastern Brewing Company, two-label 12-ounce tab top, yellow can, "CERVEZA" in red, multiversions. $40

Circle Brand Beer, Circle Brewing Company, two-label 12-ounce flat, zip, or tab top, white can, "CIRCLE" in red circle, single version of each top. All versions, ... $30

Colonial Premium Light Beer, Colonial Brewing Company, two-label 12-ounce flat top, red can, white label outlined in silver, single version. $100

Dart Drug Gold Medal Premium Beer, Eastern Brewing Company, two-label 12-ounce tab top, white can, maroon label, two versions.
"6 for $1.12," $15
No pricing, ... $3

Dart Premium Light Beer, Eastern Brewing Company, two-label 12-ounce tab top, red can, metallic gold trim, single version. $10

Davidson Premium Beer, Colonial Brewing Company, two-label 12-ounce flat or tab top, white can, oval red label, single version of each top.
Flat top, ... $50
Tab top, ... $45

Finast Lager Beer, Eastern Brewing Company, two-label 12-ounce flat top, metallic gold can, white label, single version. $75

Eastern Brewing Company, two-label 12-ounce flat or tab top, white, metallic gold, and yellow can, "FINAST" in white on red patch, multiversions. $10

Fischer's Old German Style Ale, Fischer Brewing Company, two-label 12-ounce tab top, white can, green vertical pinstripes, green label, multiversions. $3

Fischer's Old German Style Beer, Fischer Brewing Company, two-label 12-ounce tab top, white can, red vertical pinstripes, red label, multiversions. ... $3

Fox Head "400" Draft Brewed Beer, Fox Head Brewing Company, two-label 12-ounce tab top, white and woodgrain can, blue label, "DRAFT BREWED BEER" in red, multiversions. $15

G.E.M. Premium Beer, Colonial Brewing Company, two-label 12-ounce flat or tab top, red can, large white oval label, eagle, single version of each top.
Flat top, ... $50
Tab top, ... $45

G.E.X. Holburg Premium Light Beer, Colonial Brewing Company, two-label 12-ounce tab top, white can, split maroon gold label, metallic gold bands, single version. $65

G.E.X. Premium Beer, Colonial Brewing Company, two-label 12-ounce tab top, red can, large white oval label, eagle, single version. $45

Giant Food Premium Beer, Eastern Brewing Company, two-label 12-ounce tab top, white and red can, "PREMIUM BEER" in yellow, single version. $15

Grand Union Premium Beer, Eastern Brewing Company, two-label 12-ounce tab top, white can, orange and red label, multiversions. $30

Eastern Brewing Company, three-label 12-ounce tab top, metallic gold can, red and white Grand Union emblem, single version. $20

Hampden Premium Quality Beer, Hampden Brewing Company, two-label 12-ounce tab top, white can, metallic blue label and trim, single version. $10

Hedrick Lager Beer, Hedrick Brewing Company, two-label 12-ounce flat or tab top, white and metallic gold can, dark red label, single version of each top.
Flat top, ...$8
Tab top, ...$6

Holland Brand Ale, Eastern Brewing or Eastern Beverage Company, two-label 12-ounce flat top, woodgrain can, white label, single version of each. Either version, ... $65

Eastern Brewing Company, two-label 12-ounce flat top, white can, "HOLLAND" in black, red trim, single version. $50

India La Cerveza De Puerto Rico, Eastern Brewing Company, single-label 12-ounce tab top, white can, multi blue and red labels, outlined in gold, multiversions. $10

Kappy's Premium Light Beer, Eastern Brewing Company, two-label 12-ounce tab top, white can, red label, gold trim, multiversions. $20

Linden Brand Light Beer, Colonial Brewing Company, two-label 12-ounce flat or zip top, white can, "LINDEN BRAND" in black, single version of each top. Both versions, ... $50

Markmeister Premium Lager Beer, Colonial Brewing Company, two-label 12-ounce tab top, blue can, "BEER" in white on red label, single version. $10

Milwaukee Brand Bock Beer, Waukee Brewing Company, two-label 12-ounce tab top, white, brown, and yellow can, single version. $5

Milwaukee Brand Cream Ale, Waukee Brewing Company, two-label 12-ounce tab top, white, green, and red can, single version. $5

Milwaukee Brand Premium Beer, Waukee Brewing Company, two-label 12- or 16-ounce flat or tab top, white can, "MILWAUKEE" in red, red and gold trim, multiversions. $7
Hebrew on back, ... $20

Old Bohemian Bock Beer, Eastern Brewing Company, single-label 12-ounce flat top, white can, "BOHEMIAN" in white on black band, red bands, single version. $100

Eastern Brewing Company, two-label 12-ounce flat top, white can, green lettering, "BOCK" in black, single version. $25

Eastern Brewing Company, two-label 12-ounce flat top, white can, block label outlined in gold or black, green lettering, multiversions. $5

Photo 195. Old Bohemian Cream Ale.

Old Bohemian Cream Ale, Eastern Brewing Company, two-label 12-ounce flat top, white can, "BOHEMIAN" in white on black band, green bands, single version. *(See photo 195)*... $65

Eastern Brewing Company, two-label 12-ounce flat top, white can, green lettering, "CREAM" in black, single version. $25

Eastern Brewing Company, two-label 12-ounce flat top, white can, green label outlined in metallic gold, multiversions. $5

Old Bohemian Draft Beer, Eastern Brewing Company, two-label 12-ounce tab top, white can, metallic gold labels, two versions. $20

Old Bohemian Draft Brewed Beer, Eastern Brewing Company, two-label 12-ounce tab top, white can, metallic gold labels, single version. $25

Old Bohemian Light Beer, Eastern Brewing Company, two-label 12-ounce tab top, yellow can, "BOHEMIAN" in black, red bands, single version. $100

Eastern Brewing Company, two-label 12-ounce flat top, white can, red lettering, "LIGHT" in black, single version. $25

Eastern Brewing Company, two-label 12- or 16-ounce flat top, white can, red label outlined in metallic gold, multiversions. $10

Eastern Brewing Company, gallon can, woodgrain can, single version. $125

Old German Brand Beer, Eastern Brewing Company, single-label 12-ounce flat top, white can, picture of mug of beer, single version. $85

Eastern Brewing or Colonial Brewing Company, two-label 12- or 16-ounce zip or tab top, white can, red label, German eagle, multiversions. $10

Old German Brand Draft Beer, Eastern Brewing Company, two-label 12-ounce flat top, white can, metallic gold labels, single version. $25

PB Class "A" Beer, Eastern Brewing Company, two-label 12-ounce tab top, metallic gold can, large white stripe, multiversions. $5

Peoples Lager Beer, Colonial Brewing Company, two-label 12-ounce flat top, white can, woodgrain label, single version. $150

Polar Premium Quality Pilsner Beer, Polar Brewing Company, two-label 12-ounce tab top, blue can, white label, red circle, polar bear, two versions. .. $10

San Juan Brand Beer, Cerveceria San Juan, two-label 12-ounce flat top, white can, red label, "CERVEZA" in white on black ribbon, single version. $50

Shopwell Premium Beer, Colonial Brewing Company, two-label 12-ounce flat top, white can, gold trim, "SHOPWELL" in black, "BEER" in red, single version.. $50

Colonial Brewing Company, two-label 12-ounce flat or tab top, red and metallic gold can, "BEER" in white or off-white, single version of each. Either version, ... $30

Standard Dry Ale, Eastern Brewing Company, single-label 12-ounce tab top, white can, blue label, metallic gold bands and trim, single label. $10

Topper Pilsner Beer, Eastern Brewing Company, two-label 12-ounce tab top, white can, red chevron label, "BEER" in black, multiversions. $6

Waldbaum's Premium Lager Beer, Eastern Brewing Company, two-label 12-ounce tab top, red can, pilsner beer glass, single version. $100

Westover Premium Light Beer, Eastern Brewing Company, two-label 12-ounce tab top, white can, "WESTOVER" in white on red patch, single version. $75

Wilco Premium Beer, Colonial Brewing Company, two-label 12-ounce tab top, blue and green can, golf ball, two versions. $35

York Light Beer, Colonial Brewing Company, two-label 12-ounce flat top, white can, "YORK" in white on red square label, single version. $60

Eastern Brewing Company and all of its aka's have produced a multitude of brands in aluminum cans. The collector value of these cans can run as high as $3.

Harrison

PETER DOELGER BREWING COMPANY, 500 Harrison Street

Peter Doegler Ale, single-label 12-ounce flat top, gray can, tin mug of beer, OPENING INSTRUCTIONS, INTERNAL REVENUE TAX PAID, two minor versions. $400

Peter Doegler Bock Beer, single-label 12-ounce flat top, gold can, large goat's head, OPENING INSTRUCTIONS, INTERNAL REVENUE TAX PAID, single version. $400

Peter Doegler First Prize Beer, single-label 12-ounce flat top, OPENING INSTRUCTIONS, INTERNAL REVENUE TAX PAID, gold can, stein of beer, single version... $400

Maywood

BERGEN BREWERS, INC., foot of East Hunter Avenue

Jacob Brandt's Old Lager Beer, Rumor? Any information out there?

Newark

ANHEUSER-BUSCH, INC., 200 U.S. Highway 1

Budweiser Lager Beer, two-label 12-ounce flat top, gold can, split label, longneck bottle, multiversions. $20

Two-label 10-, 12-, or 16-ounce flat, zip, or tab top, white can, red lettering, multiversions. $5

Budweiser Malt Liquor, two-label 12- or 16-ounce tab top, black cans, two rows of eagles, single version of each size.
12-ounce, ... $10
16-ounce, ... $15

Busch Lager Beer, two-label 12-ounce flat top, red can, white label, metallic gold trim. single version. $150

Michelob Beer, two-label 12-ounce tab top, gold and black embossed can, multiversions. $25

Anheuser-Busch issued most brands in aluminum cans, as well as other brands not listed here. The collector value of these cans is $1.

P. BALLANTINE & SONS, 57 Freeman Street (aka: Blitz-Weinhard of Newark, Christian Feigenspan, Richards Brewing Company, Lexington Brewing Company)

Unless noted otherwise, all mandatories listed are P. BALLANTINE & SONS.

7-Eleven Premium Beer, Lexington Brewing Company, two-label 12-ounce tab top, metallic gold can, black lettering, 7-11 emblem, single version. $40

Ballantine 125th Anniversary Beer, two-label 12- or 16-ounce flat, bank, or zip top, metallic gold can, Ballantine rings, "125th anniversary" on white band, multiversions. All versions, ... $50

Ballantine Beer, two-label 12- or 16-ounce flat top, white can, red or green label, known as "Christmas" cans, single version of each. Each version, . $100

Two-label 12- or 16-ounce flat or zip top, gold can, Ballantine rings, BALLANTINE BEER in black on white label, multiversions. All versions, ... $15

Ballantine Bock Beer, single-label 12-ounce flat top, metallic gold can, red oval label, "bock" in black, OPENING INSTRUCTIONS, INTERNAL REVENUE TAX PAID, minor versions. $125

Two-label 12-ounce flat top, metallic gold can, yellow horseshoe label, "BOCK" in brown or red, single version of each. Each version, ... $60

Two-label 12-ounce flat top, metallic gold can, goat's head, "BOCK BEER" in red, single version. $75

Two-label 12-ounce tab top, metallic gold can, gold goat's head, small white Ballantine rings, single version. $20

Three-label 12-ounce aluminum tab top, metallic gold can, full-body goat, multiversions. $7

Ballantine Draft Beer, two-label 12-ounce flat or tab top, white can, "GENUINE DRAFT BEER" in red, multiversions. $10
Aluminum, ... $3

Ballantine Draught Beer, two-label gallon can, brown can, beer glasses, three versions. $150

Ballantine Draught XXX Ale, two-label gallon can, woodgrain can, beer glasses, three versions. $250

Ballantine Extra Fine Beer, two-label 12- or 16-ounce flat top, metallic gold can, round yellow label, multiversions. Either size, ... $25

Two-label 12- or 16-ounce or quart flat top, metallic gold can, horseshoe-shaped yellow label, multiversions.

12-ounce, ... $20
16-ounce, ... $30
Quart, ... $150

Ballantine Light Lager Beer, two-label 12- or 16-ounce or quart flat top, metallic gold can, horseshoe-shaped yellow label, multiversions.

12-ounce $20
16-ounce $30
Quart, ... $150

Ballantine Premium Beer, two-label 12- or 16-ounce flat or tab top, metallic gold can, white label, "PREMIUM" on metallic gold ribbon, multiversions. . $40

Ballantine Premium Lager Beer, two- or three-label 12- or 16-ounce tab top, gold can, white label, Ballantine rings, black lettering, multiversions. $3

Ballantine Premium Quality Beer, two-label 12- or 16-ounce flat or tab top, metallic gold can, white label, "PREMIUM QUALITY" on white label, multiversions.

12-ounce, ... $15
16-ounce, ... $20

Ballantine Triple Crown Malt Liquor, two-label 12-ounce tab top, white can, medals, "TRIPLE CROWN" in black, single version. $200

Ballantine XXX Ale, two-label 12- or 16-ounce flat or tab top, gold can, round yellow label, versions: "BREWER'S GOLD" with USBF seal, "BREWER'S GOLD" without USBF seal, without "BREWER'S GOLD" and without USBF seal. All versions, ... $20

Single- or two-label 12-ounce flat top or quart cone top, gold can, green oval label, OPENING INSTRUCTIONS or non-OI, INTERNAL REVENUE TAX PAID or non-IRTP, multiversions.

12 ounce, non-IRTP, non-OI, ... $75
12-ounce, non-OI, ... $100
12-ounce, OI $125
Quart cone top, ... $150

Ballantine's Export Light Beer, single-label 12-ounce flat or quart cone top, metallic gold can, single brown oval label, two lines text, with or without OPENING INSTRUCTIONS, INTERNAL REVENUE TAX PAID, multiversions 12-ounce, single version quart.

12-ounce, ... $200
Quart, ... $300

Single-label 12-ounce flat top or quart cone, metallic gold can, single brown oval label, three lines text, INTERNAL REVENUE TAX PAID, multiversions.

12-ounce, ... $175
Quart, ... $250

Single-label 12-ounce flat top, camouflage can, three versions. $250

Single- or two-label 12-ounce flat top, gold or copper can, black oval label, INTERNAL REVENUE TAX PAID, multiversions. $100

Ballantine's XXX Ale, single-label 12-ounce flat top, metallic gold can, single red label, OPENING INSTRUCTIONS, INTERNAL REVENUE TAX PAID, minor versions. (This is the first bock can.) .... Unique

Single-label 12-ounce flat top, metallic gold can, two red labels, two minor versions. $300

Bohack Draft Beer, Richards Brewing Company, two-label 12-ounce flat or tab top, brown can, glass of beer, "BOHACK" in red, multiversions. $10
Aluminum, ... $3

Bohack Premium Beer, Richards Brewing Company, two-label 12-ounce flat top, yellow woodgrain can, multiversions. $25

Two-label 12-ounce tab top, light blue-gray can, glass of beer, single version. $15

Two-label 12-ounce tab top, blue can, glass of beer, single version. $3
Aluminum, ... $1

Meister Brau Light Beer, Christian Feigenspan, two-label 12-ounce tab top, blue can, white label, "LITE" in blue, single version. $15

Munich Light Beer, Christian Feigenspan, two-label 12-ounce flat or tab top, white can, blue label outlined in metallic gold, multiversions. $5

Munich Light Lager Beer, Christian Feigenspan, two-label 12-ounce tab top, white can, blue label outlined in metallic gold, single steel version. $3
Aluminum, ... $1

Olde English 800 Malt Liquor, Blitz-Weinhard of Newark, two-label 12- or 16-ounce tab top, gold can, brown label, multiversions.
Steel, ... $2
Aluminum, ... $1

P. Ballantine & Sons issued a series of beer cans, drinking cups, banks, and can mugs beginning in the mid-1950s and running through the mid-1960s. The value of these range from $35 to $50. All are easily identified as being from P. Ballantine.

The *banks* in the series are: Jaycees Roll Out the Barrel '62–63, Maine Jaycees 1961–1962, New Jersey Jaycees 1958–1959, Pennsylvania Jaycees 1957–1958, Pennsylvania Jaycees 1958–1959, and Pennsylvania Jaycees 1960.

The *mugs* in the series are: 1963 Cornell Alumni Reunion, 1964 Cornell Alumni Reunion, 1965 Cornell Alumni Reunion, 1966 Cornell Alumni Reunion, and 1967 Cornell Alumni Reunion.

The *drinking cups* in the series are: Princeton '35, Princeton '40s 20th in 60, Princeton Class of 1937 25th, Princeton Class of 1947 15th, Princeton 1938's 25th in 63, Princeton 1948 15th Reunion, Princeton 1953 10th Reunion, Princeton 1958 5th Reunion, Princeton 1954 10th Reunion, Princeton 1959 5th Reunion, Princeton 1940 25th Reunion, Princeton 1941 25th Reunion, I Like Ike (two versions), and Over the Hill Club 1962.

CHRISTIAN FEIGANSPAN BREWING COMPANY, 50 Freeman Street

Feiganspan P.O.N. Ale, single-label 12-ounce flat top, silver can, green label and trim, OPENING INSTRUCTIONS or non-OI, INTERNAL REVENUE TAX PAID, two versions.
OI, ... $175
Non-OI, ... $150

Feiganspan P.O.N. Beer, single-label 12-ounce flat top, gold can, blue label and trim, OPENING INSTRUCTIONS or non-OI, INTERNAL REVENUE TAX PAID, multiversions.

OI, ... $150
Non-OI, ... $125

Feiganspan P.O.N. Light Beer, single-label 12-ounce flat top or quart cone top, gold can, yellow label, "P.O.N." in white on red circle, INTERNAL REVENUE TAX PAID, single version of flat top, two minor versions of quart.

Flat top, ... $75
Quart, ... $150

Feiganspan P.O.N. XXX Amber Ale, single-label 12-ounce flat top, or quart cone top, green can and label, "P.O.N." (Pride of Newark) in white on red circle, INTERNAL REVENUE TAX PAID, single version of flat top, two minor versions of quart.

Flat top, ... $85
Quart, ... $165

THE JOSEPH HENSLER BREWING COMPANY, 73 Wilson Avenue

Hensler Light Beer, single-label 12-ounce flat top, gold can, red stripe, single version. $100

Single-label 12-ounce flat top, white or yellow can, "HENSLER" in white on red oval label, single version of each.

White can, ... $75
Yellow can, ... $100

G. KRUGER BREWING COMPANY, 75 Belmont Avenue

Ambassador Export Brewed Beer, two-label 12-ounce flat top, white can, multicolored chevron label, dancers, single version. *(See photo 196)* $90

Kent Ale, single-label 12-ounce flat top, gold can, man holding stein, single version. .... Unique

Krueger A Premium Cream Ale, single-label 12- or 16-ounce flat top or quart cone top, white can, wheat stalks, green oval outlined in metallic gold, minor versions.

12-ounce, ... $40
16-ounce, ... $50
Quart, ... $75

Photo 196. Ambassador Export Brewed Beer.

Krueger A Real Premium Beer, single-label 12- or 16-ounce flat top or quart cone top, white can, wheat stalks, red oval outlined in metallic gold, minor versions.

12-ounce,.. $30
16-ounce,... $35
Quart,.. $65

Krueger Beer, single-label 12-ounce flat top, white can, metallic red label and metallic gold trim, single version. $40

Krueger Bock Beer, single-label 12-ounce flat top, red can, large metallic gold label, large goat's head, versions: OPENING INSTRUCTIONS, OPENING INSTRUCTIONS and IRTP.

OI, ...Unique
OI and IRTP,... $300

Two-label 12-ounce flat top, metallic gold can, red label, goat's head, single version. $150

Krueger Cream Ale, single-label 12-ounce flat top, or 16-ounce or quart cone top, green can, "k-man" on gold label, OPENING INSTRUCTIONS, INTERNAL REVENUE TAX PAID, multiversions.

12-ounce flat top, ...$125
12-ounce flat top, OI,..$175
16-ounce cone top, ... $300
Quart cone top, ...$150

Single-label, 12-ounce, high-profile cone top, flat top, or quart cone top, green can, red and yellow label, "k-man" in red, INTERNAL REVENUE TAX PAID, multiversions.

12-ounce flat top, ... $85
12-ounce cone top, ...$125
Quart cone top, ...$125

Single-label 12-ounce flat top, white can, green label, gold trim, single version.. $50

Krueger Extra Light Beer, single-label 12-ounce flat top, white can, "KRUEGER" in black, large red "k-man," minor versions. $65

Krueger Extra Light Cream Ale, two-label 12-ounce flat top, white can, green label, red or green "k-man," multiversions. $60

Krueger Extra Light Dry Beer, two-label 12-ounce flat top or 12-ounce high-profile cone top, white can, red label, red "k-man" on white circle, multiversions.

Flat top, ... $35
Cone top, ... $65

Krueger Finest Beer, single-label 12-ounce flat top, or 16-ounce or quart cone top, red can, gold square label, black "k-man," OPENING INSTRUCTIONS, INTERNAL REVENUE TAX PAID, WITHDRAWN FREE, multiversions.

WITHDRAWN FREE,..$150
12-ounce flat top, OI,...$100
12-ounce flat top, ... $85
16-ounce cone top, ... $300
Quart cone top, ... $200

Single-label, 12-ounce, high-profile cone or flat top, or quart cone top, INTERNAL REVENUE TAX PAID, brown can, yellow oval, brown "k-man," single version.

12-ounce flat top, ... $65
12-ounce cone top, ... $100
Quart cone top, ... $125

Krueger Finest Light Lager Beer, two-label 12-ounce flat top or cone top, yellow can, red label and bands, red "k-man," single version.

12-ounce flat top, ... $65
Quart cone top, ... $125

Krueger Light Cream Ale, single-label 12-ounce flat top, yellow can, green "k-man," "KRUEGER" in black, multiversions. $75

Krueger's Bock Beer, single-label 12-ounce flat top, red can, metallic gold label, large goat's head, OPENING INSTRUCTIONS, INTERNAL REVENUE TAX PAID, single version. $350

Krueger's Cream Ale, single-label 12-ounce flat top, green can, gold label, black "k-man," OPENING INSTRUCTIONS, INTERNAL REVENUE TAX PAID or non-IRTP.

OI, ... Exotic
OI and IRTP, ... $125

Krueger's Finest Beer, single-label 12-ounce flat top, red can, gold label, black "k-man," OPENING INSTRUCTIONS, IRTP or non-IRTP.

OI, ... Exotic
OI and IRTP, ... $125

Krueger's Special Beer, single-label 12-ounce flat top, red can, "k-man" on gold rectangle, OPENING INSTRUCTIONS, single version. .... Unique

PABST BREWING COMPANY, 391–399 Grove Street

Big Cat Malt Liquor, two-label 12-ounce tab top, white can, running tiger, "BIG CAT" in red, single version. $3

Blatz Milwaukee's Finest Beer, two-label 12-ounce flat top, yellow can, "NEWARK" on metallic gold bands, single version. $40

Blatz Milwaukee's Finest Bock Beer, two-label 12-ounce flat top, yellow can, "NEWARK" on metallic gold bands, single version. $65

Pabst Blue Ribbon Beer, single-label 12-ounce flat top, silver can, cream-colored label outlined in gold, INTERNAL REVENUE TAX PAID, "HOFFMAN BEVERAGE CO. LICENSED NEW YORK DISTRIBUTOR," single version. $150

Two-label quart cone top, gold can, cream-colored label, "SNAP ON FULL QUART," single version. $85

Two-label 12-ounce flat top, silver can, white label, gold trim, single version. $30

Two-label 12-ounce flat top, dark blue can, white label, single version. $20

Two-label 12-ounce flat top, white can, red band, "FINEST BEER SERVED ANYWHERE," single version. $15

Two-label 12- or 16-ounce flat, soft, or tab top, white can, red band, "THIS IS THE ORIGINAL PABST BLUE RIBBON BEER . . . ," multiversions.

Flat top, ...$5
Soft top, ...$5
Tab top, ...$2

Pabst Blue Ribbon Bock Beer, two-label 12-ounce flat top, silver can, white label, "BOCK" in red on blue ribbon, single version. $100

Two-label 12-ounce flat top, yellow can, blue ribbon on silver goat, single version. $150

Two-label 12-ounce flat or tab top, white can, red band, two small red goats, one version of each top. $5

Two-label 12-ounce tab top, white can, red band, white goat, "GENUINE BOCK," multiversions. $2

Pabst produced these brands as well as others under the PABST, THEODORE HAMM, BLITZ-WEINHARD, and RWB mandatories in aluminum cans. Collector value is up to $1.

Orange

LIEBMANN BREWERIES, INC., 119 Hill Street (successor to John F. Trommer, Inc.)

Rheingold Extra Dry Lager Beer, single-label 12-ounce flat top, white can, red label, "LAGER BEER" in block letters, multiversions. $30

Single-label 12-ounce flat top, white can, red label, set can, set of seven called "Rheingold Girls": Diane Baker, Beverly Christensen, Tami Conner, Margie McNally, Suzy Ruel, Kathleen Wallace, Margie McNally Miss Rheingold 1957; single version of each. Each, ...$250

Two-label 12-ounce flat top, white can, red label, "EXTRA DRY" in black on white oval, multiversions. $15

Rheingold Genuine Bock Beer, two-label 12-ounce flat top, gold can, red label, "GENUINE" in black on white oval, two versions, with or without Rheingold jingle.

With jingle, ...$300
Without jingle, ...$275

Two-label 12-ounce flat top, gold can, red label, two white goats above label, two minor versions. $400

RHEINGOLD BREWERIES, INC., 119 Hill Street (successor to Liebmann Breweries, Inc.; aka: Forrest Brewing Co., Jacob Ruppert)

Gablinger's Beer, single-label 12-ounce zip top, metallic brown can, yellow label, picture of man, single version. $15

Gablinger's Extra Light Beer, Forrest Brewing Company, two-label 12-ounce tab top, orange can, white label, multiversions. $2

Rheingold Extra Dry Lager Beer, Rheingold Brewing Company, two-label 12-ounce flat or tab top, white can, red label, "EXTRA DRY" in black on white oval, multiversions. $10

Brand was also produced in aluminum. Collector value is up to $1.

Rheingold Extra Light Beer, Rheingold Breweries, Inc., two-label 12-ounce tab top, white can, red and white label, single version. $2

Rheingold Golden Bock Beer, Rheingold Breweries, Inc., two-label 12-ounce flat top, red and white can, gold label, glass of beer, single version. $100

Ruppert Knickerbocker New York's Famous Beer, Jacob Ruppert, two-label 12-ounce tab top, metallic gold can, red, gold, and blue ribbons, multiversions. $5

Brand was also produced in aluminum cans. Collector value is $1.

JOHN F. TROMMER, INC., 119 Hill Street (predecessor to Liebmann Breweries, Inc.)

Trommer's Ale, two-label 12-ounce flat top, green can, "ALE" in red, man with mug of beer, OPENING INSTRUCTIONS, INTERNAL REVENUE TAX PAID, multiversions. ....Exotic

Trommer's Beer, single-label 12-ounce flat top, metallic gold can, red label, metals, WITHDRAWN FREE, French, Spanish, and Portuguese text on back of can, single version. ....Unique

Two-label 12-ounce flat top, bright or dull gold, red label, white lettering, INTERNAL REVENUE TAX PAID, single version of each. Either version, ... $200

Trommer's Bock Beer, single-label 12-ounce flat top, gold can, large goat's head, "BOCK" in red, OPENING INSTRUCTIONS, INTERNAL REVENUE TAX PAID, single version. ....Exotic

Two-label 12-ounce flat top, gold can, red label, red band, white goat, single version. $300

Trommer's Malt Beer, single-label 12-ounce flat top, gold can, blue label, "MALT" in red, OPENING INSTRUCTIONS, INTERNAL REVENUE TAX PAID, single version. $300

Two-label 12-ounce flat top, white can, red label, gold trim, INTERNAL REVENUE TAX PAID, single version. $150

Two-label 12-ounce flat top, gold can, red label, white lettering, two minor versions. $125

Trommer's Red Letter Beer, two-label 12-ounce flat top, red can, pilsner beer glass label, single version. $75

Paterson

BURTON PRODUCTS COMPANY, 81 Straight Street

Grahams Ale, single-label, 12-ounce, high-profile cone top, dark green and gold can, INTERNAL REVENUE TAX PAID, single version. ....Unique

Morlein Premium Beer, single-label, 12-ounce, high-profile cone top, metallic gold can, black label, white lettering, INTERNAL REVENUE TAX PAID, single version. ....Exotic

Vita Brew Beer, single-label high-profile cone top, yellow and gold can, INTERNAL REVENUE TAX PAID, single version. ....Exotic

Trenton

CHAMPALE, INC., Lalor and Lamberton Streets (aka: Metropolis Brewery of New Jersey, Champale, Banner Brewing Company, Black Horse Brewery of New Jersey, Class "A" Brewing Company, Gilt Edge Brewing Company, Hornell Brewing Company, Old Bohemian Brewing Company, Rialto Brewing Company, Roger Wilco Brewing Company, Tudor Brewing Company)

Banner Extra Dry Premium Beer, Banner Brewing Company, single-label 12-ounce tab top, white can, red label, "PREMIUM BEER" in blue, single version. $30

Black Horse Ale, Black Horse Brewery of New Jersey, single-label 12-ounce flat top, white can, oval label, black horse, single version. $75

Bock Brand Beer, Metropolis Brewery of New Jersey, single-label 12-ounce flat top, gold can, black label, large goat's head, single version. $300

Brauhaus Beer, Metropolis Brewery of New Jersey, single-label 12-ounce flat top, metallic gold can, maroon label, drinking scene, single version. $75

Champale Extra Dry Sparkling Malt Liquor, Champale, Inc. or Metropolis Brewery of New Jersey, single-label 12-ounce flat or tab top, metallic green can, white label, "SPARKLING" in red, multiversions. $20

Champale, Inc., two-label 12-ounce tab top, green can, large champagne glass, multiversions. *(See photo 197)* $10

Champale Pink Flavored Malt Liquor, Champale, Inc., pink can, Champale glass, single version. $10

Copenhagen Castle Brand Beer, Metropolis Brewery of New Jersey, single-label 12-ounce flat top, multicolored can, man's head, single version. $250

Ehret's Extra Near Beer, Metropolis Brewery of New Jersey, single-label 12-ounce flat top, red can, "EHRET'S EXTRA NEAR BEER" in blue on gold ribbon, single version. $100

Embassy Club Extra Dry Beer, Metropolis Brewery of New Jersey, single-label 12-ounce flat or tab top, metallic gold can, red label, white trim, single version. $60

Metropolis Brewery of New Jersey, single-label 12-ounce flat top, white can, red label, "BEER" in blue, single version. $30

Metropolis Brewery of New Jersey or Champale, Inc., two-label 12-ounce tab top, white can, red label, "BEER" in blue, single version of each brewery. . $20

Gilt Edge Brand Ale, Gilt Edge Brewing Company, two-label 12-ounce flat top, green can, white label, single version. $75

Photo 197. Champale Extra Dry Sparkling Malt Liquor.

Gilt Edge Brand Beer, Gilt Edge Brewing Company, two-label 12-ounce flat top, gold can, white label, "GILT EDGE" in green, single version. $50

Grand Union Premium Ale, Gilt Edge Brewing Company, two-label 12-ounce flat top, white can, red and yellow label, "PREMIUM ALE" in black, single version. $30

Grand Union Premium Beer, Gilt Edge Brewing Company, two-label 12-ounce tab top, white can, red and yellow label, two versions. $25

Horton Premium Beer, Metropolis Brewery of New Jersey, single-label 12-ounce flat top, orange can, gold bands, single version. $75

Kol Premium Quality Beer, Metropolis Brewery of New Jersey, single-label 12-ounce flat top, silver can, vertical blue stripes, blue label, single version. $25

Old Bohemian Light Beer, Old Bohemian Brewing Company, two-label 12-ounce flat top, white can, "LIGHT" in black, red lettering, single version. . $40

Old Dutch Brand Lager Premium Beer, Metropolis Brewery of New Jersey, single-label 12-ounce flat top, red can, cream label outlined in black, single version. $125

Old Ranger Premium Beer, Hornell Brewery, single-label 12-ounce tab top, white can, red labels, "OLD RANGER" in black, single version. $60

Oldbru Bavarian Style Beer, Metropolis Brewery of New Jersey, single-label 12-ounce flat top, white can, green outline, single version. $150

PB Class "A" Ale, Class "A" Brewing Company, two-label 12-ounce flat top, white can, metallic gold label, green trim, single version. $50

PB Class "A" Beer, Class "A" Brewing Company, two-label 12-ounce flat top, white can, metallic gold label, red trim, single version. $25

Pilser's Original Extra Dry Beer, Metropolis Brewery of New Jersey, single-label high-profile cone or flat top, metallic gold can, cream label outlined in red, single version of each.
Flat top, ... $60
Cone top, ... $100

Pilser's Original Maltcrest Brew, Metropolis Brewery of New Jersey, single-label 12-ounce flat top, white can, "MALTCREST" in white on blue oval, multi-versions. $50

Regent Premium Quality Ale, Metropolis Brewery of New Jersey, single-label 12-ounce flat top, white can, "PREMIUM QUALITY" in white on red band, single version. $85

Regent Premium Quality Beer, Metropolis Brewery of New Jersey, single-label 12-ounce flat top, white can, "PREMIUM QUALITY" in white on black band, single version. $60

Rialto Ale, Rialto Brewing Company, two-label 12-ounce flat top, green can, white label, single version. $85

Rialto Beer, Rialto Brewing Company, two-label 12-ounce flat top, gold can, white label, single version. $60

Roger Wilco 199 Brand Beer, Roger Wilco Brewing Company, two-label 12-ounce flat top, yellow can, blue label, single version. $150

Tudor Bock Beer, Metropolis Brewery of New Jersey or Tudor Brewing, two-label 12-ounce flat top, cream-colored can, maroon label, helmet or cornet, minor versions.

Helmet, ...$150
Cornet, ...$100

Tudor Brewing Company, two-label 12-ounce flat or tab top, white can, brown oval label, "A&P," single version of each top.

Flat top, ... $60
Tab top, ... $55

Tudor Cream Ale, Tudor Brewing Company, two-label 12-ounce flat or tab top, white can, oval green label, "A&P," single version of each top. Either top, ... $10

Tudor Pilsner Beer, Tudor Brewing Company, two-label 12-ounce flat or tab top, white can, red oval label, "A&P," single version of each top. Either top, ... $10

Tudor Premium Quality Ale, Metropolis Brewery of New Jersey, two-label 12-ounce flat top, green or white can, cornet, single version of each. $25

Tudor Premium Quality Beer, Metropolis Brewery of New Jersey, single- or two-label 12-ounce flat top, red can, blue label, multiversions. $30

Metropolis Brewery of New Jersey, two-label 12-ounce flat top, white can, red label outlined in gold, single version. $20

Tudor Premium Quality Cream Ale, Metropolis Brewery of New Jersey, single-label 12-ounce flat top, green can, white lettering, single version. $25

PEOPLES BREWING COMPANY, Lalor and Lamberton Streets (predecessor to Champale, Inc.)

Trent Cream Ale, single-label quart cone top, silver can, yellow label, INTERNAL REVENUE TAX PAID, single version. ....Exotic

Trenton Old Stock Beer, single- or two-label, 12-ounce, J-spout cone, crowntainer, or quart cone top, silver can, yellow label, "TRENTON" in red, INTERNAL REVENUE TAX PAID, WITHDRAWN FREE, minor versions.

J-spout, ...$250
Crowntainer, ...$225
WITHDRAWN FREE, ... $400
Quart, ...$350

Union City

GEORGE EHRET BREWERY, INC., 3315–3317 Hudson Avenue

Ehret's Extra Beer, single-label, 12-ounce, high-profile cone top, red can, "EHRET'S EXTRA BEER" in black on white ribbon, single version. $200

SCHULZ BREWING COMPANY, 106 44th Street

Schulz Quality Ale, single-label 12-ounce flat top, silver can, "QUALITY" on green ribbon, INTERNAL REVENUE TAX PAID, single version. ....Exotic

Schulz Quality Beer, single-label 12-ounce flat top, gold can, "QUALITY BEER" on red ribbon, INTERNAL REVENUE TAX PAID, single version. ....Exotic

New Mexico

No beer cans were ever produced in this state.

New York

/

Albany

BEVERWYCK BREWERIES, INC., 56 North Ferry Street (predecessor to F. & M. Schaefer Company)

Beverwyck Cream Ale, single-label, 12-ounce, low-profile cone top, silver can, green shamrock label, INTERNAL REVENUE TAX PAID, single version. $300

Beverwyck Famous Ale, single-label low-profile cone top, silver can, oval label, "BEVERWYCK" in red, INTERNAL REVENUE TAX PAID, minor versions. $150

Single-label, 12-ounce, low-profile cone top, gold can, oval label, "BEVERWYCK" in red, INTERNAL REVENUE TAX PAID, multiversions. $175

Beverwyck Famous Beer, single-label, 12-ounce, low-profile cone top, silver can, oval label, "BEVERWYCK" in red, INTERNAL REVENUE TAX PAID, minor versions. $100

Single-label, 12-ounce, low-profile cone top, gold can, oval label, "BEVERWYCK" in red, INTERNAL REVENUE TAX PAID, multiversions. $125

Single-label, 12-ounce, low- or high-profile cone top, or quart cone top, green can, yellow lettering, INTERNAL REVENUE TAX PAID, WITHDRAWN FREE, multiversions.

12-ounce, ...$100
12-ounce WITHDRAWN FREE, ...$150
Quart, ...$150

Two-label 12-ounce crowntainer, silver or white can, black label outlined in red, INTERNAL REVENUE TAX PAID, single version. $75

Two-label, 12-ounce, high-profile cone or flat top, gold can, white shamrock label, INTERNAL REVENUE TAX PAID, single version of each.

Flat top, ...$75
Cone top, ...$100

Beverwyck Famous Export Beer, single-label high-profile cone top, gold can, "EXPORT" in white, INTERNAL REVENUE TAX PAID, single version. ....Exotic

Beverwyck Golden Dry Beer, single-label 12-ounce flat top, gold can, white shamrock, INTERNAL REVENUE TAX PAID, multiversions. $75

Beverwyck Irish Brand Cream Ale, single-label, 12-ounce, low-profile or quart cone top, gold and green can, green shamrock, INTERNAL REVENUE TAX PAID, multiversions.
12-ounce,..$125
Quart,..$175

Single-label 12-ounce crowntainer, silver can, white label, INTERNAL REVENUE TAX PAID, multiversions. $125

Single-label, 12-ounce, high-profile cone top, green shamrock, "1845," INTERNAL REVENUE TAX PAID, multiversions. $125

Single-label, 12-ounce, high-profile cone or flat top, or quart cone top, metallic gold can, green shamrock, INTERNAL REVENUE TAX PAID, multiversions.
12-ounce flat top, ... $75
12-ounce cone top, ...$130
Quart cone top, ...$175

Beverwyck Irish Cream Ale Brand, single-label, 12-ounce, low-profile cone top, gold can, green shamrock, INTERNAL REVENUE TAX PAID, single version.
....$150

Beverwyck Irish Cream Ale Type, single-label, 12-ounce, low-profile cone top, gold can, green shamrock, INTERNAL REVENUE TAX PAID, single version. ..$150

DOBLER BREWING COMPANY, 187 South Swan Street

Dobler Bock Beer, single-label 12-ounce flat top, white can, metallic gold bands, "BOCK" in black, single version. $300

Dobler Private Seal Beer, single-label 12-ounce flat top, gold or white can, vertical red stripes, "SINCE 1865" in red or black, minor versions. $20

Dobler XXX Amber Ale, single-label 12-ounce flat top, green can, gold bands, "SINCE 1865" on large red patch, single version. $150

Single-label 12-ounce tab top, silver or gold can, white label, "SINCE 1865" on red or green patch, single version of each. Each, ...$20

HEDRICK BREWING COMPANY, 410 Central Avenue

Hedrick Lager Beer, single-label 12-ounce flat or tab top, metallic gold can, red and white label, single version of each top.
Flat top, ... $20
Tab top,... $15

F. & M. SCHAEFER BREWING COMPANY, 56 North Ferry Street (successor to Beverwyk Brewing Company)

Schaefer Beer, single-label 12-ounce flat, zip, or tab top, white can, 15 circles, multiversions. $5

Photo 198. Schaefer Irish Brand Cream Ale.

Schaefer Fine Beer, single-label 12-ounce flat top, woodgrain can, red label outlined in black or gold, multiversions. Either version, ... $50

Single-label 12-ounce flat top, white can, red label, light or dark brown trim, single version of each. Either version, ... $25

Schaefer Golden Beer, single-label 12-ounce flat top, brown barrel can, single version. $40

Schaefer Irish Brand Cream Ale, single-label 12-ounce flat top, yellow can, dull green shamrock, two versions. $50

Single-label 12-ounce flat top, cream-colored can, green shamrock, single version. *(See photo 198)* $35

Schaefer Pale Dry Beer, single-label 12-ounce flat top, cream-colored can, metallic gold bands, red label, minor versions. $40

Baldwinsville

ANHEUSER-BUSCH, INC., 2885 Belgium Road (successor to Jos. Schlitz Brewing Company [*see* Syracuse])

All cans produced at this brewery were produced in aluminum, including the time since the brewery reopened in 1983. The collector value will not exceed $1.

Buffalo

INTERNATIONAL BREWERIES, INC., 194–262 Pratt Street (successor to Iroquois Beverage Corporation; aka: International Breweries, Blackhawk Brewing Company, Frankenmuth Brewing Company, Phoenix Brewing Company)

Blackhawk Beer, Blackhawk Brewing Company, two-label 12-ounce flat top, silver can, red Indian head, "BLACKHAWK" in blue, single version. $75

Frankenmuth Genuine Bock, International Breweries, two-label 12-ounce flat top, black can, red oval label, yellow lettering, single version. $100

Frankenmuth Mel-O-Dry Ale, International Breweries, single-label 12-ounce flat top, metallic gold can, brown label outlined in white, single version. ...$100

International Breweries, single-label 12-ounce flat top, cream-colored can, brown label, red patch, minor versions. $60

Frankenmuth or International Breweries, two-label 12-ounce flat top, white can, green label, single version of each. $40

Frankenmuth Mel-O-Dry Beer, International or Frankenmuth Breweries, two-label 12-ounce flat top, white can, red label outlined in metallic gold or white, single version of each. $40

International Frankenmuth Ale, International Breweries, two-label 12-ounce flat top, white can, green label, single version. $40

International Frankenmuth Beer, International Breweries, two-label 12-ounce flat top, white can, red label, minor versions. $25

International Frankenmuth Bock, International Breweries, two-label 12-ounce flat top, gold can, red label, single version. $60

International Iroquois Ale, International Breweries, two-label 12-ounce flat or zip top, white can, green label, single version of each. Either top, ... $40

International Iroquois Beer, International Breweries, two-label 12-ounce flat or zip top, white can, red label, multiversions. $25

Iroquois Ale, International Breweries, single-label 12-ounce flat or tab top, white can, green label, single version of each top. Either top, ... $40

Iroquois Beer, International Breweries, single-label 12-ounce flat top, white can, red label outlined in metallic gold, single version. $40

Iroquois Indian Head Beer, International Breweries, single-label 12-ounce flat top, metallic gold can, hatched in white, red arrowhead label, single version. $75

International Breweries, two-label 12-ounce tab top, red can, metallic gold stripes, white label, single version. $25

Iroquois Tomohawk Ale, International Breweries, two-label 12-ounce tab top, green can, white label, silver stripes, single version. $100

Phoenix Premium Beer, International or Phoenix Breweries, two-label 12-ounce flat top, white can, blue label, single version of each. $75

Stolz Premium Beer, Phoenix or International Breweries, two-label 12-ounce flat top, white can, red lettering, yellow trim, multiversions. *(See photo 199)* $40

IROQUOIS BEVERAGE CORPORATION, 194–262 Pratt Street (predecessor to International Breweries, Inc.)

Iroquois Half & Half, single-label, 12-ounce, low-profile cone top, red can, yellow and red label outlined in black, INTERNAL REVENUE TAX PAID, single version. $350

Photo 199. Stolz Premium Beer.

Iroquois Indian Head Ale, single-label, 12-ounce, high- or low-profile cone top, blue can, INTERNAL REVENUE TAX PAID, single version of each. ....Exotic

Two-label 12-ounce crowntainer, silver can, Indian head, red bands top and bottom, single version. $150

Iroquois Indian Head Beer, single-label, 12-ounce, high- or low-profile cone top, yellow can, red oval, "IROQUOIS INDIAN HEAD BEER" in black, INTERNAL REVENUE TAX PAID, minor versions.
High- or low-profile, ... $200
Camouflage cone, ...$350

Two-label 12-ounce crowntainer, silver can, Indian head, "IROQUOIS" in red, INTERNAL REVENUE TAX PAID, single version. $150

Two-label 12-ounce crowntainer, silver can, small Indian head, green bands top and bottom, INTERNAL REVENUE TAX PAID, single version. $175

Single-label, 12-ounce, high-profile cone top, metallic red can, white label, single version. $125

Single-label, 12-ounce, high-profile cone or flat top, gold hatched can, red arrowhead label, single version of each.
Flat top, ...$125
Cone top, ...$160

IROQUOIS BREWING COMPANY (DIVISION OF IRO-QUOIS INDUSTRIES, INC.), 194–262 Pratt Street (successor to International Breweries, Inc.; aka: Iroquois Brewing, Cleveland-Sandusky Brewing Company)

Bavarian's Select Beer, Iroquois Brewing, single-label 12-ounce flat top, white can, metallic gold label, three pennants, single version. $25

Draft Beer By Iroquois, Iroquois Brewing, two-label 12-ounce flat or tab top, white can, "DRAFT BEER" in blue, multiversions (a warehouse full of these cans was found). *(See photo 200)* $1

Iroquois Draft Ale, Iroquois Brewing, two-label 12-ounce flat top, green can, white stripes, white label, "DRAFT" in red, single version. *(See photo 201)*
.... $35

Iroquois Indian Head Beer, Iroquois Brewing, two-label 12-ounce tab top, red can, gold stripes, white label outlined in metallic gold, multiversions. $20

Old Timers Ale, Cleveland-Sandusky Brewing, single-label 12-ounce flat top, white and green can, buggy and horse in red, single version. $65

Photo 200 (left).
Draft Beer By Iroquois.
Photo 201 (center).
Iroquois Draft Ale.
Photo 202 (right).
Koch's Genuine
Draft Beer.

WILLIAM SIMON BREWERY, INC., 143–145 Emslie Street

Simon Pure Beer, single-label 12-ounce flat, zip, or tab top, gold can, white label, red inner label, versions: different tops.
Flat top, ... $60
Zip and tab top, ... $50

GEORGE F. STEIN BREWERY, INC., 797 Broadway

Banner Extra Dry Premium Beer, single-label 12-ounce flat top, white can, red label, "PREMIUM BEER" in blue, single version. $25

Kol Premium Quality Beer, single-label 12-ounce flat top, silver can, vertical white stripes, blue label, single version. $25

Stein's Beer, two-label 12-ounce flat top, metallic gold can, red and white label, single version. $65

Two-label 12-ounce flat top, white can, red label, single version. $50

Stein's Canandaigua Extra Dry Beer, two-label 12-ounce flat top, metallic gold can, white stripes, white label, single version. $50

Single-label 12-ounce flat top, gray can, white label, "EXTRA DRY BEER" in red, single version. $100

Stein's Light Ale, two-label 12-ounce flat top, metallic gold can, white stripes, green and white label, single version. $85

Tudor Premium Quality Beer, single-label 12-ounce flat top, red can, blue label, white helmet, single version. $30

Tudor Premium Quality Cream Ale, single-label 12-ounce flat top, green can, white label, white helmet, single version. $40

Dunkirk

FRED KOCH BREWERY, 15–25 Courtney Street (aka: Black Horse Brewery, Iroquois Brewery/Dunkirk)

Black Horse Ale, Black Horse Brewery, two-label 12-ounce tab top, white can, multicolored oval label, black horse, single version. $75

Black Horse Premium Ale, Black Horse Brewery, two-label 12-ounce tab top, black and silver can, single version. $50

Black Horse Premium Beer, Black Horse Brewery, two-label 12-ounce tab top, black and gold can, single version. $40

Iroquois Indian Head Beer, Iroquois Brewing Company/Dunkirk, two-label 12-ounce tab top, solid red can, white label, red face, single version. $75

Koch's Deer Run Genuine Draft Beer, Fred Koch Brewery, two-label gallon can, green and white can, red and white label, "ALE" in red, single version.
.... $350

Koch's Genuine Draft Beer, Fred Koch Brewery, two-label gallon can, wood-grain can, red and white label, "BEER" in red, multiversions. *(See photo 202)*
.... $425

Koch's Golden Anniversary Beer, Fred Koch Brewery, single-label 12-ounce flat, zip, or tab top, yellow and white can, "GOLDEN ANNIVERSARY" in black, multiversions. $40

Fred Koch Brewery, two-label 12-ounce tab top, yellow can, white label, "GET THE BEST IN FLAVOR," multiversions. $25

Fulton

MILLER BREWING COMPANY, Owens Road

This brewery was built in 1976 and produced nothing but aluminum cans. The collector value of these cans does not exceed $1.

Hornell

HORNELL BREWING COMPANY, 7 Franklin Street

Bock Brand Beer, single-label 12-ounce flat top, metallic gold can, red bands, black label, large goat's head, single version. .... Exotic

Gilt Edge Brand Ale, two-label 12-ounce flat top, green can, white label, single version. $100

Gilt Edge Brand Beer, two-label 12-ounce flat top, gold can, white label, single version. $60

Old Dutch Premium Lager Beer, two-label 12-ounce flat top, red can, off-white label, single version. $100

Two-label 12-ounce flat top, red can, white label, single version. $80

Old Ranger Premium Beer, single-label 12-ounce flat top, metallic gold can, white label, "BEER" in black, single version. $200

Single-label 12-ounce flat top, white can, red target label, "IT'S A HIT," single version. $20

Tudor Bock Beer, two-label 12-ounce flat top, white can, brown label, helmet or cornet, single version of each. $75

Tudor Premium Quality Ale, two-label 12-ounce flat top, green can, white label and cornet, single version of each. $40

Tudor Premium Quality Beer, single-label 12-ounce flat top, red can, white label, helmet or cornet, single version of each. $30

Single-label 12-ounce flat top, white can, red label outlined in metallic gold, single version. $20

Tudor Premium Quality Cream Ale, single-label 12-ounce flat top, green can, white label, helmet, single version. $30

New York City

CITY BREWING CORPORATION, 912 Cypress Avenue (predecessor to Greater New York Brewery, Inc.)

Horton Ale, single-label, 12-ounce, high-profile cone or quart cone top, brown can, white lettering, INTERNAL REVENUE TAX PAID, single version of each size.
12-ounce, ... $200
Quart, ... $350

Horton Beer, single-label, 12-ounce, high-profile cone or quart cone top, orange can, " Horton Beer" in black, INTERNAL REVENUE TAX PAID, single version of can.

12-ounce,..$125
Quart,... $200

Tally-Ho Ale, single-label, 12-ounce, low-profile cone top, green can, "KOENIG-RAUCH-PAULSEN," INTERNAL REVENUE TAX PAID, single version. ....Exotic

Tally-Ho Beer, single-label, 12-ounce, low-profile cone top, yellow can, "TALLY-HO BEER" in red, INTERNAL REVENUE TAX PAID, two versions............... $300

THE EBLING BREWING COMPANY, 756 St. Anns Avenue

Ebling Premium Beer, two-label 12-ounce crowntainer, red can, "PREMIUM BEER" in black, INTERNAL REVENUE TAX PAID, single version. $150

Two-label 12-ounce crowntainer or quart cone top, white can, red label, INTERNAL REVENUE TAX PAID, multiversions. $100

Ebling White Head Ale, two-label 12-ounce crowntainer or quart cone top, silver can, green label, INTERNAL REVENUE TAX PAID, single version of each size.

12-ounce,..$125
Quart,... $200

Ebling's Bock Beer, two-label 12-ounce crowntainer, silver can, red and yellow label, goat's head, INTERNAL REVENUE TAX PAID, single version. $300

Ebling's Extra Special Beer, two-label 12-ounce crowntainer, INTERNAL REVENUE TAX PAID, yellow and red can, two versions...............................$150
WITHDRAWN FREE,... $175

Two-label, 12-ounce, high-profile cone top, yellow can, red trim, "EBLING'S" in black, paper label, INTERNAL REVENUE TAX PAID, single version. ......Exotic

Ebling's White Head Ale, single-label, 12-ounce, J-spout cone top, yellow can, red and metallic gold label, horse's head, INTERNAL REVENUE TAX PAID, two versions. Either version,... $300

Two-label 12-ounce crowntainer, silver can, INTERNAL REVENUE TAX PAID, single version. $300

Single-label, 12-ounce, high-profile cone top, gray and orange can, horse's head, paper label, INTERNAL REVENUE TAX PAID, single version. ....Exotic

Michel's Beer, two-label 12-ounce crowntainer, silver can, yellow trim, "MICHEL'S" on red ribbon, IRTP or non-IRTP, single version of each.

Non-IRTP, ... $175
IRTP, ... $185

Michel's Bock Beer, two-label 12-ounce crowntainer, silver can, yellow trim, goat's head, INTERNAL REVENUE TAX PAID, single version. $300

EDELBREW BREWERY, INC., 1 Bushwick Place (aka: Edelbrau Brewery, Inc.)

Copenhaven Castle Brand Beer, Edelbrew Brewery, single-label 12-ounce flat top, multicolored can, white label, single version. $150

Edel Brau Beer, Edelbrew Brewery, single-label 12-ounce flat top, brown can, large lion, INTERNAL REVENUE TAX PAID, single version. $300

Edel Brew Premium Beer, Edelbrew Brewery, single-label 12-ounce flat top, brown can, red label, glass of beer, single version. $150

Edelbrew Premium Beer, Edelbrew Brewery, single-label 12-ounce flat or quart cone top, brown can, yellow stripes, white lettering, IRTP or non-IRTP, single versions.
Non-IRTP flat top, ... $85
IRTP flat top, ... $90
Quart cone top, ...$350

Golden Rod Ale, Edelbrau Brewery, single-label 12-ounce flat top, green can, white label, single version. ....Exotic

Golden Rod Beer, Edelbrau Brewery, single-label 12-ounce flat top, gold can, white label, INTERNAL REVENUE TAX PAID, two versions. $350

GEORGE EHRET BREWERY, INC., 123 Melrose Avenue

Ehret's Extra Beer, single-label, 12-ounce, high-profile cone top, red can, metallic gold ribbon, INTERNAL REVENUE TAX PAID, single version. $350

THE GREATER NEW YORK BREWERY, INC., 912 Cypress Avenue (successor to City Brewing Corporation)

Bartel's Beer, single-label high-profile cone top, metallic gold can, white label outlined in red, INTERNAL REVENUE TAX PAID, single version. $200

Horton America's Finest Ale, single-label high-profile cone top, brown can, "AMERICA'S FINEST" in black on gold label, INTERNAL REVENUE TAX PAID, single version. $250

Horton Beer, single-label, 12-ounce, high-profile cone or quart cone top, orange can, metallic gold bands top and bottom, INTERNAL REVENUE TAX PAID, single version of each.
12-ounce, ... $175
Quart, ...$250

Horton Export Beer, single-label, 12-ounce, high-profile cone top, orange can, metallic gold bands, "EXPORT" on black ribbon, INTERNAL REVENUE TAX PAID, single version. $200

Lion Pilsener Beer, single-label 12-ounce flat top, black can, red label, INTERNAL REVENUE TAX PAID, single version. $300

Lion Sparkling Ale, single-label 12-ounce flat or quart cone top, red can, black label, INTERNAL REVENUE TAX PAID, single version of each. $350

New Yorker Ale, single-label 12-ounce flat top, green and red can, white lettering, INTERNAL REVENUE TAX PAID, single version. $275

New Yorker Beer, single-label 12-ounce flat top, blue and red can, white lettering, INTERNAL REVENUE TAX PAID, single version. $250

New Yorker Half and Half, single-label 12-ounce flat top, brown and red can, white lettering, INTERNAL REVENUE TAX PAID, single version. $375

HORTON PILSENER BREWING COMPANY, 460 West 128th Street

Horton America's Finest Ale, single-label, 12-ounce, low profile cone or quart cone top, brown can, "AMERICA'S FINEST" in black on gold oval, INTERNAL REVENUE TAX PAID, single version of each size.

12-ounce,	$300
Quart,	$450

Horton Old Stock Ale, single-label, 12-ounce, low-profile cone or quart cone top, brown can, "OLD STOCK ALE" in black on gold oval, INTERNAL REVENUE TAX PAID, minor versions.

12-ounce,	$150
Quart,	$225

Horton Pilsener Beer, single-label, 12-ounce, low-profile cone or quart cone top, orange can, "PILSENER BREWING COMPANY" in white, minor versions.

12-ounce,	$125
Quart,	$200

Horton's America's Finest Beer, single-label, 12-ounce, low-profile cone top, orange can, INTERNAL REVENUE TAX PAID, single version. $250

KINGS BREWERY, INC., 239–269 Pulaski

Kings Ale, two-label 12-ounce flat top, yellow can, "KING'S ALE" in red and green, OPENING INSTRUCTIONS, INTERNAL REVENUE TAX PAID, single version. $300

Kings Beer, two-label 12-ounce flat top, yellow can, "KING'S BEER" in red and green, OPENING INSTRUCTIONS, INTERNAL REVENUE TAX PAID, single version. $275

LIEBMANN BREWERIES, INC., 36 Forrest Street

Liebmann's Beer, single-label 12-ounce flat top, gold can, white label, OPENING INSTRUCTIONS, INTERNAL REVENUE TAX PAID, single version. $300

Liebmann's XXX Cream Ale, single-label 12-ounce flat top, green can, yellow label, INTERNAL REVENUE TAX PAID, single version. $175

Rheingold Ale, single-label 12-ounce flat top, green can, red label, white stars, IRTP or non-IRTP, minor versions.

IRTP,	$225
Non-IRTP,	$215

Rheingold Beer, single-label 12-ounce flat top or quart cone top, gold can, white label outlined in black, OPENING INSTRUCTIONS, INTERNAL REVENUE TAX PAID, two versions.

OI, IRTP,	$175
IRTP,	$150

Single-label 12-ounce flat top or quart cone top, woodgrain can, white label, INTERNAL REVENUE TAX PAID, multiversions. $75

WITHDRAWN FREE,	$125
Quart,	$125

Single-label 12-ounce flat top, white can, red label, "LAGER BEER" in block letters, multiversions. $30

Two-label 12-ounce flat top, white can, red label, "EXTRA DRY" in black, multiversions. $15

Single-label 12-ounce flat top, white can, red label, set can, set of seven called "Rheingold Girls": Diane Baker, Beverly Christensen, Tami Conner, Margie McNally, Suzy Ruel, Katleen Wallace, Margie McNally Miss Rheingold 1957; single version of each. $250

Single-label 16-ounce flat or tab top, white can, red label, multiversions. ... $15

Rheingold Cream Ale, two-label 12-ounce flat top, blue and white can, black and yellow label, single version. $200

Rheingold Famous Scotch Brand Ale, single-label 12-ounce flat top or quart cone top, woodgrain and multicolored label, INTERNAL REVENUE TAX PAID, multiversions.
Flat top, ... $50
Cone top, ... $85

Rheingold Genuine Bock Beer, two-label 12-ounce flat top, gold can, red label, "GENUINE" in black on white label, two versions: with or without Rheingold jingle.
With jingle, ... $300
Without jingle, ...$275

Two-label 12-ounce flat top, gold can, red label, two white goats above label, single version. $300

Rheingold Golden Bock Beer, two-label 12-ounce flat top, red can, large glass of beer label, single version. $65

Rheingold McSorley's Ale, single-label 12-ounce flat top, metallic gold can, red square label, INTERNAL REVENUE TAX PAID, single version. $350

Rheingold Pale Bock Beer, single-label 12-ounce flat top, gold can, metallic gold label outlined in black, single version. $400

Rheingold Pale Double Bock Beer, single-label 12-ounce flat top, two orange goats on large label, two versions.
OI and IRTP,..Exotic
IRTP, ... $600

Scotch Thistle Brand Ale, single-label 12-ounce flat top, brown can, brown or green oval, OPENING INSTRUCTIONS, INTERNAL REVENUE TAX PAID, multiversions.
OI and IRTP,.. $300
IRTP, ...$275

LION BREWERY OF NEW YORK CITY, 104 West 108th Street

Lion Beer, single-label 12-ounce flat top, black can, red label, OPENING INSTRUCTIONS, INTERNAL REVENUE TAX PAID, single version. ....Exotic

Lion Bock Beer, single-label 12-ounce flat top, brown can, INTERNAL REVENUE TAX PAID, single version. ....Exotic

Lion Pilsener Beer, single-label 12-ounce flat top, green can, red label, two versions.

OI and IRTP, ... $400

IRTP, ...$350

Lion Sparkling Ale, single-label 12-ounce flat top, red can, "LION ALE" in gold, OPENING INSTRUCTIONS, INTERNAL REVENUE TAX PAID, two versions.
.... $300

Single-label 12-ounce flat top, red can, "LION ALE" in white, INTERNAL REVENUE TAX PAID, single version. $275

LOEWER'S BREWERY COMPANY, 528 West 42nd Street (aka: Loewer's Brewery, Brewery Management)

Blue Crest Light Dry Beer, Loewer's Brewery, two-label 12-ounce crowntainer or single-label quart cone top, silver can, white label, INTERNAL REVENUE TAX PAID, single version of each.

12-ounce, ...$225

Quart, ... $300

Loewer's Blue Crest Light Dry Beer, Loewer's Brewery, two-label 12-ounce crowntainer, silver can, white label, "LOEWER'S BEER" in red, INTERNAL REVENUE TAX PAID, single version. $225

Loewer's Pilsener Premium Beer, Loewer's Brewery, single-label quart cone top, white can, "LOEWER'S PILSENER BEER" in black, INTERNAL REVENUE TAX PAID, single version. $300

V. R. Vat Reserve Beer, Brewery Management, two-label, 12-ounce, high-profile cone top, gray can, yellow label, "V.R." in black outlined in red, INTERNAL REVENUE TAX PAID, single version. $200

Brewery Management, two-label 12-ounce crowntainer, red can, yellow label, "V.R." in black outlined in red, INTERNAL REVENUE TAX PAID, single version.
....$225

METROPOLIS BREWERY, INC., 501 1st Avenue

Brauhaus Beer, single-label 12-ounce flat top, red can, cream label, single version. $150

Horton Beer, single-label 12-ounce flat top, orange can, silver or gold trim, single version of each. $60

Horton Premium Beer, single-label quart cone top, brown can, INTERNAL REVENUE TAX PAID, single version. $175

Lion Pilsener Beer, two-label 12-ounce crowntainer, silver can, INTERNAL REVENUE TAX PAID, single version. $150

Old Dutch Brand Lager Beer, single-label, 12-ounce, high-profile cone or flat top, and quart cone top, INTERNAL REVENUE TAX PAID, red can, white label outlined in metallic gold or silver, multiversions.

12-ounce flat top, ... $65

12-ounce cone top, ... $85

Quart cone top, ...$125

Pilser's Bock Beer, single-label 12-ounce flat top, metallic gold can, black label, large goat's head, single version. ....Exotic

Pilser's Extra Dry Ale, single-label, 12-ounce, high-profile cone top, hatched metallic gold can, yellow label, INTERNAL REVENUE TAX PAID, single version. $125

Pilser's Extra Pilsener Beer, two-label 12-ounce crowntainer, silver can, yellow label, INTERNAL REVENUE TAX PAID, single version. $125

Single-label, 12-ounce, high-profile cone or flat top, or quart cone top, gold can, white label, ''PREMIUM'' on red label, INTERNAL REVENUE TAX PAID, multiversions.
12-ounce flat top, ... $65
12-ounce cone top, ... $85
Quart cone top, ...$125

Tudor Premium Quality Beer, single-label 12-ounce flat top or quart cone top, red can, white lettering, red helmet, INTERNAL REVENUE TAX PAID, single version of each.
12-ounce flat top, ... $85
Quart cone top, ...$125

Tudor Premium Quality Cream Ale, single-label 12-ounce flat top or quart cone top, green can, white lettering, green helmet, IRTP or non-IRTP, single version of each.
Non-IRTP 12-ounce flat top,.. $85
IRTP 12-ounce flat top,... $95
Quart cone top, ...$125

OLD DUTCH BREWERS, INC., East 42nd Street and Glenwood Road

Brauhaus Ale, single-label 12-ounce flat top, blue can, white label, INTERNAL REVENUE TAX PAID, single version...$250

Brauhaus Beer, single-label 12-ounce flat top, red can, cream label, INTERNAL REVENUE TAX PAID, single version...$150

Brauhaus Half and Half, single-label 12-ounce flat top, brown can, cream label, INTERNAL REVENUE TAX PAID, single version. $175

Horton Beer, single-label 12-ounce flat top, brown can, silver or gold trim, INTERNAL REVENUE TAX PAID, single version of each. $75

Old Dutch Brand Ale, single-label, 12-ounce, high- or low-profile cone or flat top, or quart cone top, various shades of green and white cans, windmill, OPENING INSTRUCTIONS, INTERNAL REVENUE TAX PAID, multiversions.
12-ounce flat top, ...$225
12-ounce cone top, ...$160
Quart cone top, ... $200

Old Dutch Brand Beer, single-label, 12-ounce, high- or low-profile cone or quart cone top, brown and white can, windmill, single version of each.
12-ounce,..$140
Quart,..$185

Old Dutch Brand Bock Beer, single-label 12-ounce flat top, gold can, black label, goat's head, INTERNAL REVENUE TAX PAID, single version. .... Exotic

Old Dutch Brand Lager Beer, single-label 12-ounce flat top, blue and silver or gray can, windmill, OPENING INSTRUCTIONS, INTERNAL REVENUE TAX PAID, minor versions. $175

Old Dutch Extra Ale, single-label 12-ounce flat top, brown and cream can, windmill, OPENING INSTRUCTIONS, INTERNAL REVENUE TAX PAID, single version of each. Either can, ... $200

Old Dutch Superior Pilsner Beer, single-label 12-ounce flat top, blue and gray can, OPENING INSTRUCTIONS, WITHDRAWN FREE, single version. .... Exotic

Pilser's Extra Dry Pilsener Beer, single-label 12-ounce flat top, silver can, yellow label, red and blue bands, INTERNAL REVENUE TAX PAID, single version. $125

PIEL BROS., 315 Liberty Avenue, 1632 Bushwick Avenue (successor to John Trommer)

All mandatories are PIELS BROS. except Red Letter Beer, which is TROMMER'S.

Piel's Light Beer, single-label 12-ounce flat top, metallic gold can, yellow label, "LIGHT" in red, IRTP or non-IRTP, multiversions.
IRTP, ... $65
Non-IRTP, ... $60

Piel's Special Light Dortmunder Beer, single-label, 12-ounce, high- or low-profile cone top, red can, white label outlined in gold, INTERNAL REVENUE TAX PAID, single version of each can. $150

Piels Light Beer, single-label 12- or 16-ounce flat top, metallic gold can, blue label, multiversions.
12-ounce.. $30
16-ounce, ... $35

Piels Light Lager Beer, single-label 12- or 16-ounce flat, zip, or tab top, white can, gold bands, "PIELS BEER" in red, multiversions.
12-ounce,... $20
16-ounce, ... $25

Aluminum versions have a collector value of up to $5.

Piels Real Draft Beer, two-label 12-ounce flat top, white can, "PIELS" in red, "REAL DRAFT" in woodgrain, single version. $8

Piels Real Draft Premium Beer, two-label 12-ounce flat or zip top, white can, "PIELS" in red, "REAL DRAFT" in woodgrain, single version of each top. ...$8

Aluminum versions of this brand have a collector value of up to $5.

Trommer's Beer, two-label 12-ounce flat top, gold can, red label and band, two versions. $85

Trommer's Red Letter Beer, two-label 12-ounce flat top, red can, large pilsner glass label, single version. $65

Piels Light Light Beer was produced in aluminum cans only. They have a collector value of $3.

PIEL'S, INC., 191 Canal Street (successor to Rubsam and Horrmann Company)

Piel's Light Beer, single-label 12-ounce flat top, gold can, yellow label, "LIGHT" in red, IRTP or non-IRTP, minor versions.
IRTP, ... $65
Non-IRTP, ... $60

Piels Light Beer, single- or two-label 12-ounce flat top, gold can, blue label, two versions. $30

Piels Light Lager Beer, two-label 12-ounce flat top, white can, gold bands, "PIELS" in red, single version. $20

PILSER BREWING COMPANY, 161st Street and St. Ann's Avenue

Lion Pilsner Beer, two-label 12-ounce crowntainer, silver crowntainer, INTERNAL REVENUE TAX PAID, single version. $300

Single-label 12-ounce flat top, gold can, blue bands, INTERNAL REVENUE TAX PAID, single version. $250

Pilser's Export Half and Half, single-label, 12-ounce, J-spout cone or quart cone top, yellow can, red and yellow label outlined in metallic gold, single version.
12-ounce, ... $250
Quart, ... $400

Pilser's XXXX Pale Ale, single-label, 12-ounce, J-spout cone or quart cone top, green can, INTERNAL REVENUE TAX PAID, single version.
12-ounce, ... $300
Quart, ... $450

Two-label 12-ounce crowntainer, silver can, yellow label, INTERNAL REVENUE TAX PAID, single version. $150

Pilsner's Extra Dry Pilsener Light Beer, single-label, 12-ounce, J-spout cone top, or crowntainer, or quart cone top, silver can, yellow label outlined in red, single version of each.
12-ounce, ... $100
Quart, ... $225

RHEINGOLD BREWERIES, INC., 36 Forrest Street (successor to Liebmann Breweries, Inc.; aka: Rheingold Breweries, Forrest Brewing Company, Jacob Ruppert)

Esslinger Premium Beer, Jacob Ruppert, two-label 12-ounce tab top, white can, red label, full-figure man in inner circle, single version. $5

Gablinger's Beer, Rheingold Breweries, single-label 12- or 16-ounce tab top, black, brown, or metallic brown can, oval label. $5

Brand was also produced in aluminum. Collector value is $3.

Jacob Ruppert Beer, Rheingold Breweries, two-label 12-ounce tab top, blue can, white label, "JACOB RUPPERT BEER" in yellow outlined in black, multi-versions. $3

Knickerbocker Natural Beer, Rheingold Breweries, two-label 7-, 12-, or 16-ounce flat or soft top, white, red, blue can with or without yellow ribbon, multiversions.

7-ounce, ...$3
12-ounce flat top, ...$3
All others, ...$2

Brand was also produced in aluminum. The collector value is $1.

Pathmark Premium Lager Beer, Forest Brewing Company, two-label 12-ounce flat or tab top, off-white can, blue label, single version of each top. $5

Rheingold Extra Dry Lager Beer, Rheingold Breweries, two-label 7-, 12-, or 16-ounce flat, zip, or tab top, white can, red label, "EXTRA DRY" in black, multiversions.

Flat top, ...$8
All others, ...$5

Brand was also produced in aluminum cans. The collector value is $1.

Rheingold Golden Bock Beer, Rheingold Breweries, two-label 12-ounce tab top, red can, large beer glass with foam, single version. $75

Ruppert Knickerbocker Beer, Jacob Ruppert, two-label 7-, 12-, or 16-ounce tab top, white and metallic gold can, three ribbons, multiversions. All versions, ...$10

Brand was also produced in aluminum cans. The collector value is $2.

Ruppert Knickerbocker New York's Famous Beer, Jacob Ruppert, two-label 12- or 16-ounce tab top, white can, metallic gold can, three ribbons, multiversions. All versions, ...$10

Shop-Rite Super Markets Pilsener Beer, Forrest Brewing Company, two-label 12-ounce tab top, gold can, red label, single version. $15

RUBSAM & HORRMANN BREWING COMPANY, 191 Canal Street (predecessor to Piels, Inc.)

R & H Crown Premium Lager Beer, single-label 12-ounce flat top, yellow can, red crown, minor versions. $85

R & H Light Beer, single-label 12-ounce flat top, gold can, red label, "R & H LIGHT BEER" in white, single version. $100

R & H Sparkling Ale, single-label 12-ounce flat top or quart cone top, gold and green can, black stripes, INTERNAL REVENUE TAX PAID, single version of each.

Flat top, ...$100
Cone top, ...$400

R & H Special Lager Beer, single-label 12-ounce flat top, gold can, red circle, INTERNAL REVENUE TAX PAID, single version. $300

R & H Special XXX Ale, single-label 12-ounce flat top, gold can, green label, INTERNAL REVENUE TAX PAID, single version. $500

R & H Staten Island Light Beer, single-label 12-ounce flat top or quart cone top, gold can, yellow label, "R & H LIGHT BEER" in red, INTERNAL REVENUE TAX PAID, minor versions.

12-ounce flat top, ... $85
12-ounce WITHDRAWN FREE, ... $350
Quart cone top, ... $275

R & H XXX Ale, single-label 12-ounce flat top, green can, red circle, single version. $150

JACOB RUPPERT, 1639 3rd Avenue (aka: Five Star Brewing Company, Yankee Brewing Company, Esslinger, Inc., Philadelphia)

American Dry Extra Premium Beer, Jacob Ruppert, two-label 12- or 16-ounce flat or zip top, metallic gold can, red, white, and blue label, minor versions.
12-ounce, ... $30
16-ounce, ... $35

Beer, Jacob Ruppert, single-label 12-ounce flat top, OPENING INSTRUCTIONS, INTERNAL REVENUE TAX PAID, camouflage can. .... Unique

Corona Cerveza Banda Blanca, Jacob Ruppert, single-label 12-ounce flat top, blue and white can, metallic gold can, multiversions. $15

Empire Beer, Yankee Brewing Company, two-label 12-ounce flat top, white can, picture of Empire State Building, single version. $275

Esslinger Parti Quiz, single- or double-label 12-ounce flat or zip top, set cans, called "Parti Quiz," two different sets, Bock cans not issued, one-, two-, or three-color cans, basic colors: blue, bronze, green, orange, pink, silver, purple, red (all colors have a variety of tones), issued 1964, all cans have eight rows of text or facts, text can be straight or slanted, total number of cans in each set is unverified, example of text: "7 presidents died in office," "White House is at 1600 Pennsylvania Ave." (For other "Parti Quiz" cans see Esslinger's, Philadelphia.) Each, ... $100

Esslinger Premium Beer, Jacob Ruppert, two-label 12-ounce zip top, gold can, white label, single version. $25

Five Star Beer, Five Star Brewing Company, two-label 10-ounce flat top, blue can, white star, minor versions. $150

Gretz Premium Beer, Jacob Ruppert, two-label 12-ounce flat top, blue can, white label, "GRETZ" in red, single version. $85

Jacob Ruppert Ale, Jacob Ruppert, single-label 12-ounce flat top, green and woodgrain can, INTERNAL REVENUE TAX PAID, minor versions. $150

Five Star Brewing Company, single-label 12-ounce flat top, white can, "JACOB RUPPERT" in white on green ribbon, single version. $75

Jacob Ruppert Bock Beer, Jacob Ruppert, single-label 12-ounce flat top, INTERNAL REVENUE TAX PAID, OPENING INSTRUCTIONS or non-OPENING INSTRUCTIONS, single version of each.
OI, ... $400
Non-OI, ... $385

Jacob Ruppert Knickerbocker Beer, Jacob Ruppert, single-label 12-ounce flat top, white can, eagle, OPENING INSTRUCTIONS, INTERNAL REVENUE TAX PAID, two versions.
"COOL BEFORE SERVING," $300
Non-"COOL BEFORE SERVING," $285
Non-OI, ... $260

Keglet Beer, Five Star Brewing, two-label 12-ounce flat top, woodgrain can, "KEGLET BEER" in red, multiversions. $40

Knickerbocker Dark Beer, Jacob Ruppert, two-label 12-ounce flat top, metallic gold can, maroon and white label, multiversions. $75

Ruppert Ale, Jacob Ruppert, yellow can, round green label, "RUPPERT ALE" in green, IRTP or non-IRTP, single version of each.
Non-IRTP, ... $125
IRTP, ... $135

Ruppert Beer, Jacob Ruppert, single-label 12-ounce flat top, yellow can, maroon label, IRTP or non-IRTP, multiversions.
WITHDRAWN FREE, ... $100
IRTP, ... $60
Non-IRTP, ... $50

Ruppert Bock Beer, Jacob Ruppert, single-label 12-ounce flat top, white can, brown oval label, goat's head, IRTP or non-IRTP, minor versions.
Non-IRTP, ... $125
IRTP, ... $135

Ruppert Knickerbocker Beer, Jacob Ruppert, single-label 12-ounce flat top, orangish or white can, red label, IRTP or non-IRTP, multiversions.
WITHDRAWN FREE, ... $100
IRTP, ... $65
Non-IRTP, ... $60

Jacob Ruppert, two-label 12- or 16-ounce flat top, white can, gold oval label, "KNICKERBOCKER" across label, multiversions. All versions, ... $25

Ruppert Knickerbocker Bock Beer, Jacob Ruppert, two-label 12-ounce flat or zip top, off-white can, maroon can, goat's head, minor versions. $85

Ruppert Knickerbocker Draft, Jacob Ruppert, two-label gallon can, white can, three ribbons, single version. $300

Ruppert Knickerbocker New York's Famous Beer, Jacob Ruppert, two-label 12- or 16-ounce flat top, white can, gold oval, multiversions. All versions, . $20

Jacob Ruppert, two-label 12- or 16-ounce flat, zip, or tab top, white can, three ribbons, multiversions. $30

Ruppert Light Ale, Jacob Ruppert, two-label 12-ounce flat top, green can, vertical white pinstripes, "RUPPERT ALE" in green, single version. $100

Ruppert Ruppiner Dark Beer, Jacob Ruppert, single-label 12-ounce flat top, yellow can, maroon label, minor versions. $85

Jacob Ruppert, two-label 12-ounce flat top, brown can, three ribbons, single version. $60

Ruppiner Dark Beer, Jacob Ruppert, single-label 12-ounce flat top, beige can, brown label, single version. $85

Tudor Premium Quality Beer, Five Star Brewing, two-label 12-ounce flat top, gold can, red label, single version. $65

Yankee Premium Beer, Yankee Brewing Company, two-label 12- or 16-ounce flat top, white can, red label, sailing ship, single version.
12-ounce, ... $125
16-ounce, ... $110

CHAS. SCHAEFER BREWING COMPANY, 1306 Greene Avenue

Dorquest Quality Beer, single-label, 12-ounce, high-profile cone top, gold can, white label, INTERNAL REVENUE TAX PAID, single version. $175

Imperial Pilsener Beer, single-label, 12-ounce, high-profile cone top, gold can, white label, INTERNAL REVENUE TAX PAID, single version. $350

F. & M. SCHAEFER BREWING COMPANY, 430 Kent Avenue

Gunther Light Lager Beer, Gunther Brewing Company, two-label 12-ounce tab top, red can, white label, gold band(s), multiversions. $3

All other cans from this brewery carry the SCHAEFER mandatory.

Schaefer Beer, single-label 12- or 16-ounce flat, zip, or tab top, white can, 15 circles (12-ounce), 20 circles (16-ounce), multiversions. All versions, ... $3

Brand was also produced in aluminum. The collector value is $1.

Single-label 12- or 16-ounce tab top, white can, 8 circles (12-ounce), 9 circles (16-ounce), multiversions. $4

Schaefer Bock Beer, single-label 12-ounce flat top, woodgrain can, black label, large goat's head, INTERNAL REVENUE TAX PAID, single version. $175

Single-label 12-ounce flat top, woodgrain can, black label, small goat's head, IRTP or non-IRTP, single version of each.
IRTP, ... $125
Non-IRTP, ... $115

Schaefer Fine Beer, single-label 12-ounce flat top, woodgrain can, red and black label, IRTP or non-IRTP, multiversions.
IRTP, ... $60
Non-IRTP, ... $55

Single-label 12- or 16-ounce flat top, yellow woodgrain can, red label, outlined in metallic gold or silver, multiversions. $50

Single-label 12- or 16-ounce flat top, yellow can, red label, multiversions... $40

Schaefer Golden Beer, single-label 12-ounce flat top, woodgrain can, "GOLDEN" on black label, multiversions. $65

Schaefer Light Beer, single-label 12-ounce flat top, woodgrain can, red and black can, INTERNAL REVENUE TAX PAID, multiversions.
WITHDRAWN FREE, ... $300
All other versions, ... $50

Schaefer Pale Dry Beer, single-label 12-ounce flat top, yellow woodgrain can, "PALE DRY BEER" on white label, IRTP or non-IRTP, multiversions.
IRTP, ... $60
Non-IRTP, ... $50

JOS. SCHLITZ BREWING COMPANY, 193 Melrose

Schlitz Beer, single- or two-label, 12- or 16-ounce flat top, brown and yellow can, blue globe, gold bands (c. 1949, 1954, and 1957), IRTP or non-IRTP, multiversions.

IRTP, ... $15
Non-IRTP, ... $10

Two-label 12- or 16-ounce flat, soft, zip, or tab top, white can, brown label outlined in gold (c. 1960 and 1962), multiversions. $3

Rochester

AMERICAN BREWERY OF ROCHESTER, NEW YORK, INC., 444 Hudson Street

Apollo Beer, single-label 12-ounce flat top, gray can, black label, OPENING INSTRUCTIONS, INTERNAL REVENUE TAX PAID, single version. ....Unique

Tam O'Shanter Dry Hopped Ale, single-label, 12-ounce, high-profile cone top, INTERNAL REVENUE TAX PAID, gold can, red tartan label, single version. ...$250

Single-label, 12-ounce, high-profile cone or flat top, silver or gray can, red tartan label, INTERNAL REVENUE TAX PAID, single version of each.
Cone top, ... $175
Flat top, ...$225

Tam O'Shanter Lager Beer, single-label, 12-ounce, high-profile cone top, gold can, blue tartan label, INTERNAL REVENUE TAX PAID, single version. $350

Single-label, 12-ounce, high-profile cone or flat top, silver can, blue tartan label, INTERNAL REVENUE TAX PAID, single version of each.
Cone top, ...$225
Tab top, ...$250

GENESEE BREWING COMPANY, 14-23 Cataract Street

Dickens Dry Ale, single-label 12-ounce flat top, blue can, white label outlined in metallic gold, single version. $125

Fyfe & Drum Beer, two-label 12-ounce tab top, silver can, multicolored drum, "FYFE & DRUM BEER" in black, multiversions. $5

Fyfe & Drum Extra Lyte Beer, two-label 12-ounce tab top, silver can, multicolored drum, metallic gold bands, multiversions. $7

Fyfe & Drum Lyte Beer, two-label 12-ounce tab top, silver can, 125 calories, single version. $10

Genesee 12 Horse Ale, single-label 12-ounce flat top, yellow can, red and black label, OPENING INSTRUCTIONS, INTERNAL REVENUE TAX PAID, single version.
....$225

Single- or two-label 12-ounce flat top or quart cone top, gold and black can, team of horses, OPENING INSTRUCTIONS or non-OPENING INSTRUCTIONS, IRTP or non-IRTP.
Non-OI, IRTP, ...$150
OI, IRTP, ...$125
Non-OI, non-IRTP, ...$100
Quart, ...$125

Genesee Ale, two-label 12-ounce flat top, white can, green label, single version. ... $35

Two-label 12-ounce tab top, metallic green can, white label and trim, multiversions. ... $5

Genesee All Malt Beer, single-label 12-ounce flat top, metallic gold can, black label and lettering, OPENING INSTRUCTIONS, INTERNAL REVENUE TAX PAID, minor versions. ... $125

Genesee Beer, single-label 12-ounce flat top, camouflage can, OPENING INSTRUCTIONS, INTERNAL REVENUE TAX PAID, single version. ... Exotic

Two-label 12-ounce flat, zip, or tab top, white can, red oval label, multiversions.
Flat top, ... $7
All other versions, ... $5

Drinking cup for Cornell University, red can, white lettering, single version of each cup, Cornell Class Reunions:
1969, ... $35
1970, ... $35
1971, ... $35
1972, ... $30
1973, ... $30
1974, ... $30
1975, ... $30

Genesee Cream Ale, two-label 12-ounce tab top, green can, white label and lettering, multiversions. ... $3

Genesee Lager Beer, single-label 12-ounce flat top, INTERNAL REVENUE TAX PAID, metallic gold, red, and white can, single version. ... $150

Single-label 12-ounce flat top, white can, gold stripes, red and black label, IRTP or non-IRTP, multiversions.
Non-IRTP, ... $65
IRTP, ... $55

Genesee Liebotschaner All Malt Beer, single-label 12-ounce flat top, yellow can, black label and lettering, OPENING INSTRUCTIONS, INTERNAL REVENUE TAX PAID, single version. ... $350

Genesee Liebotschaner Beer, single-label 12-ounce flat top or quart cone top, gold can, blue or purple label, INTERNAL REVENUE TAX PAID, minor versions.
Flat top, ... $200
Cone top, ... $350

Genesee Light Ale, single-label 12-ounce flat top or quart cone top, gold can, red label, INTERNAL REVENUE TAX PAID, single version of each.
Flat top, ... $200
Cone top, ... $350

Genesee Light Lager Beer, two-label 12-ounce tab top, gold can, with or without white lines, white label, multiversions. ... $50

The Genesee Brewing Company has and is producing a number of brands in aluminum cans. The collector value of these cans is $1.

ROCHESTER BREWING COMPANY, 770 Emerson Street

Ar Bee Lager Beer, single-label, 12-ounce, J-spout cone top, blue can, black label, INTERNAL REVENUE TAX PAID, single version. ....Exotic

Old Topper Ale, two-label 12-ounce crowntainer, silver can, stars, "OLD TOPPER ALE" on woodgrain panel, INTERNAL REVENUE TAX PAID, single version.
.... $95

Two-label 12-ounce crowntainer, cream top and sides, brown label, IRTP or non-IRTP, multiversions.
IRTP, ...$135
Non-IRTP, ...$125

Old Topper Beer, two-label 12-ounce crowntainer, silver can, red and white label, INTERNAL REVENUE TAX PAID, single version. $100

Old Topper Bock Beer, two-label 12-ounce crowntainer, silver can, orange label, INTERNAL REVENUE TAX PAID, single version. $250

Old Topper Golden Ale, two-label high-profile cone top, yellow can, gold bands, "OLD TOPPER GOLDEN" on woodgrain panel, single version. $85

Old Topper Golden Beer, two-label, 12-ounce, high-profile cone top, red can, metallic gold bands, white letering and trim, single version. $125

Old Topper Lager Beer, single-label, 12-ounce, J-spout cone or quart cone top, yellow can, red and black label, "LAGER BEER" in red, INTERNAL REVENUE TAX PAID, single version of each.
12-ounce,.. $95
Quart,...$150

Two-label 12-ounce crowntainer, silver can, red and black label, "LAGER BEER" in red, INTERNAL REVENUE TAX PAID, single version. $85

Two-label 12-ounce crowntainer, silver can, red, yellow, or white label, "OLD TOPPER LAGER" on woodgrain panel, INTERNAL REVENUE TAX PAID, single version of each. $100

Two-label 12-ounce crowntainer, camouflage can, single version. $150

Old Topper Snappy Ale, single-label, 12-ounce, J-spout cone top, crowntainer, or quart cone top, yellow, woodgrain, and black label, INTERNAL REVENUE TAX PAID, minor versions.
J-spout,... $75
Crowntainer,.. $75
Quart,.. $85

Topper Light Dry Ale, two-label 12-ounce flat top, yellow can, with or without metallic gold bands, "TOPPER" in red, single version of each.................. $60

Topper Light Dry Beer, two-label 12-ounce flat top, yellow can, metallic gold bands, "TOPPER" in red, single version. $60

STANDARD BREWING COMPANY, 436 Lake Street

Old Ox Head Ale, two-label, 12-ounce, J-spout cone top or crowntainer, tan-colored can, INTERNAL REVENUE TAX PAID, single version either can. Either can,..$350

Snappy Dry Ale, single-label 12-ounce flat top, white can, blue bands, "DRY" in blue or black, single version either can. Either can, ... $60

Standard Light Ale, single- or two-label, 12-ounce, J-spout cone top or crowntainer, silver can, orange label, "STANDARD LIGHT ALE" in yellow, INTERNAL REVENUE TAX PAID, minor versions. $125

Standard Old Ox Cart Dry Beer, single-label 12-ounce flat top, white can, green label, "STANDARD DRY" in black, single version. $100

Standard Sparkling Ale, single-label, 12-ounce, J-spout cone top, tan-colored can, INTERNAL REVENUE TAX PAID, single version. $175

STANDARD-ROCHESTER BREWING COMPANY, 770 Rochester (aka: Standard-Rochester, Jaguar Brewing Company, Haberle-Congress, Rochester)

Haberle Light Lager Congress Beer, Haberle-Congress, Rochester, two-label 12-ounce flat top, metallic gold can, white label, brown trim, single version. $60

Jaguar Light Beer, Jaguar Brewing Company, single-label 12-ounce tab top, white can, red label, "JAGUAR LIGHT BEER" in white, single version. $150

Jaguar Light Premium Beer, Jaguar Brewing Company, single-label 12-ounce zip top, tiger-striped can, red label outlined in metallic gold, single version. $90

Jaguar Malt Liquor, Standard-Rochester or Jaguar Brewing, single-label 12-ounce zip or tap top, tiger-striped can, black label outlined in metallic gold, multiversions. *(See photo 203)* $125

Jaguar "Pub" Beer, Jaguar Brewing Company, single-label 12-ounce tab top, white can, red label, single version. $150

Standard Beer, Standard-Rochester, single-label 12-ounce flat or tab top, woodgrain can, white stripes, "STANDARD BEER" in yellow, single version of each top.
Flat top, ... $35
Tab top,.. $30

Standard Cream Ale, Standard-Rochester, single-label 12-ounce tab top, metallic gold can, large white band, metallic green label, single version. $20

Standard Dry Ale, Standard-Rochester, single-label 12-ounce flat top, white can, blue label and trim, minor versions. $20

Photo 203. Jaguar Malt Liquor.

Standard-Rochester, single-label 12-ounce zip top, metallic gold can, large white stripe, blue label, minor versions. $20

Standard Dry Beer, Standard-Rochester, two-label 12-ounce flat or zip top, white can, blue label, single version of each top.
Flat top, ... $15
Zip top, ... $12

Standard-Rochester, two-label 12-ounce flat or zip top, metallic gold can, large white band, blue label, single version of each top.
Flat top, ... $10
Zip top, ... $8

Standard Genuine Draught Beer, Standard-Rochester, two-label gallon can, white can, woodgrain label, single version. $150

Standard Genuine Draught Dry Ale, Standard-Rochester, two-label gallon can, white can, blue label, single version. $225

Standard Old Ox Cart Dry Beer, Standard-Rochester, single-label 12-ounce flat top, white can, green bands, single version. $60

Standard Ox Cart Dry Beer, Standard-Rochester, two-label 12-ounce flat top, white can, green label, "DRY" in black, single version. $85

Topper Genuine Draught Beer, Standard-Rochester, single-label gallon can, woodgrain can, red label, two versions. $150

Topper Light Dry Ale, Standard-Rochester, two-label 12-ounce flat top, yellow can, metallic gold bands, "ALE" in black, single version. $75

Standard-Rochester, two-label 12-ounce flat or tab top, white can, red label, "ALE" in white, single version of each top.
Flat top, ... $35
Tab top, ... $25

Topper Light Dry Beer, Standard-Rochester, two-label 12-ounce flat top, white can, metallic gold bands top and bottom, single version. $65

Topper Light Pilsener, Standard-Rochester, single-label 12-ounce flat top, gold can, white label, "TOPPER" in red, minor versions. $60

Topper Light Pilsener Beer, Standard-Rochester, two-label 12-ounce flat or tab top, white can, red label, "BEER" in black, minor versions. $10

Topper Real Draft Beer, Standard-Rochester, two-label 12-ounce tab top, white can, gold bands, red lettering, single version. $15

Syracuse

HABERLE-CONGRESS BREWING COMPANY, INC., 500 Butternut Street

Congress Light Beer, two-label 12-ounce flat top, white can, red label outlined in black, stars, single version. $100

Two-label 12-ounce flat top, white can, red label outlined in silver, single version. $40

Single-label 12-ounce flat top, set cans, set of 21 cans. Ducks and grouse: yellow can, white label; gold can, white label; white can, red label. Indoor activities: white can, red label; gold and white can. Carnival: white can, blue label; red can, white label. Winter sports: blue can, white label; white can, blue label. Summer sports: green can, white label. New York sites: gold can, white label; red can, white label. Automobile: red can, white label. Hunting and fishing: gold can, white label; white can, blue label. Table tennis: green can, white label; white can, red label. Lobster and shrimp: gold striped can, white label. Steins: gold can, white label. Fish: blue can, white label. Single version of each.
Each,..$100

Haberle Light Lager Congress Beer, single-label 12-ounce flat top, gold can, white label, brown trim, single version.. $85

Haberle's Congress Beer, single-label, 12-ounce, high- or low-profile cone or quart cone top, gold can, blue label, INTERNAL REVENUE TAX PAID, single version of each.
12-ounce,..$250
Quart,.. $300

Haberle's Light Ale, single-label, 12-ounce, high- or low-profile cone or quart cone top, gold can, green label, INTERNAL REVENUE TAX PAID.
12-ounce,.. $300
Quart,..$350

Steinbrau Pilsener Beer, two-label 12-ounce tab top, white can, red oval label outlined in black, single version...$100

JOS. SCHLITZ BREWING COMPANY, 2885 Baldwin Road
(predecessor to Anheuser-Busch, Inc., Baldswinville)

Schlitz Beer, single-label 12-ounce tab top, white can, brown label, "GRAND OPENING/SYRACUSE N.Y.," single version.. $25

All other cans and brands produced by Schlitz at this brewery were in aluminum. Collector value is $1.

Troy

FITZGERALD BROS. BREWING COMPANY, 498 River Street

Fitz Ale, two-label 12-ounce flat top, white can, "FITZ" in green, "ALE" in black, single version.. $20

Fitz Beer, two-label 12-ounce flat top, white can, "FITZ" in red, "BEER" in black, multiversions.. $15

Fitzgerald Bock Beer, single-label 12-ounce flat top, gold can, maroon label, goat's head, single version..$150

Fitzgerald Burgomaster Beer, single-label 12-ounce flat top, white can, gold stripes, "BURGOMASTER" in red, multiversions.................................. $65

Fitzgerald Pale Ale, single-label 12-ounce flat top, red can, metallic gold bands, single version.. $85

Fitzgerald's Burgomaster Beer, single-label, 12-ounce, J-spout cone or quart cone top, blue can, white label, black trim, INTERNAL REVENUE TAX PAID, minor versions.

12-ounce, ... $200

Quart, ... $350

Two-label 12-ounce crowntainer, white or silver can, blue label, INTERNAL REVENUE TAX PAID, multiversions. $150

Fitzgerald's Garryowen Ale, single-label, 12-ounce, J-spout cone or quart cone top, green can, white label, INTERNAL REVENUE TAX PAID, multiversions.

12-ounce, ... $350

Quart, ... $400

Two-label 12-ounce crowntainer, silver or white crowntainer, INTERNAL REVENUE TAX PAID, single version of each. Either can, ... $200

Fitzgerald's Lager Beer, single- or two-label, 12-ounce, high-profile cone top or crowntainer, INTERNAL REVENUE TAX PAID, white can, blue label, minor versions. $100

Fitzgerald's Pale Ale, single- or two-label, 12-ounce, high-profile cone top or crowntainer, white can, green label, minor versions. $125

Williams Purple Cow, single-label 12-ounce flat top, gold and purple can, white lettering, single version. .... Exotic

Utica

UTICA BREWING COMPANY, INC., OF UTICA, NEW YORK, 610 Jay Street (aka: Utica Brewing Company, Fort Schuyler Division, The West End Brewing Company)

Fort Schuyler Lager Beer, Utica Brewing and Fort Schyuler, single-label, 12-ounce, high-profile cone or flat top, metallic gold can, red label, white inner label, multiversions.

Cone top, ... $125

Flat top, ... $65

Fort Schuyler Light Ale, Utica Brewing, single-label, 12-ounce, high-profile cone top, metallic gold can, green label, white inner label, two versions... $150

Utica Brewing, single-label 12-ounce crowntainer, green can, yellow stripes and label, paper label, single version. $200

WEST END BREWING COMPANY, 811 Edward Street (aka: Fort Schyler Brewing Company, F. X. Matt Brewing Company)

Billy Beer, West End Brewing, two-label 12-ounce aluminum can, white can, orange label, single version. $2

Fort Schuyler Lager Beer, Fort Schuyler Brewing Company, single-label 12-ounce flat, soft, or zip top, gold can, red label, white inner label, single version of each. All versions, ... $15

Matt's Premium Lager Beer, West End Brewing Company, two-label 12-ounce tab top, metallic gold can, green and white label, single version. $10

F. X. Matt Brewing Company, two-label 12-ounce tab top, metallic gold or gold can, "MATT'S" in white on red, multiversions. $5

Matt's Utica Club Premium Lager Beer, West End Brewing Company, single-label 12-ounce flat or soft top, lime green can, metallic gold bands, white label outlined in gold, single version of each top. $20

Maximus Regular Beer, F. X. Matt Brewing Company, two-label 12-ounce tab top, gold can, red circle, "MAXIMUS REGULAR" in white circle, single version...$5

Maximus Super Beer, F. X. Matt Brewing Company, two-label 12-ounce tab top, dark brown can, red circle, "MAXIMUS SUPER" in yellow circle, multiversions. $5

Ole 55 Twentieth, West End Brewing Company, orange and white drinking cup, single version.. $20

Utica Club Bock Beer, West End Brewing Company, two-label 12-ounce flat, soft, or tab top, green can, goat's head in stein, single version of each top. All versions. $30

Utica Club Extra Dry Cream Ale, West End Brewing Company, two-label 12-ounce flat or tab top, gold can, green label, "Schultz and Dooley," single version of each.. $40

West End Brewing Company, two-label 12-ounce tab top, metallic gold can, white label, brown trim, minor versions. $10

Utica Club Pilsener Lager Beer, West End Brewing Company, two-label 12- or 16-ounce flat, soft, or tab top, gold can, white label, "UTICA CLUB" in red, "Schultz and Dooley," multiversions. $10

West End Brewing Company, two-label 12- or 16-ounce tab top, metallic gold can, white split label, multiversions. $3

Utica Club XX Dry Bock Beer, West End Brewing Company, two-label 12-ounce flat top, metallic gold can, green label, white lettering, single version. $40

Utica Club XX Pilsener Lager Beer, West End Brewing Company, two-label 12-ounce flat top, metallic gold can, white label, "UTICA CLUB" in red, multiversions... $25

West End Brewing Company, single-label, 12-ounce, high-profile cone top or flat top, or quart cone top, cones carry IRTP, white can, "FAMOUS PILSENER BEER" in blue, multiversions.
12-ounce flat top, ... $50
12-ounce cone top, ... $75
Quart cone top, ...$125

Utica Club XX Sparkling Ale, West End Brewing Company, single-label, 12-ounce, high- or low-profile cone or quart cone top, blue can, white lettering, INTERNAL REVENUE TAX PAID, multiversions.
12-ounce,...$125
Quart, ... $175

Utica Club XXX Dry Pale Cream Ale, West End Brewing Company, two-label 12-ounce flat top, metallic gold can, red label, white lettering, "UC FOR ME," multiversions. $60

Utica Club XX Pale Cream Ale, West End Brewing Company, single-label, 12-ounce, high- or low-profile cone or flat top, or quart cone top, red can, white lettering, cones are IRTP.

12-ounce flat top, ... $40
12-ounce cone top $65
Quart cone top, ...$100

This brewery has and is producing an array of brands in aluminum cans and the beer is of exceptional quality. Collector value of these cans is $1.

North Carolina

Charlotte

ATLANTIC COMPANY, 300 South Graham Street

Atlantic Sparkling Ale, single-label 12-ounce flat top, bright orange can, black label, "ATLANTIC" in black on metallic gold band, single version. $125

Single-label 12-ounce flat top, bright orange can, white label, "ATLANTIC" in white on black band, two versions. $110

Atlantic The Beer Of The South, single-label 12-ounce flat top, white can, orange bands, plantation scene, single version. $250

Eden

MILLER BREWING COMPANY, 863 East Meadow Road

This brewery, built in 1978, has produced only aluminum cans. The collector value of these cans is $1.

Winston-Salem

JOS. SCHLITZ BREWING COMPANY, 4791 Schlitz Avenue

This brewery, built in 1970, was acquired by the Stroh Brewery in the 1982 merger. The brewery did produce some steel cans before converting to all aluminum production. The collector value of these cans will not exceed $1.

North Dakota

Bismarck

DAKOTA MALTING AND BREWING COMPANY, 26th and Main Street

Dakota Beer, single-label 12-ounce flat top, metallic gold can, blue stripes, white label outlined in red, two versions. $65

Two-label 12-ounce flat or zip top, white can, red label, blue circle, single version of each top. Either top, ... $50

Ohio

/

Akron

BURGER BREWING COMPANY, 529 Grant Street

Burger Light Beer, two-label 12-ounce flat top, white can, red label outlined in metallic gold, single version. $50

Two-label 12-ounce flat top, white can, metallic red label, gold trim, single version. $40

Two-label 12-ounce soft top, white can, silver bands and stripes, red label, rumored test can. $60

Mug Ale, single-label 12-ounce flat top, maroon can, cream label, maroon lettering, single version. $100

BURKHARDT BREWING COMPANY, 529 Grant Street

Banner Extra Dry Premium Ale, single-label 12-ounce flat top, white can, red label, "PREMIUM ALE" in blue, single version. $50

Banner Extra Dry Premium Beer, single-label 12-ounce flat top, white can, red label, "PREMIUM BEER" in blue, minor version. $40

Burkhardt's Custom Brewed Beer, single-label 12-ounce flat top, red and yellow can, white label outlined in metallic gold, single version. $65

Burkhardt's Diamond Jubilee Beer, single-label 12-ounce flat top, yellow can, white label, "DIAMOND JUBILEE BEER" in black, single version. $125

Burkhardt's Export Master Blended Beer, single-label, 12-ounce, high-profile cone top, red and yellow can, "EXPORT BEER" in white, IRTP and non-IRTP, single version of each.

Non-IRTP, ... $75

IRTP, ... $85

Burkhardt's Master Blended Beer, single-label, 12-ounce, high-profile cone or flat top, red and yellow can, white label, single version of each.
IRTP cone top, ... $85
Non-IRTP flat top, ... $70

Burkhardt's Nut Brown Mug Ale, two-label 12-ounce flat top, maroon can, metallic gold bands, "BURKHARDT'S" in black, single version. $85

Burkhardt's Special Master Blended Beer, single-label, 12-ounce, high-profile cone top, red and yellow can, "SPECIAL BEER" in white, INTERNAL REVENUE TAX PAID, two versions. $85

Mug Ale, single-label, 12-ounce, high-profile cone or flat top, blue can, yellow label, single version of each.
Cone top, ... $175
Flat top, ... $150

Tudor Premium Quality Beer, single-label 12-ounce flat top, red can, white lettering, helmet, single version. $50

Tudor Premium Quality Cream Ale, single-label 12-ounce flat top, green can, white lettering, helmet, single version. $60

GEORGE J. RENNER BREWING COMPANY, 275 North Forge Street

Grossvater Beer, single-label, 12-ounce, J-spout cone top or crowntainer, gray can, blue label, "GROSSVATER" on red stripe, INTERNAL REVENUE TAX PAID.
J-spout, ... $175
Crowntainer, ... $150

Grossvater Special Beer, single-label, 12-ounce, high-profile cone top, white can, yellow bands, brown label, red trim, single version. $175

Old German Brand Lager Beer, single-label, 12-ounce, high-profile cone top, black can, silver bands, white lettering, red circle, single version. $175

Souvenir Fine Beer, single-label, 12-ounce, high-profile cone top, hatched metallic gold can, white label outlined in red, two versions, IRTP and non-IRTP.
Non-IRTP, ... $160
IRTP, ... $150

Chillcothe

AUGUST WAGNER BREWERIES, INC., 51 East Water Street

Wagner's Gambrinus Quality Pale Beer, single-label, 12-ounce, high-profile cone top, gold can, two versions, IRTP and non-IRTP.
Non-IRTP, ... $175
IRTP, ... $185

Cincinnati

THE BRUCKMANN COMPANY, Ludlow Avenue and Central Parkway (successors to Herschel Condon Brewing Company)

Brucks Beer, single-label, 12-ounce, J-spout cone or quart cone top, blue and white can, "BRUCKS" in red, INTERNAL REVENUE TAX PAID, minor versions.
12-ounce, ... $135
Quart, ... $165
Brucks Jubilee Ale, two-label, 12-ounce, J-spout cone or single-label quart cone top, silver can, blue band, white oval label outlined in gold, INTERNAL REVENUE TAX PAID, minor versions.
12-ounce, ... $75
Quart, ... $100
Brucks Jubilee Beer, two-label, 12-ounce, J-spout cone top, crowntainer, or quart cone top, silver can, blue band, white oval label outlined in gold, INTERNAL REVENUE TAX PAID, multiversions.
J-spout, ... $85
Crowntainer, ... $75
Quart, ... $100

BURGER BREWING COMPANY, Central Parkway and Liberty Street

Red Lion Malt Liquor uses the mandatory of RED LION BREWING COMPANY.

Bohemian Tap Lager Beer, two-label 12-ounce tab top, light or dark woodgrain can, single version of each. $5

Burger Ale, two-label 12-ounce tab top, white can, green label outlined in gold, multiversions. $8

Burger Beer, single-label, 12-ounce, low-profile cone top, yellow can, red and black bands, "BURGER BEER" in red, INTERNAL REVENUE TAX PAID, multiversions. $150

Single-label, 12-ounce, high-profile cone or flat top, white can, red label, "BEER" in black, multiversions. *(See photo 204)*
Cone top, ... $85
Flat top, ... $65

Two-label 12- or 16-ounce tab top, white can, red label, blue ribbon, metallic gold bands, multiversions.
12-ounce, ... $10
16-ounce, ... $12

Photo 204 (left). Burger Beer.
Photo 205 (right). Gotham Fine Beer.

Burger Bohemian Beer, single-label, 12-ounce, high- or low-profile cone or quart cone top, black can, red label, "BURGER" in white, INTERNAL REVENUE TAX PAID, single version of each.

12-ounce, ... $85
Quart, ... $125

Burger Bohemian Style Beer, single-label, 12-ounce, low-profile cone top, black can, red label, gold lettering, INTERNAL REVENUE TAX PAID, minor versions.
.... $100

Burger Finest Quality Beer, single-label, 12-ounce, high-profile cone top, white can, gray stripes, "BURGER" in black, single version. $75

Burger Light Beer, two-label 12-ounce flat, soft, or tab top, white can, red label, gold or silver bands, multiversions. $25

Burger Premium Ale, two-label 12-ounce tab top, white can, metallic or dull green label, single version of each. $30

Burger Premium Beer, two-label 12- or 16-ounce tab top, white can, red label, gold bands, multiversions. $20

Burger Premium Quality Ale, two-label 12-ounce tab top, white can, green label, silver bands, single version. $20

Burger Premium Quality Beer, single-label 12-ounce tab top or quart cone top, white can, gray bands, "BURGER" in black, single version of each.

12-ounce, ... $65
Quart, ... $100

Two-label 12- or 16-ounce zip or tab top, white can, metallic red label, metallic gold bands, single version.

12-ounce, ... $30
16-ounce, ... $35

Burger Sparkling Ale, single-label, 12-ounce, high-profile cone top, black can, green label, "BURGER" in white, IRTP or non-IRTP, single version.

Non-IRTP, ... $100
IRTP, ... $90

Single-label, 12-ounce, high-profile cone, flat, or zip top, white cans, "SPARKLING ALE" in black, with or without gold bands, multiversions. $30

Cincinnati Burger Brau Beer, single-label, 12-ounce, high-profile cone or quart cone top, white can, man toasting with glass of beer, INTERNAL REVENUE TAX PAID, multiversions. $135
Camouflage can, ... $225

Red Lion Malt Liquor, Red Lion Brewing Company, single-label 12-ounce tab top, white can, metallic red label, "MALT LIQUOR" in black, single version.
.... $35

Red Lion Sparkling Ale, single-label, 12-ounce, low-profile cone top, red and white can, lion head on black circle, INTERNAL REVENUE TAX PAID, two minor versions. $300

CINCINNATI BREWING COMPANY, Amity and Reading Roads

Gotham Fine Beer, single-label, 12-ounce, high-profile cone top, red and gray can, city skyline, multiversions. (*See photo 205*) $175

HERSCHEL CONDON BREWING COMPANY, Ludlow Avenue and Central Parkway

Brucks Jubilee Ale, single-label 12-ounce crowntainer, silver can, blue stripe, silver label outlined in metallic gold, INTERNAL REVENUE TAX PAID, single version. $175

Condon's Modern Style Beer, single-label 12-ounce crowntainer, silver can, red label, INTERNAL REVENUE TAX PAID, single version. ....Exotic

HUDEPOHL BREWING COMPANY, 5th and Gast Streets

Burger Beer, two-label 12-ounce tab top, white can, red label outlined in metallic gold, green ribbon, with or without "BREWED WITH PURE ARTESIAN WATER," multiversions. $3

Burger Light Beer, single-label 12-ounce tab top, white can, "LIGHT" in red, single version. $2

Chevy Ale, single-label, 12-ounce, J-spout cone top, blue can, gold bands, "ALE" in white on blue ribbon, single version. $350

Chevy 85 Ale, single-label 12-ounce flat top, white can, metallic gold label and bands, "CHEVY" in white on red ribbon, single version. $200

Hudepohl 14K Beer, two-label 12-ounce flat, zip, or tab top, metallic gold can, white label, "HUDEPOHL BEER" in red, multiversions. *(See photo 206)*
Flat top, ... $40
Zip or tab top, ... $30

Hudepohl 14K Golden Beer, two-label 12-ounce flat or tab top, metallic gold can, white label, "HUDEPOHL" in red, single version of each.
Flat top, ... $35
Tab top, ... $30

Hudepohl 14K Golden Pure Grain Beer, two-label 12-ounce flat or tab top, yellow can, white label outlined in yellow bands, single version of each.
Flat top, ...$5
Tab top, ...$3

Hudepohl 14K Pure Grain Beer, two-label 12-ounce tab top, brown or red woodgrain can, multiversions. *(See photo 207)* $7

Two-label 12-ounce tab top, gold can, white label, "HUDEPOHL" in red, multiversions. $10

Two-label 12-ounce tab top, white can, red bands, yellow label, multiversions. $5

Photo 206 (left). Hudepohl 14K Beer.
Photo 207 (right). Hudepohl 14K Pure Grain Beer.

Hudepohl Beer, two-label 12-ounce tab top, two deer and barrel, multiversions..$1

Hudepohl Golden Beer, two-label 12-ounce flat top, gold can, white label, "GOLDEN HUDEPOHL" in red, single version. $40

Hudepohl Old 85 Ale, single-label, 12-ounce, high-profile cone top, white can, red bands, oval woodgrain label, IRTP and non-IRTP.
Non-IRTP, ...$225
IRTP, ...$135

Hudepohl Original 14K Draft Beer, two-label gallon can, brown or reddish woodgrain can, three versions. $125

Hudepohl Pure Grain Beer, single-label 12-ounce tab top, brown can, white label, 1975 or 1976 World Champions, single version of each. Each, ...$2

Hudepohl Pure Lager Beer, single-label, 12-ounce, J-spout cone top, red can, white label, "PURE LAGER" in black, INTERNAL REVENUE TAX PAID, single version...$200

Single-label, 12-ounce, high-profile cone top, metallic brown can, white label, IRTP or non-IRTP, single version of each.
Non-IRTP, ...$85
IRTP, ...$90

Single-label 12-ounce crowntainer, red and silver can, white label, "PURE LAGER" in black, INTERNAL REVENUE TAX PAID, single version. $175

Single-label 12-ounce crowntainer, blue and silver can, "PURE LAGER" in red, single version. $250
Camouflage can, ...Exotic

Hudy Delight Beer, two-label 12-ounce tab top, multiversions. $1

Hudepohl Brewing Company produced several brands in aluminum cans. The collector value of these cans is $1. Hudepohl Brewing Company merged with the Schoenling Brewing Company in 1985 and operations were moved to the Schoenling plant.

RED TOP BREWING COMPANY, 1747 Central Avenue (aka: Wunderbrau Brewing Company)

20 Grand Select Cream Ale, Red Top Brewing Company, single-label, 12-ounce, high-profile cone top, metallic green can, yellow label, IRTP or non-IRTP, minor versions.
IRTP, ...$100
Non-IRTP, ...$90

Red Top Brewing Company, single-label 12-ounce flat top, green can, yellow label, single version...$20

Red Top Brewing Company, two-label 12-ounce flat top, green can, white label, single version..$15

Barbarossa Beer, Red Top Brewing Company, single-label, 12-ounce, high-profile cone or flat top, metallic gold can, scene, INTERNAL REVENUE TAX PAID.
Cone top, ...$125
Flat top, ...$100

Red Top or Wunderbrau Brewing, single-label 12-ounce flat top, red and white can, single version of each. $50

Red Top Ale, Red Top Brewing, single-label, 12-ounce, high-profile cone top, yellow can, "RED TOP" in red, "ALE" in black, IRTP or non-IRTP, single version of each.
Non-IRTP, ... $75
IRTP, ... $85

Red Top Brewing, two-label 12-ounce tab top, cream-colored can, silver or white band, OPENING INSTRUCTIONS, INTERNAL REVENUE TAX PAID, single version of each. Either version, ... $350

Red Top Export Lager Beer, Red Top Brewing Company, single-label 12-ounce flat top, red and white can, "RED TOP" in white, OPENING INSTRUCTIONS, INTERNAL REVENUE TAX PAID. $250

Red Top Extra Dry Ale, Red Top Brewing, single-label 12-ounce flat top, white can, metallic red label outlined in metallic gold, single version. $75

Red Top Brewing, two-label 12-ounce tab top, red and white checkered can, single version. $60

Red Top Extra Dry Beer, Red Top Brewing Company, single-label, 12-ounce, high-profile cone top, white can, metallic gold circle, "RED TOP" in maroon, single version. $125

Red Top Extra Pale Beer, Red Top Brewing, single-label, 12-ounce high-profile cone top, white can, "EXTRA PALE" in metallic gold, IRTP or non-IRTP, single version of each.
Non-IRTP, ... $80
IRTP, ... $85

Red Top Old Cincinnati Beer, Red Top Brewing, single-label 12-ounce flat top, red and gray can, "RED TOP" in red, "BEER" in gray, OPENING INSTRUCTIONS, INTERNAL REVENUE TAX PAID, single version. $300

Red Top Olden Flavor Ale, Red Top Brewing, single-label 12-ounce flat top, OPENING INSTRUCTIONS, INTERNAL REVENUE TAX PAID, single version. ...Exotic

Red Top Triple XXXtra Ale, Red Top Brewing, single-label 12-ounce flat top, white can, woodgrain label, single version. $90

Redtop Extra Dry Beer, single-label 12-ounce flat top, white can, metallic gold circle, "REDTOP" in maroon, minor versions. $50

Single-label 12-ounce flat top, set can, 26 to set, all colors are metallic. Playing cards: blue can, purple can; circus tent: red can, blue can; party flags: blue can, green can; haywagon: red can, purple can; musical symbols: blue can, purple can; fishing scene: blue can, green can; cooking scene: red can, purple can; bowling: red can, orange can; country scene: purple can, blue can; horse race: blue can, red can; baseball: purple can, green can; radio and wrestling: blue can, green can; golf: blue can, green can; single version of each can. Each,
.... $60

Wunderbrau Das Trocken Lager, Wunderbrau Brewing, two-label 12-ounce flat top, woodgrain can, "WUNDERBRAU" in red, single version. $85

Wunderbrau Brewing, two-label 12-ounce flat top, gold can, woodgrain label, minor versions. $75

Wunderbrau Brewing, two-label 12-ounce flat top, white can, woodgrain label, single version. $85

SCHOENLING BREWING COMPANY, Oliver Street and Central Parkway (aka: Frank Fehr Brewing Company/Cincinnati)

Fehr's X/L Beer, two-label 12-ounce tab top, white can, red label outlined in silver, two versions. $30

Schoenling Lager Beer, single-label 12-ounce flat top, black can, metallic gold bands, red label, multiversions. $85

Single-label 12-ounce flat top, black can, metallic gold bands, white label, multiversions. $75

Single-label 12-ounce flat top, gold can, white label, red bands, "LAGER" in red, multiversions. $35

Single-label 12-ounce flat or tab top, gold can, yellow label, red bands, "SCHOENLING LAGER" in metallic gold, multiversions. $30

Single-label 12-ounce tab top, white can, red label, multiversions. $3

Schoenling Old Time Bock Beer, single-label 12-ounce flat top, white can, red bands, full-bodied goat, single version. $225

Cleveland

BREWING CORPORATION OF AMERICA, 9400 Quincy Avenue (aka: Carling's, Inc., Carling Brewing Company)

Black Label Beer, Brewing Corporation of America or Carling's, Inc., single- or two-label 12-ounce zip or tab top, red can, black label outlined in white, map of the U.S. or the world, multiversions. $10

Brewing Corporation of America, single-label 12-ounce zip top, red can, black label outlined in white, map of world, test can embossed, single version. .. $300

Carling's, Inc., two-label 12-ounce tab top, red can, black label outlined in white, gold bands, multiversions. $15

Carling's, Inc., two-label 12-ounce tab top, tankard can, multiversions. $15

Black Label Bock Beer, Carling Brewing Company, single-label 12-ounce flat top, red can, black label, "BOCK BEER" in black on white patch, white goat, multiversions. $40

Carling Black Label Beer, Carling Brewing Company, single- or two-label 12-ounce flat, zip, or tab top, red can, black label outlined in white, "CARLING" on label, multiversions. $8

Carling Black Label Bock Beer, Carling Brewing Company, single-label 12-ounce flat top, white can, black label, red goat's head, "CARLING" in red, single version. $85

Carling's Ale, Brewing Corporation of America, single-label, 12-ounce, high-profile cone or quart cone top, green can, yellow label, INTERNAL REVENUE TAX PAID, single version of each.
12-ounce, ...$150
Quart, ...$225

Carling's Black Label Beer, Brewing Corporation of America, single-label, 12-ounce, high-profile cone or quart cone top, black can, white lettering, INTERNAL REVENUE TAX PAID, multiversions.
12-ounce, ... $85
Quart, ... $125

Brewing Corporation of America, single-label 12-ounce flat top, black can, white lettering, multiversions. $25

Brewing Corporation of America or Carling Brewing Company, single-label 12-ounce flat top, white can, black label, multiversions. $15

Carling's Red Cap Ale, Brewing Corporation of America or Carling's, Inc., single-label, 12-ounce, high-profile cone top, green can, horse and rider, INTERNAL REVENUE TAX PAID, single version of each. $75

Carling's, Inc. or Carling Brewing Company, single-label, 12-ounce, high-profile cone top, WITHDRAWN FREE, single version of each. $300

Brewing Corporation of America, single-label, 12-ounce, high-profile cone top, green can, yellow label with man's head, IRTP and non-IRTP, single version of each. $85

Carling Brewing Company, single-label, 12-ounce, high-profile cone top, red can, yellow label with man's head, INTERNAL REVENUE TAX PAID, single version. $125

Carling Brewing Company, single-label 12-ounce flat top, green can, yellow can with man's head, "RED CAP" in red, multiversions. $25

Heidelberg Light Pilsner Beer, Carling Brewing Company, two-label 12-ounce tab top, gold and white can, multiversions. $20

Red Cap Ale, Carling Brewing Company, two-label 12-ounce flat top, metallic green can, split orangish label, multiversions. $25

Carling Brewing Company, gold diamonds, white label, vertical red band, single version. $20

CLEVELAND HOME BREWING COMPANY, 2515 East 161st

Black Forest Light Beer, two-label, 12-ounce, high-profile cone top, red can, white label, "BLACK FOREST" in black, two versions. $300

Dee Light Beer, single-label, 12-ounce, high-profile cone top, black can, metallic gold label, single version. $350

CLEVELAND-SANDUSKY BREWING COMPANY, 2764 East 55th

Crystal Rock White Label Pilsener Beer, two-label 12-ounce flat top, white can, blue bands and lettering, single version. $60

Two-label 12-ounce flat top, white can, gold and brown bands, single version. $85

GB Lager Beer, two-label 12-ounce flat top, metallic gold can, red and brown label outlined in white, single version. $85

Gold Bond Bock Beer, two-label 12-ounce flat top, white can, metallic gold label, "GOLD BOND BOCK BEER" in green, single version. $200

Gold Bond Lager Beer, two-label 12-ounce flat top, white can, "GOLD BOND" on red and black label, single version. $300

Gold Bond Special Beer, single-label 12-ounce flat top, white can, certificate label, single version. $150

Two-label 12-ounce flat top, white can, metallic gold half label, "SPECIAL BEER" in black, single version. $125

Gold Bond The Special Beer, two-label 12-ounce flat top, white can, metallic gold label, single version. $150

New York Special Brew, single-label 12-ounce flat top, white can, blue skyline, single version. $175

Old Timers Ale, single-label 12-ounce flat top, green and white can, single version. $60

FOREST CITY BREWING COMPANY, 6900 Union Avenue

Old Bohemian Style Lager Beer, single-label 12-ounce flat top, maroon can, orange lettering, "LAGER" on gold band, OPENING INSTRUCTIONS, INTERNAL REVENUE TAX PAID, single version. $150

Old Bohemian Style Pilsner Beer, single-label 12-ounce flat top, maroon can, orange lettering, "PILSNER" on gold band, OPENING INSTRUCTIONS, INTERNAL REVENUE TAX PAID, two versions. $135

Waldorf Ale, single-label 12-ounce flat top, yellow and green can, "WALDORF ALE" in black, OPENING INSTRUCTIONS, INTERNAL REVENUE TAX PAID, three versions. $250

Waldorf Lager Champagne Of Beer, single-label 12-ounce flat top, metallic gold and orange can, "WALDORF LAGER" in black, OPENING INSTRUCTIONS, INTERNAL REVENUE TAX PAID, two versions. $225

Waldorf Red Band Beer, single-label 12-ounce flat top, woodgrain can, three red bands, white lettering, INTERNAL REVENUE TAX PAID, multiversions. $75

Waldorf Red Band Super Fine Pilsner Beer, single-label 12-ounce flat top, metallic gold can, black and red bands, OPENING INSTRUCTIONS, INTERNAL REVENUE TAX PAID, single version. $250

Waldorf Samson Ale, single-label 12-ounce flat top, gray can, black label, red lettering, OPENING INSTRUCTIONS, INTERNAL REVENUE TAX PAID, minor versions. .... Exotic

Single-label 12-ounce flat top, yellow woodgrain can, INTERNAL REVENUE TAX PAID, single version. $175

THE LEISY COMPANY, 3400 Vega Avenue

Brew 82 Extra Select Beer also lists BREW 82 Brewing Company on a can as a mandatory. All other mandatories are LEISY.

Berghoff 1887 Pale Extra Dry Beer, single-label 12-ounce flat top, white can, metallic gold bands, "BERGHOFF BEER" in black, single version. $40

Photo 208. Black Dallas Malt Liquor.

Black Dallas Malt Liquor, two-label 12-ounce flat top, blue can, black city skyline, two versions. *(See photo 208)* $75

Blackhawk Premium Beer, two-label 12-ounce flat top, hatched silver can, red Indian head, single version. $100

Brew 82 Extra Select Beer, two-label 12-ounce flat top, red can, blue label and stripes, two versions.
Leisy Brewing, ... $65
Brew 82 Brewing, ... $75

Leisy Pilsner Beer, two-label 12-ounce flat top, gold can, yellow label outlined in maroon, single version. $225

Leisy's Dortmunder Brand Beer, two-label 12-ounce flat top, red can, metallic gold bands, "DORTMUNDER" in white, single version. $85

Leisy's Dortmunder Style Beer, single-label 12-ounce high-profile cone top, red can, gold stripes and lettering, INTERNAL REVENUE TAX PAID, single version. $200

Leisy's Dortmunder Type Beer, two-label 12-ounce flat top, red can, gold stripes, "DORTMUNDER" in white, single version. $85

Leisy's Light Beer, single-label, 12-ounce, high-profile cone or flat top, metallic blue can, yellow label, IRTP or non-IRTP, multiversions.
IRTP cone top, ...$160
Non-IRTP cone top, ...$150
Non-IRTP flat top, ...$100

Leisy's Light Full Flavored Beer, single-label 12-ounce flat top, blue can, metallic gold bands and eagle, yellow label, single version. $75

Two-label 12-ounce flat top, blue and eagle can, yellow label outlined in metallic gold, single version. $75

Leisy's Mello-Gold, two-label 12-ounce flat top, metallic gold can, white diamond label, "MELLO-GOLD" in black, single version. $125

Savoy's Special Beer, two-label 12-ounce flat top, silver and maroon can, single version. $75

Stein's Beer, single-label 12-ounce flat top, white can, red label, single version. $75

PILSENER BREWING COMPANY, 6605 Clark Avenue

Half And Half, single-label 12-ounce flat top, metallic gold can, yellow stripes, red and yellow label, single version. $85

P.O.C. Pilsener Beer, single-label, 12-ounce, high-profile cone or flat top, maroon can, gold label, single version of each.

Flat top, ... $75
Cone top, ...$100

Single- or two-label 12-ounce flat top, white can, metallic gold label and bands, multiversions. $12

P.O.C. (Pilsener On Call) Pilsener Extra Dry Beer, single-label, 12-ounce, high-profile cone or flat top, blue can, metallic gold label, IRTP or non-IRTP, single version of each.

Flat top, ... $85
Non-IRTP cone top, ...$125
IRTP cone top, ...$135

SCHAEFER BREWING COMPANY OF OHIO, 5801 Train Avenue (successor to Standard Brewing Company)

Schaefer Beer, single-label 12-ounce flat top, white can, 15 circles, single version. $5

C. SCHMIDT & SONS, 5801 Train Avenue (successor to Schaefer Brewing Company)

Schmidt's Of Philadelphia Light Beer, two-label 12-ounce tab top, metallic gold and metallic red can, white label, single version. $10

Schmidt's Of Philadelphia Tiger Beer, two-label 12-ounce tab top, metallic gold and green can, white label, single version. $15

C. Schmidt & Sons produced an array of brands in aluminum cans before the brewery closed in 1987. The collector value of these cans is up to $2.

STANDARD BREWING COMPANY, 5801 Train Avenue

Erin Brew The Standard Brew, single-label 12-ounce flat top, white can, purple label, "STANDARD" in red, multiversions. $50

Red Velvet Ale, two-label 12-ounce flat top, white can, orange steins, single version. $100

Two-label 12-ounce flat top, white can, single stein, metallic orange band, single version. $110

Standard The Erin Brew, single-label 12-ounce flat top, white can, red label, single version. $75

Single-version 12-ounce flat top, metallic gold and maroon can, white trim, single version. $20

Standard Premium Beer, single-label 12-ounce flat or tab top, white can, red label outlined in metallic gold, single version. $20

Columbus

ANHEUSER-BUSCH, INC., 7000 East Schrock Road

Built in 1968, this brewery produced a few steel cans, but nothing that has a collector value of over $1. This value would include any aluminum cans produced.

FRANKLIN BREWING COMPANY, 117 North Sandusky Street

Ben Brew 100% Grain Beer, single-label 12-ounce, high-profile cone top, yellow can, wide gold bands, "BEN BREW" in black, IRTP or non-IRTP, single version of each.
Non-IRTP, ...$165
IRTP, ...$175

Ben Brew 100% Grain Krausen Beer, single-label, 12-ounce, high-profile cone top, blue can, yellow label, "BEN BREW" in white on red ribbon, INTERNAL REVENUE TAX PAID, two minor versions. $250

Kings Head Ale, single-label, 12-ounce, high-profile cone top, red can, black label outlined in yellow, INTERNAL REVENUE TAX PAID, single version. $350

PILSENER BREWING COMPANY, 117 North Sandusky Street

P.O.C. Pilsener Beer, single-label 12-ounce flat top, white label, metallic gold bands and label, single version. $15

AUGUST WAGNER BREWERIES, INC., 605–631 South Front Street

All mandatories are AUGUST WAGNER BREWERIES except Iroquois Indian Head Beer, which has IROQUOIS BREWING COMPANY as a mandatory.

ABC Premium Ale, single-label 12-ounce flat top, white can, green label, "AGED" in black, single version. $10

ABC Premium Beer, single-label 12-ounce flat top, white can, red label, "AGED" in black, single version. $10

Augustiner Beer, single-label, 12-ounce, high-profile cone or flat top, white can, metallic gold bands, "AUGUSTINER" in red, multiversions.
Cone top, ...$125
Flat top, ...$15

Gam That Good Gambrinus Beer, single-label, 12-ounce, high-profile cone or flat top, white can, gold bands, "BEER" in red, minor versions. *(See photo 209)*
Cone top, ...$100
Flat top, ...$65

Gambrinus Gold Label Beer, single-label 12-ounce flat, zip, or tab top, white can, orange and gold can, multiversions.
Flat top, ...$10
Soft top, ...$8
Tab top, ...$5

Iroquois Indian Head Beer, Iroquois Brewing Company, two-label 12-ounce tab top, red can, gold bands, white label outlined in gold, single version. .. $12

Mark V Beer, single-label 12-ounce tab top, white can, calorie statement in red, blue stripe, multiversions. $3

Mark V Slim Line Beer, single- or two-label 12-ounce tab top, white can, three bands, multiversions. $10

Wagner's Gambrinus Quality Pale Beer, single-label, 12-ounce, high-profile cone top, metallic gold can, multicolor label, IRTP or non-IRTP, single version of each.

Non-IRTP, ...$150

IRTP, ...$160

WASHINGTON BREWERIES, INC., West 2nd Avenue and Perry Street

Noch-Eins Pale Beer, single-label, 12-ounce, J-spout cone top, white or silver can, red bands, black trim, "PALE BEER" in red, INTERNAL REVENUE TAX PAID multiversions. *(See photo 210)*..$225

Single-label 12-ounce crowntainer, silver or gray can, red bands, "NOCH-EINS" on black band, multiversions. $185

Washington XX Pale Pilsener Beer, single-label, 12-ounce, high-profile cone top, white can, metallic gold band and eagle, chevron label, IRTP or non-IRTP, single version of each.

Non-IRTP, ...$125

IRTP, ...$135

Washington XX Pale Beer, single-label 12-ounce crowntainer, silver can, eagle, chevron label, INTERNAL REVENUE TAX PAID, minor versions. $135

Dayton

MIAMI VALLEY BREWING COMPANY, 315 North Beckel Street

London Bobby Ale, two-label 12-ounce crowntainer, silver or white can, red and black band, INTERNAL REVENUE TAX PAID, minor versions. $150

London Bobby Brand Beer, two-label 12-ounce crowntainer, red can, white label, INTERNAL REVENUE TAX PAID, single version. $300

Nick Thomas Pilsener Pale Beer, two-label 12-ounce crowntainer, white can, red band, INTERNAL REVENUE TAX PAID, single version. $250

Van Bek Light Lager Beer, single-label 12-ounce crowntainer, silver can, white label, single version. *(See photo 211)* $150

Photo 209 (left). Gam That
Good Gambrinus Beer.
Photo 210 (center). Noch-Eins Pale Beer.
Photo 211 (right). Van Bek Light
Lager Beer.

Defiance

CHRISTIAN DIEHL BREWING COMPANY, 24 North Clinton Street

Diehl Beer, single-label, 12-ounce, high-profile cone top, black can, white label, "DIEHL," bands and trim in metallic gold, IRTP or non-IRTP.
Non-IRTP, ... $75
IRTP, ... $85

Diehl Five Star Select Pilsener Beer, two-label, 12-ounce, high-profile cone top, white can, red labels and bands, "FIVE STAR" in white, single version.
.... $135

East Liverpool

THE WEBB CORPORATION, 242 West 8th Street

Webber's Old Lager Beer, single-label, 12-ounce, high-profile cone top, white can, gold bands, "WEBBER'S" and "BEER" in red, INTERNAL REVENUE TAX PAID, multiversions. $150

Findlay

INTERNATIONAL BREWERIES, INC., Clinton Court and Jefferson Street (successor to Krantz Brewing Company)

Franken Muth Beer, two-label 12-ounce tab top, white can, couple, "FRANKEN MUTH" in blue, single version. $125

Frankenmuth Mel-O-Dry Beer, single-label 12-ounce flat top, yellow can, red or cream label outlined in metallic gold, two versions. Either version, ... $60

International Franken Muth Beer, two-label 12-ounce flat or zip top, white can, metallic red label, single version of each. $50

International Old Dutch Beer, two-label 12-ounce flat or tab top, white can, metallic red label, multiversions. $50

"Old Dutch" Beer, two-label 12-ounce zip top, white can, red label, yellow trim, single version. *(See photo 212)* $40

"Old Dutch" Brand Beer, single-label 12-ounce flat top, black can, white label, "OLD DUTCH" in red, single version. $50

"Old Dutch" Brand The Good Beer, single-label 12-ounce flat top, black can, white label, "OLD DUTCH" in red, single version. $50

Photo 212. "Old Dutch" Beer.

KRANTZ BREWING CORPORATION, Clinton Court and Jefferson Street

"Old Dutch" Brand The Good Beer, single-label 12-ounce flat top, black can, white label, "OLD DUTCH" in red, single version. $60

Minster

THE WOODEN SHOE BREWING COMPANY, 137 South Ohio Street

Wooden Shoe Beer, single-label, 12-ounce, high-profile cone or quart cone top, white can, blue band outlined in red, "LAGER BEER" in red, IRTP or non-IRTP, multiversions.

Non-IRTP, ... $115
IRTP, ...$125
Quart,.. $200

New Philadelphia

NEW PHILADELPHIA BREWERY, INC., 646 South Broadway

John Bull Beer, single-label, 12-ounce, high- or low-profile cone top, red and yellow can, "JOHN BULL" in black, INTERNAL REVENUE TAX PAID, single version of each.

Non-IRTP, ... $300
IRTP, ... $310

Old Bohemia Pilsner Style Beer, single-label, 12-ounce, high- or low-profile cone top, metallic gold can, black bands, INTERNAL REVENUE TAX PAID, single version of each. $150

Single-label, 12-ounce, high-profile cone top, yellow can, black bands, "OLD BOHEMIA" in black, INTERNAL REVENUE TAX PAID, single version. $140

Single-label, 12-ounce, high-profile cone top, yellow can, black band, "OLD BOHEMIA" in red, INTERNAL REVENUE TAX PAID, multiversions. $150

Olde Vat Premium Beer, single-label, 12-ounce, high-profile cone top, gold can, "OLDE VAT" in black, red and black trim, minor versions. $225

Scotch Highland Brand Genuine Ale, single-label, 12-ounce, high-profile cone top, tartan can, yellow label, "GENUINE" in black, INTERNAL REVENUE TAX PAID, single version. $250

Toledo

BUCKEYE BREWING COMPANY, 1501 Michigan Street

Buckeye Export Beer, single-label, 12-ounce, high-profile cone top, blue and white can, "LITTLE BUCKY," INTERNAL REVENUE TAX PAID, minor versions.
....$150

Buckeye Pilsener Beer, single-label, 12-ounce, high-profile cone top, gold sunburst can, blue and white label, "LITTLE BUCKY," INTERNAL REVENUE TAX PAID, single version of each. $100

Buckeye Pilsener Type Beer, single-label, 12-ounce, high-profile cone top, gold sunburst can, "LITTLE BUCKY," "DEPENDABLE" in white on blue band, INTERNAL REVENUE TAX PAID, multiversions. $125

Single-label, 12-ounce, high-profile cone top, gold sunburst can, two waiters, "PILSENER TYPE" in red, INTERNAL REVENUE TAX PAID, multiversions. $135

Buckeye Sparkling Dry Ale, two-label, 12-ounce, high-profile cone or flat top, white can, green label and pinstripes, white inner label outlined in metallic gold, single label of each.
Flat top, ... $40
Cone top, ... $85

Buckeye Sparkling Dry Beer, two-label, 12-ounce, high-profile cone top, white can, round red label outlined in metallic gold, single version. $100

1 Two-label, 12-ounce, high-profile cone top, white can, square red label, white inner label, single version. $100

Two-label 12-ounce flat top, red can, white label outlined in metallic gold, "BUCKEYE SPARKLING DRY" in black, single version. $40

Two-label 12-ounce flat or tab top, metallic red and silver can, "BUCKEYE SPARKLING DRY BEER" in red, multiversions. $30

Schwegmann Brothers Giant Super Markets Premium Light Beer, two-label 12-ounce tab top, metallic maroon can, white diamond label, single version.
.... $30

LUBECK BREWING COMPANY

Cans with mandatory LUBECK BREWING COMPANY, Toledo, Ohio, were actually brewed and filled by the Manhattan Brewing Company, Chicago. For listings see Manhattan, Chicago.

MEISTER-BRAU, INC., 1501 Michigan (successor to Buckeye Brewing Company; aka: Meister-Brau, Inc., Chicago, IL 60622 and Toledo, OH 43604; Buckeye Brewing Company, Division of Meister Brau, Inc., Toledo, OH 43604; Iroquois Indian Head Beer)

Buckeye Premium Beer, Meister Brau or Buckeye, two-label 12-ounce tab top, white can, metallic red label outlined in gold, single version of each. $15

Meister Brau, Inc., two-label 12-ounce tab top, white can, red label outlined in yellow, multiversions. $12

Buckeye Sparkling Dry Beer, Meister-Brau, Inc., single-label 12-ounce tab top, metallic red and silver can, "BUCKEYE SPARKLING DRY BEER" in red, multiversions... $25

Draft Beer By Iroquois, Iroquois Brewing Company, two-label 12-ounce tab top, white can, "DRAFT BEER" in blue, "BY IROQUOIS" in red, single version.
.... $5

Iroquois Indian Head Beer, Iroquois Brewing Company, two-label 12-ounce tab top, single version. $10

Wapakoneta

KOCH BEVERAGE COMPANY, 206 North Water Street

Koch's Old Vienna Type Beer, single-label, 12-ounce, high-profile cone top, reddish brown can, yellow label, INTERNAL REVENUE TAX PAID, minor versions. $125

Old Vienna Type Premium Quality Beer, two-label, 12-ounce, high-profile cone top, white can, yellow bands, "BEER" in black, single version. $150

Youngstown

CRYSTAL TOP BREWERY, INC., Rayen and North Avenue

Crystal Top Premium Beer, single-label 12-ounce flat top, black can, "CRYSTAL TOP" on white ribbon, single version. $200

RENNER COMPANY, 203–209 Pike Street

Clipper Beer, single-label 12-ounce flat top, yellow and black can, "BEER" in black, airplane, single version. ....Exotic

Old Bavaria Style Beer, single-label, 12-ounce, low- or high-profile cone top, metallic gold can, "BAVARIA" in black, minor versions. $300

Old German Brand Lager Beer, single-label, 12-ounce, high-profile cone top, black can, white lettering, single version. $175

Old German Style Beer, single-label, 12-ounce, high-profile cone top, white can, red label and bands, yellow trim, single version. $100

Renner Golden Amber Light Beer, single-label, 12-ounce, high-profile cone top, red can, white label, "RENNER" in red, single version. $150

Single-label, 12-ounce, high-profile cone top, red can, metallic gold bands, white label outlined in yellow, single version. $150

Single-label 12-ounce flat top, white and metallic gold can, split red label, single version. $20

Renner Old Oxford Ale, single-label, 12-ounce, high- or low-profile cone top, light green can, yellow label, "RENNER" and "YOUNGSTOWN" in red, INTERNAL REVENUE TAX PAID, single version of each. $150

Single-label, 12-ounce, high-profile cone top, dark green can, yellow label, "RENNER" and "YOUNGSTOWN" in red, INTERNAL REVENUE TAX PAID, minor versions. $125

Renner Premium Beer, single-label, 12-ounce, high-profile cone top, gold can, yellow and brown label, INTERNAL REVENUE TAX PAID, single version. $150

Single-label, 12-ounce, high-profile cone top, red can, yellow label, "RENNER BEER" in black, IRTP or non-IRTP, single version of each.

Non-IRTP, ...$125

IRTP, ...$135

Oklahoma

/

Oklahoma City

PETER FOX BREWING COMPANY OF OKLAHOMA,
2 North West 3rd Street (successor to Southwestern Brewing Company)

Silver Fox Beer, single-label, 12-ounce, high-profile cone top, silver can, white label, "SILVER FOX BEER" in black, single version. $350

LONE STAR BREWING COMPANY, 501 North Douglas Avenue
(successor to Progress Brewing Company)

Colt 45 Malt Liquor, two-label 12- or 16-ounce tab top, white can, horseshoe, "UNDER LICENSE OF NATIONAL BREWING COMPANY," single version of each. Each,... $30
Lone Star Beer, single-label 12-ounce soft or flat top, white can, red label outlined in yellow, stars, multiversions. $25
Lone Star Handy Keg Draft Beer, single-label 12-ounce tab top, silver barrel can, red label, "NON-PASTEURIZED" in black, multiversions. $25

PROGRESS BREWING COMPANY, 501 North Douglas Avenue

Progress Select Beer, single-label, 12-ounce, high-profile cone top, yellow can, red label, "PROGRESS BEER" in white, IRTP or non-IRTP, single version of each.
IRTP, ... $200
Non-IRTP, ...$190

Two-label, 12-ounce, high-profile cone or flat top, white can, red label outlined in metallic gold, minor version of each.

Cone top, ... $175

Flat top, ... $150

SOUTHWESTERN BREWING COMPANY, 2 North West 3rd Street

Gold Seal Extra Dry Premium Beer, single-label high-profile cone top, red, white, and gold can, INTERNAL REVENUE TAX PAID, single version. ....Exotic

Oregon

Portland

BLITZ-WEINHARD BREWING COMPANY, 1991 Northwest Upshur (aka: Blitz-Weinhard Company, Brewing Company of Oregon, Brewing Corporation of Oregon, Great Falls Breweries, Bohemian Breweries)

Acme Beer, Blitz-Weinhard, two-label 12-ounce steel or aluminum tab top, gold or brownish can, multicolored label with woman, multiversions.
Steel, ...$5
Aluminum, ...$3

Alta America's Extra Light Beer, Blitz-Weinhard, two-label 12- or 16-ounce aluminum tab top, light blue can, mountain scene, multiversions.
12-ounce, ...$3
16-ounce, ...$5

Aspen Gold Beer, Blitz-Weinhard, two-label 12-ounce tab top, white can, blue label, yellow trim, "A GREAT LIGHT PREMIUM BEER," multiversions. $5

Big Sky Pale Light Beer, Great Falls Breweries, two-label 11-ounce flat or tab top, blue can, white label outlined in gold, single version of each top. $75

Blitz-Weinhard Beer, Blitz-Weinhard, two-label 12- or 16-ounce flat, zip, or tab top, white can, red metallic label overlaid on metallic ribbons, "TIME PER-FECTED," multiversions. *(See photo 213, next page)*
Flat top, ...$35
Soft or zip top, ...$30

Blitz-Weinhard, two-label 12- or 16-ounce tab top, white can, red label overlaid on gold ribbons, story in black box, multiversions. $12

Photo 213 (left). Blitz Weinhard Beer.
Photo 214 (center). Blitz Weinhard
Draught Beer. Photo 215 (right).
Blitz Weinhard Select Beer.

Blitz-Weinhard, two-label 12- or 16-ounce steel or aluminum tab top, white can, red label, gold or brown barrel and trim, multiversions.
Steel,...$3
Aluminum,..$2
All other Blitz-Weinhard Beer produced in aluminum cans have a collector value of $1.

Blitz-Weinhard Draught Beer, Blitz-Weinhard, two-label gallon can, white and woodgrain can, spigot pouring beer, single version. *(See photo 214)* $60

Blitz-Weinhard Light Beer, Blitz-Weinhard, two-label 11- or 15-ounce flat top, white can, metallic red label overlaid on metallic gold and blue ribbons, "LIGHT" in gold, single version of each size.
11-ounce,..$50
15-ounce,..$60

Blitz-Weinhard Select Beer, Blitz-Weinhard, two-label 12- or 16-ounce flat top, light blue can, white label, BLITZ-WEINHARD" in black, IRTP or non-IRTP, multiversions. *(See photo 215)*
12-ounce IRTP,...$75
12-ounce non-IRTP,..$65
16-ounce non-IRTP,..$75

Blitz-Weinhard The Light Refreshing Beer, Blitz-Weinhard, two-label 12- or 16-ounce flat top, white can, metallic red label overlaid on metallic blue and gold ribbons, "THE LIGHT REFRESHING BEER" in gold, multiversions.
12-ounce,...$35
16-ounce,...$40

Bohemian Club Beer, Blitz-Weinhard or Brewing Company of Oregon, two-label 11- or 15-ounce flat or tab top, metallic red and gold, off-white can, man with glass, multiversions.
11-ounce,...$40
15-ounce,...$50

Brewing Company Of Oregon, two-label 12- or 16-ounce flat top, white can, blue label, gold trim, multiversions.
12-ounce,..$3
16-ounce,..$5
Aluminum versions,...$1

Buffalo Premium Lager Beer, Blitz-Weinhard, two-label 12-ounce tab top, tan can, reddish buffalo, multiversions. $5

Cascade Beer, Blitz-Weinhard, two-label 11- or 15-ounce flat top, white can, mountain scene, multiversions.
11-ounce, ... $15
15-ounce, ... $20

Blitz-Weinhard, two-label 11-, 12-, 15-, or 16-ounce flat or tab top, white can, blue label, yellow trim, multiversions.
11- and 15-ounce, ...$5
12- and 16-ounce, ...$2
Aluminum versions, ...$1

Champagne Velvet Beer, Brewing Company of Oregon, two-label 12-ounce flat top, red and dull gold can, white champagne glass, multiversions. $50

Brewing Company of Oregon, two-label 11- or 15-ounce flat top, metallic red and gold can, white champagne glass, multiversions.
11-ounce, ... $30
15-ounce, ... $35

Brewing Company of Oregon, Bohemian Breweries, two-label 11- or 15-ounce flat top, blue and gold can, white champagne glass, multiversions.
11-ounce, ... $10
15-ounce, ...$15

Golden Velvet Premium Beer, Blitz-Weinhard, white can, blue label, yellow trim, multiversions. $5

Great Falls Select Beer, two-label 12-ounce tab top, white can, metallic red label outlined in metallic gold, multiversions. $3

Brand was also produced in aluminum cans. Collector value is $1.

Olde English Brand "600" A Malt Liquor, Brewing Corporation of Oregon, single-label 11-ounce flat top, hatched metallic gold can, white label, "600" in red, single version. $100

Olde English Brand "600" Malt Liquor, Blitz-Weinhard, two-label 12- or 16-ounce tab top, white can, metallic gold label, maroon trim, single version of each. *(See photo 216)*
12-ounce, ... $75
16-ounce, ... $85

(From left to right) Photo 216. Olde English Brand "600" Malt Liquor. Photo 217. Olde English Brand "800" Stout, A Malt Liquor. Photo 218. Old Style Pale Export Lager Beer. Photo 219. Sick's Select Beer.

Olde English Brand "800" Malt Liquor, Blitz-Weinhard, two-label 12- or 16-ounce tab top, gold can, maroon label, "MALT LIQUOR" in maroon, multiversions. $1

Brand was also produced in aluminum. Collector value is $1.

Olde English Brand "800" Stout A Malt Liquor, Blitz-Weinhard, single- or two-label 12-ounce flat or tab top, gold can, maroon label, "A MALT LIQUOR" in maroon, multiversions. *(See photo 217)* $2

Tivoli A Light Premium Beer, Blitz-Weinhard, two-label 12-ounce tab top, white can, blue label outlined in gold, single version. $10

G. HEILEMAN BREWING COMPANY, 1991 Northwest Upshur (successor to Pabst Brewing Company)

All cans produced by G. Heileman Brewing Company, Portland, Oregon, are produced in aluminum and carry a collector value of $1. These cans can be separated from other Heileman breweries by the letter "N" stamped on the bottom of the cans.

PABST BREWING COMPANY, 1991 Northwest Upshur (successor to the Blitz-Weinhard Company)

All cans produced by Pabst Brewing Company, Portland, Oregon, were produced in aluminum and carry a collector value of $1.

Salem

SALEM BREWING ASSOCIATION, 268 Commercial Street

Brown Derby Pilsener Beer, two-label 12-ounce flat top or quart cone top, yellow can, white label, "PILSENER" in red, nine lines of text, OPENING INSTRUCTIONS, INTERNAL REVENUE TAX PAID, single version.
Flat top, ... $200
Quart, ... Exotic

Single-label 12-ounce flat top, yellow can, white label, "PILSENER" in red, six lines of text, OPENING INSTRUCTIONS, INTERNAL REVENUE TAX PAID, single version. $200

Old Style Pale Export Lager Beer, single-label 12-ounce flat top, gray can, red trim, OPENING INSTRUCTIONS, INTERNAL REVENUE TAX PAID, "Manufactured by SALEM BREWING ASSOCIATION, for SILVER SPRINGS BREWING COMPANY, Port Orchard, WASH.," single version. *(See photo 218)* ....Unique

SICK'S BREWING COMPANY, 268 Commercial (successor to Salem Brewing Association)

Sick's Select Beer, single-label 12-ounce flat top, metallic maroon can, yellow label, OPENING INSTRUCTIONS, world globe inside of 6, WITHDRAWN FREE, single version. *(See photo 219)* $75

Single-label 12-ounce flat top, maroon can, yellow label, "A SICK'S QUALITY PRODUCT," OPENING INSTRUCTIONS, INTERNAL REVENUE TAX PAID, single version. $250

Pennsylvania

Allentown

HORLACHER BREWING COMPANY, 311 Gordon Street (aka: Hofbrau Brewing Company, Old Dutch Brewing Company)

Bel Aire Premium Beer, Horlacher Brewing Company, single-label 12-ounce flat top, yellow can, white label outlined in metallic gold, multiversions. ... $75

Bonanza Premium Beer, Old Dutch Brewing Company, two-label 12-ounce tab top, white, metallic red, and blue can, steins, multiversions. $12

Brew II, Horlacher Brewing Company, two-label 12-ounce tab top, tan, yellow, or gold, light or dark blue can, multiversions. $2

Coburger Extra Dry Beer, Horlacher or Old Dutch Brewing, single-label 12-ounce flat or tab top, white or off-white can, blue lettering, gold striping, multiversions. *(See photo 220)* $15

Foodtown Premium Beer, Old Dutch Brewing Company, two-label 12-ounce flat top, metallic red and gold can, "beer" in white, single version. $15

Photo 220 (left). Coburger Extra Dry Beer.
Photo 221 (right). Hofbrau Beer.

Gex Holuburg Premium Light Beer, Hofbrau Brewing Company, two-label 12-ounce flat or tab top, white can, split brown label, metallic gold trim, single version of each.

Flat top, ... $25
Tab top, ... $20

Hofbrau Beer, Hofbrau Brewing Company two-label 12-ounce flat or tab top, white can, "HOFBRAU" in red, "BEER" in blue, single version of each. *(See photo 221)*

Flat top, ... $25
Tab top, ... $20

Horlacher Pilsener Beer, Horlacher Brewing Company, single- or two-label 12-ounce flat or tab top, white can, red band, penguin, multiversions. $8

Horlacher Premium Pilsener Beer, Horlacher Brewing Company, single-label 12-ounce flat top, white can, hex, "SUMMER 1976," single version. $3

Horlacher Brewing Company, single- or two-label 12-ounce tab top, metallic gold can, hex label, white trim, multiversions $2

Hub Draft Brewed Beer, Horlacher Brewing Company, two-label 12-ounce flat top, white can, red band, "DRAFT BREWED" in blue, single label. $50

Imperial Pilsener Beer, Hoffbrau Brewing Company, two-label 12-ounce tab top, white can, black, red, and gold label, minor versions. $30

Kappy's Premium Light Beer, Horlacher or Old Dutch Brewing, two-label 12-ounce flat or tab top, white can, brown label outlined in metallic gold, minor versions.

Flat top, ... $5
Tab top, ... $3

King Kullen Premium Beer, Horlacher Brewing Company, two-label 12-ounce flat or tab top, metallic gold and white can, black trim, "BEER" in red, single version of each.

Flat top, ... $10
Tab top, ... $8

LF Holburg Premium Light Beer, Hofbrau Brewing Company, two-label 12-ounce tab top, white can, split brown label, single version. $30

Little King Premium Beer, Horlacher Brewing Company, two-label 12-ounce flat or tab top, white or off-white can, "PREMIUM" in black, multiversions.

Flat top, ... $75
Tab top, ... $70

Pathmark Premium Beer, Hofbrau Brewing Company, two-label 12-ounce flat or tab top, off-white can, split metallic blue label, single version of each.

Flat top, ... $10
Tab top, ... $8

PB Class "A" Beer, Horlacher Brewing Company, two-label 12-ounce flat or tab top, metallic gold band, wide white band, single version of each.

Flat top, ... $5
Tab top, ... $3

Penguin Extra Dry Beer, Horlacher Brewing Company, single-label 12-ounce flat top, white can, blue label, single version. $15

Perfection Premium Beer, Horlacher Brewing Company, single-label 12-ounce flat top, white can, red band, penguin, multiversions............................. $15

Renaee Premium Light Beer, Horlacher Brewing Company, two-label 12-ounce tab top, gold and white can, red and black label, single version. $60

Rheinbeck Premium Beer*, Horlacher Brewing Company, two-label 12-ounce tab top, metallic gold can, blue label, single version. $25

Shop Rite Pilsner Beer, Old Dutch Brewing Company, two-label 12-ounce tab top, gold can, red label, single version. $3

Old Dutch Brewing Company, two-label 12-ounce flat top, white can, orange label, single version. $2

Shop Rite Premium Beer, Horlacher or Old Dutch Brewing Company, two-label 12-ounce flat or tab top, white can, large or small label, multiversions.
Flat top, ... $10
Tab top,..$8

Weisbrod The Peerless Pilsner, Old Dutch Brewing Company, two-label 12-ounce tab top, cream-colored can, white label, German eagle, single version.
.... $20

Westover Premium Light Beer, Old Dutch Brewing Company, two-label 12-ounce tab top, white can, red label, "LIGHT BEER" in black, single version.
.... $75

Wilco Premium Beer, Holfbrau Brewing Company, two-label 12-ounce flat or tab top, blue and green can, golf ball, minor versions. $35

LOUIS F. NEUWEILER'S SONS, INC., 401–453 Front Street

Hochberg Beer, two-label 12-ounce flat or tab top, mountain scene, blue bands, single version of each.
Flat top, ... $85
Tab top,... $80

Neuweiler Cream Ale, two-label 12-ounce flat top, green can, gold lettering and bands, single version...$100

Neuweiler Light Lager Beer, single-label 8- or 12-ounce flat top, white can, gold bands, "LIGHT LAGER" in red or gold multiversions. *(See photo 222)*
8-ounce, ... $75
12-ounce,... $50

Neuweiler's Bock Beer, single-label 12-ounce flat top, OPENING INSTRUCTIONS, INTERNAL REVENUE TAX PAID, single version. ....Unique

Photo 222. Neuweiler Light Lager Beer.

Neuweiler's Cream Ale, single-label, 12-ounce, high-profile cone or quart cone top, blue can, gold label and trim, single version of each size.

12-ounce,...$125
Quart,... $200

Single-label 12-ounce flat top, green and gray can, OPENING INSTRUCTIONS, IN-
TERNAL REVENUE TAX PAID, single version. $100

Single-label 12-ounce flat top or quart cone top, green and silver can, OPENING
INSTRUCTIONS, INTERNAL REVENUE TAX PAID, multiversions.

12-ounce flat top, ...$100
Quart cone top, ...$150
OI, non-IRTP, ...:........Exotic

Neuweiler's Pilsener Beer, single-label, 12-ounce, high-profile cone top, crowntainer, or quart cone top, orange and silver can, black lettering, multiversions.

High-profile,...$175
Crowntainer,... $85
Quart ,..$275

Single-label 12-ounce flat top or quart cone top, gray and blue can, OPENING
INSTRUCTIONS, INTERNAL REVENUE TAX PAID, multiversions.

Flat top, ...$150
Quart,..$250
Non-IRTP, OI, ...Exotic

Bethlehem

SOUTH BETHLEHEM BREWING COMPANY, 327 Webster Street

Supreme Light Beer, single-label, 12-ounce, J-spout or quart cone top, gold
can, yellow label, "SUPREME" in black, single version.

12-ounce,..Exotic
Quart,...Unique

Brackenridge

BRACKENRIDGE BREWING COMPANY, 849 6th Avenue

Old Anchor Beer, single-label 12-ounce, J-spout cone top, white can, red and
black bands, INTERNAL REVENUE TAX PAID, single version. ....Exotic

Catasauqua

EAGLE BREWING COMPANY, 210 2nd Street

Lebanon Valley Pilsener Beer, two-label 12-ounce flat top, white can, blue
label, red circle, single version. $50
Old Dutch Brand Beer, single-label, 12-ounce, J-spout cone or quart cone top,
metallic gold can, white label, INTERNAL REVENUE TAX PAID, single version of
each.

12-ounce,...$175
Quart,..$350

Two-label 12-ounce crowntainer, white can, red face on yellow circle, INTERNAL REVENUE TAX PAID, single version. ....Exotic

Two-label 12-ounce crowntainer, silver can, white or flesh-colored face on red face, minor versions. $300

Old Dutch Modern Light Beer, two-label 12-ounce flat top, white can, "NEW" on gold circle, "OLD DUTCH" in red, single version. $50

Old Dutch Premium Lager Beer, two-label 12-ounce flat top, gold can, yellow label, face on label, single version. $125

Two-label 12-ounce flat top, white can, gold bands and label, multiversions. $60

Pennsylvania Dutch Brand Old German Beer, single-label 12-ounce flat top, white can, red and yellow label, single version. *(See photo 223)*.............. $40

Shore Club Beer, single-label 12-ounce flat top, white can, metallic gold bands, "SHORE CLUB" in white, single version. $100

Chester

CHESTER BREWERY, INC., 2400 West 2nd Street

Chester Pilsner Beer, single-label, 12-ounce, J-spout cone top, red can, yellow label, INTERNAL REVENUE TAX PAID, single version. $350

Single-label 12-ounce crowntainer or quart cone top, silver can, red and yellow label, INTERNAL REVENUE TAX PAID, single version of each.
12-ounce,... $300
Quart,...$450

Silver Dime Premium Beer, single-label, 12-ounce, J-spout cone top, blue can, white label, INTERNAL REVENUE TAX PAID, single version. ....Exotic

Du Bois

DU BOIS BREWING COMPANY, Hahnes Court and South Main Street (purchased by the Pittsburgh Brewing Company, 1967)

Du Bois Budweiser Beer, single-label 12-ounce crowntainer, white can, yellow label, single version. $125

Single-label 12-ounce tab top, metallic gold can, white label, single version. $75

Du Bois Export A Fine Lager Beer, single-label, 12-ounce, high-profile cone top, metallic gold can, white and red label, single version. $100

Photo 223. Pennsylvania Dutch Brand Old German Beer.

Du Bois Light Beer, single-label, 12-ounce, J-spout cone top, white can, blue label, INTERNAL REVENUE TAX PAID, multiversions. $125

Two-label, 12-ounce, crowntainer or quart cone top, silver or white can, blue label, INTERNAL REVENUE TAX PAID, multiversions.
12-ounce, ...$125
Quart, ...$175

Du Bois The Perfect Beer, single-label 12-ounce zip or tab top, white can, red band, waterfall scene, single version of each. $25

DU BOIS BREWING COMPANY, Hahne's Court and South

Main Street (successor to Du Bois Brewing Company [owned by Pittsburgh Brewing Company 1967–1974])

Cloud Nine Malt Lager, two-label 12-ounce tab top, metallic green can, "MALT LAGER" in yellow, single version. $30

Cloud Nine Malt Liquor, two-label 12-ounce tab top, metallic green can, "MALT LIQUOR" in yellow, single version. $40

Du Bois Export Beer, single-label 12-ounce tab top, red can, white label, "EXTRA FINE" in gold or silver, multiversions. $20

Du Bois Premium Beer, single-label 12-ounce tab top, metallic gold can, white label outlined in brown, single version. $40

Norvic Pilsener Lager Beer, two-label 12-ounce tab top, white can, "NORVIC" in metallic red, single version. $20

Easton

BUSHKILL PRODUCTS COMPANY, 58 North Locust Street

Bushkill Lager Beer, single-label, 12-ounce, J-spout or quart cone top, gold can, "BUSHKILL" in white on blue band, INTERNAL REVENUE TAX PAID, single version.
12-ounce, ... $400
Quart, ...Exotic

KUEBLER BREWING COMPANY, South Delaware Drive

Kuebler Bock Beer, single-label, 12-ounce, J-spout cone top, goat drinking beer, INTERNAL REVENUE TAX PAID, single version. ....Exotic

Kuebler Cream Ale, single-label, 12-ounce, J-spout, crowntainer, or quart cone top, yellow can, green bands, full face or silhouette, INTERNAL REVENUE TAX PAID.
J-spout, ...$225
Crowntainer, ...$200
Quart, ...$350

Kuebler Extra Dry Beer, single-label quart cone top, white can, dark red label and bands, INTERNAL REVENUE TAX PAID, single version. $125

Keubler Pale Beer single-label, 12-ounce, high-profile cone top, white can, metallic red label and bands, IRTP or non-IRTP, single version of each.
Non-IRTP, ...$90
IRTP, ...$100

Kuebler Pilsener Beer, single-label, 12-ounce, J-spout, crowntainer or quart cone top, metallic gold can, red bands, full face or silhouette, INTERNAL REVENUE TAX PAID, multiversions.

J-spout, ...$100
Crowntainer, ... $90
Quart, ... $175

Edwardsville

BARTELS BREWING COMPANY, Plymouth Street and Toby's Creek

Bartels Pure Beer, two-label 12-ounce flat top, white can, metallic gold bands, red label, multiversions. $40

Bartels Pure Extra Light Beer, two-label 12-ounce flat or tab top, white can, dark blue diamond label, gold bands, single version of each.

Flat top, ... $50
Tab top, ... $45

Erie

ERIE BREWING COMPANY, 2124–2212 State Street

The mandatory IROQUOIS BREWING COMPANY was used on the Iroquois brands. ERIE BREWING was used on all other brands.

Draft Beer By Iroquois, two-label 12-ounce tab top, white can, "DRAFT BEER" in blue, single version. $5

Iroquois Indian Head Beer, two-label 12-ounce tab top, red can, gold bands, white label, single version. $15

Koehler Beer, single-label 12-ounce flat, soft, or tab top, green or blue and white can, eagle or shield, multiversions. $3

Single-label 12-ounce aluminum tab top, set can, three to a set, blue and white can with "Minute Man," "Paul Revere's Ride," and "Spirit of '76."
Each, ...$3

Koehler Lager Beer, two-label 12-ounce tab top, white can, red label, "UNCLE JACKSON KEOHLER," single version. $2

Brand was also produced in aluminum. Collector value is $1.

Koehler Select Beer, single-label, 12-ounce, high-profile cone top or two-label 12-ounce flat top, blue and white can, eagle, single version of each.

Cone top, ...$100
Flat top, ... $30

Koehler's Beer, single-label, 12-ounce, high- or low-profile cone top, blue can, metallic gold band, red ribbon, INTERNAL REVENUE TAX PAID, multiversions. .$125

Single-label, 12-ounce, high-profile cone top, white can, red ribbon, flying eagle, single version. $125

Olde Pub Tavern Brew Beer, two-label 12-ounce tab top, brown can, white label, stein, multiversions. $3

Koehler produced several brands in aluminum cans before ceasing operations in 1978. Collector value of these cans is $1.

Harrisburg

R. H. GRAUPNER BREWING COMPANY, 829–841 Market Street

Graupner's Beer, single-label, 12-ounce, high-profile cone or quart cone top, metallic gold can, red shield label, white lettering, INTERNAL REVENUE TAX PAID, single version of each.
12-ounce, ... $300
Quart, ... $450

Graupner's Old German Brand Beer, single-label, 12-ounce, J-spout or quart cone top, white can, red and black bands, INTERNAL REVENUE TAX PAID, single version.
12-ounce, ... Exotic
Quart, ... Exotic

Single-label 12-ounce crowntainer, silver can, red and black bands, INTERNAL REVENUE TAX PAID, single version. .... Exotic

Jolly Scott Ale, single-label, 12-ounce, J-spout or quart cone top, white can, red and black bands, "ALE" in red, INTERNAL REVENUE TAX PAID, single version.
12-ounce, ... $300
Quart, ... $450

Single-label 12-ounce crowntainer, silver can, red band, INTERNAL REVENUE TAX PAID, single version. .... Exotic

Old German By Graupner's, single-label, 12-ounce, J-spout, crowntainer or quart cone top, INTERNAL REVENUE TAX PAID, single version.
12-ounce, ... Exotic
Crowntainer, ... Exotic
Quart, ... Exotic

Lancaster

WACKER BREWING COMPANY, 203 West Walnut Street

Wacker Little Dutch Brand Lager Beer, single-label, 12-ounce, J-spout or quart cone top, white can, oval yellow label, INTERNAL REVENUE TAX PAID, single version.
J-spout, ... $250
Quart, ... $350

Single-label 12-ounce crowntainer, silver can, oval white label, INTERNAL REVENUE TAX PAID, single version. $300

Single-label 12-ounce, high-profile cone top, yellow can, "LAGER BEER" in black, single version. $300

Wacker Premium Beer, single-label, 12-ounce, J-spout or quart cone top, white can, red label, INTERNAL REVENUE TAX PAID, single version.
J-spout, ... $275
Quart, ... $400

Single-label 12-ounce crowntainer, yellow can, red and blue bands and eagle, single version. $300

Lansdowne

FERNWOOD BREWING COMPANY, Baltimore and Melrose Streets

Golden Age Beer, single-label, 12-ounce, low-profile cone or quart cone top, gold and blue can, red label, INTERNAL REVENUE TAX PAID, single version.
12-ounce, ...$250
Quart, ...$350

Wolf's Beer, single-label, 12-ounce, low-profile cone or quart cone top, metallic gold can, red label, INTERNAL REVENUE TAX PAID, single version.
12-ounce, ...$250
Quart, ...$350

Latrobe

LATROBE BREWING COMPANY, 119 Ligonier Street

Rolling Rock Extra Pale Premium Beer, single-label, 12-ounce, high-profile cone, flat, or tab top, green can, white lettering, horse's head, multiversions.
Cone top, ... $75
Flat top, ... $20
Tab top, ...$5

Rolling Rock Premium Beer, single-label 7- or 12-ounce tab top, green can, white lettering, waterfall, multiversions.
7-ounce, ...$5
12-ounce, ...$2

Latrobe Brewing has produced a number of brands in aluminum cans. Collector value is $1.

Lebanon

LEBANON VALLEY BREWING COMPANY, 840 North 7th

Gold Mug Beer, single-label 12-ounce flat top, metallic gold can, white label, yellow trim, single version. $250

Lebanon Valley Pilsner Beer, single-label, 12-ounce, J-spout, high-profile, flat, or quart cone top, white can, metallic gold band and trim, single version.
J-spout, ... $200
High-profile, ... $200
Flat top, ...$100
Quart, ...$250

Single-label 12-ounce flat top, white can, blue label and bands, red trim, single version. $50

Manhattan Beer, single-label 12-ounce flat top, metallic gold and white can, skyline, red label, single version. $200

Old India Brand Beer, two-label 12-ounce flat top, red and white can, "INDIA BRAND" in white, single version. $80

Pennsylvania Dutch Old German Brand Beer, single-label, 12-ounce, high-profile cone or flat top, yellow and white can, woodgrain label, multiversions. $125

Shore Club Beer, single-label 12-ounce flat top, white can, gold bands, red label, single version. $125
Silver Mug Premium Beer, single-label 12-ounce flat top, silver can, green and gold shield, single version. $250

Lehigh Valley

F. & M. SCHAEFER BREWING COMPANY, Route 100

This brewery, built in the mid-1970s, was acquired by the Stroh Brewery in 1981 through a merger. A long list of brands have been produced, all in bi-metal or aluminum cans. Collector value is not over $1.

Mahoney City

C. D. KAIER COMPANY, 67–69 North Main Street

Kaier's Draft Beer, two-label 12-ounce tab top, white can, gold and red label, "DRAFT" in white, single version. $30
Kaier's Draft Brewed Beer, single-label 12-ounce flat top, white can, gold and red label, "BEER" in white, single version. $30
Kaier's Premium Ale, two-label 12-ounce tab top, white can, green and yellow circle, "KAIER'S" in black, single version. $30
Kaier's Special Light Lager Beer, single-label, 12-ounce, J-spout, high-profile flat or quart cone top, white can, red label, gold bands, INTERNAL REVENUE TAX PAID, single version of each.
12-ounce cone top, ...$100
12-ounce flat top, ... $60
Quart cone top, ...$160

McKeesport

TUBE CITY BREWING COMPANY, 225 12th Street

Tube City Premium Quality Beer, single-label, 12-ounce, high-profile or quart cone top, gold can, white bands, red label, single version.
12-ounce, ...$100
Quart, ... $175

New Castle

UNION BREWING COMPANY, 506–528 Sampson Street

Royal Bru Beer, single-label, 12-ounce, low- or high-profile cone top, silver or white can, shield, INTERNAL REVENUE TAX PAID, multiversions. $300

Norristown

ADAM SCHEIDT BREWING COMPANY, Marshall and Barba-does Street

Brewery was owned and operated by C. Schmidt, Philadelphia, from 1954 to 1960.

Prior Beer, single-label 12-ounce flat top, blue can, gold bands, white label, single version. $50

Prior Lager Beer, two-label 12-ounce flat top, green can, white label, circle label, minor versions. $40

Prior Tasty Lager Beer, single-label 12-ounce flat top, metallic gold can, white stripes and label, IRTP or non-IRTP, single version.
IRTP, ... $85
Non-IRTP, ... $75

Rams Head Ale, single-label 12-ounce flat top, green can, dark yellow label and stripes, multiversions. $15

Scheidt's Rams Head Ale, single-label 12-ounce flat top, or quart flat or cone top, metallic gold can, red label, ''SCHEIDT'S'' in black, OPENING INSTRUCTIONS, INTERNAL REVENUE TAX PAID, multiversions of 12-ounce flat tops only.
12-ounce flat top, ...$125
Quart flat top, ... $300
Quart cone top, ...$250

Scheidt's Valley Forge Beer, single-label 12-ounce flat top, gray can, gray letters on the red logo, OPENING INSTRUCTIONS, WITHDRAWN FREE, single version. ....Exotic

Single-label 12-ounce or quart flat or cone top, metallic gold can, red label, ''VALLEY FORGE BEER'' in yellow, OPENING INSTRUCTIONS, INTERNAL REVENUE TAX PAID, multiversions.
12-ounce flat top, ...$100
Quart flat top, ... $300
Quart cone top, ...$225

Schedit's Valley Forge Bock Beer, single-label 12-ounce flat top, green can, green label, ''BOCK BEER'' in yellow, OPENING INSTRUCTIONS, INTERNAL REVENUE TAX PAID, minor versions. $225

Valley Forge Beer, single-label 12-ounce flat top, silver can, red circle, multiversions.. $50

Single-label 12-ounce flat top, blue can, red label, head, multiversions...... $30

Single-label 12-ounce flat top, white can, red label, blue bands, multiversions. $20

Valley Forge Bock Beer, single-label 12-ounce flat top, white can, green label, ''BOCK BEER'' in yellow, single version. $125

C. SCHMIDT & SONS, Marshall and Barbadoes Street (aka: Valley Forge Brewing Company, Prior Brewery)

Name was changed to C. Schmidt & Sons February 15, 1960. Brewery closed December 31, 1963.

Prior Lager Beer, C. Schmidt & Sons, two-label 12-ounce flat top, white can, green bands, two lions, multiversions. $40

Prior Preferred Beer, C. Schmidt & Sons, two-label 12-ounce flat top, gold can, split label, ''PRIOR'' in black on white circle, multiversions. $50

C. Schmidt & Sons or Prior Brewery, two-label 12-ounce tab top, white can, gold trim, ''PRIOR'' in metallic red, ''LIQUID LUXURY,'' multiversions. $60

Rams Head Ale, Valley Forge or C. Schmidt & Sons, two-label 12-ounce flat or tab top, green can, dark yellow label, stripes, multiversions. $10

Schmidt's Light Beer, C. Schmidt & Sons, single-label 12-ounce flat top, silver can, white label outlined in gold "SILVER NOGGIN," multiversions. $75

C. Schmidt & Sons, two-label 12-ounce flat or tab top, metallic red and gold can, white label, multiversions. $20

Valley Forge Beer, Valley Forge Brewing Company, two-label 12-ounce flat or tab top, white can, red label, blue bands, multiversions. $20

Valley Forge Bock Beer, Valley Forge Brewing Company, two-label 12-ounce flat or tab top, yellow can, green label, "BOCK BEER" in yellow, single version of each.
Flat top, ...$125
Tab top, ...$100

Valley Forge Old Tavern Beer, C. Schmidt & Sons, two-label 12-ounce flat or tab top, metallic gold can, white label, red lettering, multiversions. $20

C. Schmidt & Sons, two-label 12-ounce tab top, off-yellow can, white label, red lettering, single version. $2

Northampton

NORTHAMPTON BREWING COMPANY, 1247 Newport Avenue

Blue Crest Light Dry Beer, single-label quart cone top, gray and blue can, "BLUE CREST" in blue outlined in black, INTERNAL REVENUE TAX PAID, single version. $400

Loewer's Blue Crest Beer, two-label 12-ounce crowntainer, silver can, white label, "LOEWER'S BEER" in red, INTERNAL REVENUE TAX PAID, single version. $200

Tru Blu Ten Star Ale, single-label, 10-ounce, J-spout cone top, green and silver can, INTERNAL REVENUE TAX PAID, single version. ....Exotic

Two-label 12-ounce crowntainer or quart cone top, green and silver can, INTERNAL REVENUE TAX PAID, single version of each.
Crowntainer, ...$250
Quart, ... $400

Single- or two-label 12-ounce flat top, black and gold can, OPENING INSTRUCTIONS, IRTP or non-IRTP, single version of each.
Single-label, ...Unique
Two-label, ...Exotic

Two-label 12-ounce flat top, green and silver can, OPENING INSTRUCTIONS, INTERNAL REVENUE TAX PAID, multiversions. $300

Tru Blu White Seal Pilsener Beer, two-label, 10-ounce, J-spout cone top, silver can, red ribbons, blue band and lettering, single version. ....Exotic

Two-label 12-ounce crowntainer, flat top, or quart cone top, silver can, blue band and lettering, red trim, WITHDRAWN FREE, OPENING INSTRUCTIONS, INTERNAL REVENUE TAX PAID, multiversions.
Crowntainer, WITHDRAWN FREE, ...$350

Flat top, WITHDRAWN FREE, ... $300
Flat top, ...$250
Crowntainer, ...$225
Quart cone top, ...$350

Philadelphia

CLASS & NACHOD BREWING COMPANY, Philadelphia

Cans with the mandatory CLASS & NACHOD BREWING COMPANY, Philadelphia, were actually brewed and filled by the Manhattan Brewing Company, Chicago, IL.

COOPER BREWING COMPANY, 173 Carson Street Manyunk (successor to Liebert & Obert Brewing Company)

Namar Premium Beer, single-label, 12-ounce, high-profile cone or quart cone top, metallic gold can, blue label outlined in red, "CAREFULLY BREWED OF THE FINEST INGREDIENTS," INTERNAL REVENUE TAX PAID, multiversions.
12-ounce, ...$125
Quart, ...$225

Two-label 12-ounce crowntainer, silver can, blue label, red band, "CAREFULLY BREWED OF THE FINEST INGREDIENTS," INTERNAL REVENUE TAX PAID, single version. $175

OTTO ERLANGER BREWING COMPANY, 845 North Orianna Street

Erlanger's Pilsener Beer, single-label, 12-ounce, high- or low-profile cone or quart cone top, green can, yellow label outlined in gold, IRTP or non-IRTP, multiversions.
12-ounce, ...$185
12-ounce non-IRTP, ...$175
Quart, ...$250

Erlanger's Pilsner Deluxe Beer, single-label, 12-ounce, high-profile cone or quart cone top, white can, "DELUXE" counter stamped over label, IRTP or non-IRTP, minor versions.
12-ounce, ...$150
12-ounce non-IRTP, ...$135
Quart, ...$185

Perone Beer, single-label quart cone top, brown can, red and white label, INTERNAL REVENUE TAX PAID, single version. ....Unique

ESSLINGER'S, INC., 10th and Callowhill Streets

Camden Lager Beer, single-label 12-ounce flat top, white can, orange bands and ribbon, single version. $85

Esslinger Little Man Ale, single-label 12-ounce flat top or quart cone top, metallic green and gold can, "ALE" in white, IRTP or non-IRTP, multiversions.
12-ounce flat top, ...$175
IRTP quart cone top, ...$260
Non-IRTP quart cone top, ...$250

Esslinger Parti Quiz, single- or double-label 12-ounce flat top, set cans, called "Parti Quiz," nine different sets, one-, two- or three-color cans, issued 1953–1964, basic colors: blue, bronze, green, orange, pink, purple, red, silver (all colors have a variety of tones), all cans have eight rows of text or facts, text can be straight or slanted, sets also issued in Bock cans, total number of cans in each set is unverified, example of text: "25th President William H. Taft," "Corn is largest farm crop in the U.S.," "Babe Ruth record for strikeouts 330."

Beer cans, ... $75
Bock cans, ... $125

Jacob Ruppert, New York City, produced two sets after Esslinger, Inc. folded.

Esslinger Premium Beer, single-label 12-ounce flat top or quart cone top, white can, maroon label, red ribbon, multiversions. $60
Esslinger Special Beer, single-label 12-ounce flat top, white can, maroon label, red ribbon, multiversions. $60
Esslinger's Bock Beer, single-label 12-ounce crowntainer, flat top, or quart cone top, yellow can, waiter riding goat, red trim, INTERNAL REVENUE TAX PAID, single version.
Crowntainer, ... $300
Flat top, ... $275
Cone top, ... $400
Esslinger's Premium Ale, single-label 12- or 32-ounce flat top or quart cone top, yellow can, "BEER" in red, waiter, OPENING INSTRUCTIONS, INTERNAL REVENUE TAX PAID, single version.
12-ounce flat top, ... $100
12-ounce cone top, ... $125
Quart cone top, ... $200
Single-label, 12-ounce, high-profile cone or flat top, metallic gold and green can, IRTP or non-IRTP, single version of each.
Cone top, ... $200
Non-IRTP cone top, ... $185
Flat top, ... $150
Esslinger's Premium Beer, single-label, 12-ounce, high-profile cone or flat top, or quart flat or cone top, yellow can, waiter, red trim, INTERNAL REVENUE TAX PAID, single version of each.
12-ounce cone top, ... $150
12-ounce flat top, ... $125
Quart flat top, ... Exotic
Quart cone top, ... $300
Single-label, 12-ounce, high-profile cone or flat top, or quart cone or flat top, metallic red and gold can, little man, INTERNAL REVENUE TAX PAID, single version of each.
12-ounce cone top, ... $175
12-ounce flat top, ... $150
Quart flat top, ... Exotic
Quart cone top, ... $325
Gretz Premium Beer, two-label 12-ounce flat top, blue can, white label, gold or silver ribbons, single version of each. Either version, ... $40
Keglet Beer, two-label 12-ounce flat top, woodgrain can, gold bands, single version. $60

PB Class "A" Beer, two-label 12-ounce flat top, gold can, minor versions.
.... $35

WILLIAM GRETZ BREWING COMPANY, 1536 Germantown Avenue

Betts Premium Beer, two-label 12-ounce flat top, white can, single version.
.... $200

Bond Hill Deluxe Lager Beer, two-label 12-ounce flat top, red can, single version. $350

Bond Hill Premium Lager Beer, two-label 12-ounce flat top, blue can, red lettering, single version. $300

Diamond State Light Beer, single-label 12-ounce flat top, metallic gold can and ribbon, white label and stripes, single version. $350

Exeter Beer, single-label 12-ounce flat top, metallic gold can and label, white and blue stripes, single version. $450

Germantown Extra Light Beer, single-label 12-ounce flat top, brown and yellow can, single version. ....Exotic

Gretz Ale, single-label 12-ounce crowntainer, silver can, yellow label, INTERNAL REVENUE TAX PAID, single version. ....Exotic

Gretz Beer, single-label, 12-ounce, J-spout or crowntainer, or quart cone top, silver can, blue striping, yellow label, INTERNAL REVENUE TAX PAID, multiversions.
12-ounce J-spout, ...$250
12-ounce crowntainer, ...$300
Quart cone top, ...$250

Single-label 12-ounce crowntainer, high-profile, or quart cone top, blue can, yellow label, "GRETZ" in red, bicyclist, INTERNAL REVENUE TAX PAID, multiversions.
Crowntainer, ... $175
Quart, ...$300
High-profile, ... $175

Single-label, 12-ounce, high-profile cone or flat top, yellow can, white diamond label, "GRETZ" in red, multiversions.
Flat top, ...$100
Cone top, ...$160

Single-label 12-ounce flat top, yellow can, metallic gold ribbon, black or red bicycle, single version of each. $75

Single-label 12-ounce flat top, yellow can with sports car in red, two sets, called "G B Car Fleet" (printed in red or black), 12 cars to each set: Alfa Romero, Austin Healy, Corvette, Fiat 600, Fiat 1100, Ford Thunderbird, Isetta BMW, Mercedes Benz, MGA Convertible, MGA Hardtop, Porsche 1500, Saab 93. *(See photo 224)* Each can, each version, ...$150

Gretz Bock Beer, single-label 12-ounce flat top, yellow can, "BOCK BEER" in red, red stripes, single version. $160

Gretz Half & Half, single-label 12-ounce flat top, cream-colored can, white label outlined in gold, single version. $300

Photo 224. Gretz Beer.

Gretz Tooner Schooner Beer, single-label 12-ounce flat top, set cans, set of 21 cans called "Tooner Schooner." Lyrics to a song, illustrated by cartoons: "A Bird in a Gilded Cage," "After the Ball," "Casey Jones," "Everybody Works but Father," "Good Old Summertime," "Hello, My Baby," "Hot Time in the Old Town Tonight," "Ida, Sweet as Apple Cider," "I Want a Girl," "I Wonder Who's Kissing Her Now," "Kentucky Babe," "Let Me Call You Sweetheart," "My Gal Sal," "Sweet Rosie O'Grady," "Take Me Out to the Ballgame," (lyrics in red and blue), "The Sidewalks of New York," "Wait Til the Sun Shines, Nellie," "When You Were Sweet Sixteen," "Wild Irish Rose." Single version of each can. Each, ... $85

York Light Beer, two-label 12-ounce flat top, white can, "YORK" in black, single version. $100

JOHN HOHENADEL BREWING, INC., Conrad Street and Indian Queen Lane

Hohenadel Beer, two-label 12-ounce crowntainer, silver can, black bands, "BEER" in red, INTERNAL REVENUE TAX PAID, single version. $150

Two-label 12-ounce crowntainer, white can, black and red bands, "BEER" in red, INTERNAL REVENUE TAX PAID, single version. $175

Single-label, 12-ounce, high-profile cone or quart cone top, white can, red and metallic gold can, "BEER" in black, IRTP or non-IRTP, minor versions.
12-ounce non-IRTP, ... $175
12-ounce IRTP, ... $185
Quart, ... $300

Hohenadel Bock Beer, single-label, 12-ounce, J-spout cone top, goat above HOHENADEL, INTERNAL REVENUE TAX PAID, single version. .... Exotic

Hohenadel Indian Queen Ale, single-label, 12-ounce, J-spout cone or quart cone top, yellow can, red and metallic gold bands, INTERNAL REVENUE TAX PAID, single version.
12-ounce, ... $350
Quart, ... Exotic

Hohenadel Light Beer, single-label, 12-ounce, J-spout cone or quart cone top, white can, red and metallic gold bands, INTERNAL REVENUE TAX PAID, single version.
12-ounce, ... $175
Quart, ... $300

Indian Queen Ale, single-label, 12-ounce, J-spout cone or quart cone top, yellow can, red and metallic gold bands, INTERNAL REVENUE TAX PAID, single version.

12-ounce,... $300
Quart,..$450

JACOB HORNUNG BREWING COMPANY, 1420 North Randolph Street

Hornung Light Beer, single-label, 12-ounce, high-profile cone or flat top, metallic gold can, yellow label, "DIAMOND ANNIVERSARY," OPENING INSTRUCTIONS, WITHDRAWN FREE, INTERNAL REVENUE TAX PAID, multiversions.
Cone top, ...$250
Flat top, ... $300
WITHDRAWN FREE,.. $400

Hornung Premium Beer Dry Lager, single-label 12-ounce flat top, gold can, cream label, single version. $100

Hornung's Bock Beer, single-label 12-ounce flat top, metallic gold can, yellow label, "BOCK" in white, OPENING INSTRUCTIONS, INTERNAL REVENUE TAX PAID, single version...$250

Hornung's Cream Ale, single-label 12-ounce flat top, metallic gold can, yellow label, "ALE" in red, OPENING INSTRUCTIONS, IRTP or non-IRTP, single version of each.
IRTP, ...$250
Non-IRTP, ...$325

Hornung's Light Beer, single-label 12-ounce flat top or quart cone top, metallic gold can, yellow label, "LIGHT" in black, single version.
Flat top, ...$250
Cone top, ... $400

Hornung's Pilsner Beer, single-label 12-ounce flat top, metallic gold can, yellow label, OPENING INSTRUCTIONS, INTERNAL REVENUE TAX PAID, single version...Exotic

India Cerveza, single-label 12-ounce flat top, yellow can, red vertical stripes, white label, WITHDRAWN FREE, single version. $300

LIEBERT & OBERT BREWING COMPANY, 173 Carson Street, Manyunk

Cooper's Old Bohemian Beer, single-label, 12-ounce, J-spout or quart cone top, metallic gold can, white label, black band, INTERNAL REVENUE TAX PAID, minor versions.
12-ounce,.. $200
Quart,...$275

Two-label 12-ounce crowntainer, silver can, white, red, and black label, INTERNAL REVENUE TAX PAID, single version. $200

Cooper's Yorktown Brand Ale, two-label 12-ounce crowntainer or quart cone top, silver can, red, black, and white label, INTERNAL REVENUE TAX PAID, single version.

12-ounce, ...$150
Quart, ...$250

HENRY F. ORTLIEB BREWING COMPANY, American and Poplar Streets

Before closure in 1981, the Henry F. Ortlieb Brewing Company brewed a wide variety of brands using several mandatories. These cans were produced in bi-metal and aluminum and have a collector value of $1.

In addition, Henry F. Ortlieb produced a set of 14 Ortlieb's Collector's Series and a set of six Ortlieb's Americana Collection. These cans were also produced in aluminum and bi-metal and have a collector value of $2.

The mandatory CHARLES D. KAIER COMPANY, Philadelphia, is used on Kaier's Special Beer. All other brands carry the ORTLIEB mandatory.

Kaier's Special Beer, two-label 12-ounce tab top, white can, red circle, horseman, multiversions. $5

Ortlieb's Ale, single-label 12-ounce crowntainer, silver can, yellow label, INTERNAL REVENUE TAX PAID, single version. $250

Ortlieb's Bock Beer, single-label, 12-ounce, J-spout cone top, "BOCK ALE" on ribbon, goat, single version. ....Exotic

Ortlieb's Draught Beer, two-label 16-ounce tab top, white can, red oval label, "DRAUGHT BEER" in red, multiversions. $3

Ortlieb's Export Lager Beer, single-label, 12-ounce, high-profile cone or quart cone top, metallic gold can, white label, "LAGER BEER" in red, single version.

12-ounce, ...$100
Quart, ...$125

Single-label 12-ounce crowntainer, silver can, white label, single version. .. $85

Ortlieb's Genuine Draught Beer, two-label 12-ounce tab top, white can, oval red label, blue lettering, single version. $3

Ortlieb's Lager Beer, single-label, 12-ounce, J-spout or quart cone top, yellow can, gold label, red ribbon, INTERNAL REVENUE TAX PAID, single version.

12-ounce, ...$100
Quart, ...$125

Single-label 12-ounce crowntainer, silver can, red band, "IRTP" in red, minor versions. $100

Ortlieb's Philadelphia's Famous Beer, single-label 12-ounce flat, zip, or tab top, white can, dark red label outlined in gold, multiversions. $10

Single-label 12-ounce tab top, white can, red label outlined in silver, text or no text, multiversions. $3

Ortlieb's Premium Beer, single-label 12-ounce flat or tab top, dark red label outlined in gold, "PREMIUM" in black, single version of each top. Either version, ... $10

Ortlieb's Premium Lager Beer, single-label, 12-ounce, high-profile or quart cone top, metallic gold can, white label, "LAGER BEER" in red, multiversions.

12-ounce, ... $100
Quart, ... $125

Single-label 12-ounce flat top, white can, red oval or ribbon label, "PREMIUM" in black, multiversions. $20

PHILADELPHIA BREWING COMPANY, 6th and Clearfield Streets

P.O.S. Lager Beer, two-label, 12-ounce, high-profile cone top, cream-colored can, red label, "P. O. S. BEER" in white, INTERNAL REVENUE TAX PAID, two versions. $175

POTH BREWING COMPANY, 1811–1823 North 10th Street

Poth's Ale, single-label 12-ounce flat top, brown can, OPENING INSTRUCTIONS, INTERNAL REVENUE TAX PAID, single version. .... Exotic

Poth's Beer, single-label 12-ounce flat top, brown can, white lettering, OPENING INSTRUCTIONS, INTERNAL REVENUE TAX PAID, single version. .... Exotic

Poth's Special Pilsener Beer, single-label 12-ounce flat top, metallic gold can, red label, "POTH'S SPECIAL BEER" in white, OPENING INSTRUCTIONS, INTERNAL REVENUE TAX PAID, two versions. $250

C. SCHMIDT & SONS, INC., 127 Edward Street (aka: Valley Forge Brewing Company, Duquesne Brewing Company, Pilsener Brewing Company)

C. Schmidt & Sons brewed a wide variety of beers under a wide array of labels and mandatories. These brands were canned in aluminum and bi-metal cans. The collector value of these cans does not exceed $1.

  C. Schmidt & Sons issued a 14-can bicentennial set in 1976. These brands were filled in bi-metal and aluminum cans and the collector value is $3.

Casey's Lager Beer, single-label 12-ounce tab top, multicolored can featuring baseball stars, set of four: Duke Snider, Richie Ashburn, Monte Irvin, Whitey Ford; single version of each. *(See photo 225)* Each, ... $5

Photo 225. Casey's Lager Beer.

Duke Beer, C. Schmidt and Duquesne Brewing, two-label 12-ounce tab top, white can, prince, multiversions. $2

Duquesne Bavarian Beer, C. Schmidt and Duquesne Brewing, two-label 12-ounce tab top, blue can, mountain scene, white label, multiversions. $1

P.O.C. Pilsenser Beer, Pilsenser Brewing Company, two-label 12-ounce tab top, white can, gold label, red ribbon, multiversions. $1

Ram's Head Old Stock Ale, C. Schmidt & Sons, single- or two-label 12-ounce tab top, green can, orange label, multiversions. $3

C. Schmidt & Sons, C. Schmidt & Sons, two-label 12-ounce flat or tab top, green and gold can, white label, tiger, multiversions. $25

Schmidt's Ale, C. Schmidt & Sons, single-label, 12-ounce, high-profile cone or quart cone top, silver can, white label, tiger, multiversions.
12-ounce, ...$85
Quart, ...$135

Schmidt's Bock Beer, C. Schmidt & Sons, single-label 12-ounce flat top, silver can, red label outlined in white, goat, single version. $100

C. Schmidt & Sons, single-label 12-ounce flat or tab top, gold can, red label outlined in white, goat, single version of each top,
Flat top, ...$125
Tab top, ...$115

Schmidt's Cream Ale, C. Schmidt & Sons, single-label, 12-ounce, J-spout or quart cone top or crowntainer, silver or gray can, white label, blue lettering, multiversions.
Crowntainer, ...$85
J-spout, ...$100
Quart, ...$125

Schmidt's Lager Beer, C. Schmidt & Sons, two-label 12-ounce flat top, red and gold can, white label, single version. $20

Schmidt's Light Beer, C. Schmidt & Sons, single-label, 12-ounce, J-spout cone, crowntainer, or quart cone top, silver metallic can, red trim, white label outlined in metallic gold, ''SCHMIDT'S'' in black, some cans say ''SILVER NOGGIN,'' INTERNAL REVENUE TAX PAID, multiversions. *(See photo 226)*
J-spout, ...$150
Crowntainer, ...$140
Quart, ...$200

C. Schmidt & Sons, two-label 12- or 16-ounce flat or tab top, red and metallic gold can, white label, multiversions. $5

Photo 226. Schmidt's Light Beer.

Schmidt's Old Style Bock Beer, C. Schmidt & Sons, single-label 12-ounce crowntainer or quart cone top, silver can, red label, INTERNAL REVENUE TAX PAID, single version.
Crowntainer, ...Exotic
Quart, ...Exotic

Schmidt's Tiger Brand Ale, C. Schmidt & Sons, single-label 12-ounce flat top, silver can, yellow and blue label, minor versions. $65

Silver Top Beer, Duquesne Brewing Company, two-label 12-ounce tab top, red can, silver label, minor versions. $5

Tudor Premium Ale, Valley Forge Brewing, two-label 12-ounce tab top, green can, black label, single version. $5

Tudor Premium Beer, Valley Forge Brewing, two-label 12-ounce tab top, gold and yellow can, black label, single version. $3

Pittsburgh

DUQUESNE BREWING COMPANY, South 22nd and Mary
Streets (aka: Pilsenser Brewing Company)

Astro Premium Beer, Pilsener Brewing Company, two-label 12-ounce tab top, white can, light or dark blue band, yellow or gold circles, two versions. $20

Duke Beer, Duquesne Brewing Company, single- or two-label 12-ounce tab top, metallic gold can, white label, red trim, multiversions. $8

Duquesne Brewing Company, single-label 12-ounce tab top, white can, prince, multiversions. $5

Duquesne Bavarian Beer, Duquesne Brewing Company, two-label 12-ounce tab top, blue can, white label, mountain scene, multiversions. $4

Duquesne Can-O-Beer, Duquesne Brewing Company, two-label, 12-ounce, high-profile cone or 12-ounce flat top, white can, red label with prince, single version of each.
Cone top, ... $85
Flat top, ... $60

Duquesne Brewing Company, single-label, 12-ounce, high-profile cone top, woodgrain can, yellow bands, white lettering, single version. $75

Duquesne Brewing Company, single-label, 12-ounce, high-profile cone top, WITHDRAWN FREE, single version. $300

Duquesne Keg-O-Beer, Duquesne Brewing Company, single-label, 12-ounce, high-profile cone top, single version. $100

Duquesne Pilsener Beer, Duquesne Brewing Company, single-label, 12-ounce, high-profile cone or flat top, or two-label 12-ounce tab top, gold can, open-ended diamond-shaped white label, multiversions.
Cone top, ... $85
Flat top, ... $15
Tab top, ...$8

P.O.C. Pilsener Beer, Pilsener Brewing Company, two-label 12-ounce soft or tab top, white can, metallic gold label and bands, multiversions. $5

Silver Top Old Time Lager Beer, Duquesne Brewing Company, two-label 12-ounce tab top, red can, split label, black lettering, multiversions. $15

Silver Top Premium Beer, Duquesne Brewing Company, two-label 12-ounce flat top, silver can, white label, "PREMIUM" on red band, single version. .. $60

Silver Top Premium Lager Beer, Duquesne Brewing Company, two-label 12-ounce flat top, silver can, INTERNAL REVENUE TAX PAID, single version. ...$100

Silver Top Premium Special Lager Beer, Duquesne Brewing Company, two-label 12-ounce flat top, green or white can, white label, "PREMIUM SPECIAL LAGER" in white on red band, single version of each. $75

FORT PITT BREWING COMPANY, 16th and Mary Streets

Fort Pitt Ale, single-label 12-ounce flat top, green can, silver label and lettering, OPENING INSTRUCTIONS, INTERNAL REVENUE TAX PAID, two minor versions. $300

Fort Pitt Beer, two-label 12-ounce crowntainer, silver can, red lettering, INTERNAL REVENUE TAX PAID, WITHDRAWN FREE, two versions. (*See photo 227*)
Crowntainer, ... $150
WITHDRAWN FREE, ... $300

Single-label 12-ounce flat top, silver can, running waiter, OPENING INSTRUCTIONS, INTERNAL REVENUE TAX PAID, two versions. $300

Fort Pitt Extra Special Pilsener Beer, single-label, 12-ounce, high-profile cone top, white can, blue label surrounded by metallic gold, single version. $175

Fort Pitt Pale Ale, single-label, 12-ounce, high-profile cone top, metallic blue can, "PALE ALE" in red, IRTP or non-IRTP, single version of each.
IRTP, ... $150
Non-IRTP, ... $140

Fort Pitt Special Beer, two-label 12-ounce crowntainer or high-profile cone top, red and yellow can, "FORT PITT" in black, INTERNAL REVENUE TAX PAID, multiversions.
Crowntainer, ... $125
Cone top, ... $125

Old Shay Deluxe Beer, two-label 12-ounce crowntainer, black and silver can, red label, INTERNAL REVENUE TAX PAID, single version. $150

PITTSBURGH BREWING COMPANY, 16th and Mary Streets

Pittsburgh Brewing Company has and is producing a multitude of brands in bi-metal and aluminum cans under the PITTSBURGH mandatories. Other mandatories used are DUBOIS and MAGNA CARTA BREWING COMPANIES. The collector value of these cans does not exceed $1.

Photo 227. Fort Pitt Beer.

Photos 228 and 229. Brickskeller Beer.

American Beer, two-label 12-ounce tab top, white can, metallic red diamond-shaped label, minor versions. $2

American Brewers Historical Beer, two-label 12-ounce flat or tab top, set can, set of six, Nos. 13–18. For can Nos. 1–12, see Jos. Huber Brewing Company, Monroe, WI. Multicolored cans, brewery pictured, each can numbered: No. 13, The Old Salmon Brewery; No. 14, Grenier's; No. 15, T. M. Morton; No. 16, Meyer's Brewery; No. 17, Mack & Simon; No. 18, C. L. Centlivre. Versions: each can comes in both flat and tab tops. This is the *only* set that has tab tops.
Flat top, each,..$5
Tab top, each, ...$7.50

Augustiner Beer, two-label 12-ounce tab top, white can, yellow bands, "AUGUSTINER" in red, multiversions. $2

Brickskeller Beer, two-label 12-ounce "sta-put" tab, set can, set of 12 cans known as "Endangered Species" set: American alligator, American peregrine falcon, bald eagle, brown pelican, California condor, Colorado squawfish, Florida panther, grizzly bear, Houston toad, leatherneck sea turtle, Sonoran pronghorn, Texas red wolf; single version of each. *(See photos 228, 229, and 230)*
Each,...$5

Photo 230.
Brickskeller Beer.

Photo 231 (left). Brickskeller Saloon Style Beer.
Photo 232 (right). Brickskeller Saloon Style Lager Beer.

Brickskeller Saloon Style Beer, single-label 12-ounce "sta-put" tab, blue or cream-colored can, single version of each. *(See photo 231)* Each, ...$3

Brickskeller Saloon Style Lager Beer, single-label 12-ounce "sta-put" tab, blue or cream-colored can, single version of each. *(See photo 232)* Each,......$3

Brown Derby Lager Beer, two-label 12-ounce flat top, brown and orange label, UPC code, multiversions...$3

Dubois Premium Quality Beer (mandatory reads DUBOIS BREWING COMPANY), two-label 12-ounce tab top, metallic gold can, white label, single version.....$3

Dutch Club Beer, single-label, 12-ounce, high- or low-profile cone top, blue can, dark blue label outlined in white, INTERNAL REVENUE TAX PAID, single version of each. Either version, ... $175

Single-label, 12-ounce, high-profile cone top, metallic gold can, red label outlined in yellow, IRTP or non-IRTP, single version of each.
IRTP, ...$100
Non-IRTP, ... $90

Dutch Club Brand Beer, single-label, 12-ounce, low-profile cone top, blue can, white label, single version. $225

Gambrinus Gold Label Beer, two-label 12-ounce tab top, white can, metallic gold bands, metallic gold and red label, multiversions. $3

Heritage House Premium Beer, two-label 12-ounce tab top, yellow can, red label, multiversions. $2

Hop'n Gator Flavored Beer, two-label 12-ounce tab top, white can, "FLAVORED BEER" in black, single version. $3

Hop'n Gator Lemon-Lime Lager, two-label 12-ounce tab top, yellow can, stein with fruit, single version. $100

Hop'n Gator Malt Liquor, two-label 12-ounce tab top, white can, glass with palm tree, single version. $10

Iron City Beer, single-label, 12-ounce, high- or low-profile cone top, red can, "IRON CITY" in white on black ribbon, INTERNAL REVENUE TAX PAID, single version of each. $175

Single-label 12-ounce flat top, gray can, black circle, OPENING INSTRUCTIONS, INTERNAL REVENUE TAX PAID, single version................................... $300

Single-label, 12-ounce, high- or low-profile cone or flat top, white can, red circle, gold bands, cone has IRTP, multiversions.

Cone top, ... $85
Flat top, ... $35

Single-label, 12-ounce, high-profile cone or flat top, white can, red circle, silver or gray bands, "IT'S REAL BEER," multiversions.

Cone top, ... $100
Flat top, ... $35

Single-label, 12-ounce, high-profile cone or flat, soft, or zip top, white can, red circle, "PREMIUM QUALITY," single version of each top.

Cone top, ... $75
All others, ... $10

Single-, two-, or three-label 12- or 16-ounce zip or tab top, white can, red circle, various slogans: "New" (two versions), "No 1" (one version), "Beer Drinker's Beer" (four versions), "The Big Iron" (two versions), "Goodwill for Good People" (one version). $3

Single-label 12-ounce tab top, white can, red label, set cans, set of six cans called "Pittsburgh Scenes": "Cathedral of Learning," "Civic Area," "Fort Pitt Blockhouse," "Old North Side Post Office," "The Incline," "Three Rivers Stadium"; single version of each. Each, ... $5

Single-label 12- or 16-ounce tab top, white can, red label, set can, set of four cans called "Pour it on, Steelers": "1972 Record/1973 Schedule," "Offense Signatures," "Defense Signatures," "Defense Helmets"; single version of each. Each, ... $5

Single-label 12-ounce tab top, white can, red label, set can, set of three called "Good Friends, Good Cheer": "Country Scene," "Covered Bridge," "Hearth"; single version of each. Each, ... $5

Single-label 12-ounce tab top, white can, red label, set can, set of nine called "Pour it on, Pirates": "Letter from Brewery President," "World Series Record," "1974 Roster" (pitchers and catchers), "1974 Roster" (infielders and outfielders), "1974 TV Schedule," "Pirates Team Record," "1974 Home Schedule," "1960 World Series," "1971 World Series"; single version of each. Each, ... $5

Single-label 12-ounce tab top, white can, red label, set can, set of five called "Pro Sports Championships": "Baseball World Championships," "Golf Tourneys," "Leading PBA Averages," "NBA Champions," "Stanley Cup Champions," "Super Bowl Winners"; single version of each. Each, ... $3

Single-label 12-ounce tab top, white can, red label, set can, set of six cans called "Bicentennial Flag Series": "Confederate Battle Flag," "Cowpens," "Grand Union," "Sons of Liberty," "Star Spangled Banner," "Tauton"; single version of each. Each, ... $5

Single-label 12- or 16-ounce tab top, white can, red label, non-set cans: "Mountaineer Basketball" (one version), "Penn State Numero Uno" (one version), "Penn State 1974 Football Schedule" (one version), "Pitt Helmet" (one version), "West Virginia 1976" (two versions), "Running Mountaineer" (one version), "Standing Mountaineer" (one version), "Two Great Names on Ice" (one version), "1982 Pittsburgh Penguins" (one version), "1979 World Champion Pirates" (one version), "Pitt #1 in '80" (two versions), "Renaissance 2" (one version), "Marine Corps League" (one version), "Men of Iron & Steel" (one version), "1975 Super Steelers" (one version), "1975 Super Bowl Champs" (one version), "1976 Super Bowl Champs" (one version), "The 1976 Pittsburgh Steelers" (one version), "Super Super Super Steelers" (one version), "The Team of the Decade" (two versions), "Pittsburgh's Pride Our Steelers" (two versions), "Steelers 50th Anniversary" (one version), "The Steel Can Team" (one version), "Weirton Pride" (one version), "Title Drive 85" (one version). Each,..$5

Iron City Draft Beer, two-label 12-ounce tab top, white can, red label, "DRAFT BEER" in black or red letters, multiversions..$5

Single-label 12-ounce tab top, white can, red label, "DRAFT BEER" in black, set can, set of three called "Good Friends, Good Cheer": "Country Scene," "Covered Bridge," "Hearth"; single version of each. Each,....................$5

Single-label 12-ounce tab top, white can, red label, "DRAFT BEER" in black, set can, set of nine cans called "Pour it on, Pirates": "Letter from Brewery President," "World Series Record," "1974 Roster" (pitchers and catchers), "1974 Roster" (infielders and outfielders), "1974 TV Schedule," "Pirates Team Record," "1974 Home Schedule," "1960 World Series," "1971 World Series"; single version of each. Each,...$3

Single-label 12-ounce tab top, white can, red label, "DRAFT BEER" in black, set cans, set of six cans called "Discover New Jersey": "Atlantic City Boardwalk," "Historic Barnegat Light House," "Map of New Jersey," "The Great Falls of the Passaic River," "The Twin Lights of Highlands," "Washington's Headquarters"; single version of each. Each, ...$4

Single-label 12-ounce tab top, white can, red label, "DRAFT BEER" in black, set cans, set of six cans called "Pro Sports Championships": "Baseball World Championships," "Golf Championships," "Leading PBA Averages," "NBA Champions," "Stanley Cup Champions," "Super Bowl Winners"; single version of each. Each,...$5

Mark V Beer, two-label 12-ounce tab top, white can, red and blue stripes, multiversions. $2

Mustang Malt Lager, two-label 12- or 16-ounce tab top, black can, gold horse, single version.
12-ounce,.. $10
16-ounce,.. $15

Mustang Malt Liquor, two-label 12- or 16-ounce tab top, black can, gold label, single version.
12-ounce,..$8
16-ounce,.. $12

Mustang Premium Malt Lager, two-label 12-ounce tab top, red can, black horse, single version. $20

Mustang Premium Malt Liquor, two-label 12- or 16-ounce tab top, red can, black horse, metallic gold trim, multiversions. $10

Old Dutch Brand The Good Beer, two-label 12-ounce tab top, white can, red bands, scene, multiversions. $3

Old Export Premium Beer, two-label 12-ounce tab top, red can, white label, "PREMIUM" in red, single version. $3

Old German Brand Premium Lager Beer, two-label 12-ounce tab top, white can, red label, multiversions. $3

Photo 233 (left). Olde Frothingslosh Beer.
Photo 234 (right). Olde Frothingslosh Beer.

Old Heidel Brau Lager Beer, two-label 12-ounce tab top, red and white can, minor versions. $2

Olde Frothingslosh Beer, single-label 12-ounce tab top, set can, 31 cans total: "Bathing Beauty"—brown can, ecology statement; brown can, no ecology statement; orange can; blue can; red can; silver can (wide seam); silver can (narrow seam); purple can (wide seam); purple can (narrow seam); yellow can; red, white, and blue can; red, white, and blue can (crimped); multicolored. (*See photo 233*). "Pin-up Girl"—ballet, on bear skin rug, tied to trolley tracks, leading parade, on wharf, cutting ribbon. (*See photo 234*). "Sir Reggie"—"Opening Soon," "Foam on the Bottom," red can, purple can, green can, blue can, "Political Campaign," "Nine to Five" (two versions), "Spa" (two versions). Each, ...$5

Seven Springs Mountain Beer, two-label 12-ounce tab top, set can, set of five cans: dark blue, brown, gold, green, light blue; single version of each. Each, ...$3

Sir Lady Frothingslosh Pale Stale Ale, single-label 8-ounce flat top, white can, yellow band, "PALE STALE ALE" in black, single version. $300

Tech Golden Beer, single-label 8- or 12-ounce flat top, white can, metallic green label, minor versions.
8-ounce, ... $60
12-ounce, ... $40

Tech Premium Ale, single-label 8-ounce flat top, gold can, white label, minor versions. $75

Tech Premium Beer, single-label 8-ounce flat top, gold can, white label, minor versions. $60

Single-label 12-ounce flat or tab top, white can, plaid label, two versions. $3

Ultra Light Premium Beer, two-label 12-ounce tab top, white can, blue and yellow ribbon, multiversions. $2

Waynesboro FD Lager Beer, single-label 12-ounce tab top, set can, set of four, red, gold, blue, or yellow can, single version of each. Each, ...$2

Weir Radio/Steel Premium Beer, single-label 12-ounce tab top, white can, multicolored photographs, single version. $2

WFBG Radio's Keystone Country, single-label 12-ounce tab top, blue can, multicolored pictures, single version. $2

Wild Mustang Super Premium Malt Liquor, single-label 12-ounce tab top, gold can, black horse, multiversions. $1

WKIS Beer, two-label 12-ounce tab top, cream-colored can, white label, single version. $2

Pottsville

MOUNT CARBON BREWERY, 716 Centre Street

Bavarian Premium Beer, single-label, 12-ounce, high-profile cone or flat top, or quart cone top, brown can, cream label, single label of each.
12-ounce cone top, ...$100
Quart cone top, ...$175
Two-label 12-ounce tab top, white can, black oval label outlined in metallic gold, single version. $10

Bavarian Type Beer, single-label, 12-ounce, high-profile cone or quart cone top, brown can, cream label, IRTP or non-IRTP, single version of each.
12-ounce non-IRTP, ...$100
12-ounce IRTP, ...$110
Quart non-IRTP, ...$175
Quart IRTP, ...$185

Bavarian Type Premium Beer, single-label 12-ounce flat top, woodgrain label, metallic gold oval label, single version. $50

Two-label 12-ounce flat or tab top, white can, black oval label outlined in metallic gold, minor versions of each top.
Flat top, ...$10
Tab top, ...$8

M.C. Deluxe Pilsener Beer, single-label, 12-ounce, low-profile cone or quart cone top, gold can, blue label, INTERNAL REVENUE TAX PAID, single version.
12-ounce, ...$85
Quart, ...$150

Mount Carbon Old Bohemian Beer, single-label 12-ounce flat top, metallic gold and red can, single version. $150

D.G. YUENGLING & SON BREWING COMPANY, 5th and Mahantongo Streets

The MOUNT CARBON BREWERY mandatory is used on Bavarian Type Premium Beer only. All other brands use the D.G. YUENGLING & SON mandatory.

Bavarian Type Premium Beer, two-label 12-ounce tab top, white can, black oval label outlined in metallic gold, minor versions. $5

Brau Fest Beer, single-label 12-ounce tab top, multicolored can, single version. $3

Coal Cracker Beer, single-label 12-ounce tab top, multicolored can, single version. $3

D.G. Yuengling & Son Premium Beer, single-label 12-ounce tab top, multicolored can, factory scene, versions: "Our 150th Year," "Our 151st Year," "Our 152nd Year," "Our 153rd Year." $3

Collector value for aluminum versions is $2.

Food Fair Prize Beer, two-label 12-ounce flat top, white can, black label outlined in yellow, single version. $75

Haentjens Ale, single-label 12-ounce tab top, multicolored can, single version. $2

Lord Chesterfield Ale, single-label 12-ounce tab top, yellow can, white label, single version. $2

Pocono Mountain Premium Beer, single-label 12-ounce tab top, multicolored cans, set can, set of five cans: "Spring Sports," "Summer Sports," "Autumn Sports," "Winter Sports," "1980 Winter Carnival"; single version of each. Each, ...$5

Royal Hibernia Premium Beer, single-label 12-ounce tab top, multicolored can, single version. $3

Shenanigans Premium Beer, single-label 12-ounce tab top, multicolored can, single version. $3

Yuengling Beer, single-label, 12-ounce, high-profile cone or quart cone top, red can, yellow lettering, minor versions.
12-ounce, ...$125
Quart, ...$175

Yuengling Premium Beer, single-label, 12-ounce, high-profile cone, flat, or tab top, or quart cone top, white can, red label, gold stars, single version of cones, multiversions of others.
12-ounce cone top, ...$125
Quart cone top, ...$185
12-ounce flat top, ...$50
12-ounce tab top, ...$40

Two-label 12-ounce flat or tab top, white can, split metallic red label, multiversions. $7

Yuengling's Beer, single-label, 12-ounce, low- or high-profile cone or quart cone top, red can, gold label, white lettering, INTERNAL REVENUE TAX PAID, minor versions.
12-ounce, ...$100
Quart, ...$150

Yuengling's Old Oxford Brand Cream Ale, single-label, 12-ounce, high- or low-profile cone or quart cone top, yellow can, maroon label, red ribbon, single version.
12-ounce, ...$200
Quart, ...$350

D.G. Yuengling & Son produced an array of brands in aluminum cans. The collector value is $1.

Reading

BARBEY'S, INC., West Elm and Gordon Streets

Sunshine Beer, single-label 12-ounce crowntainer, silver can, red and brown bands, INTERNAL REVENUE TAX PAID, single version. ....Exotic

Sunshine Extra Light Beer, single-label 12-ounce crowntainer, silver can, red and brown bands, IRTP or non-IRTP, single version of each.

IRTP, ... $215
Non-IRTP, ... $200

Single-label quart cone top, gold can, red and brown bands, INTERNAL REVENUE TAX PAID, single version. $250

Sunshine Light Beer, single label, 12-ounce, J-spout or quart cone top, gold can, red and brown bands, INTERNAL REVENUE TAX PAID, minor versions.
12-ounce, ...$225
Quart, ...$250

OLD READING BREWERY, INC., South 9th and Little Laurel Streets

Bergheim Beer, two-label 12-ounce flat top, white can, farm and waterfall, single version. $10

Manheim Premium Beer, two-label 12-ounce flat top, white can, red label, "PREMIUM" in gold, single version. $15

Old Reading Ale, single-label, 12-ounce, J-spout or quart cone top, metallic green can, old man raising stein, INTERNAL REVENUE TAX PAID, single version.
12-ounce, ... $200
Quart, ...$275

Old Reading Beer, single-label, 12-ounce, J-spout or quart cone top, metallic blue can, old man raising stein, INTERNAL REVENUE TAX PAID, single version.
12-ounce, ... $185
Quart, ...$250

Two-label 12-ounce crowntainer, silver can, blue label, old man raising stein, INTERNAL REVENUE TAX PAID, single version. $200

Two-label, 12-ounce, high-profile cone or flat top, white can, blue label outlined in yellow, "TRADITIONALLY PENNSYLVANIA DUTCH," single version.
Cone top, ...$125
Flat top, ... $65

Old Reading Pilsner Beer, two-label 12-ounce crowntainer, silver or cream-colored can, brown label, silver can IRTP, cream-colored both, minor versions.
IRTP, ... $175
Non-IRTP, ...$165

Old Reading Premium Golden Dry Beer, single label, 12-ounce, high-profile cone top, yellow can, red label, "PREMIUM" in gold, single version. $100

Old Reading Premium Quality Beer, single label, 12-ounce, high-profile cone top, yellow can, red label, "PREMIUM QUALITY" in silver, single version. .$100

Prizer Extra Dry Premium Beer, two-label 12-ounce flat top, yellow can, "EXTRA DRY" in yellow on red band, yellow stein, single version. $50

Two-label 12-ounce flat top, white can, red and metallic gold bands, silver stein, single version. $15

Reading Light Premium Beer, two-label 12-ounce flat or tab top, white can, blue label, metallic gold circles, single version of each top.
Flat top, ... $10
Tab top, ...$8

Reading Premium Beer, two-label 12-ounce flat top, white can, gold bird with or without eye, single version of each. Either can, ... $30

Yorktown Extra Fine Premium Beer, single-label 12-ounce flat top, white can, red bands, gold or silver shield, single version of each. $15

READING BREWING COMPANY, South 9th and Little Laurel Streets (successor to Old Reading Brewery, Inc.; aka: Bergheim Brewing Company, Mein Brewing Company)

Bergheim Beer, Reading Brewing or Bergheim Brewing, two-label 12-ounce flat or tab top, white can, farm, waterfall, multiversions. *(See photo 235)*
Flat top, ...$5
Tab top, ...$3

Manheim Premium Beer, Reading Brewing Company, single-label 12-ounce flat or tab top, white can, red label, ''Premium'' in gold, single version of each top. *(See photo 236)*
Flat top, ... $10
Tab top, ...$8

Mein Beer, Mein Brewing Company, two-label 12-ounce tab top, multicolored can, waterfall, single version. $8

Prizer Extra Dry Premium Beer, Reading Brewing Company, two-label 12-ounce flat or tab top, white can, red and gold bands, silver stein, single version of each top.
Flat top, ... $10
Tab top, ...$8

Reading Light Premium Beer, Reading Brewing Company, two label 12- or 16-ounce flat top, white can, blue label, gold circles, multiversions.
12-ounce, ...$5
16-ounce, ...$7

Reading Brewing Company, two-label 12-ounce tab top, set of two called ''Bicentennial Collector's Series'': ''Declaration of Independence,'' ''The Star Spangled Banner''; single version of each. *(See photo 237)* $3

(From left to right)
Photo 235. Bergheim Beer.
Photo 236. Manheim
Premium Beer.
Photo 237. Reading
Light Premium Beer.
Photo 238. Reading
Light Premium Beer.

Reading Brewing Company, single- or two-label 12- or 16-ounce tab top, white can, blue label, red circles, multiversions. *(See photo 238)*

12-ounce,...$2
16-ounce,...$3

Yorktown Extra Fine Premium Beer, Reading Brewing Company, single-label 12-ounce flat or tab top, white can, red bands, silver shield, single version of each top.

Flat top,...$8
Tab top,...$6

SUNSHINE BREWING COMPANY, West Elm and Gordon Streets (successor to Barbey, Inc.; aka: Bavarian Brewing Company, Esslingler Brewing Company, Jamaica Brewing Company, Knickerbocker Brewing Company, Mulheim Brewing Company)

Big Apple Premium Beer, Sunshine Brewing Company, two-label 12-ounce flat top, white can, blue label outlined in silver, single version. $125

Dart Premium Light Beer, Bavarian Brewing Company, two-label 12-ounce tab top, red can, split metallic gold label, single version. $35

Esslinger Premium Beer, Esslinger Brewing Company, two-label 12-ounce tab top, gold can, white label outlined in red, pirate, single version. $20

Giant Food Premium Beer, two-label 12-ounce tab top, red and white can, Giant Food logo, multiversions. $5

Jamaica Sun Premium Beer, Jamaica Brewing Company, two-label 12-ounce tab top, metallic gold can, white label, single version. $50

Mulheim Draft Beer, Mulheim Brewing Company, two-label 12-ounce tab top, red can, gold barrel, black lettering, single version. $30

Mulheim Brewing Company, two-label 12-ounce tab top, red can, gold barrel, gold bands, multiversions. $15

Playmate Malt Liquor, Sunshine Brewing Company, two-label 12-ounce tab top, white can, stylized woman's mouth, eye, and eyebrow, single version. $250

Playmate Premium Beer, Sunshine Brewing Company, two-label 12-ounce tab top, white can, stylized woman's mouth, eye, and eyebrow, single version. $250

Royal Farms Super Premium Beer, Sunshine Brewing Company, two-label 12-ounce flat top, white can, red and blue label, "PREMIUM" in blue, single version...$200

Ruppert Knickerbocker New York's Famous Beer, Knickerbocker Brewing Company, two-label 12-ounce tab top, metallic gold can, white label, three ribbons, single version. $5

Shopwell Premium Beer, Sunshine Brewing Company, two-label 12-ounce flat top, white can, metallic gold bands, red lettering, single version. $25

Sunshine Bock Beer, Sunshine Brewing Company, two-label 12-ounce flat top, white can, red label, metallic gold trim, single version. $125

Sunshine Extra Light Premium Beer, Bavarian Brewing Company, two-label, 12-ounce, high-profile cone top, white or yellow can, red label, metallic gold trim, single version of each. *(See photo 239)* Either version,.................$125

Sunshine Premium Beer, Sunshine Brewing Company, single-label 12-ounce flat top or quart cone top, white can, metallic gold bands, red label outlined in gold, single version.

12-ounce,.. $35

Quart,...$225

Sunshine Brewing Company, two-label 12-ounce flat or tab top, white can, yellow sun, "SUNSHINE" in black, multiversions. $40

Town & Country VVS Sparkling Malt Liquor, Sunshine Brewing Company, single-label 12-ounce flat top, white can, blue label, "vvs" in red, single version.. $200

Scranton

STANDARD BREWING COMPANY, Walnut Street and Pennsylvania Avenue

Cardinal Premium Beer, single-label, 12-ounce, high-profile cone top, white can, gold stripes, "CARDINAL" in red, minor versions. $175

Shamokin

FUHRMANN & SCHMIDT BREWING COMPANY, 301 East Commerce Street (aka: Fuhrmann & Schmidt, Innsbrau Brewing Company, Brewmasters International, Charles D. Kaier)

F & S Beer, Fuhrmann & Schmidt, two-label 12-ounce flat or tab top, white can, red label, metallic gold bands, minor versions.

Flat top, ... $15

Tab top,.. $12

Photo 239 (left). Sunshine Extra Light Premium Beer. Photo 240 (right). State Fair Premium Beer.

F & S Pilsener Beer, Fuhrmann & Schmidt, single-label, 12-ounce, high-profile or quart cone top, red can, yellow scroll label, INTERNAL REVENUE TAX PAID, WITHDRAWN FREE, single version of each.
12-ounce, ... $175
12-ounce, WITHDRAWN FREE, camouflage can, ... $300
Quart, ... $200
Fuhrmann & Schmidt, single-label, 12-ounce, high-profile or quart cone top, white can, metallic gold label and bands, red oval, IRTP or non-IRTP, single version of each.
12-ounce non-IRTP, ... $150
12-ounce IRTP, ... $160
Quart non-IRTP, ... $185
Quart IRTP, ... $200
F & S Premium Beer, Fuhrmann & Schmidt, two-label 12-ounce flat top, white can, red oval label outlined in metallic gold, multiversions. $40

Fuhrmann & Schmidt, two-label 12-ounce flat top, white can, square red label, metallic gold square, multiversions. $30

F & S Premium Bock Beer, Fuhrmann & Schmidt, two-label 12-ounce flat top, white can, red square label, single version. $150

F & S Royale Ale, Fuhrmann & Schmidt, single-label, 12-ounce, high-profile or quart cone top, white can, metallic gold label overlaid with green, minor versions.
12-ounce, ... $150
Quart, ... $250

G.E.M. Premium Beer, Fuhrmann & Schmidt, two-label 12-ounce flat top, white can, "G.E.M." in red, white, and blue, single version. $40

G.E.X. Premium Beer, Fuhrmann & Schmidt, two-label 12-ounce flat or tab top, white can, "G.E.X." in red, white, and blue, minor versions. $40

Kaier's Special Beer, Charles D. Kaier, two-label 12-ounce tab top, white can, red circle label, multiversions. $5

L.F. Rheinbrau Lager Beer, Fuhrmann & Schmidt or Innsbrau Brewing, two-label 12-ounce tab top, gold can, blue label, multiversions. $5

Master Premium Beer, Fuhrmann & Schmidt, two-label 12-ounce flat top, white can, red triangle label, "beer" in black, single version. $50

Parks Beverages Super Quality Premium Beer, Fuhrmann & Schmidt, red can, large white label, single version. $300

State Fair Premium Beer, Fuhrmann & Schmidt, two-label 12-ounce flat or zip top, silver can, blue label and lettering, single version of each. *(See photo 240)*
Flat top, ... $85
Zip top, ... $80
Fuhrmann & Schmidt, two-label 12-ounce tab top, white can, blue label outlined in red, single version. $115

Thrifty Lager Beer, Brewmasters International, two-label 12-ounce tab top, black and silver can, single version. $35

United Milwaukee Premium Beer, Fuhrmann & Schmidt, two-label 12-ounce flat top, black and white can, "PREMIUM" in red, single version. $65

United Renaee Premium Beer, Fuhrmann & Schmidt, two-label 12-ounce flat top, red and white can, "PREMIUM" in black, single version. $75

Shenandoah

COLUMBIA BREWING COMPANY, 101-115 South Ferguson Street

Columbia Preferred Beer, two-label 12-ounce flat top, white can, red label outlined in metallic gold, gold stars, minor versions. $75

Senator's Club Draft Beer, single-label 12-ounce flat top, white can, gold bands, "DRAFT BEER" in black, single version. $85

Senator's Club Premium Beer, single-label 12-ounce flat top, white can, gold bands, "PREMIUM BEER" in black, single version. $75

Whitman & Lord Extra Dry Beer, two-label 12-ounce flat top, silver green can, black label, single version. $100

Two-label 12-ounce flat top, green can, black label, single version. $85

Smithtown

JONES BREWING COMPANY, 2nd Street and B & O Railroad

Esquire Premium Beer, two-label 12-ounce tab top, brown or tan woodgrain can, white label, multiversions. $3

Fort Pitt Beer, two-label 12-ounce tab top, gold can, red label outlined in white, single version. $10

Fort Pitt Special Beer, two-label 12-ounce tab top, red and yellow filigree can, white label, single version. $3

Old Shay Golden Cream Ale, two-label 12-ounce tab top, yellow can, black label, single version. $3

Stoney's Pilsener Beer, two-label, 12-ounce, high-profile cone, flat, or tab top, split white and orange label, "STONEY'S" in white, multiversions.
Cone top, ... $75
Flat top, ... $50
Tab top, ... $45

Two-label 12-ounce tab top, white can, gold bands, "STONEY'S" in red or black, multiversions. $5

Jones Brewing Company has produced a number of brands in aluminum cans. The collector value of these cans is $1.

Stowe Township

DUQUESNE BREWING COMPANY PLANT #2, Thomas Street and McKee Avenue

Carnegie Beer, single-label, 12-ounce, high- or low-profile, or quart cone top, white can, red band, man and dog label, INTERNAL REVENUE TAX PAID, single version of each.
Low-profile, ... $250
High-profile, ... $235
Quart, ... $350

Duquesne Can-O-Beer, single-label, 12-ounce, high- or low-profile, or quart cone top, brown woodgrain can, gold bands, multiversions.

12-ounce,... $85

Quart,.. $150

Single-label, 12-ounce, high-profile cone top, camouflage can, WITHDRAWN FREE, single version. $300

Two-label, 12-ounce, high-profile cone top, white can, prince on red label, IRTP or non-IRTP, single version of each.

Non-IRTP, ... $75

IRTP, ... $85

Duquesne Keg-O-Beer, single-label, 12-ounce, low-profile cone top, brown woodgrain can, gold bands, INTERNAL REVENUE TAX PAID, minor versions.

.... $100

Stroudsburg

STROUDSBURG BREWING COMPANY, 1st Street and Lincoln Avenue

Stroud Cream Ale, two-label 12-ounce flat top, no "New York Distributor," OPENING INSTRUCTIONS, INTERNAL REVENUE TAX PAID, single version. ..Unique

Stroud Export Beer, two-label 12-ounce flat top, with or without "New York Distributor," OPENING INSTRUCTIONS, INTERNAL REVENUE TAX PAID, single version of each. Either version,...Unique

Wilkes-Barre

THE LION, INC., 5 and 6 Hart Street

Bartels Pure Beer, single-label 12-ounce tab top, yellow can, brown label, single version. $20

Gibbons Ale, single-label, 12-ounce, low-profile or quart cone top, gold can, black label, INTERNAL REVENUE TAX PAID, multiversions 12-ounce, single-version quart.

12-ounce,.. $135

Quart,.. $200

Gibbons Beer, single-label, 12-ounce, low- or high-profile, or quart cone top, gold can, red label, INTERNAL REVENUE TAX PAID, multiversions.

Low-profile, ... $75

High-profile,... $75

Quart,.. $135

Gibbons Bock Beer, single-label, 12-ounce, low-profile cone top, gold can, blue label, goat, single version. $250

Gibbons Premium Beer, two-label 12-ounce flat, soft, or tab top, gold can, red "G," white label, multiversions.

Flat and soft top, ...$3

Tab top,..$2

Gibbons Premium Quality Beer, single-label, 12-ounce, high-profile, or quart cone top, metallic gold can, red label, single versions.

12-ounce, ... $75
Quart, ... $125

The Lion, Inc. has and is producing a wide variety of brands in aluminum and bi-metal cans. Mandatories used include THE LION, POCONO BREWING COMPANY, and STEGMAIER BREWING COMPANY. Collector value is $1.

STEGMAIER BREWING COMPANY, Market and Baltimore Streets (aka: Gold Medal Brewing Company)

Gold Medal Beer, Stegmaier Brewing Company, single-label, 12-ounce, low- or high-profile, or quart cone top, brown can, red or brown shields, INTERNAL REVENUE TAX PAID, WITHDRAWN FREE—camouflage can, multiversions.

Low- or high-profile, ... $90
Quart, ... $135
WITHDRAWN FREE—camouflage can, ... $225

Gold Medal Select Pennsylvania Beer, Gold Medal Brewing Company, two-label 12-ounce tab top, dull or metallic gold can, red band and label, single version of each. $35

Stallion XII Brand Malt Liquor, Gold Medal Brewing Company, two-label 12-ounce tab top, white can, gold label, "STALLION XII" in red, two versions. $75

Stegmaier Gold Medal Beer, Stegmaier Brewing Company, single-label, 12-ounce, high-profile cone or flat top, white and metallic gold can, "QUALITY SINCE 1857," single version of each.

Flat top, ... $75
Cone top, ... $110

Stegmaier Brewing Company, single-label, 12-ounce, high-profile cone or flat top, red can, white label outlined in metallic gold, single version of each.

Flat top, ... $85
Cone top, ... $125

Stegmaier Brewing Company, single- or two-label 12-ounce flat or tab top, metallic gold can, white label, red trim, minor versions.

Flat top, ... $40
Tab top, ... $35

Stegmaier Brewing Company, two-label 12-ounce tab top, metallic gold can, vertical red and white stripes, multiversions. $5

Stegmaier's Ale, Stegmaier Brewing Company, single-label, 12-ounce, low-profile or quart cone top, green can, red label, INTERNAL REVENUE TAX PAID, single version.

12-ounce, ... $125
Quart, ... $225

Stegmaier's Gold Medal Beer, Stegmaier Brewing Company, single-label, 12-ounce, high-profile or quart cone top, white can, brown label, single version.

12-ounce, ... $85
Quart, ... $125

Rhode Island

Cranston

FALSTAFF BREWING COMPANY, Garfield Avenue and Cranston Street (successor to Narragansett Brewing Company; aka: Croft Brewing Company, Haffenreffer & Company, James Hanley Company, G. Krueger Brewing Company)

Ambassador Export Brewed Beer, G. Kruger Brewing Company, two-label 12-ounce flat, zip, or tab top, white woodgrain can, dancers, red, gold, and blue label, single version of each top.
Flat top, ... $85
Zip top, ... $80
Tab top, ... $75
Boh Bohemian Lager Beer, Haffenreffer & Company, two-label 12-ounce tab top, white can, metallic gold square label, "LAGER" in red, multiversions. ..$8
Croft Imported Quality Ale, Falstaff Brewing and Haffenreffer & Company, two-label 12- or 16-ounce flat or zip top, gold can, green and white label, multiversions.
12-ounce, either top, ... $35
16-ounce, either top, ... $40
Croft The Champion Ale, Croft Brewing Company, single-label 12-ounce flat top, white can, green and yellow label, single version. $40
Falstaff Beer, Falstaff Brewing Company, two-label 12- or 16-ounce tab top, white can, stars, blue band, maroon and yellow shield, multiversions.
12-ounce, ... $5
16-ounce, ... $7.50
Haffenreffer Lager Beer, Haffenreffer & Company, two-label 12-ounce tab top, white can, red label, single version. $50

Hanley Export Beer, James Hanley Company, single-label 12-ounce flat top, yellow can, bluish label, single version. $15

Hanley Lager Beer, James Hanley Company, single-label 12-ounce tab top, yellow can, bluish label, white lettering, multiversions. $3

Hanley Pilsener Beer, James Hanley Company, single-label 12-ounce flat, zip, or tab top, yellow can, bluish label, white lettering, multiversions. All versions, ... $15

Kruger Beer, G. Kruger Brewing, single-label 12-ounce flat top, white can, dark metallic red label, metallic gold trim, multiversions. $35

G. Kruger Brewing, single-label 12-ounce flat, soft, zip, or tab top, white can, red label, "K-man" on green circle, multiversions. All versions, ... $50

G. Kruger Brewing, single-label 12-ounce zip or tab top, white can, red label, gold or silver trim, multiversions. $10

Kruger Cream Ale, G. Kruger Brewing, single-label 12- or 16-ounce flat top, white can, green label, gold trim, single version of each.
12-ounce, ... $50
16-ounce, ... $65

G. Kruger Brewing, single-label 12- or 16-ounce flat or zip top, white can, green label, "K-man" on red circle, multiversions.
12-ounce, ... $60
16-ounce, ... $75

G. Kruger Brewing, two-label 12- or 16-ounce flat or tab top, white can, green label, gold trim, "K-man" on red patch, multiversions. $25

Kruger Pilsener Beer, Kruger Brewing, two-label 12-ounce tab top, white or gold can, "PILSENER" in red, multiversions. $5

Kruger Pilsener Draft Beer, Kruger Brewing, two-label 12-ounce tab top, white can, gold bands and stripes, "DRAFT" in red, single version. $10

Pickwick Ale, Haffenreffer & Co., single-label 12-ounce tab top, red can, white label, black lettering, single version. $60

Falstaff Brewing brewed a wide array of brands using many mandatories in aluminum and bi-metal cans. A few brands might command as much as $5 collector value, but the vast majority are only worth $2 or less to the collector.

THE JAMES HANLEY COMPANY, 35 Jackson Street

Hanley Extra Dry Lager Beer, single-label 12-ounce flat top, greenish can, white label, green band, single version. $60

Hanley Extra Pale Ale, single-label 12-ounce flat top, gold can, white label, green band, single version. $75

Hanley Premium Export Lager Beer, two-label 12-ounce flat top, white can, blue label, white lettering, single version. $65

Hanley Select Export Lager Beer, two-label 12-ounce flat top, gold can, blue label, single version. $150

Hanley Special ** Ale,** single-label 12-ounce flat top, white can, green label outlined in gold, gold bands, single version. $65

Hanley's Extra Dry Lager Beer, single-label 12-ounce crowntainer, silver can, red label, single version. $300

Hanley's Extra Pale Ale, single-label, 12-ounce, J-spout cone top, light or dark purple can, INTERNAL REVENUE TAX PAID, single version of each. Either can, ... $125

Single-label 12-ounce crowntainer, silver can, purple label, INTERNAL REVENUE TAX PAID, two versions. $125

Single-label 12-ounce crowntainer or quart cone top, silver can, purple basket-weave and label, INTERNAL REVENUE TAX PAID, single version.
Crowntainer, ... $75
Quart, ... $125

Hanley's Extra Pale Lager Beer, single-label 12-ounce crowntainer, INTERNAL REVENUE TAX PAID, silver can, red label, single version. $250

NARRAGANSETT BREWING COMPANY, Garfield Avenue and Cranston Streets (predecessor to Falstaff Brewing Company)

Gold Label Ale, single-label 12-ounce flat top, gold can, hops, red label, multiversions. $200

Narragansett Ale, single-label 12-ounce flat top, metallic gold can, red label outlined in white, multiversions. $65

Single-label 12-ounce flat top, brown can, red label outlined in white, single version. $40

Single-label 12-ounce flat or zip top, white can, metallic gold label, ''HI NEIGHBOR,'' multiversions. $40

Two-label 12-ounce tab top, off-white can, white label outlined in green, red circle, multiversions. $20

Two-label 12-ounce tab top, gold can, diamonds, white label, green band, multiversions. $5

Narragansett Banquet Ale, single-label 12-ounce flat top or quart cone top, yellow label, ''ALE'' in red, OI or non-OI, INTERNAL REVENUE TAX PAID, multiversions.
12-ounce OI, ... $200
12-ounce non-OI, ... $175
Quart, ... $300

Narragansett Draft Beer, two-label 12-ounce tab top, greenish can, white label, ''DRAFT'' in white on red patch, single version. $60

Narragansett Extra Light Beer, single-label 12-ounce flat top, ''BEER'' in red, OPENING INSTRUCTIONS, INTERNAL REVENUE TAX PAID, single version. $300

Narragansett Lager Beer, single-label 12- or 16-ounce flat, soft, or zip top, white or greenish can, gold trim, ''HI NEIGHBOR,'' ''FLIP TOP'' in white on red patch some versions, multiversions.
12-ounce flat top, ... $25
12-ounce soft top, ... $25
12-ounce zip top, ... $40
16-ounce flat top, ... $35
16-ounce soft top, ... $40
16-ounce zip top, ... $50

Two-label 12- or 16-ounce flat, zip, or tab top, green can, white label, "HI NEIGHBOR . . . HAVE A GANSETT," multiversions.

12-ounce,... $10
16-ounce,... $12

Single-label 12-ounce tab top, blue or gold and white can, gold ships, single version of each.

Blue can,... $40
Gold can,... $30

Two-label 12- or 16-ounce tab top, gold can, white label, red band, multiversions.

12-ounce,..$7
16-ounce,... $10

Narragansett Light Ale, single-label 12-ounce flat top, metallic gold can, blue label, INTERNAL REVENUE TAX PAID, single version. $75

Narragansett Select Stock Lager, single-label 12-ounce flat top, gold can, green label, black trim, INTERNAL REVENUE TAX PAID, single version. $250

Single-label 12-ounce flat top, gold can, white label, black trim, IRTP or non-IRTP, multiversions.

IRTP, ...$100
Non-IRTP, ... $90

Williams Purple Cow, single-label 12-ounce tab top, gold can, purple label, single version...Exotic

ROGER WILLIAMS BREWING CORPORATION, 61 Troy Street

Roger Williams Ale, single-label 12-ounce flat top, enamel or metallic paint, INTERNAL REVENUE TAX PAID, single version of each. Either version, ...Exotic

Union Cream Ale, single-label 12-ounce flat top, gold can, white label, red lettering, INTERNAL REVENUE TAX PAID, single version. ....Exotic

South Carolina

No operating breweries since 1934. No beer cans produced.

South Dakota

No operating breweries since 1939. No beer cans produced.

Tennessee

/

Memphis

APOLPH COORS COMPANY, 5151 Raines Road

Purchased from the Stroh Brewery in 1990, this brewery produces nothing but aluminum cans with a collector value of $1.

JOS. SCHLITZ BREWING COMPANY, 5151 Raines Road

Built in 1971, the tab top, bi-metal, and aluminum cans produced by Schlitz carry a collector value of $1.

JOS. SCHLITZ BREWING COMPANY, DIVISION OF STROH BREWING, 5151 Raines Road (successor to Jos. Schlitz Brewing Company)

Brands of Schlitz and Stroh were produced in only aluminum cans with a collector value of $1.

TENNESSEE BREWING COMPANY, 11 West Butler Street

Berghoff 1887 Extra Dry Beer, single-label 12-ounce flat top, white can, metallic red and gold bands, ''BERGHOFF'' in black, single version. $300

De Soto Beer, single-label 12-ounce flat top, blue can, Cavalier, single version. .... Exotic

Goldcrest 51 Beer, single-label, 12-ounce, high profile cone top, blue can, white lines, metallic gold label outlined in white, dark blue band, INTERNAL REVENUE TAX PAID, single version. $350

Photo 241. Goldcrest 51 Premium Beer.

Goldcrest 51 Premium Beer, single-label, 12-ounce, high-profile or quart cone top, light blue can, white lines, light gold label outlined in white, light blue band, two versions 12-ounce, single-version quart.

12-ounce, ... $300

Quart, ... $400

Two-label 12-ounce flat top, metallic red can, metallic gold bands, white label outlined in metallic gold, single-version. *(See photo 241)* $125

Goldcrest 51 Select Beer, two-label, 12-ounce, high-profile or quart cone top, white can, metallic gold lines and label, red circle, single version.

12-ounce, ... $175

Quart, ... $300

Nashville

WILLIAM GERST BREWING COMPANY, 821 6th Avenue

Gerst 57 Premium Beer, two-label 12-ounce crowntainer, silver can, black label, "GERST" in red outlined in yellow, single version. $175

Gerst 77 Beer, two-label, 12-ounce, high-profile cone top, metallic gold can, red and white label, single version. $200

Texas

/

Dallas

DALLAS–FORT WORTH BREWING COMPANY, 1026 Young Street

Bluebonnet Extra Pale Beer, single-label, 12-ounce, high-profile cone top, metallic gold can, blue and white label, IRTP or non-IRTP, single version of each.
IRTP, ...$250
Non-IRTP, ...$235

SCHEPPS BREWING CORPORATION, Dallas

Cans with mandatory SCHEPPS BREWING CORPORATION, Dallas, TX, were actually brewed and filled by the Manhattan Brewing Company, Chicago, IL. For listings see Manhattan, Chicago.

TIME BREWING COMPANY, 1026 Young Street

Time Lager Beer, single-label, 12-ounce, high-profile cone top, gold can, red label, INTERNAL REVENUE TAX PAID, single version. ....Exotic

El Paso

FALSTAFF BREWING CORPORATION, 3801 Frutas (successor to Mitchell Brewing Company)

Falstaff Beer, single-label 12-ounce flat top, white can, gold and brown "FALSTAFF" shield, "THE CHOICEST PRODUCT OF THE BREWER'S ART,"
multiversions. $10

Two-label 12-ounce flat, zip, or tab top, white can, gold and brown "FALSTAFF" shield, "AMERICA'S PREMIUM QUALITY BEER," single version of each.

Flat top, ... $15
Others, ... $12

MITCHELL BREWING COMPANY, 3801 Frutas Street

Golden Grain Beer, two-label 12-ounce flat top, white can, checkerboard maroon label, metallic gold trim, single version. $40

Mitchell's Extra Dry Premium Beer, single-label 12-ounce flat top, metallic red can, metallic gold label outlined in white, IRTP or non-IRTP, minor versions.

IRTP, ... $225
Non-IRTP, ... $215

Mitchell's Premium Beer, two-label 12-ounce flat top, metallic red can, white label and stripes, "PREMIUM BEER" in black, multiversions. $125

Fort Worth

CARLING BREWING COMPANY, 7001 South Freeway

Carling Black Label Beer, single-label 12-ounce zip top, red can, black label outlined in white, "CARLING" on label, single version. $15

MILLER BREWING COMPANY, 7001 South Freeway (successor to Carling Brewing Company)

Cans produced at this plant, both aluminum and steel, are common and carry a collector value of not more than $1.

Galveston

ANHEUSER-BUSCH, INC., 775 Gellhorn Drive

Built in the mid-'60s, this plant produced very few steel cans. All Anheuser-Busch brands have been produced at this plant with a collector value of $1.

FALSTAFF BREWING CORPORATION, 3301 Church Street (successor to Galveston–Houston Breweries, Inc.)

Only cans that specially say "Galveston" are listed. Other cans could have been brewed and filled at Galveston but there is no way of knowing by the information provided on the cans.

Falstaff Beer, two-label 12-ounce flat top, white can, gold and brown "FALSTAFF" shield, gold bands, multiversions. $10

Two-label 12-ounce tab top, white can, gold and brown "FALSTAFF" shield, multiversions. $10

Falstaff Draft Beer, two-label 12-ounce tab top, white can, gold and maroon label, "DRAFT" on blue ribbon, single version. $10

This brewery produced a wide array of brands using several outside mandatories in aluminum cans before it closed in 1981. Collector value of these cans does not exceed $2.

Photo 242. Southern Select Beer.

GALVESTON–HOUSTON BREWERIES, INC., 3312 Church Street

Southern Select Beer, two-label, 12-ounce, J-spout cone or crowntainer, white or silver can, brown label, INTERNAL REVENUE TAX PAID, multiversions. ...$125

Southern Select Premium Quality Beer, single-label 12-ounce flat top, red and brown can, red trim, single version. $85

Two-label 12-ounce flat top, metallic gold can, yellow label, single version. *(See photo 242)*.. $60

GULF BREWING COMPANY, 5301 Polk Avenue

Buccaneer Beer, two-label 12-ounce flat top, gold can, white label, pirate, single version. $200

Charro Cerveza Beer, single-label 12-ounce flat top, white, red, yellow can, horse and rider, single version. $250

Grand Prize Beer, single-label 12-ounce flat top, gray or silver can, medals, "GRAND PRIZE" in red, OPENING INSTRUCTIONS, INTERNAL REVENUE TAX PAID, single version of each. $125

Single-label 12-ounce flat top, metallic gold can, red label and bands, IRTP or non-IRTP, single version of each.
IRTP, ... $85
Non-IRTP, ... $75

Single-label 12-ounce flat top, white can, blue sunburst, single version. $50

Grand Prize Lager Beer, single-label 12-ounce flat top, metallic silver label, "GRAND PRIZE" in red, OPENING INSTRUCTIONS, INTERNAL REVENUE TAX PAID, single version. $200

Grand Prize Light Dry Beer, single-label 12-ounce flat top, gold can, white bands, white label, single version. $75

Grand Prize Pale Dry Beer, single-label 12-ounce flat top, metallic gold can, white lines, white label, red trim, single version. $85

Single- or two-label 12-ounce flat top, silver can, white label, "PALE DRY" in red, single version of each. Either version, ... $65

Grand Prize Premium Quality Beer, single-label 12-ounce flat top, white and metallic gold can, red label, single version. $50

Kol Premium Quality Beer, single-label 12-ounce flat top, silver can, white stripes, blue label, single version. $15

THEO. HAMM BREWING COMPANY, 5301 Polk Avenue (successor to Gulf Brewing Company)

Grand Prize Premium Quality Beer, two-label 12-ounce tab top, white can, red label, gold bands and stripes, single version. $75

Hamm's Beer, single-label 12-ounce aluminum tab top, blue can, white crown, "HAMM'S" in red, message from brewery president, single version. $40

Two-label 12-ounce aluminum tab top, blue can, white crown, "HAMM'S" in red, "REFRESHING AS THE LAND OF SKY BLUE WATERS," multiversions. $5

Longview

JOS. SCHLITZ BREWING COMPANY, 1400 West Cotton

Old Milwaukee American Light Genuine Draft Beer, two-label 14-ounce tab top, red and white can, multiversions. $3

Schlitz Beer, two-label 10-ounce flat or tab top, white can, globe, gold or silver bands, multiversions. $4

Two-label 10-ounce tab top, white can, globe, no bands, multiversions. $4

JOS. SCHLITZ BREWING COMPANY, DIVISION OF STROH BREWING COMPANY, 1400 West Cotton Street

All cans produced by Stroh Brewing at this plant are aluminum cans with a collector value of $1.

San Antonio

G. HEILEMAN BREWING COMPANY, 542 Lone Star Lane (successor to Olympia Brewing Company)

Only aluminum cans were produced by Heileman at this plant. The collector value of these cans is $1.

LONE STAR BREWING COMPANY, 542 Lone Star Boulevard

Brut Super Premium Beer, two-label 12-ounce tab top, black can, red label outlined in metallic gold, two versions. *(See photo 243)* $40

Lime Lager Ultra Light Beer, two-label 12-ounce tab top, white can, green label, "LIME LAGER" in white, single version. *(See photo 244)* $40

Lone Star Beer, two-label 12-ounce flat top, brown can with yellow tinge, brown label, IRTP or non-IRTP, multiversions.

IRTP, ... $75

Non-IRTP, ... $65

Two-label 12-ounce flat top, white can, red label outlined in metallic gold, blue ribbon, multiversions. $50

Photo 243 (left). Brut Super Premium Beer.
Photo 244 (center). Lime Lager Ultra Light Beer.
Photo 245 (right). Lone Star Beer.

Two-label 12-ounce flat top, white can, silver or gold outlined star on red label, multiversions. *(See photo 245)* $30

Two-label 12-ounce flat, soft, or tab top, white can, solid gold star on red label, silver or gold patch, multiversions. $15

Two-label 12-ounce tab top, white can, small red labels, small gold metallic circles, multiversions. $5

Two-label 12-ounce tab top, white can, red label in gold circles, small gold circles, multiversions. $5

Lone Star Handy Draft Beer, two-label 12-ounce tab top, good woodgrain can, red label, black lettering, Anniversary can, limited distribution, single version. $100

Two-label 12-ounce tab top, silver can, red shield label, black lettering, "NON-PASTEURIZED," multiversions. $5

Two-label 12-ounce tab top, silver can, red shield label, "HONEST TO GOODNESS" or "CHARCOAL FILTERED," multiversions. $5

OLYMPIA BREWING COMPANY, 542 Lone Star Boulevard
(successor to Lone Star Brewing Company)

Purchased in 1978, Olympia Brewing Company produced only aluminum cans at this brewery. Collector value will not exceed $1.

PEARL BREWING COMPANY, 312 James Street (successor to
San Antonio Brewing Association)

Brown Derby Lager Beer, two-label 12-ounce tab top, white can, red label outlined in brown, multiversions. $2

Country Club Malt Liquor, two-label, 8-, 12-, and 16-ounce tab top, white can, metallic gold label, "COUNTRY CLUB" in red outlined in gold, multiversions. $2

County Club Premium Light Beer, two-label 8- or 12-ounce tab top, yellow can, red circle, "COUNTRY CLUB" in black, multiversions.
8-ounce, ... $15
12-ounce, ... $10
12-ounce aluminum, ... $5

Country Club Stout Malt Liquor, two-label 12-ounce tab top, white can, gold lettering, "XXX" on blue oval, single version. $3

Country Tavern Beer, two-label 12-ounce tab top, woodgrain label, "COUNTRY TAVERN" in brown, single version. $2

Goetz Beer, single-label 12-ounce tab top, white can, blue label, single version. $2

Pearl Beer, two-label 12- or 16-ounce tab top, light or dark gold can, red label outlined in white, multiversions. $10

Pearl Dark Draft Beer, two-label 12-ounce tab top, metallic gold can, black label, red circle, single version. $100

Pearl Draft Beer, two-label 12-ounce tab top, gold can, large red label outlined in white, "PEARL" in black, multiversions. $15

Pearl Fine Lager Beer, two-label 12- or 16-ounce tab top, white can, red circle label, full-color waterfall scene, multiversions. $10

Two-label 12- or 16-ounce tab top, yellow can, red circle, black, white, and silver waterfall scene, multiversions. $3

Two-label 8- or 12-ounce tab top, white can, red label, full-color waterfall scene, "PREMIUM LIGHT," single version.
8-ounce, ...$5
12-ounce, ...$3

Pearl Genuine Draft Lager Beer, two-label 12-ounce tab top, blue can, red label and "PEARL" outlined in silver, single version. $20

Pearl Lager Beer, single-label 12-ounce flat top, woodgrain barrel can, red label, "PREMIUM XXX QUALITY," minor versions. $75

Two-label 12-ounce flat top, gold can, red label, white stripes, single version. $50

Two-label 12-ounce flat top, yellow can, red label, "THE GEM OF FINE BEER," multiversions. $35

Two-label 12-ounce flat top, yellow or white can, sunburst, "THE GEM OF FINE BEER," multiversions. $40

Two-label 12- or 16-ounce flat or soft top, white can, red label, "FAMOUS SPRING WATER, FAMOUS AS THE COUNTRY OF 10,000 SPRINGS," multiversions.
12-ounce, ...$5
16-ounce, ...$7

Pearl Brewing has and is putting out a wide array of brands, using a wide array of mandatories, in aluminum or bi-metal cans. The collector value of these cans will not exceed $1.

SAN ANTONIO BREWING ASSOCIATION, 312 James Street

Pearl Lager Beer, single-label 12-ounce flat top, woodgrain barrel can, "PREMIUM XXX QUALITY," IRTP or non-IRTP, single version of each. *(See photo 246)*
IRTP, ...$100
Non-IRTP, ...$90

Shiner

SPOETLZ BREWING COMPANY, Brewery Street, Block 60 East End Addition

Chilympiad Beer, two-label 12-ounce flat top, "10th ANNIVERSARY," single version. $2

Photo 246. Pearl Lager Beer.

Czhilispel Premium Beer, two-label 12-ounce tab top, couple making chili, multiversions. $2

Shiner Premium Beer, two-label 12-ounce tab top, gold can, white label, red ribbon, multiversions. $2

Two-label 12-ounce tab top, white can, red lettering, multiversions. $1

Wurstest '79 Dark Beer, two-label 12-ounce tab top, white can, man dressed in German costume, single version. $1

Spoetzl Brewing also has produced other brands in aluminum cans. These cans have a collector value of up to $1.

Utah

Ogden

BECKER BREWING COMPANY, 1900 Lincoln Avenue (successor to Becker Products)

Becker's Best Pale Premium Quality Beer, two-label 12-ounce flat top, silver can, "BECKER'S BEST" in black red trim, single version. $65

Becker's Mellow Premium Beer, two-label 12-ounce flat top, white can, red and blue label, single version. $25

Golden Pilsener Premium Quality Beer, two-label 11- or 12-ounce flat top, metallic gold and red can, single version. $50

Unita Club Aged Golden Lager Beer, two-label 12-ounce flat top, metallic gold can, split red, white, and blue can, single version. $75

BECKER PRODUCTS, 1900 Lincoln Avenue

Becker's Best Pale Premium Quality Beer, single-label 12-ounce flat top, silver can, "BECKER'S BEST BEER" in black, red trim, OPENING INSTRUCTIONS, INTERNAL REVENUE TAX PAID, multiversions. *(See photo 247).* $100

Photo 247. Becker's Best Pale Premium Quality Beer.

Photo 248. Becker's Mellow Beer.

Single-label 12-ounce flat top, silver can, "BECKER'S BEST BEER" in black, red trim, single version. $75

Becker's Mellow Beer, two-label 11- or 12-ounce flat top, yellow can, metallic or enamel gold bands, "MELLOW" in red, multiversions. *(See photo 248)* .. $20

Becker's Unita Club Mellow Beer, two-label 12-ounce flat top, silver can, red and blue label, "MELLOW" in red, multiversions. $75

Brewer's Choice Premium Pale Dry Beer, two-label 12-ounce flat top, brown and white can, "PREMIUM PALE DRY" in red, single version. $125

Golden Pilsener Premium Quality Beer, two-label 11- or 12-ounce flat top, metallic gold and red can, multiversions. $60

Unita Club Aged Golden Lager Beer, two-label 12-ounce flat top, metallic gold can, red, white, and blue split label, multiversions. $85

Unita Club Old Style Lager Beer, single-label 12-ounce flat top, gray can, wide red band, split blue label, OPENING INSTRUCTIONS, INTERNAL REVENUE TAX PAID, multiversions. $150

Unita Club Old Type Lager Beer, single-label 12-ounce flat top, gray can, wide red band, split blue label, "TYPE" instead of "STYLE," OPENING INSTRUCTIONS, INTERNAL REVENUE TAX PAID, single version. $250

Salt Lake City

FISHER BREWING COMPANY, 160 South 10th West Street

Fisher Beer, two-label 12-ounce flat top, metallic gold can, white stripes, blue label, multiversions. $50
"EXPORT BEER, NOT FOR SALE IN UTAH," $75

Two-label 11-, 12-, or 15-ounce flat top, metallic gold can, white stripes, red label, minor versions.
11-ounce, ... $30
12-ounce, ... $25
15-ounce, ... $40

Fisher Premium Light Beer, two-label 12- or 16-ounce flat top, white can, red label, gold stripes, "PREMIUM LIGHT" on blue band, minor versions.
12-ounce, ... $7
16-ounce, ... $10

Fisher Premium Pilsener Beer, two-label 11- or 15-ounce flat top, white can, red label, gold bands and stripes, "PREMIUM PILSENER" on blue band, single version.

11-ounce, ... $15

15-ounce, ... $20

Super X Markets Pale Dry Beer, two-label 11-ounce flat top, metallic red and white can, "PALE DRY BEER" in white, single version. $150

GENERAL BREWING CORPORATION, 160 South 10th West Street (successor to Fisher Brewing Company)

Fisher Premium Light Beer, two-label 12- or 16-ounce flat or tab top, white can, red label, gold stripes, "PREMIUM LIGHT" on blue band, multiversions.
.... $5

Lucky Extra Light Beer, two-label 12-ounce tab top, gold and white can, small red "x," single version. $10

Lucky Fine Light Beer, two-label 12-ounce tab top, gold and white can, small red "x," single version. $10

Lucky Lager Aged For Flavor Beer, two-label 12- or 16-ounce zip or tab top, yellow can, white label, red "x," "AGED FOR FLAVOR," multiversions. $5

Lucky Light Draft Beer, two-label 12-ounce tab top, white and metallic gold can, small red "x," multiversions. $5

Super X Markets Pale Dry Beer, two-label 12-ounce flat top, metallic red and white can, "PALE DRY" in white, single version. $140

LUCKY LAGER BREWING COMPANY, 160 South 10th West Street (successor to General Brewing Company)

Fisher Premium Light Beer, single-label 12- or 16-ounce flat top, white can, red label, gold stripes, multiversions. $5

Lucky Lager Age Dated Beer, two-label 12- or 16-ounce flat top, white and gold can, large "x" in square label, "AGE DATED" with no text in label, single version of each. $15

Lucky Lager Age Dated Premium Beer, two-label 12- or 16-ounce flat top, yellow can, white label outlined in metallic gold, "AGE DATED," multiversions. $5

Lucky Lager Aged For Flavor, two-label 12-ounce flat top, yellow can, white label, red "x," multiversions. $5

Vermont

No operating breweries since 1893. No cans.

Virginia

Norfolk

CENTURY BREWING CORPORATION, 710 Washington Street (successor to Jacob Ruppert–Virginia, Inc.)

Banner Extra Dry Premium Beer, single-label 12-ounce flat top, white can, red label, "PREMIUM BEER" in blue, single version. *(See photo 249)* $25

Brown Derby Lager Beer, single-label 11-ounce flat or zip top, white can, "BROWN DERBY" in brown outlined in gold, single version of each. $20

Champale Extra Sparkling Malt Liquor, single-label 12-ounce flat top, green can, white label, "SPARKLING" in red, multiversions. $15

Embassy Club Extra Dry Beer, single-label 12-ounce flat top, metallic gold can, red label, white trim, single version. $50

Gilt Edge Brand Ale, two-label 12-ounce flat top, green can, white label, red trim, single version. $60

Gilt Edge Brand Beer, two-label 12-ounce flat top, gold can, white label, red trim, single version. $50

Photo 249. Banner Extra Dry Premium Beer.

Grand Union Brand Premium Beer, two-label 12-ounce tab top, white can, yellow and red label, "PREMIUM BEER" in red, single version................. $25

Grenay Malt Liquor, single-label 12-ounce tab top, white can, square label, "MALT LIQUOR" in red, single version. $75

Old Dutch Brand Premium Lager Beer, single-label 12-ounce flat, zip, or tab top, red can, white label, black ribbon, single version of each.
Flat top, ... $75
Zip top,... $70
Tab top,... $60

Olde Virginia Special Premium Beer, single-label 12-ounce flat top, red can, black label outlined in yellow, single version. $175

Red Fox Premium Beer, single-label 12-ounce flat top, red can and white can, "RED FOX" in white, single version. $175

Regent Beer, single-label 16-ounce flat or tab top, white can, red label, "KING SIZE" in yellow, "BREWERY FRESH," single version of each top.
Flat top, ... $35
Tab top,... $30

Regent Premium Ale, single-label 12-ounce flat or tab top, white can, green label, yellow trim, "BREWERY FRESH," single version of each top.
Flat top, ... $75
Tab top,... $65

Regent Premium Beer, single-label 12-ounce flat top, white can, maroon label, single version. $35

Single-label 12-ounce flat top, white can, dark red label, "JAMESTOWN FESTIVAL YEAR," minor versions. $85

Single-label 12- or 16-ounce flat, zip, or quart cone top, white can, dark red label, multiversions.
12-ounce,... $40
16-ounce,... $50
Quart,.. $100

Seven-Eleven Premium Quality Beer, two-label 12-ounce flat top, white can, square metallic gold label, "7" in red, "11" in green, single version. $85

Spearman Ale, two-label 12-ounce tab top, green can, "SPEARMAN" in white on red band, single version. $35

Spearman Bavarian Style Beer, two-label 12-ounce tab top, white and metallic gold can, red ribbon, single version. $100

Tudor Premium Quality Beer, single-label 12-ounce flat top, red can, blue label, helmet, single version. $25

Tudor Premium Quality Cream Ale, single-label 12-ounce flat top, green can, white label, helmet, single version. $35

Viking Premium Beer, two-label 12-ounce flat top, white can, yellow label, "VIKING" in red, single version. $100

CHAMPALE PRODUCTS, INC., 710 Washington Street (successor to Century Brewing Corporation; aka: Champale Products, Embassy Club Brewing Company, Grenay Brewing Company, Monticello Brewery Company, Spearman Brewing Company, Tudor Brewing Company, Tuxedo Brewing Company)

Brown Derby Lager Beer, Champale Products, two-label 12-ounce flat top, white can, "BROWN DERBY" in brown outlined in gold, single version. $40

Champale Extra Dry Sparkling Malt Liquor, Champale Products, two-label 12-ounce tab top, green and yellow can, champale glass, multiversions. $15

Embassy Club Extra Dry Beer, Embassy Club Brewing, single-label 12-ounce flat top, gold can, red label, white lettering, single version. $50

Grand Union Premium Beer, Champale Products, two-label 12-ounce flat or tab top, metallic gold and yellow can, red label, "BEER" in red, multiversions. $15

Grenay Malt Lager, Grenay Brewing, white can, large square metallic gold label, "MALT LAGER" in red, single version. $175

Grenay Malt Liquor, Champale Products or Grenay Brewing, single-label 12-ounce tab top, white can, large square metallic gold label, "MALT LIQUOR" in red, single version of each. $100

Monticello Premium Ale, Monticello Brewing Company, two-label 12-ounce flat or zip top, green can, building outline in brown, white lettering, minor versions. $85

Monticello Brewing Company, two-label 12-ounce flat or zip top, green can, white circle label, building, minor versions. $65

Old Dutch Brand Premium Beer, Champale Products, two-label 12-ounce tab top, red can, white label, black ribbon, single version. $85

Regent Premium Beer, two-label 12- or 16-ounce tab top, white can, red label, "BREWERY FRESH" in yellow, single version of each.
12-ounce, ... $15
16-ounce, ... $20

Tudor Cream Ale, Tudor Brewing Company, two-label 12-ounce tab top, white can, green label, "A&P" in circle, single version. $20

Tudor Pilsner Beer, Tudor Brewing Company, two-label 12-ounce flat or tab top, white can, red label outlined in metallic gold, single version of each.
Flat top, ... $20
Tab top, ... $15

Tudor Premium Quality Ale, Tudor Brewing, two-label 12-ounce flat top, green can, white label, cornet, single version. $25

Tudor Brewing, two-label 12-ounce flat top, white can, green label outlined in metallic gold, single version. $35

Tudor Premium Quality Beer, Tudor Brewing Company, single-label 12-ounce flat top, red can, white lettering, helmet, multiversions. $25

Tudor Brewing Company, two-label 12- or 16-ounce flat top, red can, white lettering, cornet, single version of each.
12-ounce, ... $25
16-ounce, ... $30

Tudor Premium Quality Cream Ale, Tudor Brewing Company, single-label 12- or 16-ounce flat top, green can, white lettering, helmet, single version.
12-ounce, ... $30
16-ounce, ... $40

Tuxedo 51 Premium Beer, Tuxedo Brewing Company, two-label, 12- or 16-ounce flat or zip top, metallic red can, white label outlined in black, minor versions.
12-ounce, ... $50
16-ounce, ... $65

GLASGOW BREWING COMPANY, Boush and Brooke Avenue

Glasgo Select Beer, single-label, 12-ounce, high-profile cone top, black can, red square, "GLASGO" in yellow, IRTP or non-IRTP, single version of each.
Non-IRTP, ... $135
IRTP, ... $125

JACOB RUPPERT–VIRGINIA, INC., 710 Washington Street

Red Fox Premium Beer, single-label 12-ounce flat top, red and white can, "RED FOX" in white, IRTP or non-IRTP, single version of each.
Non-IRTP, ... $125
IRTP, ... $135

Ruppert Beer, single-label, 12-ounce flat top, yellow can, white label outlined in maroon, multiversions. $60

Richmond

HOME BREWING COMPANY, Harrison and Clay Streets

Pub Malt Lager, two-label 12-ounce tab top, brown and yellow can, "PUB" in white, single version. $50

Richbrau Beer, two-label, 12-ounce, high-profile cone, flat, or quart cone top, gold can, "RICHBRAU" in white on red band, single version of each.
Cone top, ... $75
Flat top, ... $60
Quart cone top, ... $100

Richbrau Bock Beer, two-label 12-ounce flat or zip top, silver can, black label, blue band, with or without goats, multiversions. $50

Richbrau Premium Beer, two-label, 12-ounce, high-profile cone or quart cone top, silver can, black label, red band, single version of each.
12-ounce, ... $60
Quart, ... $100

Two-label, 12-ounce, high-profile cone, flat, or quart cone top, gold can, black label, red band, multiversions.
Cone top $75
Flat top, ... $40
Quart, ... $100

Two-label 12- or 16-ounce flat, zip, or tab top, white or silver can, black label, red bar, multiversions. All versions, ... $15

Roanoke

MOUNTAIN BREWING COMPANY, 1218 Wise Avenue Southeast (successor to Virginia Brewing Company)

Dixie Beer, single-label 12-ounce flat top, metallic gold can, white label, single version. $150

Olde Virginia Special Premium Beer, single-label 12-ounce flat top, red can, black label outlined in yellow, single version. $150

VIRGINIA BREWING COMPANY, 1218 Wise Avenue Southeast

Olde Virginia Beer, single-label, 12-ounce, high-profile cone top, blue can, white label, "OLDE VIRGINIA" in white, single version. $100

Olde Virginia Special Export Beer, two-label, 12-ounce, high-profile cone top, red, white, and blue can, "SPECIAL" in white on red, single version. $100

Virginia's Famous Lager Beer, two-label, 12-ounce, high-profile cone top, white can, red lettering, "FAMOUS" in black, single version. $225

Williamsburg

ANHEUSER-BUSCH, INC., 200 Pocahontas Trail

Built in 1972, this plant has produced nothing but aluminum cans with a collector value not over $1.

Washington

Ellensburg

MUTUAL BREWING COMPANY, 414 West 5th

Gold Seal Beer, two-label, 12-ounce, low-profile or quart cone top, metallic gold can, blue bottom band, red circle label, no blue band across label, INTERNAL REVENUE TAX PAID, single version of each size. *(See photo 250)*
12-ounce,.. $400
Quart,...Exotic
Two-label, 12-ounce, low-profile or quart cone top, metallic gold can, blue bottom band, red circle label, blue ribbon across label, INTERNAL REVENUE TAX PAID, single version.
12-ounce,..Exotic
Quart,...Exotic

Olympia

OLYMPIA BREWING COMPANY, 1 Schmidt Place

Hamm's Beer, two-label 7-ounce aluminum tab top, red, white, and blue can, gold trim, single version. ....Exotic

Photo 250. Gold Seal Beer.

Olympia Export Type Beer, two-label 12- or 16-ounce aluminum tab top, yellow can, vertical pinstripes, called "Yankee" can, single version of each. *(See photo 251)*
12-ounce, ... $15
16-ounce, ... $35

Olympia Light Beer, two-label 12- or 16-ounce aluminum tab top, silver and white can, gold "v" band, test market can, called "Chevron" can, single version of each. *(See photo 252)*
12-ounce, ... $3
16-ounce, ... $5

Olympia Little Oly Beer, two-label 7-ounce steel tab top, silver and white can, gold "v" band, test market can, called "Chevron" can, single version. $5

Single-label 7-ounce flat top, white can, metallic gold bands and trim, orange horseshoe label, multiversions. $25

Single-label 7-ounce soft, zip, or tab top, white can, olive or olive-gold bands, yellow horseshoe label, multiversions. $3

Single-label 7-ounce tab top, white can, no bands, yellow horseshoe label, multiversions. $1

Single-label 12-ounce flat top, white can, metallic gold bands and trim, orange horseshoe label, "A LIGHT TABLE BEER," multiversions. $20

Two-label 11-, 12-, 15-, or 16-ounce flat, soft, zip, or tab top, white can, metallic gold bands and trim, orange horseshoe label, multiversions.
11-ounce, ... $8
12-ounce, ... $5
15-ounce, ... $10
16-ounce, ... $5

Two-label 12- or 16-ounce tab top, white can, olive or olive-gold bands, yellow horseshoe label, multiversions. $2

Port Orchard

SILVER SPRINGS BREWING COMPANY, East of Bay Street
on waterfront

Gold Seal Beer, two-label, 12-ounce, high- or low-profile cone or quart cone top, metallic gold band, wide blue bottom band, red circle label, single version of each.
12-ounce, ... Exotic
Quart, ... Exotic

*Photo 251 (left). Olympia Export
Type Beer.
Photo 252 (center). Olympia Light Beer.
Photo 253 (right). Oldstyle Pale Export
Lager Beer.*

Oldstyle Pale Export Lager Beer, single-label 12-ounce flat top, gray can, red trim, OPENING INSTRUCTIONS, INTERNAL REVENUE TAX PAID, "MANUFACTURED BY SALEM BREWERY ASSOCIATION FOR THE SILVER SPRINGS BREWING COMPANY, PORT ORCHARD, WASH.," single version. *(See photos 254 and 255)*.......Unique

Single-label quart cone top, gray can, red trim, INTERNAL REVENUE TAX PAID, single version. *(See photo 253)* $400

Seattle

APEX BREWING COMPANY, 2910 Airport Way South

Apex Beer, single label, 12-ounce, low-profile cone top, red can, gold label, INTERNAL REVENUE TAX PAID, single version.................................Unique

CENTURY BREWING ASSOCIATION, 606 Westlake Avenue North (successor to Horluck Brewing Company)

Rainier Beer, single-label 12-ounce flat top, yellow can, "RAINIER" in red over full-color mountain, OPENING INSTRUCTIONS, INTERNAL REVENUE TAX PAID, single version. *(See photo 256)* ....Exotic

Rheinlander Beer, single label 12-ounce flat top, yellow can, black band, single version...Exotic

G. HEILEMAN BREWING COMPANY, 3100 Airport Way South (successor to Rainier Brewing Company)

Heileman has produced a wide array of Heileman brands in aluminum cans. The collector value of these cans does not exceed $1.

HORLUCK BREWING COMPANY, 606 Westlake Avenue North

Horluck's Vienna Style Beer, single-label 12-ounce flat top, metallic gold can, white checkerboard, white label, "HORLUCK'S" in black, "BREWED ESPECIALLY FOR EXPORT," OPENING INSTRUCTIONS, INTERNAL REVENUE TAX PAID, single version...Exotic

Single-label 12-ounce flat top, metallic gold can, white checkerboard, white label, "HORLUCK'S" in red, "BREWED ESPECIALLY FOR EXPORT," OPENING INSTRUCTIONS, INTERNAL REVENUE TAX PAID, single version. ....Exotic

Photo 254 (left). Oldstyle Pale Export Lager Beer.
Photo 255 (center). Oldstyle Pale Export Lager Beer.
Photo 256 (right). Rainier Beer.

Single-label 12-ounce flat top, orange can, white label, "HORLUCK'S" in red outlined in gold, "FIRE BREWED," OPENING INSTRUCTIONS, INTERNAL REVENUE TAX PAID, single version. ....Exotic

RAINIER BREWING COMPANY, 3100 Airport Way South (successor to Sick's Rainier Brewing Company)

Rainier Ale, two-side 12-ounce aluminum tab top, green can, gold label, story on back of can, single version. $15

Rainier Beer, two-label 12- or 16-ounce steel tab top, white can, "RAINIER" in red, "MOUNTAIN FRESH LIGHT," multiversions. $5

Rainier Bold Malt Liquor, two-label 12-ounce aluminum tab top, black can, gold label, red trim, single version. $20

Rainier Old Stock Ale, two-label 12- or 16-ounce tab top, green can, light gold oval, multiversions. $3

Rainier Brewing Company, although not the first to use aluminum cans (Coors was in 1959), was the first brewery in the country to go to all aluminum cans (1971). All cans after 1971 have a collector value of up to $1, except as noted above.

SEATTLE BREWING AND MALTING COMPANY, 3100 Airport Way South

Beer, single-label 12-ounce flat top, green and gray can, airplane propeller, INTERNAL REVENUE TAX PAID, single version. *(See photo 257)* ....Exotic

Rainier Special Export Pale Beer, single-label 12-ounce flat top, white can, metallic gold bands, "RAINIER" in red outlined in metallic gold, "COOL BEFORE SERVING," OPENING INSTRUCTIONS, INTERNAL REVENUE TAX PAID, minor versions..$250

Rheinlander Brand Extra Pale Beer, single-label 12-ounce flat top, yellow can, orange castle, OPENING INSTRUCTIONS, INTERNAL REVENUE TAX PAID, single version. *(See photo 258)*..Exotic

SICK'S RAINIER BREWING COMPANY, 3100 Airport Way South (successor to Sick's Seattle Brewing and Malting; aka: Highlander Brewing Company, Rheinlander Brewing Company)

Highlander and Rheinlander brands will carry the HIGHLANDER BREWING and the RHEINLANDER mandatories. All other entries will carry the SICK'S RAINIER BREWING COMPANY mandatory.

(From left to right)
Photo 257. Beer.
Photo 258. Rheinlander
Brand Extra Pale Beer.
Photo 259. Rainier Beer.
Photo 260. Rainier Old
Stock Ale.

Highlander Premium Beer, two-label 12-ounce zip top, plaid can, white label, single version. $20

Two-label 12-ounce zip or tab top, white can, yellow bands, "HIGHLANDER" in blue, minor versions. All versions, ... $10

Rainier Beer, single-label 11-, 12-, 15-, or 16-ounce flat top, *not* all designs appear in all sizes, set can, called "Party Series," for description see "Party Series" under Seattle, Sick's Seattle Brewing and Malting, Rainier Beer. *(See photo 259)*

11-ounce, ... $40
12-ounce, ... $20
15-ounce, ... $50
16-ounce, ... $30

Single-label 11-, 12-, 15-, or 16-ounce flat or zip top, *not* all designs appear in all sizes, set can, called "Brewery Series," set of six cans: "Brewed Naturally," "Choicest Ingredients," "More Life Naturally," "Naturally Aged," "Naturally Light," "Specially Care," 21 colors: black, turquoise, dark purple, light purple, metallic blue, blue, blue-green, yellow-green, metallic green, green, metallic red, orange-red, metallic pink, metallic brown, bronze, gold, red-gold, yellow, blue-green, metallic orange, yellow-green (*not* all colors appeared on all cans; unlisted colors *do* appear at random on cans); 15- and 16-ounce variations included: "KING SIZE" on both front and back bottom, "KING SIZE" on bottom front, "KING SIZE RAINIER BEER" on bottom rear, "HALF QUART" on both front and back bottom, "HALF QUART" on bottom front, "HALF QUART RAINIER BEER" on rear; not all versions appear in all colors.

11-ounce, ... $40
12-ounce, ... $20
15-ounce, ... $50
16-ounce, ... $30

Two-label 12- or 16-ounce soft or tab top, white can, metallic or dull gold trim, "RAINIER" in red, "A TOUCH OF WORLD FLAVOR IN A LIGHT WESTERN BEER," multiversions.

Metallic soft top (12-ounce only), ... $25
12-ounce tab top, ... $15
16-ounce tab top, ... $20
Dull trim all versions, ... $10

Two-label 12- or 16-ounce tab top, white can, "light" in red, many "light" in yellow or gold covering can, multiversions.

12-ounce, ... $10
16-ounce, ... $12

Rainier Exposition Ale, two-label 12-ounce flat top, paper label, brown can, gold label, single version. $200

Rainier Light Light, two-label 12-ounce tab top, gold can, black lettering, single version. $100

Rainier Not-So-Light, two-label 12-ounce tab top, blue can, white lettering, two versions. $75

Rainier Old Stock Ale, two-label 12-ounce tab top, green can, black ribbon, lion and unicorn, single version. $5

Two-label 11-, 12-, or 16-ounce flat top, green can, woodgrain label, single version of each. *(See photo 260)* All sizes, ... $10

Photo 261 (left). Rainier Premium Malt Liquor.
Photo 262 (center). Rainier Spur Stout Malt Liquor.
Photo 263 (right). Brew 66 Sick's Select Beer.

Two-label 11-, 15-, or 16-ounce flat, zip, or tab top, green can, gold speckled label, multiversions.
11-ounce, ... $10
15-ounce, ... $20
16-ounce, ... $10
Two-label 12-ounce flat top, green can, light gold oval label, multiversions...$3

Rainier Premium Malt Liquor, two-label 16-ounce tab top, white can, yellow label, crown, single version. *(See photo 261)* .... Exotic

Rainier Spur Stout Malt Liquor, two-label 12- or 16-ounce zip or tab top, white can, metallic gold spur, "SPUR" in silver, red, or blue, "A SOPHISTICATED MALT LIQUOR," multiversions. *(See photo 262)*
12-ounce silver, ... $125
12-ounce red, ... $85
12-ounce blue, ... $150
16-ounce red, ... $65

Rheinlander Light Pale Beer, two-label 11- or 12-ounce flat, soft, zip, or tab top, white, orange, and yellow can, crown, multiversions.
11-ounce, ... $10
12-ounce soft top, ... $10
All others, ... $5

SICK'S SEATTLE BREWING AND MALTING COMPANY,
3100 Airport Way South (successor to Seattle Brewing and Malting Company)

Brew 66 A Lighter Beer, single-label 12-ounce flat top, metallic red can, yellow pinstripes and labels, single version. $150

Brew 66 Sick's Select Beer, single-label 12-ounce flat top, metallic red can, yellow pinstripes and label, single version. *(See photo 263)*.................. $125

Rainier Beer. The total number of variations for *all* "Rainier Jubilee" cans is somewhere between 1,000 and 1,100.

Single-label 12- or 16-ounce flat top, set cans, known as "Cartoon Series," six different cartoons: "Barbeque," "Do It Yourself," "Dutchman," "In the Northwest," "Outdoor Life," "Surprise Party"; 16 colors: black, turquoise, deep purple, metallic blue, blue, blue-green, yellow-green, metallic green, green, metallic red, red-orange, pink, gray, bronze, yellow, violet (*not all* colors appeared on all cans; unlisted colors *do* appear at random on cans). *(See photo 264)* Each, ... $30

Single-label 11-, 12-, 15-, or 16-ounce flat top (*not* all cans were produced in all sizes), set cans, known as "Party Series," 12 different designs: "Beer Garden," "Diamond Jubilee," "Drinking Songs," "Food," "Games," "Geographic," "Home & Entertainment," "Hunting & Fishing," "Parties & Music," "Paul Bunyan," "Sports," "Toasts"; 20 different colors: black, turquoise, dark purple, violet, light purple, metallic blue, blue, blue-green, yellow-green, metallic green, green, metallic red, red-orange, gray, bronze, yellow, flesh, pink, blue-green, metallic brown (*not all* colors appear on all cans; unlisted colors *do* appear at random on cans), cans may have a blank gold band or "RAINIER FOR LIFE" on gold band. *(See photos 265 and 266)* Each, ... $20

Rainier Extra Pale Beer, single-label 12-ounce flat top, silver hatched can, white label outlined in metallic gold, with or without "SICK'S SYMBOL OF QUALITY," minor versions.
With, ...$125
Without, ... $110

Rainier Famous Old Stock Ale, single-label 12-ounce flat top, green can, maroon and white label, single version. $65

Rainier Old Stock Ale, two-label 12-ounce flat top, green can, yellow label, orange star, multiversions. $30

Two-label 12- or 16-ounce flat top, green can, yellow label, unicorn and lion, minor versions.
12-ounce, ... $25
16-ounce, ... $40

Rainier Special Export Pale Beer, single-label 12-ounce flat top, white can, metallic gold bands, "RAINIER" in red outline in metallic gold, OPENING INSTRUCTIONS, INTERNAL REVENUE TAX PAID, minor versions. *(See photo 267)*
....$225

Rainier Truly Mild Beer, single-label 12-ounce flat top, silver and gold hatched can, white label, red lettering, known as "TRANSITION" can, single version. *(See photo 268)* $300

Single-label 12-ounce flat top, set cans, known as "Christmas Series," cartoon drawing of turkey, Christmas bells, and candelabra, band reads "BREWED IN WASHINGTON," colors: red and blue, red and purple, red and green, red and yellow. $100

(From left to right) Photo 264. Rainier Beer, "Cartoon Series."
Photo 265. Rainier Beer, "Party Series." Photo 266. Rainier Beer,
"Party Series." Photo 267. Rainier Special Export Pale Beer.
Photo 268. Rainier Truly Mild Beer.

Sick's Select Beer, single-label 12-ounce flat top, red can, yellow label, red "6," "EMIL SICK SELECT," OPENING INSTRUCTIONS, INTERNAL REVENUE TAX PAID, single version. $250

Single-label 12-ounce flat top, red can, yellow label, red "6," "SICK'S SELECT, THE BEST BEER IN TOWN," OPENING INSTRUCTIONS, INTERNAL REVENUE TAX PAID, single version. $225

Single-label 12-ounce flat top, red can, yellow label, red "6," "THAT FAMOUS BEER FROM SEATTLE," OPENING INSTRUCTIONS, INTERNAL REVENUE TAX PAID, two versions. $225
Camouflage can, ...Exotic

Single-label 12-ounce flat top, metallic red can, yellow label outlined in metallic gold, single version. *(See photo 269)* $100

Selah

YAKIMA VALLEY BREWING COMPANY, Selah

Martin's Beer, single-label, 12-ounce, high- or low-profile cone top, blue can, metallic gold stripes, white label outlined in metallic gold, IRTP or non-IRTP, single version of each. *(See photo 270)* Three cans total, ...Exotic

Spokane

BOHEMIAN BREWERIES, 1402 West 2nd

Bohemian Club Beer, two-label 12-ounce flat top, white can, gold bands and trim, "TASTES SO GOOD," minor versions. *(See photo 271)*......................$60

Two-label 12-ounce flat top, metallic red, white, and silver can, "BO BELONGS," minor versions. All versions, ...$45

Bohemian Club Light Export Lager Beer, single-label, 12-ounce, high- or low-profile cone top, red and green can, gold bands, white label, IRTP or non-IRTP, multiversions.
Non-IRTP, ...$90
IRTP, ...$100

(From left to right) Photo 269. Sick's Select Beer.
Photo 270. Martin's Beer. Photo 271. Bohemian Club Beer.
Photo 272. Excell Lager Beer. Photo 273. Washington's Viking Beer.

Bohemian Club Pale Beer, two-label 12-ounce flat top, white can, gold stripes, orange label, man, "OUR FINEST BEER IN 60 YEARS," minor versions. $40

BOHEMIAN DIVISION ATLANTIC BREWING COMPANY,
1402 West 2nd (successor to Bohemian Breweries, Inc.; aka: Bohemian Breweries, Atlantic Breweries, Durst Brewing Company, Tuxedo Brewing Company, K. C. Best Brewing Company)

Bohemian Club Beer, Bohemian Breweries, two-label 11- or 12-ounce flat top, metallic red, white, and silver can, "BO BELONGS," multiversions.
11-ounce, ... $60
12-ounce, ... $45
Brown Derby Lager Beer, Atlantic Brewing, two-label 11- or 12-ounce flat top, white can, "BROWN DERBY" in brown outlined in metallic gold, metallic gold oval, multiversions. $50
Champagne Velvet Beer, Atlantic Brewing, two-label 11-ounce flat top, gold can, white champagne glass, multiversions. $25
Atlantic Brewing, two-label 12-ounce flat top, gold can, white champagne glass, "NEW BOHEMIAN'S GOLDEN ANNIVERSARY SPECIAL BREW" on red, single version. $250
Durst Premium Quality Beer, Atlantic or Durst Brewing, single-label 12-ounce flat top, dark blue label, dull or metallic gold label, multiversions. $20
Excell Lager Beer, Atlantic Brewing, two-label 12-ounce flat top, blue and silver can, "EXCELL" in red, single version. *(See photo 272)* $50
Kol Premium Quality Beer, Atlantic Brewing, single-label 12-ounce flat top, silver can, white vertical bands, blue label, single version. $60
Olde English Brand "600" A Malt Liquor, Bohemian Breweries, single-label 12-ounce flat top, metallic gold can, red checkerboard, white label, "600" in red, multiversions. $100
Olde English Brand "600" A Stout Malt Liquor, Bohemian Breweries, single-label 11- or 12-ounce flat top, metallic gold can, red checkerboard, white label, "STOUT" in black, multiversions.
11-ounce, ... $150
12-ounce, ... $135
Tuxedo Premium 51 Beer, Atlantic or Tuxedo Brewing, single-label 12-ounce flat top, metallic red can, metallic gold bands and trim, white label, "TUXEDO PREMIUM 51 BEER" in red, multiversions. $50
Atlantic Brewing, single-label 12-ounce flat top, metallic red can, metallic gold bands and trim, white label, "TUXEDO PREMIUM BEER" in black, single version. $40
Washington's Viking Beer, single-label 11- or 12-ounce flat top, blue can, mountain scene, white label outlined in gold, single version of each size. *(See photo 273)* .... Exotic

GOLDEN AGE BREWERIES, 301 North Sheridan Street

Golden Age Beer, single-label low-profile cone top, camouflage can, single version. .... Unique

Golden Age Premium Beer, single-label, 12-ounce, low-profile cone top, red can, metallic gold bands, white label, WITHDRAWN FREE, single version. Exotic

Single-label, 12-ounce, low-profile cone top, metallic gold can, blue and white label, INTERNAL REVENUE TAX PAID, multiversions. *(See photo 274)* $250

Golden Age Select Beer, single-label, 12-ounce, low-profile or quart cone top, black can, red ribbon and stripe, single version of each size. *(See photo 275)*
12-ounce, ...$300
Quart, ...$450

Single-label quart cone top, yellow can, red ribbon and stripe, INTERNAL REVENUE TAX PAID, single version. $300

Golden Age Select Export Beer, single-label, 12-ounce, low-profile or quart cone top, yellow can, red ribbon and stripe, INTERNAL REVENUE TAX PAID, minor versions, single versions. *(See photo 276)*
12-ounce, ...$150
Quart, ...$250

Golden Age Select Export Pale Beer, single-label, 12-ounce, low-profile or quart cone top, yellow can, red label and ribbon, black and gold shield, INTERNAL REVENUE TAX PAID, single version.
12-ounce, ...$175
Quart, ...$300

SICK'S RAINIER BREWERY, INC., 901 West Broadway (successor to Sick's Spokane Brewery, Inc.)

Rainier Beer. This is the Rainier "Jubilee Series." For a complete description, see "Party Series" (under Seattle, Sick's Seattle Brewing and Malting, Rainier Beer) and "Brewery Series" (under Seattle, Sick's Rainier Brewing Company, Rainier Beer). Value of these cans is $5 which is more per can due a much smaller issue. *(See photo 277)*

SICK'S SPOKANE BREWERY, INC., 901 West Broadway

Rainier Beer. This is the Rainier "Jubilee Series." For a complete description see "Cartoon Series" and "Party Series" (under Seattle, Sick's Seattle Brewing and Malting, Rainier Beer). Value of these cans is $5, which is more per can than the Seattle versions due to a much smaller issue.

(From left to right) Photo 274. Golden Age Premium Beer.
Photo 275. Golden Age Select Beer. Photo 276. Golden Age Select
Export Beer. Photo 277. Rainier Beer, "Jubilee Series."
Photo 278. Rainier Special Export Pale Beer.

Rainier Extra Pale Beer, single-label 12-ounce flat top, silver hatched can, white label outlined in metallic gold, with or without "SICK'S SYMBOL OF QUALITY," single version of each.

With, ...$150

Without, ...$125

Rainier Special Export Pale Beer, single-label 12-ounce flat top, white can, metallic gold bands, "RAINIER" in red outlined in metallic gold, "COOL BEFORE SERVING," "OPENING INSTRUCTIONS," "INTERNAL REVENUE TAX PAID," minor versions. *(See photo 278)* $300

Rainier Truly Mild Beer, single-label 12-ounce flat top, silver hatched can, white label, "RAINIER" in red with mountain, called "Transition" can, single version. $250

Rheinlander Light Pale Beer, mandatory reads SPOKANE BREWING COMPANY, SPOKANE, WASHINGTON U.S.A., two-label 11-ounce flat top, white, orange, and yellow can, crown, single version. $25

Tacoma

CARLING BREWING COMPANY, 2120-2142 South "C" Street (successor to Heidelberg Brewing Company)

Black Label Beer, single- or two-label 12- or 16-ounce tab top, red can, black label outlined in white, map of the U.S. or world, multiversions. $10

Two-label 12- or 16-ounce tab top, red can, black label outlined in white, gold bands, minor versions. $15

Two-label 12-ounce tab top, tankard can, minor versions. $15

Carling Black Label Beer, single-label 11-, 12-, 15-, or 16-ounce flat or zip top, red can, black label outlined in white, "CARLING" on red label, multiversions.

11-ounce, ... $10

12-ounce, ...$8

15-ounce, ... $15

16-ounce, ... $10

Carling Heidelberg Beer, single-label 11-, 12-, 15-, or 16-ounce flat, zip, or tab top, yellow can, white round triangle label outlined in metallic gold, "HEIDELBERG" in red, "THE SLOW BREWED BEER," multiversions. $15

Single-label 12- or 16-ounce tab top, gold can, white round triangle label, "HEIDELBERG" in red, "THE SLOW BREWED BEER," multiversions. $20

Two- or three-label 12- or 16-ounce tab top, gold can, wide red band, four-line text in white, multiversions.

Three-label, ... $30

Two-label, ... $15

Two- or three-label 12- or 16-ounce tab top, gold can, two or three labels on wide red band.

Three-label, ... $35

Two-label, ... $20

Two-label 12- or 16-ounce tab top, gold can, wide red band, white label outlined in metallic gold, multiversions. $3

Two-label 12-ounce tab top, green can, white label and bands, gold trim, multiversions.
Steel, ... $3
Aluminum, ... $1

Heidelberg Beer, single-label 11- or 15-ounce flat top, yellow can, white label outlined in metallic gold, metallic red "STUDENT PRINCE," "THE SLOW BREWED BEER," minor versions.
11-ounce, ... $25
15-ounce, ... $40

Red Cap Ale, single-label 12- ounce zip top, gold diamonds, white label, red vertical band, single version. $10

Single-label 11-ounce flat top, green can, "CARLING" in oval, multiversions.
.... $10

Brewery produced Heidelberg and Tuborg in aluminum cans. Collector value is $1.

CARLING-NATIONAL BREWERIES, INC., 2120-2142 South "C" Street (successor to Carling Brewing Company)

All cans were produced in aluminum. Collector value is $1 *except*:

Heidelberg Beer, two-label 12- or 16-ounce tab top, gold and red can, "75 year anniversary" on lid, single version of each size.
12-ounce, ... $3
16-ounce, ... $5

COLUMBIA BREWERY, INC., 2120-2142 South "C" Street

Alt Heidelberg Brand Beer, single-label 12-ounce flat top, white can, "HEIDELBERG" in red, student prince on ribbon, two versions.
"TOAST OF THE COAST," $15
"BREWED IN THE NOR'WEST," $20

Alt Heidelberg Guest Beer, single-label 12-ounce flat top, gray can, wide red band, student prince in blue, OPENING INSTRUCTIONS, INTERNAL REVENUE TAX PAID, two versions, with or without red triangle. *(See photo 279)* .... Exotic

Alt Heidelberg Premium Pale Beer, single-label 12-ounce flat top, white can, pinstripes, gold student prince, two versions. *(See photos 280 and 281)* $100
"DU FINE," $250

Photo 279 (left). Alt Heidelberg Guest Beer.
Photo 280 (center). Alt Heidelberg Premium Pale Beer.
Photo 281 (right). Alt Heidelberg Premium Pale Beer.

Brown Derby Pilsner Beer, single-label 12-ounce flat top, gray can, dark brown label, "BROWN DERBY" in green, OPENING INSTRUCTIONS, INTERNAL REVENUE TAX PAID, single version. $350

Columbia Beer, single-label 12-ounce flat top, metallic gold can, white label, OPENING INSTRUCTIONS, INTERNAL REVENUE TAX PAID, single version. *(See photo 282)* ....Exotic

Columbia Extra Pale Export Beer, single-label 12-ounce flat top, white can, wide red band, gold band, Statue of Liberty within light or dark circle, OPENING INSTRUCTIONS, INTERNAL REVENUE TAX PAID, single version of each. $300

Finer Flaver Brand Beer, single-label 12-ounce flat top, gray can, blue lettering, mug on red label, single version. *(See photo 283)* ....Exotic

Heidelberg Beer, single-label 12-ounce flat top, white can, yellow bands, student prince on red circle, minor versions. $20

HEIDELBERG BREWING COMPANY, 2120-2142 South "C" Street (successor to Columbia Brewing Company)

Columbia Ale, two-label 12-ounce flat top, cream-colored can, brown square label and bands, "COLUMBIA" in red, two versions. $125

Heidelberg Beer, two-label 12- or 16-ounce flat top, white can, yellow bands, student prince on red, single version of each size. *(See photo 284)*
12-ounce, ... $25
16-ounce, ... $40

Two-label 12- or 16-ounce flat top, white can, gold bands, student prince on gold, multiversions.
12-ounce, ... $40
16-ounce, ... $50

Two-label 12- or 16-ounce flat top, yellow can, white label outlined in metallic gold, "THE SLOW BREWED LIGHT BEER," minor versions.
12-ounce, ... $25
16-ounce, ... $40

Tumwater

PABST BREWING COMPANY, 1 Schmidt Place (successor to The Olympia Brewing Company)

All cans brewed by Pabst Brewing Company are aluminum and carry a collector value of $1 *except* the Lodi brands.

Photo 282 (left). Columbia Beer.
Photo 283 (center). Finer Flaver Brand Beer.
Photo 284 (right). Heidelberg Beer.

Photo 285. Olympia Lodi.

Hamm's Lodi, two-label 12-ounce aluminum tab top, white can, "LODI" in blue, on gold band, "HAMM'S BEER" in metallic red, single version. $40

Olympia Lodi, two-label 12-ounce aluminum tab top, white can, orange label, "LODI" in blue outlined in white, single version. *(See photo 285)* $25

Pabst Lodi, two-label 12-ounce aluminum tab top, white can, blue label, "LODI" outlined in metallic gold, single version. $25

PK's Special Selection Lodi Beer, two-label 12-ounce aluminum tab top, yellow can, "LODI" in metallic red outlined in metallic gold, single version. $15

Two-label 12-ounce aluminum tab top, black can, "LODI" in metallic red outlined in white, gold lettering, single version. $10

PK's Special Selection Lodi Malt Liquor, black can, "LODI" in metallic red outlined in white, gold lettering, single version. $10

SILVER SPRINGS BREWING COMPANY, 105 East 26th Street

Brown Derby Lager Beer, two-label 12-ounce flat top, white can, "BROWN DERBY" in gold outlined in brown, gold circle label, two versions. *(See photo 286)* $60

Dunkel Bräu Bavarian Style Beer, two-label 11-ounce flat or zip top, black can, Pioneer emblem, "DUNKEL BRÄU" in white, single version of each. *(See photo 287)*
Flat top, ... $400
Zip top,..$450

Durst Premium Quality Beer, single-label 11-ounce flat top, blue and metallic gold can, single version. $60

Photo 286 (left). Brown Derby Lager Beer.
Photo 287 (right). Dunkel Bräu
Bavarian Style Beer.

Hartz Western Style Pilsener Beer, single-label 12-ounce flat top or 11-ounce flat or zip top, white can, metallic red can, totem poles, 12-ounce flat top two versions, 11-ounce flat top two versions, 11-ounce zip top one version.

11-ounce zip top,.. $35

All other versions,.. $25

Köl Premium Quality Beer, single-label 11-ounce flat top, white can, dark blue stripes and label, single version. *(See photo 288)*............................... $15

Vancouver

GENERAL BREWING COMPANY, 615 Columbia Street (successor to Lucky Lager Brewing Company)

All cans produced by General Brewing Company were aluminum and bi-metal and carry a collector value of $1, including Mash 4077 and Billy Beer.

INTERSTATE BREWERY COMPANY, 2110 West 7th Street (successor to Star Brewing Company)

Hop Gold Pale Export True Lager Beer, single-label 12-ounce flat top, metallic gold can, white label, blue trim, "BREWED FROM THE BUBBLING SPRING WATERS OF THE NORTH," OPENING INSTRUCTIONS, INTERNAL REVENUE TAX PAID, two versions. *(See photo 289)*...Exotic

Lucky Lager Age Dated Beer, single-label 12-ounce flat top, gold can, full-can red "x," INTERNAL REVENUE TAX PAID, single version. $150

Silver Springs Beer, single-label 12-ounce flat top, blue and gray can, OPENING INSTRUCTIONS, INTERNAL REVENUE TAX PAID, single version. ....Exotic

Town Club Lager Beer, single-label 12-ounce flat top, gray and blue can, "BREWED FOR PIGGLEY-WIGGLEY MARKETS, TACOMA, WASH.," OPENING INSTRUCTIONS, INTERNAL REVENUE TAX PAID, single version. *(See photo 290)* ....Exotic

LUCKY LAGER BREWING COMPANY, 215 West 7th Street (successor to Interstate Brewing Company)

Lucky Lager Age Dated Beer, single-label 12-ounce flat top, gold can, horizontal lines, large red "x," multiversions. $50

Single-label 12-ounce flat top, gold can, large red "x," single version. $25

Two-label 11- or 12-ounce flat top, white can, red "x" on gold label, "LUCKY LAGER" in red, multiversions. $10

Photo 288 (left). Köl Premium Quality Beer.
Photo 289 (center). Hop Gold Pale Export True Lager Beer.
Photo 290 (right). Town Club Lager Beer.

Photo 291 (left). Ye Old English Style Ale By Hop Gold.

Lucky Lager Age Dated Premium Beer, two-label 12-ounce flat top, yellow can, white label outlined in metallic gold, "AGE DATED," multiversions. $5

STAR BREWERY COMPANY, 215 West 7th Street

Hop Gold Beer, single-label 12-ounce flat top, metallic gold can, blue star label, OPENING INSTRUCTIONS, INTERNAL REVENUE TAX PAID, two versions......Exotic

Hop Gold Pale Export True Lager Beer, single-label 12-ounce flat top, metallic gold can, white label, blue trim, OPENING INSTRUCTIONS, INTERNAL REVENUE TAX PAID, single version. ....Exotic

Silver Springs Beer, single-label 12-ounce flat top, blue and gray can, OPENING INSTRUCTIONS, INTERNAL REVENUE TAX PAID, single version. ....Exotic

Town Club Lager Beer, single-label 12-ounce flat top, blue and gray can, "BREWED FOR PIGGLEY-WIGGLEY STORES, TACOMA, WASH.," OPENING INSTRUCTIONS, INTERNAL REVENUE TAX PAID, single version. ....Exotic

Ye Old English Style Ale By Hop Gold, single-label 12-ounce flat top, silver and gold can, OPENING INSTRUCTIONS, INTERNAL REVENUE TAX PAID, single version. *(See photo 291)* ....Unique

West Virginia

/

Huntington

FESSENMEIER BREWING COMPANY, 14th Street and Madison Avenue

Fessenmeier Centennial Beer, two-label 12-ounce soft top, copper can, enamel red, white, and blue, single version. $35

Two-label 12-ounce soft or zip top, white can, metallic gold bands and trim, "FESSENMEIER BEER" in metallic red, single version of each. Either version, ... $25

West Virginia Light Beer, two-label 12-ounce flat top, white can, metallic gold bands, blue oval label, single version. $75

Two-label 12-ounce soft top, white can, silver bands, blue oval label, single version. $65

Virginia Special Export Beer, two-label, 12-ounce, high-profile cone top, white can, West Virginia map, "SPECIAL EXPORT" in blue, single version. $100

LITTLE SWITZERLAND BREWING COMPANY, 14th Street and Madison Avenue (successor to Fessenmeier Brewing Company)

Charge Premium Beer, two-label 12-ounce tab top, white can, cavalry scene, "THE BOLD AMERICAN" in metallic red, two versions. $20

West Virginia Pilsner Beer, two-label 12-ounce tab top, white can, metallic gold bands, "WEST VIRGINIA" in metallic red, two versions. $35

Wisconsin

Appleton

GEORGE WALTER BREWING COMPANY, 200–220 South
Walnut Street

Adler Brau Appleton Beer, two-label 12-ounce flat or zip top, silver can, white
label, red banner, minor versions. All versions,.................................. $30

Adler Brau Beer, two-label 12-ounce flat top, metallic or yellow-gold can, white
or yellow label, single version of each. Either version,.......................... $15
Two-label 12-ounce zip or tab top, red can, black and gold label, multiversions.
Zip top,... $12
Tab top,... $10

Beaver Dam

LOUIS ZIEGLER BREWING COMPANY, 516 Madison Street

Arrowhead Pale Lager Beer, single-label high-profile cone top, white can, metallic gold bands, red arrowhead label, single version. $150

Ziegler's Premium Lager Beer, single-label, 12-ounce, high-profile cone top,
yellow or white can, accordian player label, minor versions.
Yellow can, ... $175
White can, ... $160

Burlington

BURLINGTON BREWING COMPANY, 425–443 McHenry Street

Van Merritt Brand Beer, single-label, 12-ounce, high-profile cone top, metallic green can, white label, "VAN MERRITT" in blue, IRTP or non-IRTP, minor versions.

IRTP, ...$100

Non-IRTP, ... $85

VAN MERRITT BREWING COMPANY, 425–443 McHenry Street (successor to Burlington Brewing Company)

Van Merritt Brand Beer, single-label 12-ounce flat top, metallic green can, white label, "VAN MERRITT" on red band, single version. $60

WISCONSIN BREWING COMPANY, 425–443 McHenry Street (successor to Van Merritt Brewing Company)

Wisconsin Premium Beer, single-label 12-ounce flat top, white can, black and red bands, "WISCONSIN BEER" in black, single version. $40

Single-label 12-ounce flat top, white can, black and red bands, "WISCONSIN PREMIUM" in black block letters, single version. $60

Chippewa Falls

JACOB LEINENKUGEL BREWING COMPANY, 1–3 Jefferson Avenue

Action in Jackson Beer, two-label 12-ounce tab top, blue can, single version. $1

Big D Beer, single-label 12-ounce tab top, white can, single version. $1

Bosch Premium Beer, single-label 12-ounce flat top, metallic gold can, white label, single version. $1

Cadott Nabor Days Beer, single-label 12-ounce flat top, white can, single version. $1

Chippewa Pride Light Premium Beer, two-label 12-ounce tab top, yellow can, brown and tan label, minor versions. *(See photo 292)* $2

Photo 292 (right). Chippewa Pride Light Premium Beer.

Two-label 12-ounce tab top, yellow can, white label, "CHIPPEWA PRIDE" in white, single version. $2

Leinenkugel's Beer, two-label 12-ounce flat or tab top, white can, wide metallic gold bands, red band, Indian maiden, multiversions. $15

Leinenkugel's Chippewa Pride Beer, two-label 12-ounce crowntainer or flat top, yellow can, "CHIPPEWA PRIDE" in red, Indian maiden, multiversions.
Crowntainer,...$85
Flat top, ...$50

Leinenkugel's Genuine Bock Beer, two-label 12-ounce tab top, "GENUINE BOCK BEER" on one or two lines, multiversions...$2

Leinie's Light Beer, two-label 12-ounce tab top, white or yellow can, minor versions..$2

Little Muskego Beer, two-label 12-ounce tab top, white or gold can, two versions.
1978, ...$3
1979, ...$2

Pure Water Days Beer, two-label 12-ounce tab top, one can issued for every year 1980–1986, single version each year. Each, ...$1

Pure Water Days Light Premium Beer, two-label 12-ounce tab top, one can issued for each year, 1977–1979, single version each year. Each, ...$2

Rolling Meadows Anniversary Beer, two-label 12-ounce tab top, blue can, single version. $1

Wngea 1979 Beer, two-label 12-ounce tab top, blue can, single version. $1

Brewery has produced its brands in aluminum cans since the mid-1980s. Collector value is $1.

Eau Claire

WALTER BREWING COMPANY, 318 Elm Street

Acee Ducee Beer, single-label 12-ounce tab top, black can, single version. ..$1

Anoka County Humane Society Beer, single-label 12-ounce tab top, blue can, rainbow, single version. $1

Barker's Island Four Seasons Beer, single-label 12-ounce tab top, white, blue, and yellow can, single version. $1

Bean And Bacon Days Premium Beer, single-label 12-ounce tab top, versions: gold can, 1978; bronze can, 1979; yellow can, 1980. Each,......................$1

Benefit Beer, two-label 12-ounce tab top, white can, single version. $1

Bilow Garden State Bock Beer, two-label 12-ounce tab top, brown and white can, single version. $1

Bilow Garden State Light Beer, two-label 12-ounce tab top, "ERIN GO BRAUGH" single version. $1

Bilow Garden State Premium Beer, single- or two-label 12-ounce tab top, set cans, set of 10 cans: "Ashbury Park–Jersey Shore Chapter," "The Beer of the Jersey Shore," "Drakula's October Guest," "Fourth of July 1979," "Happy

New Year 1979,'' ''Happy New Year 1980,'' ''Happy St. Patrick's Day 1980,'' ''Jersey Shore Chapter,'' ''Superswap IV–Garden State Chapter,'' ''Winter at the Jersey Shore.'' Each can,...$1

Bilow Octoberfest Beer, single-label 12-ounce tab top, woodgrain can, single version. Each, ...$1

Bilow Premium Beer, two-label 12-ounce tab top, set can, set of six cans, ''Beer Cans Monthly 1st National Convention,'' ''Gertrude Browns Tinton Falls N.J.,'' ''Great American Beer Book,'' ''Happy Birthday,'' ''Happy New Year 1981,'' ''St. Patrick's Day 1981.'' Each,..$1

Breunig's Lager Beer, two-label 12-ounce tab top, gold can, purple label, single version. $1

Two-label 12-ounce tab top, red and white can, single version. $1

Two-label 12-ounce tab top, silver and blue can, single version. $1

Bub's Beer, two-label 12-ounce tab top, white can, bright or dull gold trim, multiversions.
Bright gold can,..$3
Dull gold can, ...$2

Two-label 12-ounce tab top, red and white can, multiversions. $1

Cashton's Centennial Beer, single-label 12-ounce tab top, red and white can, single version. $1

Elm Grove Bock Beer, single-label 12-ounce tab top, red and white can, single version. $2

Elm Grove Wisconsin Beer, single-label 12-ounce tab top, green and yellow can, single version. $1

Extra Light Ale From Walter's, two-label 12-ounce tab top, white can, two versions. $2

Lammer's Private Stock Premium Beer, two-label 12-ounce tab top, black can, single version. $1

Light Ale From Walter's, two-label, 12-ounce tab top, white can, multiversions..$2

Old Timer's Lager Beer, two-label 12-ounce tab top, red and white can, single version. $1

Otto's Bock Beer, two-label 12-ounce tab top, gold can, single version.......$2

Otto's Wisconsin Beer, two-label 12-ounce tab top, cream can, single version. $1

Owen Brew Premium Quality Beer, two-label 12-ounce tab top, white can, red or yellow label, single version of each. Each version, ...$1

Protivin Centennial Pivo Beer, single-label 12-ounce tab top, blue can, white label, single version. $1

Sawdust City Days Beer, single-label 12-ounce tab top, blue or brown can, single version of each. Each, ...$1

The Great American Beer Book, two-label 12-ounce tab top, blue can, single version. $1

The Master Brew, two-label 12-ounce tab top, white can, gold bands, red circle, single version. $3

Two-label 12-ounce tab top, red and white can, single version. $1

Walter's '76 Light Beer, single-label 12-ounce flat top, "WISCONSIN JAYCEES," two versions. $1

Walter's Beer, two-label 12-ounce zip or tab top, red can, white label, single version of each top. Either can,...$20

Two-label 12-ounce tab top, red, black, and white can, black pinstripes, single version. $5

Walter's Pilsener Beer, single-label, 12-ounce, high-profile cone or flat top, yellow can, green and gold bands, single version of each.
Flat top, ...$30
Cone top, ...$85

Single-label 12-ounce flat top, white can, red and gold bands, single version.
....$25

Walter's Premium Quality Beer, two-label 12-ounce flat top, "THE BEER THAT IS BEER," multiversions. $1

Walter's Premium Quality Bock, two-label 12-ounce tab top, gold and brown can, single version. $2

West Bend Old Timer's Lager Beer, single-label 12-ounce tab top, white can, metallic gold bands, drinking scene, two versions. $15

White Bear Strong Beer, two-label 12-ounce flat or soft top, red can, standing bear, single version of each.
Flat top, ...$50
Soft top, ...$30

Wisconsin Indian Head Country Beer, single-label 12-ounce flat top, white can, single version. $1

Wisconsin's Old Timer's Lager Beer, single-label 12-ounce tab top, white can, gold stripes, drinking scene. $1

Walter's has produced a number of brands in aluminum cans. Collector value is $1.

Fountain City

FOUNTAIN CITY BREWING COMPANY, Main Street

Fountain Brew Beer, two-label, 12-ounce, high-profile cone top, yellow can, green label, "FOUNTAIN BREW" in red, single version. $75

Fountain Brew Export Beer, two-label, 12-ounce, high-profile cone top, yellow can, green label, "FOUNTAIN BREW" in red, single version. $75

Photo 293 (left). Rahr's All Star Beer.
Photo 294 (right). Rahr's Beer.

Fountain Brew Strong Beer, two-label, 12-ounce, high-profile cone top, yellow can, green label, "FOUNTAIN BREW" in red, single version. $75

Green Bay

RAHR–GREEN BAY BREWING CORPORATION, 1331 Main Street (aka: All Star Brewing Company)

All Star Brand Beer, All Star Brewing Company, two-label 12-ounce flat top, white can, silver bands, large blue star label, single version. $100

Old Imperial Beer, Rahr–Green Bay Brewing, two-label 12-ounce crowntainer, white can, blue bands, "BEER" in red, "1st PRIDE OF WISCONSIN," single version. $100

Rahr's All Star Beer, Rahr–Green Bay Brewing, two-label 12-ounce flat top, white can, metallic red star, silver bands, two versions. *(See photo 293)* $40

Rahr's Beer, Rahr–Green Bay Brewing, single-label, 12-ounce, high-profile cone or two-label 12-ounce flat top, metallic dark red label, white label, single version of each. *(See photo 294)*
Flat top, ... $35
Cone top, ... $75

Two-label 12-ounce crowntainer, white can, "BEER" in red, single version. $85

La Crosse

G. HEILEMAN BREWING COMPANY, 1000–1023 South 3rd Street (aka: Ace Brewing Company, Blatz Brewing Company, Duluth Brewing Company, Fox Head Brewing, Gluek Division, Heidel Brau Brewing Company, Kingsbury Division, Pioneer Brewing Company, Weber Waukesha Brewing, Wisconsin Brewing Company)

Ace Wisconsin Pilsener Beer, G. Heileman or Ace Brewing Company, two-label 12-ounce flat top, white can, "ACE" in blue, yellow trim, single version from each brewery.
G. Heileman, ... $40
Ace Brewing, ... $60

Blatz Milwaukee's Finest Beer, two-label 12- or 16-ounce tab top, woodgrain can, brown Blatz triangle, "BARREL OF BLATZ," two versions. $15

Blatz Brewing, two-label 12- or 16-ounce tab top, gold can, dark brown Blatz triangle, multiversions. $5

G. Heileman Brewing Company, two-label 12-ounce tab top, white can, wide gold band, maroon "BLATZ" triangle, single version. $10

G. Heileman Brewing Company, two-label 12-ounce tab top, white can, no "DRAFT BREWED," single version. $5

G. Heileman Brewing Company, two-label 12- or 16-ounce tab top, white can, maroon Blatz triangle, yellow trim, multiversions. All versions, ... $1

Braumeister Special Pilsener Beer, G. Heileman Brewing Company, two-label 12-ounce tab top, white can, vertical pinstripes, maroon label. $1

Drewrys Beer, G. Heileman Brewing Company, two-label 12- or 16-ounce tab top, silver can, white label, red ribbon, multiversions.
12-ounce, ...$2
16-ounce, ...$3

Drewrys Draft Beer, G. Heileman Brewing Company, two-label 12-ounce tab top, silver can, white label, blue ribbon, multiversions. $2

Fox Deluxe Beer, G. Heileman Brewing Company or Fox Head Brewing, two-label 12-ounce tab or flat top, white can, wide metallic gold band, "BREWED ONLY IN WISCONSIN," multiversions.
Tab top, ...$3
Flat top, ...$5

Gluek Division, two-label 12-ounce gold can, white label, "BEER" in red, "BREWED ONLY IN WISCONSIN," single version. $15

Fox Head 97 Malt Liquor, G. Heileman Brewing Company, two-label 12-ounce flat or soft top, dark gold and white can, black trim, single version of each.
.... $200

Fox Head 97 Stout Malt Liquor, G. Heileman Brewing Company, two-label 12-ounce flat or soft top, dark gold and white can, black trim, single version of each. $185

Fox Head "400" Beer, Fox Head Brewing or Gluek Division, two-label 12-ounce flat, soft, or tab top, gold and white can, red or blue label, multiversions.
Blue-label flat top, ... $15
Blue-label soft or tab top, ... $12
Red-label flat top, ... $12
Red-label tab top, ... $10

Fox Head Sparkling Malt Liquor, Fox Head Brewing, two-label 12-ounce tab top, white can, "FOX HEAD" on black band, "SPARKLING" in red, single version. $10

Gluek Finest Pilsener Beer, Gluek Division, two-label 12-ounce flat or tab top, yellow and gold can, multiversions.
Flat top, ...$5
Tab top, ...$2

Heidel Brau Pilsener Beer, Heidel Brau Brewing, two-label 12-ounce flat or tab top, white can, "PILSENER BEER" in black or gray, multiversions.
Black flat top, ... $10
Gray flat top, ...$5
Tab top, ...$2

Heileman's Lager Beer, G. Heileman Brewing, two-label 12-ounce flat top, blue and white can, mountain scene, "HEILEMAN" in black or brown multiversions. *(See photo 295)* All versions, ... $15

Heileman's Old Style Lager Beer, G. Heileman Brewing Company, single-label, 12-ounce, low-profile cone top, yellow or white can, "BEER" on red band, "OLD STYLE LAGER" on black band, IRTP or non-IRTP, multiversions. *(See photo 296)*
IRTP, ... $85
Non-IRTP, ... $80

Photo 295 (left). Heileman's Lager Beer.
Photo 296 (right). Heileman's Old Style Lager Beer.

G. Heileman Brewing Company, single-label, 12-ounce, low-profile cone top, black can, yellow and red label, INTERNAL REVENUE TAX PAID, minor versions. $125

G. Heileman Brewing Company, single-label 12-ounce flat top, multicolored can, monk scene, "HEILEMAN'S" on green band, multiversions. $35

Heileman's Old Style Light Beer, G. Heileman Brewing Company, two-label 12-ounce flat top, white and metallic gold can, blue shield, red triangle, multiversions. $20

G. Heileman Brewing Company, two-label 12-ounce flat top, white can, gold bands, blue shield, red triangle, single version. $15

G. Heileman Brewing Company, two-label 12-ounce soft, zip, or tab top, white can, blue shield, "SPARKLING PURE WATER" or "SPARKLING PURE SPRING WATER," multiversions. $5

Heileman's Old Style Light Lager Beer, G. Heileman Brewing Company, two-label 12-ounce aluminum can, special "Sports" issue cans: "1982–83 Milwaukee Bucks," "Badger 1983 Football," "Milwaukee Bucks Do It with Style 1983–1984," "Illinois State 1983–1984 Basketball Schedule," "Illinois State 1983 Football Schedule," "Waukegan 125th Anniversary"; single version of each. Each can, ... $10

Heileman's Special Export Beer, G. Heileman Brewing Company, two-label 12-ounce flat top, green and white can, ship on globe, multiversions. $25

G. Heileman Brewing Company, two-label 12-ounce flat top, gold, green and white can, ship on globe, single version. $35

G. Heileman Brewing Company, two-label 12-ounce flat, soft, or tab top, white can, green stripe, metals, "SPECIAL EXPORT" in red, multiversions. $1

Heileman's Special Export Malt Lager, G. Heileman Brewing Company, two-label 12-ounce flat top, white can, yellow label, "SPECIAL EXPORT" in red, single version. $125

Heileman's Special Export Malt Liquor, G. Heileman Brewing Company, two-label 8- or 12-ounce flat top, white can, yellow label, "SPECIAL EXPORT" in red, single version of each.
8-ounce, ... $75
12-ounce, ... $100

Heileman's Special Export Old Style Lager, G. Heileman Brewing Company, two-label 12-ounce flat top, green and white can, gold filigree, ship on globe, single version. $40

Heileman's Special Export Stout Malt Liquor, G. Heileman Brewing Company, white can, yellow label, sailing ship, two versions. Either version, ... $60

Karlsbrau Old Time Beer, Duluth Division, single-label 12-ounce flat or tab top, white can, maroon and woodgrain label, viking ship, multiversions. $2

Kingsbury Beer, G. Heileman Brewing Company or Kingsbury Brewing, two-label 12-ounce tab top, white can, red label and lettering, multiversions. $2

Kingsbury Genuine Draft Beer, Kingsbury Breweries, two-label gallon can, white can, red label, blue trim, "HEILEMAN" label, single version. $175

Kingsbury Light Beer, Kingsbury Breweries, two-label 12-ounce tab top, white can, red label, blue trim, "HEILEMAN" label, multiversions. $3

Old Style Lager Beer, G. Heileman Brewing Company, single-label, 12-ounce, high-profile cone top, white can, monastery scene, red and black bands, INTERNAL REVENUE TAX PAID, multiversions. $100

G. Heileman Brewing Company, single-label, 12-ounce, high-profile cone or flat top, green and white can, monastery scene, IRTP or non-IRTP, multiversions.

IRTP, ... $85
Non-IRTP, ... $75
Flat top, ... $40

Pioneer Beer, Pioneer Brewing Company, two-label 12-ounce flat top, white can, split yellow and woodgrain label, buffalo, multiversions. $25

Royal 58 Beer, Duluth Division, two-label 12-ounce tab top, white can, light blue label, "ROYAL" in royal blue, single version. $150

Sparkling Stite Malt Liquor, Gluek Division or G. Heileman Brewing Company, two-label 8- or 12-ounce flat or tab top, white can, red band, "STITE" in black, multiversions.

8-ounce, ... $15
12-ounce, ... $10

Weber Special Premium Beer, Weber Waukesha or G. Heileman Brewing Company, two-label 12-ounce flat top, brown can, metallic gold metals, minor versions. $65

Wisconsin Premium Beer, Wisconsin Brewing, two-label 12-ounce flat top, metallic gold can, state map of Wisconsin in white, minor versions. $35

Wisconsin Brewing, two-label 12-ounce flat, soft, or tab top, white can, small Wisconsin state map, multiversions. $10

G. Heileman has and is producing a wide variety of brands, using the HEILEMAN mandatory as well as other mandatories, in aluminum and bi-metal cans. The collector value of these cans will run up to $1.

LA CROSSE BREWERIES, INC., 727 South 3rd

Peerless Beer, single-label, 12-ounce, high-profile cone top, white can, metallic gold band, red lettering, IRTP or non-IRTP, multiversions.

IRTP, ... $100
Non-IRTP, ... $85

Peerless Extra Premium Beer, single-label, 12-ounce, high-profile cone top, green, red, and white can, minor versions.

IRTP, ... $125
Non-IRTP, ... $115

Lomira

HAROLD C. JOHNSON BREWING COMPANY, Pleasant Hill Avenue (aka: A.B.D. Co.)

333 Pilsener Brand Beer, Harold C. Johnson, single-label, 12-ounce, high-profile cone top, white can, red and gold bands, single version. $100

Champagne Pilsener Brand Beer, Harold C. Johnson, single-label, 12-ounce, high-profile cone top, white can, red and gold bands, red lettering, single version.. $110

Trophy Beer, A.B.D. Company, single-label, 12-ounce, high-profile cone top, white can, gold bands, beer glass, single version. $300

Madison

BLATZ BREWING COMPANY, 1120 North Broadway

Blatz Ale, single-label, 12-ounce, low-profile cone top, yellow can, brown oval label, INTERNAL REVENUE TAX PAID, two versions. $150

Blatz Beer, single-label 12-ounce flat top, "FINEST BEER BREWED IN MILWAU-KEE," brown triangle label, can in six colors: green, chartreuse, pale blue, dark blue, pink, orange; single version of each can. Each, ... $75

Single-label 12- or 16-ounce flat top, gold can, brown triangle outlined in metallic gold, multiversions.
12-ounce,... $15
16-ounce,... $20

Blatz English Type Ale, single-label, 12-ounce, low-profile cone top, yellow can, brown label and bands, two versions. $200

Blatz Milwaukee Beer Select Lager, single-label, 12-ounce, high- or low-profile cone top, yellow can, blue label, "SELECT LAGER" in blue or red, INTERNAL REVENUE TAX PAID, multiversions. $65

Blatz Old Heidelberg Pilsener Type Beer, single-label 12-ounce low-profile cone top, yellow can, blue label, "OLD HEIDELBERG" on red band, INTERNAL REVENUE TAX PAID, multiversions. $65

Blatz Old Heidelberg Special Pilsener Beer, single-label, 12-ounce, low-profile cone top, yellow can, blue label, "SPECIAL PILSENER" in red, INTERNAL REVE-NUE TAX PAID, single version. $75

Blatz Old Heidelberg Special Pilsener Brew, single-label, 12-ounce, low-profile cone top, yellow can, blue label, "SPECIAL PILSENER" in red, INTERNAL REVE-NUE TAX PAID, minor versions. $75

Blatz Pilsener Beer, single-label, 12-ounce, J-spout or high-profile cone top, camouflage can, single version of each. $300

Single-label, 12-ounce, high-profile cone top, yellow can, blue label, "PILSE-NER" on red band, single version. $65

Single-label 12-ounce flat top, yellow can, gold bands, "PILSENER" in white on red band, IRTP or non-IRTP, minor versions.
IRTP, ... $65
Non-IRTP, ... $60

Single-label 12-ounce flat top, yellow can, gold label, red shield, "MILWAUKEE'S FIRST BOTTLED BEER," IRTP or non-IRTP, minor versions.

IRTP, ... $50
Non-IRTP, ... $45

Milwaukee's Finest Beer, single-label 12-ounce flat top, gold can, brown triangle outlined in orange, multiversions. $15

Tempo Beer, two-label 12-ounce flat top, red can, metallic gold bands, two versions. $125

FAUERBACH BREWING COMPANY, 647–653 Williamson Street

Fauerbach CB Pilsener Beer, single-label, 12-ounce, high-profile cone top, white can, red label, single version. $85

Single-label 12-ounce flat top, red can, white label, silver bands, single version. $45

Two-label 12-ounce tab top, light blue can, metals, dark blue ribbon, single version. $85

GETTLEMAN BREWING COMPANY, 4400 West State Street

$1000 Natural Process, two-label 12-ounce flat top, yellow can, shields, minor versions. $25

Gettleman $1000 Natural Process, two-label 12-ounce flat top, yellow can, brown label, red trim, single version. $60

Gettleman Milwaukee Beer, single-label, 12-ounce, high-profile cone or flat top, white can, brown label, filigree, single version. $65

Two-label 12-ounce flat top, white can, metallic green label, cartoon, single version. *(See photo 297)* $30

Two-label 12-ounce flat top, series can, 16 cans, four drawings, four colors, drawings: fishing and hunting, Rathskellar and picnic, TV and barbecue, "Sweet Adeline"; colors: blue, green, red, and yellow; single version of each can. $65

Gettleman Rathskellar Milwaukee Beer, single-label, 12-ounce, high-profile cone top, yellow can, brown label, IRTP or non-IRTP, single version of each.

IRTP, ... $65
Non-IRTP, ... $60

Two-label 12-ounce flat top, white can, brown label outlined in metallic gold, single version. $50

Photo 297. Gettleman Milwaukee Beer.

Milwaukee's "Best" Beer, two-label 12-ounce flat top, green and white can, stein, single version. $20

Two-label 12-ounce flat top, white can, maroon and yellow label, multiversions. $10

GETTLEMAN DIVISION, MILLER BREWING COMPANY, 4400 West State (successor to Gettleman Brewing Company)

$1000 Natural Process Beer, two-label 12-ounce flat or tab top, yellow can, shields or red ribbon, minor versions.
Flat top, ... $10
Tab top, ... $5

Gettleman Beer, two-label 12-ounce flat or tab top, white can, maroon label, enamel or metallic gold bands, "DRAFT FRESH," multiversions.
Flat top, ... $5
Tab top, ... $3

Gettleman Bock Beer, two-label gallon can, woodgrain and yellow can, white, brown, and yellow label, single version. $350

Gettleman Milwaukee Beer, two-label gallon can, woodgrain and yellow can, white, brown, and yellow label, two versions. $250

Two-label 12-ounce flat top, cream can, maroon label, metallic gold ribbon, single version. $5

Milwaukee's "Best" Beer, two-label 12-ounce flat or tab top, white can, maroon and yellow label, multiversions. $5

University Club Malt Liquor, single-label 8- or 12-ounce flat top, white can, green and gold trim, "MALT LIQUOR" in gold, single version of each.
8-ounce, ... $50
12-ounce, ... $65

University Club Stout Malt Liquor, single-label 8- or 12-ounce flat top, white can, green and gold trim, "STOUT MALT LIQUOR" in gold.
8-ounce, ... $60
12-ounce, ... $75

INDEPENDENT MILWAUKEE BREWERY, 2701 South 13th Street

Bierman Beer, two-label 12-ounce flat top, white can, drinking scene, "BEER" in red, "BREWED AND PACKED IN MILWAUKEE," single version. .... Exotic

Braumeister Special Pilsener Beer, single-label, 12-ounce, high-profile cone top, blue can, metallic gold band, pinstripes and label, IRTP and non-IRTP, multiversions.
IRTP, ... $85
Non-IRTP, ... $75

Single-label 12-ounce flat top, white can, blue label outlined in metallic gold, single version. $12

MILLER BREWING COMPANY, 4002–4026 West State

Buckeye Premium Beer, two-label 12-ounce tab top, white can, red label, gold trim, minor versions. $5

Clipper The Dark Light Beer, two-label 12-ounce aluminum tab top, gold and white can, brown label, multiversions. $5

Gettleman Bock Beer, two-label 12-ounce tab top, brown, gold, and white can, single version. $15

Meister Brau Premium Beer, three-label 12- or 16-ounce tab top, gold can, white label, multiversions.
12-ounce, ...$2
16-ounce, ...$3

Meister Brau Premium Bock Beer, two-label 12-ounce tab top, white can, gold trim, "MEISTER BRAU" in brown, multiversions. $3

Meister Brau Premium Draft Beer, three-label 12- or 16-ounce tab top, brown can, white label outlined in metallic gold, multiversions. $2

Miller Ale, two-label 12-ounce tab top, olive green can, metallic gold trim, "MILLER ALE" in white, minor versions. $10
Aluminum versions, ...$5

Miller High Life Beer, single-label 12-ounce flat top, black can, red bands, white label outlined in metallic gold, "girl on moon," bottle or story on quarter panel, IRTP or non-IRTP, multiversions.
IRTP, ... $35
Non-IRTP, ... $30

Single-label 12- or 16-ounce flat, zip, or tab top, white can, metallic gold bands and trim, "CHAMPAGNE OF BOTTLE BEER," multiversions. All versions, ...$5

Two-label 10-, 12-, or 16-ounce flat or tab top, gold can, white label outlined in green, "THE CHAMPAGNE OF BOTTLE BEERS," multiversions.
10-ounce, ... $10
All other versions, ...$1

Miller Lite A Fine Pilsner Beer, two-label 12-ounce aluminum tab top, white can, "MILLER" in white on red circle, single version. $40

Miller Malt Liquor, two-label 12- or 16-ounce aluminum can, red can, gold eagle, "MALT LIQUOR" in black, multiversions.
12-ounce, ...$5
16-ounce, ...$7.50

Miller $1000 Natural Process, two-label 12-ounce tab top, brown and black can, multiversions. $10

Miller Select Beer, single-label 12-ounce tab top, red can, Miller girl on moon on blue circle, OPENING INSTRUCTIONS, INTERNAL REVENUE TAX PAID, multiversions. $50

Miller Select Beer High Life Beer, single-label 12-ounce flat top, red can, Miller girl on moon on blue circle, "HIGH LIFE" in white, OPENING INSTRUCTIONS, INTERNAL REVENUE TAX PAID, single version. $75

Milwaukee's "Best" Beer, two-label 12-ounce tab top, white can, red shield, single version. $2

Milwaukee's Best Beer, two-label 12-ounce tab top, white can, stein and lions, multiversions. $1

Player's Lager Beer, two-label 12-ounce aluminum tab top, white can, blue and gold label, multiversions. $3

Miller Brewing Company has and is producing a wide variety of brands in aluminum cans. These cans, for the most part, are common, but would still carry a collector value of up to $1 if needed.

PABST BREWING COMPANY, 917 West Juneau Avenue

Andeker The Beer Of America, two-label 12-ounce tab top, gold and metallic gold can, black lettering, multiversions. $3

Big Cat Malt Liquor, two-label 12- or 16-ounce flat, zip, or tab top, white can, leopard, "BIG CAT" in red, multiversions. $15

Blatz Milwaukee's Finest Beer, two-label 12- or 16-ounce flat top, gold can, brown triangle, multiversions.
12-ounce, ...$5
16-ounce, ... $10

Two-label 12- or 16-ounce tab top, gold can, brown triangle, "NO OPENER NEEDED," multiversions.
12-ounce, ...$5
16-ounce, ... $10

Two-label 12-ounce flat top, gold can, brown triangle, special issue cans: "Purdue Class '23," "Purdue Class '28," "Purdue Class '37," single version of each. Each, ... $25

Blatz Milwaukee's Finest Bock, two-label 12-ounce flat top, gold can, brown triangle, "BOCK" in brown, single version. $35

Burgie Light Golden Beer, two-label 12-ounce tab top, yellow can, picture of San Francisco Bay, multiversions. $5

Old Tankard Ale, single-label 12-ounce flat top, silver and black can, red band, "OLD TANKARD" in red, OPENING INSTRUCTIONS, INTERNAL REVENUE TAX PAID, minor versions. $85

Pabst Blue Ribbon Ale, single-label 12-ounce flat top, silver can, green ribbon, "PABST ALE" in red, minor versions. $100

Pabst Blue Ribbon Beer, single-label 12-ounce flat top, silver can, blue band and ribbon, "PABST" in red, INTERNAL REVENUE TAX PAID, two versions. . $40

Single-label 12-ounce flat top, camouflage can or WITHDRAWN FREE, single version.
Camouflage can, ...$250
WITHDRAWN FREE, ...$100

Single-label 12-ounce flat top, silver can, cream label, blue ribbon, IRTP or non-IRTP, WITHDRAWN FREE stamped on lid, multiversions.
Non-IRTP, ... $50
IRTP, ... $60
WITHDRAWN FREE, ... $65

Photo 298 (left). Pabst Blue Ribbon Beer.
Photo 299 (right). Pabst Blue Ribbon Beer.

Two-label 12-ounce flat top, silver can, blue pinstripes, large white label and ribbon, multiversions. *(See photo 298)* $30

Two-label 12-ounce flat top, silver can, metallic gold pinstripes and bands, yellow label, single version. $35

Two-label 12- or 16-ounce flat top, metallic gold hatched can and bands, white label, multiversions.
12-ounce,.. $20
16-ounce,.. $25

Two-label 12- or 16-ounce flat top or quart cone top, dark blue and white can, silver trim, multiversions.
12-ounce,.. $20
16-ounce,.. $25
Quart,.. $75

Two-label 10-, 12-, or 16-ounce flat, soft, or tab top, or quart cone top, white can, blue ribbon, gold bands, red stripe, multiversions. *(See photo 299)*
10-ounce flat top, ... $10
12-ounce flat top, ...$5
12-ounce soft top, ...$5
12-ounce tab top, ...$2
16-ounce flat top, ...$7
16-ounce tab top, ...$3
Quart cone top, ... $45

Pabst Blue Ribbon Bock Beer, single-label 12-ounce flat top, silver can, red band, goat, OPENING INSTRUCTIONS, INTERNAL REVENUE TAX PAID, single version..$125

Two-label 12-ounce flat top, silver can, cream label, "BOCK" in red, single version.. $65

Two-label 12-ounce flat top, hatched gold can, "BOCK" in blue, single version.
.... $65

Two-label 12-ounce flat top, yellow can, blue ribbon, one silver goat, single version.. $75

Two-label 12-ounce tab top, white can, large blue ribbon, one silver goat, single version. $75

Two-label 12-ounce tab top, white can, large blue ribbon, two red goats, single version. $5

Two-label 12-ounce flat top, white can, large blue ribbon, one red goat, multiversions..$2

Pabst Blue Ribbon Export Beer, single-label 12-ounce flat top, silver can, blue band, "EXPORT" in blue, OPENING INSTRUCTIONS, INTERNAL REVENUE TAX PAID, multiversions. $65

Pabst Blue Ribbon Genuine Dry Ale, single-label 12-ounce flat top, green can, yellow label, pinstripes, two versions. $65

Pabst Bock Beer, single-label 12-ounce flat top, silver can, red band, goat's head, OPENING INSTRUCTIONS, INTERNAL REVENUE TAX PAID, multiversions. $125

Pabst Export Beer, single-label 12-ounce flat top, silver can, blue band, "PABST" in red, OPENING INSTRUCTIONS, INTERNAL REVENUE TAX PAID, multiversions. $65

Pabst Old Tankard Ale, single-label 12-ounce flat top, silver can, "PABST" in block letters, OPENING INSTRUCTIONS, INTERNAL REVENUE TAX PAID, single version. $100

Single-label 12-ounce flat top, silver can, cavalier, blue band, OPENING INSTRUCTIONS, INTERNAL REVENUE TAX PAID, multiversions. $85

Two-label 12-ounce flat top, gold and cream can, multiversions. $20

Two-label 12-ounce tab top, green can, white label, multiversions. *(See photo 300)* $1

Red White & Blue Special Lager Beer, two-label 12-ounce tab top, white can, red, white, blue ribbon, multiversions. $1

Pabst Brewing Company has and is producing a wide variety of brands in aluminum cans. Although most are quite common, they are worth up to $1 to the collector.

JOS. SCHLITZ BREWING COMPANY, 235 West Galena Street

Beer, single-label, 12-ounce, high-profile cone top, WITHDRAWN FREE, camouflage can, single version. .... Exotic

Encore Brewmaster's, two-label 12-ounce tab top, gold and white can, multiversions. $20

Milwaukee Club Beer, single-label, 12-ounce, low-profile cone top, black can, INTERNAL REVENUE TAX PAID, multiversions. $125

Single-label, 12-ounce, low- or high-profile cone top, brown and white can, "SCHLITZ" in white oval, INTERNAL REVENUE TAX PAID, multiversions. Either version, ... $85

Photo 300. Pabst Old Tankard Ale.

Single-label, 12-ounce, high-profile cone top, maroon and yellow can, building, INTERNAL REVENUE TAX PAID, multiversions. $100

Old Milwaukee America's Light Beer, two-label 12- or 16-ounce flat, soft, zip, or tab top, white or yellow can, red square label, multiversions.
12-ounce flat, soft, or zip top,...$5
12-ounce tab top, ...$2
16-ounce flat, soft, or zip top,..$8
16-ounce tab top, ...$3

Old Milwaukee America's Light Genuine Draft Beer, two-label 12- or 16-ounce flat or tab top, white can, red label, vertical lines, multiversions.
12-ounce flat top, ...$5
12-ounce tab top, ...$2
16-ounce flat top, ...$7
16-ounce tab top, ...$3

Old Milwaukee Beer, single-label 12-ounce flat top, blue can, red and yellow label, waiter or building on label, INTERNAL REVENUE TAX PAID, multiversions.
.... $85

Two-label 12-ounce flat top, white can, red label, winter scene, single version.
.... $15

Two-label 12- or 16-ounce tab top, white can, red label, red circle, multiversions.
12-ounce,..$3
16-ounce,..$5

Old Milwaukee Genuine Draft Beer, two-label 10-, 12-, 14-, or 16-ounce tab top, white can, red label, multiversions.
10-ounce,..$5
12-ounce,..$1
14-ounce,..$5
16-ounce,..$2

Old Milwaukee Pale Gold Beer, single-label 12-ounce flat top, gold or green can, horses and coach, single version of each. Each, ...$50

Two-label 12- or 16-ounce flat top, white can, red label, horses and coach, single version of each size.
12-ounce,.. $20
16-ounce,.. $25

Schlitz, "College Reunion" cans (16-ounce drinking cups): "Colgate," "North Carolina State University," "Princeton Class of 31 35th Reunion," "Princeton Class of 32 35th Reunion," "Princeton Class of 38 30th Reunion," "Princeton Class of 59 10th Reunion," "Princeton Class of 63 5th Reunion," "University of Illinois," "University of Iowa"; single version of each can. Each, ... $25

Single-label 12-ounce bank can, cities with Schlitz breweries: Los Angeles, Longview, Memphis, Milwaukee, Tampa, Winston-Salem; single version of each can. *(See photo 301)* Each,.. $20

Two-label 12-ounce bank can, "Cerebral Palsy," single version. $10

When Schlitz merged with the Stroh Brewery in 1981, it was producing all of its brands in aluminum or bi-metal cans. The collector value of these cans is up to $1.

Photo 301. Schlitz.

Schlitz Beer, single-label, 12-ounce, low-profile cone top, light gold can, brown label, blue globe, "SUNSHINE VITAMIN D," INTERNAL REVENUE TAX PAID, multiversions. $85

Single-label, 12-ounce, low- or high-profile cone top, brown can, white bands, "SUNSHINE VITAMIN D," INTERNAL REVENUE TAX PAID, multiversions. $100

Single-label, 12-ounce, high-profile cone top, dark gold can, brown label, blue globe, INTERNAL REVENUE TAX PAID, multiversions. $85
Camouflage can, ... $200

Single-label, 12-ounce, high-profile cone or flat top, white can, brown bands and label, globe center top face (c. 1946 or 1949), IRTP or non-IRTP, multiversions.
Cone top, ...$125
Flat top, ... $10

Two-label 10-, 12-, 16-, or 24-ounce flat top, white can, brown bands (c. 1954, 1956, or 1958), multiversions.
10-ounce, ... $15
12-ounce, ...$5
16-ounce, ... $10
24-ounce, ... $10

Two-label 10-, 12-, 16-, or 24-ounce flat, soft, zip or tab top, white can, brown label outlined in gold or silver, gold or silver bands (c. 1960, 1962, or 1966), multiversions.
10-ounce, ... $10
12-ounce, ...$3
16-ounce, ...$8
24-ounce, ...$5

Two-label 10-, 12-, 16-, or 24-ounce tab top, white can, brown label, no bands (c. 1968, 1969, 1971, 1972, or 1973), multiversions.
10-ounce, ...$5
12- or 16-ounce, ...$1
24-ounce, ...$5

Schlitz Export Beer, single-label 12-ounce flat top, copper, brown, and white can (c. 1938), panel text in Spanish, single version. ....Exotic

Schlitz Genuine Draft Beer, two-label 12- or 16-ounce tab top, white can, brown split label (c. 1966), "GENUINE DRAUGHT BEER" on brown patch, single version of each.
12-ounce, ... $20
16-ounce, ... $30

Schlitz Lager Beer, single-label, 12-ounce, low-profile cone top, brown can, yellow bands, "SCHLITZ" in white, INTERNAL REVENUE TAX PAID, multiversions. $110

Schlitz Malt Liquor, single-label 8-, 12-, 16-, or 24-ounce flat, soft, zip, or tab top, white can, silver metals, multiversions. All versions, not over $3

Schlitz Stout Malt Liquor, single-label 8-, 12-, 16-, or 24-ounce zip or tab top, white can, silver metals, multiversions. All versions, not over $3

Schlitz Sunshine Vitamin D Beer, single-label, 12-ounce, low-profile cone top, brown can, yellow bands, INTERNAL REVENUE TAX PAID, multiversions. ... $125
WITHDRAWN FREE, ... $175

Mineral Point

MINERAL SPRING BREWING COMPANY, 272 Hoard Street

Mineral Spring Beer, single-label, 12-ounce high-profile cone top, yellow and white can, "MINERAL SPRING" in black, two versions. Either version, ... $85

Monroe

JOS. HUBER BREWING COMPANY, 1200-1208 14th Avenue (aka: Heim-Brau Brewing Company, Swiss Brewing Company, United Brewing Company)

Alpine Lager Beer, two-label 12-ounce tab top, white, blue, and gold can, mountain scene, single version. $5

American Brewers Historical Beer, two-label 12-ounce flat or tab top, Nos. 1–12 set cans, set of 12, (for can Nos. 13–18, see Pittsburgh Brewing Company, Pittsburgh, Pennsylvania), multicolored cans, brewery pictured, each can numbered: 1: "Engel-Wolf," 2: "Gustavus Bergner's," 3: "Benedictine Society," 4: "Peter Barbey," 5: "Keystone State," 6: "F. A. Poth & Sons," 7: "Lili & Diversey," 8: "Peter Schoenhofen," 9: "John A. Huck," 10: "Bartholomae & Roesing," 11: "Gottfried," 12: "Michael Brand; Nos. 7–12 also come in tab tops, single version each can, total 18 cans.
Flat top, each, ... $5
Tab top, each, ... $7.50

Augsburger Bock Old World Bavarian Style Beer, Jos. Huber Brewing, two-label 12-ounce tab top, red can, white label, single version. $5

Augsburger Dark Old World Bavarian Style Beer, Jos. Huber Brewing, two-label 12-ounce tab top, brown can, white label, single version. $5

Augsburger Old Style Bavarian Style Beer, Jos. Huber Brewing, two-label 12-ounce tab top, green can, white label, single version. $5

Bavarian Club Premium Beer, Jos. Huber Brewing, two-label 12-ounce tab top, white can, blue oval label, man with accordian, multiversions. $3

Bohemian Club Old Fashion Lager Beer, Jos. Huber Brewing, two-label 12-ounce tab top, black can, metallic gold oval, red label and bands, multiversions $5

Brown Derby Lager Beer, Jos. Huber Brewing, two-label 12-ounce tab top, white can, orange label outlined in brown, single version. $3

Golden Glow Pilsner Beer, Jos. Huber Brewing, two-label 12-ounce flat top, gold can, white label, metallic dark red label, single version. $50

Heim-Brau Wisconsin Beer, Heim-Brau Brewing, two-label 12-ounce flat top, yellow can, red label outlined in orange, single version. $3

Hi-Brau Beer, Jos. Huber Brewing, two-label 12-ounce flat top, white can, diamond label, gold bands, single version. $20

Hi-Brau Premium Beer, Jos. Huber Brewing, two-label 12-ounce flat or tab top, gold, red, and black can, white label, multiversions.
Flat top, ...$5
Tab top, ...$3

Jos. Huber Brewing Company, two-label 12-ounce tab top, red can, metallic gold filigree, black label, lion, multiversions. $3

Holiday Wisconsin Beer, Jos. Huber Brewing, two-label 12-ounce tab top, yellow can, red label, multiversions. $3

Huber All Grain Beer, Jos. Huber Brewing, single-label, 12-ounce, high-profile cone top, yellow or white can, red label outlined in metallic gold, multiversions. $75

Huber Bock Beer, Jos. Huber Brewing, two-label 12-ounce tab top, white can, maroon label outlined in metallic gold, goat, multiversions. $10

Huber Premium Beer, Jos. Huber Brewing, two-label 12-ounce flat or tab top, white can, red label outlined in metallic gold and bands, multiversions.
Flat top, ...$5
Tab top, ...$3

Jos. Huber Brewing, two-label 12-ounce tab top, white can, red label, multiversions. $2

Our Beer, Jos. Huber Brewing, single-label 12-ounce tab top, black can, beer glass, multiversions. *(See photo 302)* $5

Regal Brau Bavarian Style Beer, Jos. Huber Brewing, two-label 12-ounce flat or tab top, black and white can, "REGAL BRAU" in metallic red, multiversions. $2

Rheinlander Export Premium Beer, Jos. Huber Brewing, two-label 12-ounce tab top, silver and white can, tree scene, "RHEINLANDER" in metallic red, multiversions. ..../... $20

Jos. Huber Brewing, two-label 12-ounce tab top, silver and white can, metallic green bands, multiversions. $5

Wisconsin Club Premium Pilsner Beer, Jos. Huber or Swiss Brewing, metallic gold can, white label, "WISCONSIN CLUB" in white on metallic blue ribbon, multiversions. $3

Photo 302. Our Beer.

Jos. Huber Brewing, two-label 12-ounce tab top, silver and white can, blue label, multiversions. *(See photo 303)* $3

Wisconsin Gold Label Beer, Swiss Brewing Company, two-label 12-ounce flat top, silver can, three medals, single version. $85

Wisconsin Gold Label Light Label Beer, Jos. Huber Brewing, two-label 12-ounce tab top, metallic gold can, white label, red and black trim, multiversions...$10

Jos. Huber Brewing, two-label 12-ounce tab top, white can, black round label, gold trim, multiversions. $4

Wisconsin Gold Label Premium Beer, Jos. Huber Brewing, two-label 12-ounce flat top, gray and white can, three metals, single version......................$85

Jos. Huber has also produced many brands in aluminum and bi-metal cans. The collector value of these cans will not exceed $2.

Oconto

OCONTO BREWING COMPANY, INC., 1017 Superior Street
(aka: Oconto Brewing Company, Fox Brewing Company, Bohemian Brewing Company, Oconto)

18-K Beer, Oconto Brewing, single-label 12-ounce flat or soft top, white can, metallic gold label and bands, black trim, "BRIGHT AS GOLD," single version of each top.
Flat top, ...$50
Soft top, ...$55

Bohemian Club Old Fashion Lager Beer, Bohemian Brewing Company, two-label 12-ounce flat top, black can, red label and bands, metallic gold oval, single version. $50

Fox Brew Non-Alcoholic Dry Beverage, Fox Brewing Company, single-label 12-ounce flat top, white can, metallic blue bands, picture of a fox head, single version. $35

Oconto Premium Beer, Oconto Brewing, two-label 12-ounce flat, zip, or tab top, blue and white can, gold bands, "PREMIUM" on red patch, minor versions. *(See photo 304)*
Flat top, ...$35
Zip and tab top,...$30

Photo 303 (left). Wisconsin Club Premium Pilsner Beer.
Photo 304 (center). Oconto Premium Beer.
Photo 305 (right). Alpen Brau Beer.

Old Craft Brew Premium Beer, Oconto Brewing, single-label 12-ounce flat or zip top, blue can, white label, red and black trim, single version of each top.
Flat top, ... $60
Zip top, ... $55

Oshkosh

OSHKOSH BREWING COMPANY, 1642 Doty Street (aka: Rahr–Green Bay Brewing)

Chief Oshkosh Beer, Oshkosh Brewing, single-label, 12-ounce, high-profile cone or flat top, red and gold can, white arrowhead, single version.
Cone top, ... $85
Flat top, ... $65
Oshkosh Brewing, two-label 12-ounce flat top, gold can, red arrowhead outlined in white, multiversions. $30
Oshkosh Brewing, two-label 12-ounce flat or tab top, multicolored scene, red arrowhead outlined in white, three versions: "The Pride of Winnebagoland," "Brewed on the Shores of Beautiful Lake Winnebago," "A True Wisconsin Beer." $10

Chief Oshkosh Pilsener Beer, Oshkosh Brewing Company, two-label 12-ounce crowntainer, yellow or white can, red and black bands, Indian, INTERNAL REVENUE TAX PAID, multiversions. $175

Rahr's All Star Beer, Rahr–Green Bay, two-label 12-ounce tab top, white can, metallic red star, silver bands, single version. $50

Rahr's Beer, Rahr–Green Bay, two-label 12-ounce tab top, metallic red can, white label, single version. $30

PEOPLES BREWING COMPANY, 1511-1513 South Main Street

Chief Oshkosh Beer, two-label 12-ounce tab top, multicolored can, red arrowhead outlined in white, "A TRUE WISCONSIN BEER," single version. $30

People's Beer, two-label 12-ounce flat, soft, or tab top, white can, metallic blue label, gold bands, "HITS THE SPOT," minor versions. $15

Potosi

POTOSI BREWING COMPANY, Van Buren Addition (aka: Alpen Brau Brewing Company, Alpine Brewing Company, Bohemian Brewing Company, Garten Brau Brewing Company, Holiday Brewing Company)

Alpen Brau Beer, Alpen Brau Brewing, two-label 12-ounce tab top, blue and white can, mountain scene, silver bands, single version. *(See photo 305)* ... $10

Alpine Lager Beer, Potosi or Alpine Brewing, two-label 12-ounce flat or tab top, white can, blue and gold mountain scene, minor versions.
Flat top, ... $10
Tab top, ... $8

Armanetti's Holiday Beer, Holiday Brewing, two-label 12-ounce flat top, white can, gold band, "ARMANETTI'S" in gold, minor versions.......................... $40

Bohemian Club Old Fashion Lager Beer, Potosi or Bohemian Brewing, two-label 12-ounce flat, soft, or tab top, black can, red label, metallic gold oval, single version of each top.
Flat top, ... $15
Soft or tab top, ... $12

Garten Brau Bavarian Style Beer, Garten Brau Brewing, two-label 12-ounce flat or tab top, white and metallic brown can, "GARTEN BRAU" in white, minor versions.
Flat top, ... $10
Tab top, ... $8

Holiday Bock Beer, Holiday Brewing, two-label 12-ounce tab top, red can, white lettering and goat, single version. *(See photo 306)*.......................... $15

Holiday Special Beer, Potosi Brewing, two-label 12-ounce flat top, white can, metallic red label outlined in metallic blue, blue bands, line drawings, single version. $15

Holiday Wisconsin Beer, Holiday Brewing, two-label 12-ounce tab top, off-white can, red label outlined in orange, multiversions. $10

Keller's Holiday Beer, Holiday Brewing, two-label 12-ounce flat top, white can, yellow and blue label, single version. $75

Peerless Beer, Potosi Brewing, single-label 12-ounce flat top, metallic gold can, white hatching and label, single version. $60

Potosi Good Old Beer, Potosi Brewing, single-label, 12-ounce, high-profile cone or flat top, yellow can, brown label outlined in metallic gold, multiversions.
Flat top, ... $50
Cone top, ... $85

Potosi Brewing, two-label 12-ounce tab top, white can, red label outlined in metallic gold, single version. *(See photo 307)*..................................... $30

Potosi Pilsener Beer, Potosi Brewing, two-label 12-ounce crowntainer, silver can, white label outlined in gold, INTERNAL REVENUE TAX PAID, multiversions.
.... $100

Potosi Brewing, single-label, 12-ounce, high-profile cone top, gold can, red bands, white label, INTERNAL REVENUE TAX PAID, multiversions.
IRTP, ... $160
Non-IRTP, ... $150

Photo 306 (left). Holiday Bock Beer.
Photo 307 (right). Potosi Good Old Beer.

Random Lake

WM. G. JUNG BREWERY, Carroll Street

Jung Pilsener Beer, two-label 12-ounce crowntainer, silver can, green label, IRTP or non-IRTP, single version of each.

IRTP, ... $100
Non-IRTP, ... $85

Two-label 12-ounce crowntainer, silver can, dark red label, IRTP or non-IRTP, single version of each.

IRTP, ... $115
Non-IRTP, ... $100

Rheinlander

RHEINLANDER BREWING COMPANY, 1 West and 4 East Ocala Street

Rhinelander Export Beer, single-label, 12-ounce, high-profile cone top, black can, green band, "EXPORT BEER" in gold, IRTP or non-IRTP, single version of each.

IRTP, ... $85
Non-IRTP, ... $75

Single-label, 12-ounce, high-profile cone top, silver can, snowflakes, green band, multiversions. $65

Single-label, 12-ounce, high-profile cone or flat top, silver can, snowflakes, "RHEINLANDER" in red, multiversions.

Cone top, ... $65
Flat top, ... $20

Schoen's Old Lager Beer, two-label 12-ounce flat top, white can, red label and bands, "PROPERLY AGED," single version. $40

Rice Lake

RICE LAKE BREWING COMPANY, 816 Hammond Street

Breunig's Lager Beer, single-label, 12-ounce, high-profile cone top, metallic gold can, blue label outlined in white, minor versions. $100

Two-label 12-ounce flat top, light or dark gold can, blue or purple label and bands, "4 GENERATIONS OF BREWING EXPERIENCE," minor versions. $10

Sternwirth Beer King Lager Beer, single-label 12-ounce flat top, red can, white label, "STERNWIRTH" in blue, single version. $100

Sheboygan

G. HEILEMAN BREWING COMPANY, 1012 New York Avenue
(successor to Kingsbury Breweries Company; aka: Fox Head Brewing, Independent Milwaukee Brewery, Kingsbury Breweries, Weber Brewing Company, Geo. Weidemann Brewing Company)

Braumeister Special Pilsener Beer, G. Heileman Brewing, two-label 12-ounce flat or tab top, white and gold can, blue label outlined in metallic gold, single version. $15

Independent Milwaukee Brewery, two-label 12-ounce flat or tab top, white can, maroon label outlined in metallic gold, multiversions.
Flat top, ...$5
Tab top,..$3

Fox Head "400" Beer, Fox Head Brewing, two-label 12-ounce flat top, white and metallic gold can, blue and white label, multiversions. $20

Fox Head "400" Real Draft Beer, Fox Head Brewing, two-label 12-ounce flat top, white and metallic gold can, blue and white label, "REAL DRAFT BEER" in red, multiversions. $10

Fox Head Bock Beer, Fox Head Brewing, two-label 12-ounce flat top, white and yellow can, maroon label outlined in yellow, single version. $40

Fox Head Extra Dry Sparkling Malt Liquor, Fox Head Brewing, two-label 12-ounce tab top, white can, "FOX HEAD" on black bar, "SPARKLING" in red, multiversions. $10

Fox Head Real Draft Bock Beer, Fox Head Brewing, two-label 12-ounce flat top, white and yellow can, maroon label outlined in yellow, "REAL DRAFT BOCK BEER" in maroon, single version. $50

Kingsbury Beer, Kingsbury Breweries, two-label 12-ounce flat or zip top, white can, red label, Heileman shield, "DRAFT SMOOTH," single version of each.
Flat top, ... $30
Zip top,... $25

Kingsbury Brew Near Beer, Kingsbury Breweries, single-label 12-ounce flat top, metallic gold can, map of Wisconsin in yellow, red bands, multiversions.
.... $15

Kingsbury Light Beer, Kingsbury Breweries, two-label 12-ounce soft or tab top, white can, red label, blue trim, Heileman shield, single version of each top.
.... $15

Kingsbury Real Draft Beer, Kingsbury Breweries, two-label 12-ounce tab top, white and woodgrain can, red circle, minor versions. $30

Kingsbury Sparkling Malt Tonic, Kingsbury Breweries, two-label 12-ounce tab top, metallic gold can, map of Saudi Arabia in yellow, single version. *(See photo 308)* $30

Photo 308 (left). Kingsbury Sparkling Malt Tonic.
Photo 309 (center). Kingsbury Aristocrat of Beer.
Photo 310 (right). Kingsbury Bock Beer.

Reidenbach Wisconsin Pale Dry Beer, Kingsbury Breweries, two-label 12-ounce tab top, dark brown woodgrain can, gold bands, single version. $30

Weidemann Bohemian Special Brew Fine Beer, Geo. Weidemann Brewing, two-label 12-ounce tab top, white can, red and black bands, "WEIDEMANN" in red, single version. $5

KINGSBURY BREWERIES COMPANY, 1012 York Avenue (aka: Heidel-Brau Brewing Company, Sheboygan, WI)

Fox Head Bock Beer, Kingsbury Breweries, two-label 12-ounce flat top, white can, brown and silver label, goat's head, "BREWED ONLY IN WISCONSIN," single version. $65

Heidel-Brau Premium Quality Light Beer, Heidel-Brau Brewing, two-label 12-ounce flat top, gold-flecked can, white label outlined in red, single version. $50

Kingsbury Aristocrat Of Beer, Kingsbury Breweries, two-label 12-ounce crowntainer, silver can, red, green, and yellow label outlined in black, IRTP or non-IRTP, multiversions. *(See photo 309)*

IRTP, ... $75

Non-IRTP, ... $65

Kingsbury Beer, Kingsbury Breweries, two-label 12-ounce crowntainer, silver can, metallic or enamel blue label, "BEER" in yellow, IRTP or non-IRTP, single version of each.

Non-IRTP, ... $115

IRTP, ... $125

Kingsbury Bock Beer, Kingsbury Breweries, single-label 12-ounce flat top, yellow can, brown label, yellow goat's head, minor versions. *(See photo 310)* . $85

Kingsbury Pale Beer, Kingsbury Breweries, two-label 12-ounce crowntainer, silver can, white or yellow label, blue lettering, INTERNAL REVENUE TAX PAID, multiversions. $75

Kingsbury Breweries, two-label 12-ounce flat top, metallic gold can, wide red bands, white label, "FIT FOR A KING," multiversions. $50

Kingsbury Sparkling Malt Tonic, Kingsbury Breweries, two-label 12-ounce soft top, metallic gold can, map of Saudi Arabia in yellow, single version. . $50

Kingsbury Wisconsin's Pale Beer, Kingsbury Breweries, two-label 12-ounce flat top, white can, red trim, "KINGSBURY WISCONSIN'S PALE BEER" in blue, multiversions. $30

Stevens Point

STEVENS POINT BEVERAGE COMPANY, 1108 Water Street

Point Special Beer, two-label 12-ounce flat top, metallic dark blue can, orange label outlined in gold, single version. $35

Two-label 12-ounce flat top, metallic blue can, red label outlined in gold, single version. $25

STEVENS POINT BREWERY, 1106 Water Street (successor to Stevens Point Beverage Company)

A F Base Brau Appleton Foxes, two-label 12-ounce tab top, set can, set of seven brewed for local baseball team, issued over four-year period: 1978 with red symbol, 1978 with orange symbol, 1979 blue and red can, 1979 yellow and red can, 1980 blue can, 1981 red, white, and blue can, single version of each. Each,...$3

Old Cars Beer, two-label 12-ounce tab top, set can, set of four, last three in aluminum: orange can, "Old Cars" in orange; blue can, "Old Cars" in orange; red can, "Old Cars" in blue; bronze can, "Old Cars" in white; single version of each can. Each,..$3

Point 125 A Commemorative Beer, two-label 12-ounce aluminum can, black can, blue label, "POINT 125" in gold, single version. $2

Point Bicentennial Beer, two-label 12-ounce tab top, white can, blue label, red eagle, single version. $3

Point Bock Beer, two-label 12-ounce tab top, blue label red goat, or red label blue goat, single version of each. $2

Point Special Beer, two-label 12-ounce tab top, metallic blue can, red label outlined in gold, multiversions. $3

Stevens Point Brewery has produced its brands since the mid-1980s in aluminum cans. The collector value is not over $1.

Superior

NORTHERN BREWING COMPANY, 702-724 North 8th Street

Northern Beer, single-label, 12-ounce, high-profile cone top, white can, metallic gold bands, multicolored label, IRTP or non-IRTP, multiversions.
Non-IRTP, ...$125
IRTP, ...$135

Single-label, 12-ounce, high-profile cone or flat top, yellow or white can, brown label, multiversions.
Cone top, ...$65
Flat top, ...$15

Two Rivers

TWO RIVERS BEVERAGE COMPANY, 1608 Adams Street

White Cap Beer, two-label, 12-ounce, high-profile cone top, white can, metallic gold bands, "WHITE CAP" in red, single version. $100

White Cap Select Beer, two-label, 12-ounce, high-profile cone top, white can, blue ship's wheel, IRTP or non-IRTP, single version of each.
IRTP, ...$125
Non-IRTP, ...$115

Waukesha

FOX HEAD BREWING COMPANY, 227 Maple Street (aka: Eulberg Brewing Company, Paul Bunyan Division–Wisconsin Brewing Company, Peter Fox Brewing Company, Reserve Division–Wisconsin Brewing Company, Spring City Brewing Company, Wisconsin Brewing Company)

Bierman Beer, Fox Head Brewing, two-label 12-ounce flat top, white or brown can, drinking scene label, single version of each. $150

Eulberg Crown Select Premium Beer, Eulberg Brewing, two-label 12-ounce flat top, white can, red ribbon, crown, single version. $150

Fox Brew Non-Alcohol Dry Beverage, Fox Head Brewing, single-label 12-ounce flat top, metallic blue can, white label, fox's head, single version. $60

Fox Deluxe Beer, Fox Head or Peter Fox Brewing, two-label 12-ounce flat top, metallic gold can, white label, man in red with trumpet, multiversions. $25

Fox Deluxe Bock Beer, Peter Fox Brewing, two-label 12-ounce flat top, white can, brown label, man in red with trumpet, single version. $175

Fox Deluxe Waukesha Beer, Fox Head Brewing or Peter Fox Brewing, two-label 12-ounce flat top, blue can, metallic gold bands, white label, multiversions.. $50

Fox Head 97 Malt Liquor, Fox Head Brewing, two-label 12-ounce flat top, woodgrain gold and white can, black lettering, single version. $125

Fox Head Brewing, two-label 12-ounce flat or soft top, woodgrain gold and white can, black lettering, single version.
Flat top, ...$150
Soft top, ...$135

Fox Head "400" Beer, Fox Head Brewing, single-label 12-ounce flat top, yellow can, nickel-size red fox's head, IRTP or non-IRTP, single version of each.
Non-IRTP, ... $65
IRTP, ... $75

Fox Head Brewing, single-label 12-ounce flat top, white can, metallic red bands, square label, minor versions. $50

Fox Head Brewing, two-label 12-ounce flat top, white can, blue label, metallic gold trim, minor versions. $40

Fox Head Bock Beer, Fox Head Brewing, two-label 12-ounce tab top, white can, maroon and gold label, gold head, single version. $65

Fox Head Brewing, two-label 12-ounce tab top, white and yellow can, gold checkerboarding and trim, maroon and white label, single version. $50

Fox Head Malt Liquor, Fox Head Brewing, two-label 12-ounce flat top, white can, metallic gold bands, "FOX HEAD MALT LIQUOR" in red, single version.
.... $200

Fox Head Old Waukesha Ale, Fox Head Brewing, single-label 12-ounce flat top, green can, yellow oval, fox's head, "BREWED WITH WAUKESHA WATER," minor versions. $150

Fox Head Vat Age Lager Beer, Fox Head Brewing, two-label 12-ounce flat top, cream-colored can, metallic gold bands, yellow label, single version. $125

Kol Premium Quality Beer, Wisconsin Brewing Company, two-label 12-ounce flat top, silver can, white vertical stripes, blue label, minor versions......... $25

Mr. Lager Beer, Fox Head Brewing, single-label 12-ounce flat top, blue can, white label, "FOR MEN ONLY," single version. ....Exotic

Old England Beer, Fox Head Brewing, single-label 12-ounce flat top, white can, black label, red ribbon, single version. $200

Paul Bunyan Beer, Paul Bunyan Division–Wisconsin Brewing, two-label 12-ounce flat top, white can, standing "PAUL BUNYAN" figure, multiversions. . $65

Reserve Of Wisconsin, Reserve Division–Wisconsin Brewery or Wisconsin Brewing, two-label 12-ounce flat top, metallic gold or white can, red label, minor versions.
Metallic gold can, ... $75
White can, ... $60

Weber Private Club Beer, Fox Head Brewing or Spring City Brewing, two-label 12-ounce flat top, white can, blue label, single version of each brewery.
.... $50

Wisconsin Club Beer, Fox Head Brewing, single-label 12-ounce flat top, white can, metallic red label, "WORLD FAMOUS WAUKESHA WATER," single version.
.... $50

Wisconsin Premium Beer, Fox Head and Wisconsin Brewing, two-label 12-ounce flat top, metallic gold can, white pinstripes, map of Wisconsin in white, multiversions. $40

Wisconsin Premium Quality Beer, Wisconsin Brewing, two-label 12-ounce flat top, white can, red and black stripes, multiversions. $40

Fox Head Brewing or Spring City Brewing, two-label 12-ounce flat top, white can, metallic maroon label, single version of each brewery. $85

WEBER WAUKESHA BREWING COMPANY, 220 North Street

Weber Special Premium Beer, two-label 12-ounce flat top, metallic or enamel blue can, gray or silver trim, red "w," single version of each.
Metallic can,... $50
Enamel can, ... $40

Two-label 12-ounce flat top, gold can, white label, red or maroon trim, single version of each. Either version, ... $60

*Photo 311 (left). Black Pride
Lager Beer.
Photo 312 (right). West Bend
Old Timer's Lager Beer.*

Weber Waukesha Beer, single-label, 12-ounce, high-profile cone top, yellow can, green bands, gold trim, "WEBER BEER" in red, IRTP or non-IRTP, single version of each.

Non-IRTP, ... $90

IRTP, ... $100

Single-label 12-ounce flat top, black can, white label, large red "w," silver trim, minor versions. $50

Wausau

MATHIE-RUDER BREWING COMPANY, 505–516 Grand Avenue

Red Ribbon Beer, single-label, 12-ounce, high-profile cone top, silver can, white label, red ribbon, "BEER" in white on black patch, single version. $135

WAUSAU BREWING COMPANY, 622–644 South 7th

Rib Mountain Lager Beer, single-label 12-ounce flat top, metallic blue can, oval yellow label, "RIB MOUNTAIN" in red, single version. $250

Schoen's Old Lager Beer, two-label 12-ounce flat top, white can, dark red label, "KNOWN FOR QUALITY," minor versions. $60

West Bend

WEST BEND LITHIA COMPANY, 445 North Main

Black Pride Lager Beer, two-label 12-ounce tab top, metallic gold can, yellow label, single version. *(See photo 311)* $35

Milwaukee Valley Beer, two-label 12-ounce flat top, multicolored can, map of Wisconsin in white, single version. $175

West Bend Old Timer's Lager Beer, single-label 12-ounce flat or tab top, yellow or white can, drinking scene, gold or silver bands, single version of each. *(See photo 312)*

Gold can, ... $25

White can, ... $15

Whitewater

WHITEWATER BREWING COMPANY

Cans with mandatory WHITEWATER BREWING COMPANY or WHITEWATER–MANHATTAN BREWING COMPANY were actually brewed and filled by the Manhattan Brewing Company, Chicago. For listings, see Manhattan, Chicago.

Wyoming

Evanston

BECKER BREWING AND MALTING COMPANY, 300 Front
Street

Becker's Unita Club Mellow Beer, two-label, 12-ounce, high-profile cone top,
gray can, cowboy, red trim, "BECKER'S UNITA CLUB" in blue, single version.
.... $150

Sheridan

SHERIDAN BREWING COMPANY, 200 Paul Street

Sheridan Export Beer, single-label 12-ounce flat top, yellow can, black band,
"SHERIDAN" in red outlined in black, IRTP or non-IRTP, single version of each.
Non-IRTP, ... $40
IRTP, ... $50
Sheridan Lager Beer, single-label, 12-ounce, low-profile cone top, silver can,
red and gold bands, INTERNAL REVENUE TAX PAID, single version. $300